# sed & awk

# sed & awk
## *Second Edition*

Dale Dougherty and Arnold Robbins

O'REILLY™

*Cambridge · Köln · Paris · Sebastopol · Tokyo*

**sed & awk, Second Edition**
by Dale Dougherty and Arnold Robbins

Copyright © 1997, 1990 O'Reilly & Associates, Inc.  All rights reserved.
Printed in the United States of America.

**Editor:** Tim O'Reilly
**Update Editor:** Gigi Estabrook
**Production Editor:** Nicole Gipson Arigo

**Printing History:**

|           |        |
|-----------|--------|
| November 1990: | First Edition. |
| March 1991:    | Minor corrections. |
| July 1992:     | Minor corrections. |
| November 1992: | Minor corrections. |
| March 1997:    | Second Edition. |

This book is printed on acid-free paper with 85% recycled content, 15% post-consumer waste.
O'Reilly & Associates is committed to using paper with the highest recycled content available
consistent with high quality.

ISBN:  1-56592-225-5                                                                      [5/97]

*To Miriam, for your love and patience.*

—Arnold Robbins

# Table of Contents

# *Preface*

This book is about a set of oddly named UNIX utilities, **sed** and **awk**. These utilities have many things in common, including the use of regular expressions for pattern matching. Since pattern matching is such an important part of their use, this book explains UNIX regular expression syntax very thoroughly. Because there is a natural progression in learning from **grep** to sed to awk, we will be covering all three programs, although the focus is on sed and awk.

Sed and awk are tools used by users, programmers, and system administrators—anyone working with text files. Sed, so called because it is a stream editor, is perfect for applying a series of edits to a number of files. Awk, named after its developers Aho, Weinberger, and Kernighan, is a programming language that permits easy manipulation of structured data and the generation of formatted reports. This book emphasizes the POSIX definition of awk. In addition, the book briefly describes the original version of awk, before discussing three freely available versions of awk and two commercial ones, all of which implement POSIX awk.

The focus of this book is on writing scripts for sed and awk that quickly solve an assortment of problems for the user. Many of these scripts could be called "quick-fixes." In addition, we'll cover scripts that solve larger problems that require more careful design and development.

## *Scope of This Handbook*

Chapter 1, *Power Tools for Editing*, is an overview of the features and capabilities of sed and awk.

Chapter 2, *Understanding Basic Operations*, demonstrates the basic operations of sed and awk, showing a progression in functionality from sed to awk. Both share a similar command-line syntax, accepting user instructions in the form of a script.

Chapter 3, *Understanding Regular Expression Syntax*, describes UNIX regular expression syntax in full detail. New users are often intimidated by these strange expressions, used for pattern matching. It is important to master regular expression syntax to get the most from sed and awk. The pattern-matching examples in this chapter largely rely on **grep** and **egrep**.

Chapter 4, *Writing sed Scripts*, begins a three-chapter section on sed. This chapter covers the basic elements of writing a sed script using only a few sed commands. It also presents a shell script that simplifies invoking sed scripts.

Chapter 5, *Basic sed Commands*, and Chapter 6, *Advanced sed Commands*, divide the sed command set into basic and advanced commands. The basic commands are commands that parallel manual editing actions, while the advanced commands introduce simple programming capabilities. Among the advanced commands are those that manipulate the hold space, a set-aside temporary buffer.

Chapter 7, *Writing Scripts for awk*, begins a five-chapter section on awk. This chapter presents the primary features of this scripting language. A number of scripts are explained, including one that modifies the output of the **ls** command.

Chapter 8, *Conditionals, Loops, and Arrays*, describes how to use common programming constructs such as conditionals, loops, and arrays.

Chapter 9, *Functions*, describes how to use awk's built-in functions as well as how to write user-defined functions.

Chapter 10, *The Bottom Drawer*, covers a set of miscellaneous awk topics. It describes how to execute UNIX commands from an awk script and how to direct output to files and pipes. It then offers some (meager) advice on debugging awk scripts.

Chapter 11, *A Flock of awks*, describes the original V7 version of awk, the current Bell Labs awk, GNU awk (gawk) from the Free Software Foundation, and mawk, by Michael Brennan. The latter three all have freely available source code. This chapter also describes two commercial implementations, MKS awk and Thomson Automation awk (**tawk**), as well as VSAwk, which brings awk-like capabilities to the Visual Basic environment.

Chapter 12, *Full-Featured Applications*, presents two longer, more complex awk scripts that together demonstrate nearly all the features of the language. The first script is an interactive spelling checker. The second script processes and formats the index for a book or a master index for a set of books.

Chapter 13, *A Miscellany of Scripts*, presents a number of user-contributed scripts that show different styles and techniques of writing scripts for sed and awk.

Appendix A, *Quick Reference for sed*, is a quick reference describing sed's commands and command-line options.

Appendix B, *Quick Reference for awk*, is a quick reference to awk's command-line options and a full description of its scripting language.

Appendix C, *Supplement for Chapter 12*, presents the full listings for the **spellcheck.awk** script and the **masterindex** shell script described in Chapter 12.

# *Availability of sed and awk*

Sed and awk were part of Version 7 UNIX (also known as "V7," and "Seventh Edition") and have been part of the standard distribution ever since. Sed has been unchanged since it was introduced.

The Free Software Foundation GNU project's version of sed is freely available, although not technically in the public domain. Source code for GNU sed is available via anonymous FTP* to the host *ftp.gnu.ai.mit.edu*. It is in the file */pub/gnu/sed-2.05.tar.gz*. This is a tar file compressed with the **gzip** program, whose source code is available in the same directory. There are many sites worldwide that "mirror" the files from the main GNU distribution site; if you know of one close to you, you should get the files from there. Be sure to use "binary" or "image" mode to transfer the file(s).

In 1985, the authors of awk extended the language, adding many useful features. Unfortunately, this new version remained inside AT&T for several years. It became part of UNIX System V as of Release 3.1. It can be found under the name of nawk, for new awk; the older version still exists under its original name. This is still the case on System V Release 4 systems.

On commercial UNIX systems, such as those from Hewlett-Packard, Sun, IBM, Digital, and others, the naming situation is more complicated. All of these systems have some version of both old and new awk, but what each vendor names each program varies. Some have **oawk** and **awk**, others have **awk** and **nawk**. The best advice we can give is to check your local documentation.† Throughout this book, we use the term **awk** to describe POSIX awk. Specific implementations will be referred to by name, such as "gawk," or "the Bell Labs awk."

---

* If you don't have Internet access and wish to get a copy of GNU sed, contact the Free Software Foundation, Inc., 59 Temple Place, Suite 330, Boston, MA 02111-1307 U.S.A. The telephone number is 1-617-542-5942, and the fax number is 1-617-542-2652.

† Purists refer to the new awk simply as **awk**; the new one was intended to replace the original one. Alas, almost 10 years after it was released, this still has not really happened.

Chapter 11 discusses three freely available awks (including where to get them), as well as several commercial ones.

---

*NOTE*   Since the first edition of this book, the awk language was standardized as part of the POSIX Command Language and Utilities Standard (P1003.2). All modern awk implementations aim to be upwardly compatible with the POSIX standard.

The standard incorporates features that originated in both new awk and gawk. In this book, you can assume that what is true for one implementation of POSIX awk is true for another, unless a particular version is designated.

---

## DOS Versions

Gawk, mawk, and GNU sed have been ported to DOS. There are files on the main GNU distribution site with pointers to DOS versions of these programs. In addition, gawk has been ported to OS/2, VMS, and Atari and Amiga microcomputers, with ports to other systems (Macintosh, Windows) in progress.

**egrep**, sed, and awk are available for MS-DOS-based machines as part of the MKS Toolkit (Mortice Kern Systems, Inc., Ontario, Canada). Their implementation of awk supports the features of POSIX awk.

The MKS Toolkit also includes the Korn shell, which means that many shell scripts written for the Bourne shell on UNIX systems can be run on a PC. While most users of the MKS Toolkit have probably already discovered these tools in UNIX, we hope that the benefits of these programs will be obvious to PC users who have not ventured into UNIX.

Thompson Automation Software[*] has an awk compiler for UNIX, DOS, and Microsoft Windows. This version is interesting because it has a number of extensions to the language, and it includes an awk debugger, written in awk!

We have used a PC on occasion because Ventura Publisher is a terrific formatting package. One of the reasons we like it is that we can continue to use **vi** to create and edit the text files and use sed for writing editing scripts. We have used sed to write conversion programs that translate **troff** macros into Ventura stylesheet tags. We have also used it to insert tags in batch mode. This can save having to manually tag repeated elements in a file.

Sed and awk are also useful for writing conversion programs that handle different file formats.

---

[*] 5616 SW Jefferson, Portland, OR 97221 U.S.A., 1-800-944-0139 within the U.S., 1-503-224-1639 elsewhere.

## *Other Sources of Information About sed and awk*

For a long time, the main source of information on these utilities was two articles contained in Volume 2 of the *UNIX Programmer's Guide*. The article *awk—A Pattern Scanning and Processing Language* (September 1, 1978) was written by the language's three authors. In 10 pages, it offers a brief tutorial and discusses several design and implementation issues. The article *SED—A Non-Interactive Text Editor* (August 15, 1978) was written by Lee E. McMahon. It is a reference that gives a full description of each function and includes some useful examples (using Coleridge's *Xanadu* as sample input).

In trade books, the most significant treatment of sed and awk appears in *The UNIX Programming Environment* by Brian W. Kernighan and Rob Pike (Prentice-Hall, 1984). The chapter entitled "Filters" not only explains how these programs work but shows how they can work together to build useful applications.

The authors of awk collaborated on a book describing the enhanced version: *The AWK Programming Language* (Addison-Wesley, 1988). It contains many full examples and demonstrates the broad range of areas where awk can be applied. It follows in the style of the *UNIX Programming Environment*, which at times makes it too dense for some readers who are new users. The source code for the example programs in the book can be found in the directory */netlib/research/awkbookcode* on *netlib.bell-labs.com*.

The IEEE Standard for Information and Technology Portable Operating System Interface (POSIX) Part 2: Shell and Utilities (Standard 1003.2-1992)[*] describes both sed and awk.[†] It is the "official" word on the features available for portable shell programs that use sed and awk. Since awk is a programming language in its own right, it is also the official word on portable awk programs.

In 1996, the Free Software Foundation published *The GNU Awk User's Guide*, by Arnold Robbins. This is the documentation for gawk, written in a more tutorial style than the Aho, Kernighan, and Weinberger book. It has two full chapters of examples, and covers POSIX awk. This book is also published by SSC under the title *Effective AWK Programming*, and the Texinfo source for the book comes with the gawk distribution.

It is one of the current deficiencies of GNU sed that it has no documentation of its own, not even a manpage.

---

[*] Whew! Say *that* three times fast!

[†] The standard is not available online. It can be ordered from the IEEE by calling 1-800-678-IEEE(4333) in the U.S. and Canada, 1-908-981-0060 elsewhere. Or, see *http://www.ieee.org/* from a Web browser. The cost is U.S. $228, which includes Standard 1003.2d-1994—Amendment 1 for Batch Environments. Members of IEEE and/or IEEE societies receive a discount.

Most general introductions to UNIX introduce sed and awk in a long parade of utilities. Of these books, Henry McGilton and Rachel Morgan's *Introducing the UNIX System* offers the best treatment of basic editing skills, including use of all UNIX text editors.

*UNIX Text Processing* (Hayden Books, 1987), by the original author of this hand-book and Tim O'Reilly, covers sed and awk in full, although we did not include the new version of awk. Readers of that book will find some parts duplicated in this book, but in general a different approach has been taken here. Whereas in the textbook we treat sed and awk separately, expecting only advanced users to tackle awk, here we try to present both programs in relation to one another. They are different tools that can be used individually or together to provide interesting opportunities for text processing.

Finally, in 1995 the Usenet newsgroup *comp.lang.awk* came into being. If you can't find what you need to know in one of the above books, you can post a question in the newsgroup, with a good chance that someone will be able to help you.

The newsgroup also has a "frequently asked questions" (FAQ) article that is posted regularly. Besides answering questions about awk, the FAQ lists many sites where you can obtain binaries of different versions of awk for different systems. You can retrieve the FAQ via FTP in the file called */pub/usenet/comp.lang.awk/faq* from the host *rtfm.mit.edu.*

## Sample Programs

The sample programs in this book were originally written and tested on a Mac IIci running A/UX 2.0 (UNIX System V Release 2) and a SparcStation 1 running SunOS 4.0. Programs requiring POSIX awk were re-tested using gawk 3.0.0 as well as the August 1994 version of the Bell Labs awk from the Bell Labs FTP site (see Chapter 11 for the FTP details). Sed programs were retested with the SunOS 4.1.3 sed and GNU sed 2.05.

# Obtaining Example Source Code

You can obtain the source code for the programs presented in this book from O'Reilly & Associates through their Internet server. The example programs in this book are available electronically in a number of ways: by FTP, Ftpmail, BITFTP, and UUCP. The cheapest, fastest, and easiest ways are listed first. If you read from the top down, the first one that works for you is probably the best. Use FTP if you are directly on the Internet. Use Ftpmail if you are not on the Internet, but can send and receive electronic mail to Internet sites (this includes CompuServe users). Use BITFTP if you can send electronic mail via BITNET. Use UUCP if none of the above works.

## *FTP*

To use FTP, you need a machine with direct access to the Internet. A sample session is shown, with what you should type in boldface.

```
$ ftp ftp.ora.com
Connected to ftp.ora.com.
220 FTP server (Version 6.21 Tue Mar 10 22:09:55 EST 1992) ready.
Name (ftp.ora.com:yourname): anonymous
331 Guest login ok, send domain style e-mail address as password.
Password: yourname@domain.name    (Use your user name and host here)
230 Guest login ok, access restrictions apply.
ftp> cd /published/oreilly/nutshell/sedawk_2
250 CWD command successful.
ftp> binary    (Very important! You must specify binary transfer for compressed files.)
200 Type set to I.
ftp> get progs.tar.gz
200 PORT command successful.
150 Opening BINARY mode data connection for progs.tar.gz.
226 Transfer complete.
ftp> quit
221 Goodbye.
```

The file is a **gzip** compressed **tar** archive; extract the files from the archive by typing:

```
$ gzcat progs.tar.gz | tar xvf -
```

System V systems require the following **tar** command instead:

```
$ gzcat progs.tar.gz | tar xof -
```

If **gzcat** is not available on your system, use separate **gunzip** and **tar** commands.

```
$ gunzip progs.tar.gz
$ tar xvf progs.tar
```

## *Ftpmail*

Ftpmail is a mail server available to anyone who can send electronic mail to and receive it from Internet sites. This includes any company or service provider that allows email connections to the Internet. Here's how you do it. You send mail to **ftpmail@online.ora.com**. In the message body, give the FTP commands you want to run. The server will run anonymous FTP for you and mail the files back to you.

To get a complete help file, send a message with no subject and the single word "help" in the body. The following is a sample mail session that should get you the examples. This command sends you a listing of the files in the selected directory and the requested example files. The listing is useful if there's a later version of the examples you're interested in.

```
$ mail ftpmail@online.ora.com
Subject:
reply-to yourname@domain.name        (Where you want files mailed)
open
cd /published/oreilly/nutshell/sedawk_2
dir
mode binary
uuencode
get progs.tar.gz
quit
.
```

A signature at the end of the message is acceptable as long as it appears after "quit."

## BITFTP

BITFTP is a mail server for BITNET users. You send it electronic mail messages requesting files, and it sends you back the files by electronic mail. BITFTP currently serves only users who send it mail from nodes that are directly on BITNET, EARN, or NetNorth. To use BITFTP, send mail containing your **ftp** commands to *BITFTP@PUCC*. For a complete help file, send **HELP** as the message body. The following is the message body you send to BITFTP:

```
FTP  ftp.ora.com  NETDATA
USER  anonymous
PASS  yourname@yourhost.edu    Put your Internet email address here (not your BITNET address)
CD /published/oreilly/nutshell/sedawk_2
DIR
BINARY
GET  progs.tar.gz
QUIT
```

Once you've got the desired file, follow the directions under FTP to extract the files from the archive. Since you are probably not on a UNIX system, you may need to get versions of **uudecode**, **gunzip**, **atob**, and **tar** for your system. VMS, DOS, and Mac versions are available.

## *UUCP*

UUCP is standard on virtually all UNIX systems and is available for IBM-compatible PCs and Apple Macintoshes. The examples are available by UUCP via modem from UUNET; UUNET's connect-time charges apply. If you or your company has an account with UUNET, you have a system somewhere with a direct UUCP connection to UUNET. Find that system, and type:

```
uucp uunet\!~/published/oreilly/nutshell/sedawk_2/progs.tar.gz yourhost\!~/yourname/
```

The backslashes can be omitted if you use a Bourne-style shell (**sh**, **ksh**, **bash**, **zsh**, **pdksh**) instead of **csh**. The file should appear some time later (up to a day or more) in the directory */usr/spool/uucppublic/yourname*. If you don't have an account, but would like one so that you can get electronic mail, contact UUNET at 703-206-5400. It's a good idea to get the file */published/oreilly/ls-lR.Z* as a short test file containing the filenames and sizes of all the files available. Once you've got the desired file, follow the directions under FTP to extract the files from the archive.

# *Conventions Used in This Handbook*

The following conventions are used in this book:

**Bold**

is used for statements and functions, identifiers, and program names.

*Italic*

is used for file and directory names when they appear in the body of a paragraph as well as for data types and to emphasize new terms and concepts when they are introduced.

`Constant Width`

is used in examples to show the contents of files or the output from commands.

**`Constant Bold`**

is used in examples to show command lines and options that should be typed literally by the user. (For example, **rm foo** means to type "rm foo" exactly as it appears in the text or the example.)

""

are used to identify a code fragment in explanatory text. System messages and symbols are quoted as well.

$   is the UNIX Bourne shell or Korn shell prompt.

[]   surrounds optional elements in a description of program syntax. (The brackets themselves should never be typed, unless otherwise noted.)

...   stands for text (usually computer output) that's been omitted for clarity or to save space.

☐   indicates a literal space. This symbol is used to make spaces visible in examples, as well as in the text.

•   indicates a literal TAB character. This symbol is used to make tabs visible in examples, as well as in the text.

The notation CTRL-X or ^X indicates use of control characters. It means hold down the "control" key while typing the character "x". We denote other keys similarly (e.g., RETURN indicates a carriage return). All examples of command lines are followed by a RETURN unless otherwise indicated.

## *About the Second Edition*

Since this book was first published in 1990, it has become one of the most fundamental of the O'Reilly & Associates Nutshell Handbooks. Three important events occurred after it was written. The first was the publication of the POSIX standard for sed, and more importantly for awk. The second (perhaps due to the first) was the widespread availability of some version or other of new awk on all modern UNIX systems, both commercial ones and the freely available UNIX-like systems such as NetBSD, FreeBSD, and Linux. The third was the source code availability of GNU sed, and three versions of awk, instead of just gawk.

For these and other reasons, O'Reilly & Associates decided that this handbook needed to be updated. The goals of the revision were to keep the flavor of the book intact ("if it ain't broke, don't fix it"), reorient the awk part of the book around POSIX awk, correct mistakes, and bring the book up to date.

I would like to thank Gigi Estabrook, Chris Reilley, and Lenny Muellner of O'Reilly & Associates for their help, Marc Vauclair, the French translator of the first edition, for many helpful comments, and John Dzubera for his comments on the first edition. Michael Brennan, Henry Spencer, and Ozan Yigit acted as technical reviewers for this edition, and I would like to thank them for their input. Ozan Yigit, in particular, deserves extra thanks for forcing me to be very rigorous in my testing. Pat Thompson of Thompson Automation Software graciously provided an evaluation copy of **tawk** for review in this book. Richard Montgomery of Videosoft provided me with information about VSAwk.

The following people provided the scripts in Chapter 13: Jon L. Bentley, Tom Christiansen, Geoff Clare, Roger A. Cornelius, Rahul Dhesi, Nick Holloway, Norman Joseph, Wes Morgan, Tom Van Raalte, and Martin Weitzel. Their contributions are gratefully acknowledged.

Thanks also to the staff at O'Reilly & Associates. Nicole Gipson Arigo was the production editor and project manager. David Sewell was the copyeditor, and Clairemarie Fisher O'Leary proofread the book. Jane Ellin and Sheryl Avruch performed quality control checks. Seth Maislin wrote the index. Erik Ray, Ellen Siever, and Lenny Muellner worked with the tools to create the book. Chris Reilley fine-tuned the figures. Nancy Priest and Mary Jane Walsh designed the interior book layout, and Edie Freedman designed the front cover.

My in-laws, Marshall and Elaine Hartholz of Seattle, deserve special thanks for taking our children camping for a week, allowing me to make significant progress during an important phase of the update. ☺

Finally, I would like to thank my wonderful wife Miriam for her patience during this project.

*Arnold Robbins*

# *Acknowledgments from the First Edition*

To say that this book has been long anticipated is no understatement. I published three articles on awk in *UNIX/World* in the spring and summer of 1987, making the mistake of saying that these articles were from the upcoming Nutshell Handbook, *Sed & Awk.* I proposed to Tim O'Reilly that I adapt the articles and create a book as a project I could work on at home shortly after the birth of my son, Benjamin. I thought I'd finish it in several months. Well, my son turned three around the time I was completing the first draft. Cathy Brennan and the customer service representatives have been patiently handling requests for the book ever since the *UNIX/World* articles appeared. Cathy said that she even had people call to order the book, swearing it was available because they knew other people who had read it. I owe a debt of gratitude to her and her staff and to the readers I've kept waiting.

My thanks to Tim O'Reilly for creating a great company in which one can easily get sidetracked by a number of interesting projects. As editor, he pushed me to complete the book but would not allow it to be complete without his writing all over it. As usual, his suggestions made me work to improve the book.

Thanks to all the writers and production editors at O'Reilly & Associates, who presented interesting problems to be solved with sed and awk. Thanks to Ellie Cutler who was the production editor for the book and also wrote the index. Thanks to Lenny Muellner for allowing me to quote him throughout the book. Thanks as well to Sue Willing and Donna Woonteiler for their efforts in getting the book into print. Thanks to Chris Reilley who did the illustrations. Thanks to the individual contributors of the sed and awk scripts in Chapter 13. Thanks also to Kevin C. Castner, Tim Irvin, Mark Schalz, Alex Humez, Glenn Saito, Geoff Hagel, Tony Hurson, Jerry Peek, Mike Tiller, and Lenny Muellner, who sent me mail pointing out typos and errors.

Finally, dearest thanks to Nancy and Katie, Ben and Glenda.

*Dale Dougherty*

## Comments and Questions

Please address comments and questions concerning this book to the publisher:

> O'Reilly & Associates, Inc.
> 101 Morris Street
> Sebastopol, CA 95472
> 1-800-998-9938 (in the U.S. or Canada)
> 1-707-829-0515 (international or local)
> 1-707-829-0104 (FAX)

You can send us messages electronically. To be put on the mailing list or request a catalog, send email to:

> *info@ora.com*        (via the Internet)
> *uunet!ora!info*      (via UUCP)

To ask technical questions or comment on the book, send email to:

> *bookquestions@ora.com*      (via the Internet)
> *uunet!ora!bookquestions*      (via UUCP)

# 1

# *Power Tools for Editing*

My wife won't let me buy a power saw. She is afraid of an accident if I use one. So I rely on a hand saw for a variety of weekend projects like building shelves. However, if I made my living as a carpenter, I would have to use a power saw. The speed and efficiency provided by power tools would be essential to being productive. [D.D.]

For people who create and modify text files, sed and awk are power tools for editing. Most of the things that you can do with these programs can be done interactively with a text editor. However, using sed and awk can save many hours of repetitive work in achieving the same result.

Sed and awk are peculiar and it takes time to learn them, but the capabilities they provide can repay the learning many times over, especially if text editing is a normal part of your trade.

## *May You Solve Interesting Problems*

The primary motivation for learning sed and awk is that they are useful for devising general solutions to text editing problems.[*] For some people, myself included, the satisfaction of solving a problem is the difference between work and drudgery. Given the choice of using **vi** or sed to make a series of repeated edits over a number of files, I will choose sed, simply because it makes the problem more interesting to me. I am refining a solution instead of repeating a series of keystrokes. Besides, once I accomplish my task, I congratulate myself on being clever. I feel like I have done a little bit of magic and spared myself some dull labor.

---

[*] I suppose this section title is a combination of the ancient Chinese curse "May you live in interesting times" and what Tim O'Reilly once said to me, that someone will solve a problem if he finds the problem interesting. [D.D.]

Initially, using sed and awk will seem like the long way to accomplish a task. After several attempts you may conclude that the task would have been easier to do manually. Be patient. You not only have to learn how to use sed and awk but you also need to learn to recognize situations where using them pays off. As you become more proficient, you will solve problems more quickly and solve a broader range of problems.

You will also begin to see opportunities to find general solutions to specific problems. There is a way of looking at a problem so you see it related to a class of problems. Then you can devise a solution that can be reused in other situations.

Let me give you an example (without showing any program code). One of our books used a cross-referencing naming scheme in which the reference was defined and processed by our formatting software (**sqtroff**). In the text file, a reference to a chapter on error handling might be coded as follows:

    \*[CHerrorhand]

"CHerrorhand" is the name giving the reference and "\*[" and "]" are calling sequences that distinguish the reference from other text. In a central file, the names used for cross references in the document are defined as **sqtroff** strings. For instance, "CHerrorhand" is defined to be "Chapter 16, Error Handling." (The advantage of using a symbolic cross-referencing scheme like this, instead of explicit referencing, is that if chapters are added or deleted or reordered, only the central file needs to be edited to reflect the new organization.) When the formatting software processes the document, the references are properly resolved and expanded.

The problem we faced was that we had to use the same files to create an online version of the book. Because our **sqtroff** formatting software would not be used, we needed some way to expand the cross references in the files. In other words, we did not want files containing "\*[CHerrorhand]"; instead we wanted what "CHerrorhand" referred to.

There were three possible ways to solve this problem:

1.  Use a text editor to search for all references and replace each of them with the appropriate literal string.

2.  Use sed to make the edits. This is similar to making the edits manually, only faster.

3.  Use awk to write a program that (a) reads the central file to make a list of reference names and their definitions, (b) reads the document searching for the reference calling sequence, and (c) looks up the name of the reference on the list and replaces it with its definition.

The first method is obviously time-consuming (and not very interesting!). The second method, using sed, has an advantage in that it creates a tool to do the job. It is pretty simple to write a sed script that looks for "\*[CHerrorhand]" and replaces it with "Chapter 16, Error Handling" for instance. The same script can be used to modify each of the files for the document. The disadvantage is that the substitutions are hard-coded; that is, for each cross reference, you need to write a command that makes the replacement. The third method, using awk, builds a tool that works for *any* cross reference that follows this syntax. This script could be used to expand cross references in other books as well. It spares you from having to compile a list of specific substitutions. It is the most general solution of the three and designed for the greatest possible reuse as a tool.

Part of solving a problem is knowing which tool to build. There are times when a sed script is a better choice because the problem does not lend itself to, or demand, a more complex awk script. You have to keep in mind what kinds of applications are best suited for sed and awk.

# A Stream Editor

Sed is a "non-interactive" stream-oriented editor. It is stream-oriented because, like many UNIX programs, input flows through the program and is directed to standard output. (**vi**, for instance, is not stream-oriented. Nor are most DOS applications.) Input typically comes from a file but can be directed from the keyboard.[*] Output goes to the terminal screen by default but can be captured in a file instead. Sed works by interpreting a script specifying the actions to be performed.

Sed offers capabilities that seem a natural extension of interactive text editing. For instance, it offers a search-and-replace facility that can be applied globally to a single file or a group of files. While you would not typically use sed to change a term that appears once in a particular file, you will find it very useful to make a series of changes across a number of files. Think about making 20 different edits in over 100 files in a matter of minutes, and you get an idea of how powerful sed can be.

Using sed is similar to writing simple shell scripts (or batch files in DOS). You specify a series of actions to be performed in sequence. Most of these actions could be done manually from within **vi**: replacing text, deleting lines, inserting new text, etc. The advantage of sed is that you can specify all editing instructions in one place and then execute them on a single pass through the file. You don't have to go into each file to make each change. Sed can also be used effectively to edit very large files that would be slow to edit interactively.

---

[*] Doing so, however, is not particularly useful.

There are many opportunities to use sed in the course of creating and maintaining a document, especially when the document consists of individual chapters, each placed in a separate file. Typically, after a draft of a document has returned from review, there are a number of changes that can be applied to all files. For instance, during the course of a software documentation project, the name of the software or its components might change, and you have to track down and make these changes. With sed, this is a simple process.

Sed can be used to achieve consistency throughout a document. You can search for all the different ways a particular term might be used and make them all the same. You can use sed to insert special typesetting codes or symbols prior to formatting by **troff**. For instance, it can be used to replace quotation marks with the ASCII character codes for forward and back double quotes ("curly quotes" instead of "straight" quotes).

Sed also has the ability to be used as an editing *filter*. In other words, you could process an input file and send the output to another program. For instance, you could use sed to analyze a plain text file and insert **troff** macros before directing the output to **troff** for formatting. It allows you to make edits on the fly, perhaps ones that are temporary.

An author or publisher can use sed to write numerous conversion programs—translating formatting codes in Scribe or TEX files into **troff**, for example, or converting PC word processing files, such as WordStar. Later on, we will look at a sed script that converts **troff** macros into stylesheet tags for use in Ventura Publisher. (Perhaps sed could be used to translate a program written in the syntax of one language to the syntax of another language.) When Sun Microsystems first produced Xview, they released a conversion program for converting SunView programs to XView, and the program largely consisted of sed scripts, converting the names of various functions.

Sed has a few rudimentary programming constructs that can be used to build more complicated scripts. It also has a limited ability to work on more than one line at a time.

All but the simplest sed scripts are usually invoked from a "shell wrapper," a shell script that invokes sed and also contains the commands that sed executes. A shell wrapper is an easy way to name and execute a single-word command. Users of the command don't even need to know that sed is being used. One example of such a shell wrapper is the script **phrase**, which we'll look at later in this book. It allows you to match a pattern that might fall over two lines, addressing a specific limitation of **grep**.

In summary, use sed:

1. To automate editing actions to be performed on one or more files.

2. To simplify the task of performing the same edits on multiple files.

3. To write conversion programs.

# A Pattern-Matching Programming Language

Identifying awk as a programming language scares some people away from it. If you are one of them, consider awk a different approach to problem solving, one in which you have a lot more control over what you want the computer to do.

Sed is easily seen as the flip side of interactive editing. A sed procedure corresponds closely enough to how you would apply the editing commands manually. Sed limits you to the methods you use in a text editor. Awk offers a more general computational model for processing a file.

A typical example of an awk program is one that transforms data into a formatted report. The data might be a log file generated by a UNIX program such as **uucp**, and the report might summarize the data in a format useful to a system administrator. Another example is a data processing application consisting of separate data entry and data retrieval programs. Data entry is the process of recording data in a structured way. Data retrieval is the process of extracting data from a file and generating a report.

The key to all of these operations is that the data has some kind of structure. Let us illustrate this with the analogy of a bureau. A bureau consists of multiple drawers, and each drawer has a certain set of contents: socks in one drawer, underwear in another, and sweaters in a third drawer. Sometimes drawers have compartments allowing different kinds of things to be stored together. These are all structures that determine where things go—when you are sorting the laundry—and where things can be found—when you are getting dressed. Awk allows you to use the structure of a text file in writing the procedures for putting things in and taking things out.

Thus, the benefits of awk are best realized when the data has some kind of structure. A text file can be loosely or tightly structured. A chapter containing major and minor sections has some structure. We'll look at a script that extracts section headings and numbers them to produce an outline. A table consisting of tab-separated items in columns might be considered very structured. You could use an awk script to reorder columns of data, or even change columns into rows and rows into columns.

Like sed scripts, awk scripts are typically invoked by means of a shell wrapper. This is a shell script that usually contains the command line that invokes awk as well as the script that awk interprets. Simple one-line awk scripts can be entered from the command line.

Some of the things awk allows you to do are:

- View a text file as a textual database made up of records and fields.
- Use variables to manipulate the database.
- Use arithmetic and string operators.
- Use common programming constructs such as loops and conditionals.
- Generate formatted reports.
- Define functions.
- Execute UNIX commands from a script.
- Process the result of UNIX commands.
- Process command-line arguments more gracefully.
- Work more easily with multiple input streams.

Because of these features, awk has the power and range that users might rely upon to do the kinds of tasks performed by shell scripts. In this book, you'll see examples of a menu-based command generator, an interactive spelling checker, and an index processing program, all of which use the features outlined above.

The capabilities of awk extend the idea of text editing into computation, making it possible to perform a variety of data processing tasks, including analysis, extraction, and reporting of data. These are, indeed, the most common uses of awk but there are also many unusual applications: awk has been used to write a Lisp interpreter and even a compiler!

# *Four Hurdles to Mastering sed and awk*

There are a number of introductory UNIX books that will acquaint you with sed and awk. The goal of this book is to take you much further—to help you *master* sed and awk and to reduce the amount of time and effort that it takes you to reach that goal.

There are four hurdles on the way to mastering sed and awk. You must learn:

1. *How to use sed and awk.* This is a relatively low hurdle to clear because, fortunately, sed and awk work in a very similar manner, based on the line editor **ed**. Chapter 2, *Understanding Basic Operations*, covers the mechanics of using sed and awk.

2.  *To apply UNIX regular expression syntax.* Using UNIX regular expression syntax for pattern matching is common to both sed and awk, and many other UNIX programs. This can be a difficult hurdle for two reasons: the syntax is arcane, and though many people have some experience using regular expressions, few have persevered to master the complete syntax. The more facile you are in using this syntax, the easier sed and awk are to use. That is why we spend a good deal of time covering regular expressions in Chapter 3, *Understanding Regular Expression Syntax.*

3.  *How to interact with the shell.* While not directly related to sed and awk themselves, managing the interaction with the command shell is often a frustrating problem, since the shell shares a number of special characters with both programs. If you can, avoid the problem by putting your script in a separate file. If not, use a Bourne-compatible shell for your scripts (the quoting rules are more straightforward), and use single quotes to contain your script. If you are using **csh** as your interactive shell, remember to escape any exclamation points with a backslash ("\!"). There is no other way to get **csh** to leave the exclamation point alone.

4.  *The knack of script writing.* This is the most difficult, rather like a series of high hurdles. Because of this, the bulk of the book is devoted to script writing. With sed, you have to learn a set of single-letter commands. With awk, you have to learn the statements of a programming language. To get the knack of script writing, though, you simply must pore over lots of examples and, of course, must try your hand at writing scripts yourself.

If you were running the high hurdles, the ability to clear the hurdles does not win the race—clearing them swiftly does. In writing scripts, learning the scripting command set or language is simply clearing the hurdle. Acquiring the ability to attack interesting problems with your scripts is running fast enough to compete.

# 2

## Understanding Basic Operations

If you are starting out to learn sed and awk, you can benefit from looking at how much they have in common.

- They are invoked using similar syntax.
- They are both stream-oriented, reading input from text files one line at a time and directing the result to standard output.
- They use regular expressions for pattern matching.
- They allow the user to specify instructions in a script.

One reason they have so much in common is that their origins can be found in the same line editor, **ed**. In this chapter, we begin by taking a brief look at **ed** and show how sed and awk were logical steps towards the creation of a programmable editor.

Where sed and awk differ is in the kind of instructions that control the work they do. Make no mistake—this is a major difference, and it affects the kinds of tasks that can best be performed with these programs.

This chapter looks at the command-line syntax of sed and awk and the basic structure of scripts. It also offers a tutorial, using a mailing list, that will give you a taste of script writing. It is valuable to see sed and awk scripts side-by-side before you concentrate on either one of them.

## Awk, by Sed and Grep, out of Ed

You can trace the lineage of awk to sed and **grep**, and through those two programs to **ed**, the original UNIX line editor.

Have you ever used a line editor? If so, it will be much easier for you to understand the line orientation of sed and awk. If you have used **vi**, a full-screen editor,
then you are familiar with a number of commands that are derived from its underlying line editor, **ex** (which in turn is a superset of the features in **ed**).

Let's look at some basic operations using the line editor **ed**. Don't worry—this is
an exercise intended to help you learn sed and awk, not an attempt to convince
you of the wonders of line editors. The **ed** commands that are shown in this exercise are identical to the **sed** commands you'll learn later on. Feel free to experiment with **ed** on your own to get a sense of how it works. (If you're already
familiar with **ed**, feel free to skip to the next section.)

To use a line editor, you work on one line at a time. It is important to know what
line you are positioned at in the file. When you open a file using **ed**, it displays
the number of characters in the file and positions you at the last line.

```
$ ed test
339
```

There is no prompt. If you enter a command that **ed** does not understand, it prints
a question mark as an error message. You can enter the print command, **p**, to display the current line.

```
p
label on the first box.
```

By default, a command affects only the current line. To make an edit, you move to
the line that you want to edit and then apply the command. To move to a line,
you specify its *address*. An address might consist of a line number, a symbol indicating a specific position in the file, or a regular expression. You can go to the first
line by entering the line number 1. Then you can enter the delete command to
remove that line.

```
1
You might think of a regular expression
d
```

Entering "1" makes the first line the current line, displaying it on the screen. The
delete command in **ed** is **d** and here it deletes the current line. Rather than moving
to a line and then editing it, you can prefix an editing command with an address
that indicates which line or range of lines is the object of the command. If you
enter "1d", the first line would be deleted.

You can also specify a regular expression as an address. To delete a line containing the word "regular," you could issue this command:

```
/regular/d
```

where slashes delimit the regular expression and "regular" is the string you want to match. This command deletes the first line containing "regular" and makes the line following it the current line.

---

NOTE          Make sure you understand that the delete command deletes the whole line. It does not just delete the word "regular" on the line.

---

To delete *all* the lines that contain the regular expression, you'd prefix the command with the letter **g** for global.

```
g/regular/d
```

The global command makes all lines that match the regular expression the object of the specified command.

Deleting text can take you only so far. Substituting text (replacing one bit of text with another) is much more interesting. The substitution command, **s**, in **ed** is:

```
[address]s/pattern/replacement/flag
```

*pattern* is a regular expression that matches a string in the current line to be replaced by *replacement.* For example, the following command replaces the first occurrence of "regular" with "complex" on the current line.

```
s/regular/complex/
```

No address is specified, so it affects only the first occurrence on the current line. It is an error if "regular" is not found on the current line. To look for multiple occurrences on the *same* line, you must specify **g** as a flag:

```
s/regular/complex/g
```

This command changes all occurrences on the current line. An address must be specified to direct this command to act upon more than the current line. The following substitution command specifies an address:

```
/regular/s/regular/complex/g
```

This command affects the first line that matches the address in the file. Remember, the first "regular" is an address and the second is a pattern to match for the substitution command. To make it apply to all lines, use the global command, putting **g** before the address.

```
g/regular/s/regular/complex/g
```

Now the substitution is made everywhere—all occurrences on all lines.

---

NOTE          Note the different meanings of "g." The "g" at the beginning is the
              global command that means make the changes on all lines matched
              by the address. The "g" at the end is a flag that means change each
              occurrence on a line, not just the first.

---

The address and the pattern need not be the same.

```
g/regular expression/s/regular/complex/g
```

On any line that contains the string "regular expression," replace "regular" with
"complex." If the address and the pattern are the same, you can tell **ed** by specifying two consecutive delimiters (//).

```
g/regular/s//complex/g
```

In this example, "regular" is specified as the address and the pattern to be
matched for substitution is the same. If it seems that we've covered these commands quickly and that there is a lot to absorb, don't worry. We will be covering
these commands again later on.

The familiar UNIX utility **grep** is derived from the following global command in **ed**:

```
g/re/p
```

which stands for "global regular expression print." Grep is a line-editing command
that has been extracted from **ed** and made available as an external program. It is
hard-wired to perform one editing command. It takes the regular expression as an
argument on the command line and uses it as the address of lines to print. Here's
an example, looking for lines matching "box":

```
$ grep 'box' test
You are given a series of boxes, the first one labeled "A",
label on the first box.
```

It prints all lines matching the regular expression.

One more interesting feature of **ed** is the ability to *script* your edits, placing them
in a separate file and directing them as input to the line editor. For instance, if a
series of commands were put in a file named *ed-script*, the following command
executes the script:

```
ed test < ed-script
```

This feature makes **ed** a programmable editor—that is, you can script any action
that you might perform manually.

Sed was created as a special-purpose editor that was meant to execute scripts exclusively; unlike **ed**, it cannot be used interactively. Sed differs from **ed** primarily in that it is stream-oriented. By default, all of the input to sed passes through and goes to standard output. The input file itself is not changed. If you actually do want to alter the input file, you typically use the shell mechanism for output redirection, and when you are satisfied with the edits you've made, replace the original file with the modified version.

**ed** is not stream-oriented and changes are made to the file itself. An **ed** script must contain commands to save the file and quit the editor. It produces no output to the screen, except what may be generated by a specific command.

The stream orientation of sed has a major impact on how addressing is applied. In **ed**, a command without an address affects only the current line. Sed goes through the file, a line at a time, such that each line becomes the current line, and the commands are applied to it. The result is that sed applies a command without an address to *every* line in the file.

Look at the following substitution command:

```
s/regular/complex/
```

If you entered this command interactively in **ed**, you'd substitute "complex" for the first occurrence of "regular" on the current line. In an **ed** script, if this was the first command in the script, it would be applied only to the last line of the file (**ed**'s default current line). However, in a sed script, the same command applies to all lines. That is, sed commands are implicitly global. In sed, the previous example has the same result as the following global command in **ed**:

```
g/regular/s//complex/
```

---

*NOTE*        Understanding the difference between current-line addressing in **ed** and global-line addressing in sed is very important. In **ed** you use addressing to *expand* the number of lines that are the object of a command; in sed, you use addressing to *restrict* the number of lines affected by a command.

---

Sed also was designed with a number of additional commands that support script writing. We will look at many of these commands in Chapter 6, *Advanced sed Commands*.

Awk was developed as a programmable editor that, like sed, is stream-oriented and interprets a script of editing commands. Where awk departs from sed is in discarding the line-editor command set. It offers in its place a programming language modeled on the C language. The **print** statement replaces the **p** command, for example. The concept of addressing is carried over, such that:

```
/regular/ { print }
```

prints those lines matching "regular". The braces ({}) surround a series of one or more statements that are applied to the same address.

The advantage of using a programming language in scripts is that it offers many more ways to control what the programmable editor can do. Awk offers expressions, conditional statements, loops, and other programming constructs.

One of the most distinctive features of awk is that it *parses*, or breaks up, each input line and makes individual words available for processing with a script. (An editor such as **vi** also recognizes words, allowing you to move word by word, or make a word the object of an action, but these features can only be used interactively.)

Although awk was designed as a programmable editor, users found that awk scripts could do a wide range of other tasks as well. The authors of awk never imagined it would be used to write large programs. But, recognizing that awk was being used in this way, the authors revised the language, creating **nawk** to offer more support for writing larger programs and tackling general-purpose programming problems. This new version, with minor improvements, is now codified by the POSIX standard.

## *Command-Line Syntax*

You invoke sed and awk in much the same way. The command-line syntax is:

```
command [options] script filename
```

Like almost all UNIX programs, sed and awk can take input from standard input and send the output to standard output. If a *filename* is specified, input is taken from that file. The output contains the processed information. Standard output is the display screen, and typically the output from these programs is directed there. It can also be sent to a file, using I/O redirection in the shell, but it must not go to the same file that supplies input to the program.

The *options* for each command are different. We will demonstrate many of these options in upcoming sections. (The complete list of command-line options for sed can be found in Appendix A, *Quick Reference for sed*; the complete list of options for awk is in Appendix B, *Quick Reference for awk*.)

The *script* specifies what instructions to perform. If specified on the command line, the script must be surrounded in single quotes if it contains a space or any characters that might be interpreted by the shell ($ and * for instance).

One option common to both sed and awk is the *-f* option that allows you to specify the name of a script file. As a script grows in size, it is convenient to place it in a file. Thus, you might invoke sed as follows:

```
sed -f scriptfile inputfile
```

Figure 2-1 shows the basic operation of sed and awk. Each program reads one input line at a time from the input file, makes a copy of the input line, and executes the instructions specified in the script on that copy. Thus, changes made to the input line do not affect the actual input file.

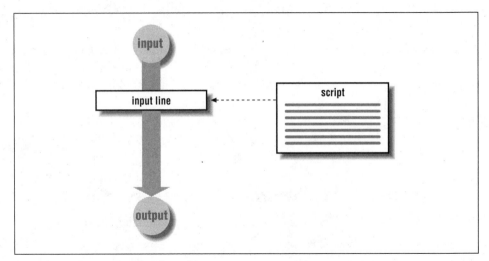

*Figure 2-1: How sed and awk work*

## Scripting

A script is where you tell the program what to do. At least one line of instruction is required. Short scripts can be specified on the command line; longer scripts are usually placed in a file where they can easily be revised and tested. In writing a script, keep in mind the sequence in which instructions will be executed and how each instruction changes the input line.

In sed and awk, each instruction has two parts: a *pattern* and a *procedure*. The pattern is a regular expression delimited with slashes (/). A procedure specifies one or more actions to be performed.

As each line of input is read, the program reads the first instruction in the script and checks the *pattern* against the current line. If there is no match, the *procedure* is ignored and the next instruction is read. If there is a match, then the action or actions specified in the *procedure* are followed. All of the instructions are read, not just the first instruction that matches the input line.

When all the applicable instructions have been interpreted and applied for a single line, sed outputs the line and repeats the cycle for each input line. Awk, on the other hand, does not *automatically* output the line; the instructions in your script control what is finally done with it.

The contents of a procedure are very different in sed and awk. In sed, the procedure consists of editing commands like those used in the line editor. Most commands consist of a single letter.

In awk, the procedure consists of programming statements and functions. A procedure must be surrounded by braces.

In the sections that follow, we'll look at a few scripts that process a sample mailing list.

### Sample Mailing List

In the upcoming sections, the examples use a sample file, named *list*. It contains a list of names and addresses, as shown below.

```
$ cat list
John Daggett, 341 King Road, Plymouth MA
Alice Ford, 22 East Broadway, Richmond VA
Orville Thomas, 11345 Oak Bridge Road, Tulsa OK
Terry Kalkas, 402 Lans Road, Beaver Falls PA
Eric Adams, 20 Post Road, Sudbury MA
Hubert Sims, 328A Brook Road, Roanoke VA
Amy Wilde, 334 Bayshore Pkwy, Mountain View CA
Sal Carpenter, 73 6th Street, Boston MA
```

If you like, create this file on your system or use a similar one of your own making. Because many of the examples in this chapter are short and interactive, you can enter them at your keyboard and verify the results.

## Using sed

There are two ways to invoke sed: either you specify your editing instructions on the command line or you put them in a file and supply the name of the file.

## *Specifying Simple Instructions*

You can specify simple editing commands on the command line.

    sed [-e] '*instruction*' file

The *-e* option is necessary only when you supply more than one instruction on the command line. It tells sed to interpret the next argument as an instruction. When there is a single instruction, sed is able to make that determination on its own. Let's look at some examples.

Using the sample input file, *list*, the following example uses the **s** command for substitution to replace "MA" with "Massachusetts."

```
$ sed 's/MA/Massachusetts/' list
John Daggett, 341 King Road, Plymouth Massachusetts
Alice Ford, 22 East Broadway, Richmond VA
Orville Thomas, 11345 Oak Bridge Road, Tulsa OK
Terry Kalkas, 402 Lans Road, Beaver Falls PA
Eric Adams, 20 Post Road, Sudbury Massachusetts
Hubert Sims, 328A Brook Road, Roanoke VA
Amy Wilde, 334 Bayshore Pkwy, Mountain View CA
Sal Carpenter, 73 6th Street, Boston Massachusetts
```

Three lines are affected by the instruction but all lines are displayed.

Enclosing the instruction in single quotes is not required in all cases but you should get in the habit of always doing it. The enclosing single quotes prevent the shell from interpreting special characters or spaces found in the editing instruction. (The shell uses spaces to determine individual arguments submitted to a program; characters that are special to the shell are expanded before the command is invoked.)

For instance, the first example could have been entered without them but in the next example they are required, since the substitution command contains spaces:

```
$ sed 's/ MA/, Massachusetts/' list
John Daggett, 341 King Road, Plymouth, Massachusetts
Alice Ford, 22 East Broadway, Richmond VA
Orville Thomas, 11345 Oak Bridge Road, Tulsa OK
Terry Kalkas, 402 Lans Road, Beaver Falls PA
Eric Adams, 20 Post Road, Sudbury, Massachusetts
Hubert Sims, 328A Brook Road, Roanoke VA
Amy Wilde, 334 Bayshore Pkwy, Mountain View CA
Sal Carpenter, 73 6th Street, Boston, Massachusetts
```

In order to place a comma between the city and state, the instruction replaced the space before the two-letter abbreviation with a comma and a space.

There are three ways to specify multiple instructions on the command line:

1.  Separate instructions with a semicolon.

    ```
    sed 's/ MA/, Massachusetts/; s/ PA/, Pennsylvania/' list
    ```

2.  Precede each instruction by *-e*.

    ```
    sed -e 's/ MA/, Massachusetts/' -e 's/ PA/, Pennsylvania/' list
    ```

3.  Use the multiline entry capability of the Bourne shell.[*] Press RETURN after entering a single quote and a secondary prompt (>) will be displayed for multiline input.

    ```
    $ sed '
    > s/ MA/, Massachusetts/
    > s/ PA/, Pennsylvania/
    > s/ CA/, California/' list
    John Daggett, 341 King Road, Plymouth, Massachusetts
    Alice Ford, 22 East Broadway, Richmond VA
    Orville Thomas, 11345 Oak Bridge Road, Tulsa OK
    Terry Kalkas, 402 Lans Road, Beaver Falls, Pennsylvania
    Eric Adams, 20 Post Road, Sudbury, Massachusetts
    Hubert Sims, 328A Brook Road, Roanoke VA
    Amy Wilde, 334 Bayshore Pkwy, Mountain View, California
    Sal Carpenter, 73 6th Street, Boston, Massachusetts
    ```

    This technique will not work in the C shell. Instead, use semicolons at the end of each instruction, and you can enter commands over multiple lines by ending each line with a backslash. (Or, you could temporarily go into the Bourne shell by entering **sh** and then type the command.)

In the example above, changes were made to five lines and, of course, all lines were displayed. Remember that nothing has changed in the input file.

## Command garbled

The syntax of a sed command can be detailed, and it's easy to make a mistake or omit a required element. Notice what happens when incomplete syntax is entered:

```
$ sed -e 's/MA/Massachusetts' list
sed: command garbled: s/MA/Massachusetts
```

Sed will usually display any line that it cannot execute, but it does not tell you what is wrong with the command.[†] In this instance, a slash, which marks the search and replacement portions of the command, is missing at the end of the substitute command.

---

[*] These days there are many shells that are compatible with the Bourne shell, and work as described here: **ksh**, **bash**, **pdksh**, and **zsh**, to name a few.

[†] Some vendors seem to have improved things. For instance, on SunOS 4.1.x, sed reports "sed: Ending delimiter missing on substitution: s/MA/Massachusetts".

GNU sed is more helpful:

```
$ gsed -e 's/MA/Massachusetts' list
gsed: Unterminated 's' command
```

## Script Files

It is not practical to enter longer editing scripts on the command line. That is why it is usually best to create a script file that contains the editing instructions. The editing script is simply a list of sed commands that are executed in the order in which they appear. This form, using the *-f* option, requires that you specify the name of the script file on the command line.

```
sed -f scriptfile file
```

All the editing commands that we want executed are placed in a file. We follow a convention of creating temporary script files named *sedscr*.

```
$ cat sedscr
s/ MA/, Massachusetts/
s/ PA/, Pennsylvania/
s/ CA/, California/
s/ VA/, Virginia/
s/ OK/, Oklahoma/
```

The following command reads all of the substitution commands in *sedscr* and applies them to each line in the input file *list*:

```
$ sed -f sedscr list
John Daggett, 341 King Road, Plymouth, Massachusetts
Alice Ford, 22 East Broadway, Richmond, Virginia
Orville Thomas, 11345 Oak Bridge Road, Tulsa, Oklahoma
Terry Kalkas, 402 Lans Road, Beaver Falls, Pennsylvania
Eric Adams, 20 Post Road, Sudbury, Massachusetts
Hubert Sims, 328A Brook Road, Roanoke, Virginia
Amy Wilde, 334 Bayshore Pkwy, Mountain View, California
Sal Carpenter, 73 6th Street, Boston, Massachusetts
```

Once again, the result is ephemeral, displayed on the screen. No change is made to the input file.

If a sed script can be used again, you should rename the script and save it. Scripts of proven value can be maintained in a personal or system-wide library.

### Saving output

Unless you are redirecting the output of sed to another program, you will want to capture the output in a file. This is done by specifying one of the shell's I/O redirection symbols followed by the name of a file:

```
$ sed -f sedscr list > newlist
```

Do not redirect the output to the file you are editing or you will clobber it. (The ">" redirection operator truncates the file before the shell does anything else.) If you want the output file to replace the input file, you can do that as a separate step, using the **mv** command. But first make very sure your editing script has worked properly!

In Chapter 4, *Writing sed Scripts*, we will look at a shell script named **runsed** that automates the process of creating a temporary file and using **mv** to overwrite the original file.

### Suppressing automatic display of input lines

The default operation of sed is to output every input line. The *-n* option suppresses the automatic output. When specifying this option, each instruction intended to produce output must contain a print command, **p**. Look at the following example.

```
$ sed -n -e 's/MA/Massachusetts/p' list
John Daggett, 341 King Road, Plymouth Massachusetts
Eric Adams, 20 Post Road, Sudbury Massachusetts
Sal Carpenter, 73 6th Street, Boston Massachusetts
```

Compare this output to the first example in this section. Here, only the lines that were affected by the command were printed.

### Mixing options (POSIX)

You can build up a script by combining both the *-e* and *-f* options on the command line. The script is the combination of all the commands in the order given. This appears to be supported in UNIX versions of sed, but this feature is not clearly documented in the manpage. The POSIX standard explicitly mandates this behavior.

### Summary of options

Table 2-1 summarizes the sed command-line options.

*Table 2–1: Command-Line Options for sed*

| Option | Description |
| --- | --- |
| *-e* | Editing instruction follows. |
| *-f* | Filename of script follows. |
| *-n* | Suppress automatic output of input lines. |

# *Using awk*

Like sed, awk executes a set of instructions for each line of input. You can specify instructions on the command line or create a script file.

## *Running awk*

For command lines, the syntax is:

**awk** *'instructions' files*

Input is read a line at a time from one or more *files* or from standard input. The *instructions* must be enclosed in single quotes to protect them from the shell. (Instructions almost always contain curly braces and/or dollar signs, which are interpreted as special characters by the shell.) Multiple command lines can be entered in the same way as shown for sed: separating commands with semicolons or using the multiline input capability of the Bourne shell.

Awk programs are usually placed in a file where they can be tested and modified. The syntax for invoking awk with a script file is:

**awk -f** *script files*

The *-f* option works the same way as it does with sed.

While awk instructions have the same structure as sed, consisting of *pattern* and *procedure* sections, the procedures themselves are quite different. Here is where awk looks less like an editor and more like a programming language. There are statements and functions instead of one- or two-character command sequences. For instance, you use the **print** statement to print the value of an expression or to print the contents of the current input line.

Awk, in the usual case, interprets each input line as a record and each word on that line, delimited by spaces or tabs, as a field. (These defaults can be changed.) One or more consecutive spaces or tabs count as a single delimiter. Awk allows you to reference these fields, in either patterns or procedures. $0 represents the entire input line. $1, $2, ... refer to the individual fields on the input line. Awk splits the input record before the script is applied. Let's look at a few examples, using the sample input file *list*.

The first example contains a single instruction that prints the first field of each line in the input file.

```
$ awk '{ print $1 }' list
John
Alice
Orville
Terry
```

```
Eric
Hubert
Amy
Sal
```

"$1" refers to the value of the first field on each input line. Because there is no pattern specified, the print statement is applied to all lines. In the next example, a pattern "/MA/" is specified but there is no procedure. The default action is to print each line that matches the pattern.

```
$ awk '/MA/' list
John Daggett, 341 King Road, Plymouth MA
Eric Adams, 20 Post Road, Sudbury MA
Sal Carpenter, 73 6th Street, Boston MA
```

Three lines are printed. As mentioned in the first chapter, an awk program can be used more like a query language, extracting useful information from a file. We might say that the pattern placed a condition on the selection of records to be included in a report, namely that they must contain the string "MA". Now we can also specify what portion of a record to include in the report. The next example uses a **print** statement to limit the output to the first field of each record.

```
$ awk '/MA/ { print $1 }' list
John
Eric
Sal
```

It helps to understand the above instruction if we try to read it aloud: *Print the first word of each line containing the string "MA".* We can say "word" because by default awk separates the input into fields using either spaces or tabs as the field separator.

In the next example, we use the *-F* option to change the field separator to a comma. This allows us to retrieve any of three fields: the full name, the street address, and the city and state.

```
$ awk -F, '/MA/ { print $1 }' list
John Daggett
Eric Adams
Sal Carpenter
```

Do not confuse the *-F* option to change the field separator with the *-f* option to specify the name of a script file.

In the next example, we print each field on its own line. Multiple commands are separated by semicolons.

```
$ awk -F, '{ print $1; print $2; print $3 }' list
John Daggett
 341 King Road
 Plymouth MA
Alice Ford
 22 East Broadway
 Richmond VA
Orville Thomas
 11345 Oak Bridge Road
 Tulsa OK
Terry Kalkas
 402 Lans Road
 Beaver Falls PA
Eric Adams
 20 Post Road
 Sudbury MA
Hubert Sims
 328A Brook Road
 Roanoke VA
Amy Wilde
 334 Bayshore Pkwy
 Mountain View CA
Sal Carpenter
 73 6th Street
 Boston MA
```

Our examples using sed changed the content of incoming data. Our examples using awk rearrange the data. In the preceding awk example, note how the leading blank is now considered part of the second and third fields.

## Error Messages

Each implementation of awk gives you different error messages when it encounters problems in your program. Thus, we won't quote a particular version's messages here; it'll be obvious when there's a problem. Messages can be caused by any of the following:

- Not enclosing a procedure within braces ({})
- Not surrounding the instructions within single quotes ('')
- Not enclosing regular expressions within slashes (//)

## Summary of Options

Table 2-2 summarizes the awk command-line options.

*Table 2–2: Command-Line Options for awk*

| Option | Description |
|--------|-------------|
| *-f* | Filename of script follows. |
| *-F* | Change field separator. |
| *-v* | *var=value* follows. |

The *-v* option for specifying parameters on the command line is discussed in Chapter 7, *Writing Scripts for awk.*

# Using sed and awk Together

In UNIX, pipes can be used to pass the output from one program as input to the next program. Let's look at a few examples that combine sed and awk to produce a report. The sed script that replaced the postal abbreviation of a state with its full name is general enough that it might be used again as a script file named **name-State**:

```
$ cat nameState
s/ CA/, California/
s/ MA/, Massachusetts/
s/ OK/, Oklahoma/
s/ PA/, Pennsylvania/
s/ VA/, Virginia/
```

Of course, you'd want to handle all states, not just five, and if you were running it on documents other than mailing lists, you should make sure that it does not make unwanted replacements.

The output for this program, using the input file *list*, is the same as we have already seen. In the next example, the output produced by **nameState** is piped to an awk program that extracts the name of the state from each record.

```
$ sed -f nameState list | awk -F, '{ print $4 }'
Massachusetts
Virginia
Oklahoma
Pennsylvania
Massachusetts
Virginia
California
Massachusetts
```

The awk program is processing the output produced by the sed script. Remember that the sed script replaces the abbreviation with a comma and the full name of the state. In effect, it splits the third field containing the city and state into two fields. "$4" references the fourth field.

What we are doing here could be done completely in sed, but probably with more difficulty and less generality. Also, since awk allows you to replace the string you match, you could achieve this result entirely with an awk script.

While the result of this program is not very useful, it could be passed to **sort | uniq -c**, which would sort the states into an alphabetical list with a count of the number of occurrences of each state.

Now we are going to do something more interesting. We want to produce a report that sorts the names by state and lists the name of the state followed by the name of each person residing in that state. The following example shows the **byState** program.

```
#! /bin/sh
awk -F, '{
        print $4 ", " $0
        }' $* |
sort |
awk -F, '
$1 != LastState {
        LastState = $1
        print $1
        print "\t" $2
}
$1 == LastState {
        print "\t" $2
}'
```

This shell script has three parts. The program invokes awk to produce input for the **sort** program and then invokes awk again to test the sorted input and determine if the name of the state in the current record is the same as in the previous record. Let's see the script in action:

```
$ sed -f nameState list | byState
California
        Amy Wilde
Massachusetts
        Eric Adams
        John Daggett
        Sal Carpenter
Oklahoma
        Orville Thomas
Pennsylvania
        Terry Kalkas
Virginia
        Alice Ford
        Hubert Sims
```

The names are sorted by state. This is a typical example of using awk to generate a report from structured data.

To examine how the **byState** program works, let's look at each part separately. It's designed to read input from the **nameState** program and expects "$4" to be the name of the state. Look at the output produced by the first line of the program:

```
$ sed -f nameState list | awk -F, '{ print $4 ", " $0 }'
Massachusetts, John Daggett, 341 King Road, Plymouth, Massachusetts
Virginia, Alice Ford, 22 East Broadway, Richmond, Virginia
Oklahoma, Orville Thomas, 11345 Oak Bridge Road, Tulsa, Oklahoma
Pennsylvania, Terry Kalkas, 402 Lans Road, Beaver Falls, Pennsylvania
Massachusetts, Eric Adams, 20 Post Road, Sudbury, Massachusetts
Virginia, Hubert Sims, 328A Brook Road, Roanoke, Virginia
California, Amy Wilde, 334 Bayshore Pkwy, Mountain View, California
Massachusetts, Sal Carpenter, 73 6th Street, Boston, Massachusetts
```

The **sort** program, by default, sorts lines in alphabetical order, looking at characters from left to right. In order to sort records by state, and not names, we insert the state as a sort key at the beginning of the record. Now the **sort** program can do its work for us. (Notice that using the **sort** utility saves us from having to write sort routines inside awk.)

The second time awk is invoked we perform a programming task. The script looks at the first field of each record (the state) to determine if it is the same as in the previous record. If it is not the same, the name of the state is printed followed by the person's name. If it is the same, then only the person's name is printed.

```
$1 != LastState {
        LastState = $1
        print $1
        print "\t" $2
}
$1 == LastState {
        print "\t" $2
}'
```

There are a few significant things here, including assigning a variable, testing the first field of each input line to see if it contains a variable string, and printing a tab to align the output data. Note that we don't have to assign to a variable before using it (because awk variables are initialized to the empty string). This is a small script, but you'll see the same kind of routine used to compare index entries in a much larger indexing program in Chapter 12, *Full-Featured Applications*. However, for now, don't worry too much about understanding what each statement is doing. Our point here is to give you an overview of what sed and awk can do.

In this chapter, we have covered the basic operations of sed and awk. We have looked at important command-line options and introduced you to scripting. In the next chapter, we are going to look at regular expressions, something both programs use to match patterns in the input.

# 3

*In this chapter:*
- *That's an Expression*
- *A Line-Up of Characters*
- *I Never Metacharacter I Didn't Like*

# Understanding Regular Expression Syntax

When a young child is struggling to understand the meaning of an idiomatic expression, such as "Someone let the cat out of the bag," you might help by explaining that it's an *expression*, and doesn't literally mean what it says.

An expression, even in computer terminology, is not something to be interpreted literally. It is something that needs to be evaluated. An expression describes a result.

In this chapter, we are going to look at regular expression syntax. A regular expression describes a pattern or a particular sequence of characters, although it does not necessarily specify a single exact sequence.

While regular expressions are a basic part of UNIX, not everyone has a complete understanding of the syntax. In fact, it can be quite confusing to look at an expression such as:

```
^□□*.*
```

which uses *metacharacters* or special symbols to match a line with one or more leading spaces. (A square box, □, is used to make spaces visible in our examples.)

If you use any UNIX text editor on a routine basis, you are probably somewhat familiar with regular expression syntax. **grep**, sed, and awk all use regular expressions. However, not all of the metacharacters used in regular expression syntax are available for all three programs. The basic set of metacharacters was introduced with the **ed** line editor, and made available in **grep**. Sed uses the same set of metacharacters. Later a program named **egrep** was introduced that offered an *extended* set of metacharacters. Awk uses essentially the same set of metacharacters as **egrep**.

To understand regular expression syntax, you have to learn the functions performed by various metacharacters. But you also have to see many examples of them working in various combinations. That is our approach in this chapter, to introduce each metacharacter and provide a lot of examples, that for the most part use **grep**, and its cousin, **egrep**, to demonstrate practical applications.

If you already understand regular expression syntax, feel free to skip this chapter. A complete listing of regular expression metacharacters can be found in Table 3-1, as well as in Appendix A, *Quick Reference for sed*, and Appendix B, *Quick Reference for awk*. For those who are interested, O'Reilly's *Mastering Regular Expressions*, by Jeffrey E. F. Friedl, provides exhaustive coverage of regular expression construction and use.

# *That's an Expression*

You are probably familiar with the kinds of expressions that a calculator interprets. Look at the following arithmetic expression:

```
2 + 4
```

"Two plus four" consists of several constants or literal values and an operator. A calculator program must recognize, for instance, that "2" is a numeric constant and that the plus sign represents an operator, not to be interpreted as the "+" character.

An expression tells the computer how to produce a result. Although it is the result of "two plus four" that we really want, we don't simply tell the computer to return a six. We instruct the computer to evaluate the expression and return a value.

An expression can be more complicated than "2 + 4"; in fact, it might consist of multiple simple expressions, such as the following:

```
2 + 3 * 4
```

A calculator normally evaluates an expression from left to right. However, certain operators have precedence over others: that is, they will be performed first. Thus, the above expression will evaluate to 14 and not 20 because multiplication takes precedence over addition. Precedence can be overridden by placing the simple expression in parentheses. Thus, "(2 + 3) * 4" or "the sum of two plus three times four" will evaluate to 20. The parentheses are symbols that instruct the calculator to change the order in which the expression is evaluated.

A regular expression, by contrast, describes a pattern or sequence of characters. Concatenation is the basic operation implied in every regular expression. That is, a pattern matches adjacent characters. Look at the following regular expression:

```
ABE
```

Each literal character is a regular expression that matches only that single character. This expression describes an "A followed by a B then followed by an E" or simply "the string ABE". The term "string" means each character concatenated to the one preceding it. That a regular expression describes a *sequence* of characters can't be emphasized enough. (Novice users are inclined to think in higher-level units such as words, and not individual characters.) Regular expressions are case-sensitive; "A" does not match "a".[*]

Programs such as **grep** that accept regular expressions must first evaluate the syntax of the regular expression to produce a pattern. They then read the input line-by-line trying to match the pattern. An input line is a string, and to see if a string matches the pattern, a program compares the first character in the string to the first character of the pattern. If there is a match, it compares the second character in the string to the second character of the pattern. Whenever it fails to make a match, it goes back and tries again, beginning one character later in the string. Figure 3-1 illustrates this process, trying to match the pattern "abe" on an input line.

A regular expression is not limited to literal characters. There is, for instance, a metacharacter—the dot (.)—that can be used as a "wildcard" to match any single character. You can think of this wildcard as analogous to a blank tile in Scrabble where it means any letter. Thus, we can specify the regular expression "A.E" and it will match "ACE," "ABE", and "ALE". It will match any character in the position following "A".

The metacharacter *, the asterisk, is used to match zero or more occurrences of the *preceding* regular expression, which typically is a single character. You may be familiar with * as a *shell* metacharacter, where it means "zero or more characters." But that meaning is very different from * in a regular expression. By itself, the asterisk metacharacter does not match anything; it modifies what goes before it. The regular expression .* matches any number of characters, whereas in the shell, * has that meaning. (For instance, in the shell, **ls** * will list all the files in the current directory.) The regular expression "A.*E" matches any string that matches "A.E" but it will also match any number of characters between "A" and "E": "AIRPLANE," "A FINE," "AFFABLE," or "A LONG WAY HOME," for example. Note that "any number of characters" can even be zero!

If you understand the difference between "." and "*" in regular expressions, you already know about the two basic types of metacharacters: those that can be evaluated to a single character, and those that modify how preceding characters are evaluated.

---

[*] Some other programs that use regular expressions offer the option of having them be case-insensitive, but sed and awk do not.

It should also be apparent that by use of metacharacters you can expand or limit the possible matches. You have more control over what's matched and what's not.

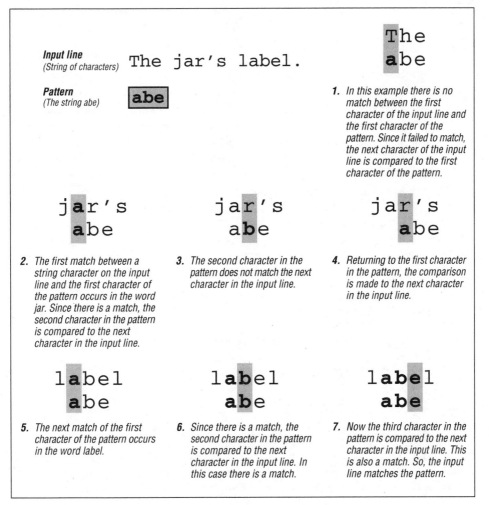

**Input line**
(String of characters)  `The jar's label.`

**Pattern**
(The string abe)  `abe`

**The**
**abe**

1. In this example there is no match between the first character of the input line and the first character of the pattern. Since it failed to match, the next character of the input line is compared to the first character of the pattern.

**j** a r ' s
**a** b e

2. The first match between a string character on the input line and the first character of the pattern occurs in the word *jar*. Since there is a match, the second character in the pattern is compared to the next character in the input line.

j **a** r ' s
**ab** e

3. The second character in the pattern does not match the next character in the input line.

j **a** r ' s
**a** b e

4. Returning to the first character in the pattern, the comparison is made to the next character in the input line.

**l** a b e l
**a** b e

5. The next match of the first character of the pattern occurs in the word *label*.

l **ab** e l
**ab** e

6. Since there is a match, the second character in the pattern is compared to the next character in the input line. In this case there is a match.

l **abe** l
**abe**

7. Now the third character in the pattern is compared to the next character in the input line. This is also a match. So, the input line matches the pattern.

*Figure 3–1: Interpreting a regular expression*

# A Line-Up of Characters

We have seen two basic elements in an expression:

1.  A value expressed as a literal or a variable.

2.  An operator.

A regular expression is made up of these same elements. Any character, except the metacharacters in Table 3-1, is interpreted as a literal that matches only itself.

*Table 3-1:  Summary of Metacharacters*

| Special Characters | Usage |
| --- | --- |
| . | Matches any *single* character except *newline.*  In awk, dot can match *newline* also. |
| * | Matches any number (including zero) of the single character (including a character specified by a regular expression) that immediately precedes it. |
| [ . . . ] | Matches any *one* of the class of characters enclosed between the brackets. A circumflex (ˆ) as first character inside brackets reverses the match to all characters except newline and those listed in the class. In awk, newline will also match.  A hyphen (-) is used to indicate a range of characters. The close bracket (]) as the first character in class is a member of the class. All other metacharacters lose their meaning when specified as members of a class. |
| ˆ | First character of regular expression, matches the beginning of the line. Matches the beginning of a string in awk, even if the string contains embedded newlines. |
| $ | As last character of regular expression, matches the end of the line.  Matches the end of a string in awk, even if the string contains embedded newlines. |
| \{*n,m*\} | Matches a range of occurrences of the single character (including a character specified by a regular expression) that immediately precedes it.  \{*n*\} will match exactly *n* occurrences, \{*n*,\} will match at least *n* occurrences, and \{*n,m*\} will match any number of occurrences between *n* and *m*. (sed and **grep** only, may not be in some very old versions.) |
| \ | Escapes the special character that follows. |

### Extended Metacharacters  (**egrep** and **awk**)

| Special Characters | Usage |
| --- | --- |
| + | Matches one or more occurrences of the preceding regular expression. |
| ? | Matches zero or one occurrences of the preceding regular expression. |
| \| | Specifies that either the preceding or following regular expression can be matched (alternation). |
| ( ) | Groups regular expressions. |
| {*n,m*} | Matches a range of occurrences of the single character (including a character specified by a regular expression) that immediately precedes it. {*n*} will match exactly *n* occurrences, {*n*,} will match at least *n* occurrences, and {*n,m*} will match any number of occurrences between *n* and *m*. (POSIX **egrep** and POSIX awk, not in traditional **egrep** or awk.)[a] |

[a] Most awk implementations do not yet support this notation.

Metacharacters have a special meaning in regular expressions, much the same way as + and * have special meaning in arithmetic expressions. Several of the metacharacters (+ ? () |) are available only as part of the extended set used by programs such as **egrep** and awk. We will look at what each metacharacter does in upcoming sections, beginning with the backslash.

## *The Ubiquitous Backslash*

The backslash (\) metacharacter transforms metacharacters into ordinary characters (and ordinary characters into metacharacters). It forces the literal interpretation of any metacharacter such that it will match itself. For instance, the dot (.) is a metacharacter that needs to be escaped with a backslash if you want to match a period. This regular expression matches a period followed by three spaces.

    \.□□□

The backslash is typically used to match **troff** requests or macros that begin with a dot.

    \.nf

You can also use the backslash to escape the backslash. For instance, the font change request in **troff** is "\f". To search for lines containing this request, you'd use the following regular expression:

    \\f

In addition, sed uses the backslash to cause a group of ordinary characters to be interpreted as metacharacters, as shown in Figure 3-2.

---

$$\backslash(\quad\backslash)\quad\backslash\{\quad\backslash\}\quad\backslash n$$

---

*Figure 3-2: Escaped metacharacters in sed*

The *n* in the "\*n*" construct represents a digit from 1 to 9; its use will be explained in Chapter 5, *Basic sed Commands*.

## *A Wildcard*

The *wildcard* metacharacter, or dot (.), might be considered equivalent to a variable. A variable represents any value in an arithmetic expression. In a regular expression, a dot (.) is a wildcard that represents any character except the newline. (In awk, dot can even match an embedded newline character.)

Given that we are describing a sequence of characters, the wildcard metacharacter allows you to specify a position that any character can fill.

For instance, if we were searching a file containing a discussion of the Intel family of microprocessors, the following regular expression:

```
80.86
```

would match lines containing references to "80286," "80386," or "80486."[*] To match a decimal point or a period, you must escape the dot with a backslash.

It is seldom useful to match just any character at the beginning or end of a pattern. Therefore, the wildcard character is usually preceded and followed by a literal character or other metacharacter. For example, the following regular expression might be written to search for references to chapters:

```
Chapter.
```

It searches for "the string 'Chapter' followed by any character." In a search, this expression would turn up virtually the same matches as the fixed string pattern "Chapter". Look at the following example:

```
$ grep 'Chapter.' sample
you will find several examples in Chapter 9.
"Quote me 'Chapter and Verse'," she said.
Chapter Ten
```

Searching for the string "Chapter" as opposed to "Chapter." would have matched all of the same lines. However, there is one case that would be different—if "Chapter" appeared at the end of a line. The wildcard does not match the newline, so "Chapter." would not match that line, while the fixed-string pattern would match the line.

## Writing Regular Expressions

For all practical purposes, you can rely on a program to produce the correct result. However, that doesn't mean the program always works correctly as far as you are concerned. Most of the time, you can bet that if a program does not produce the output that you expected, the real problem (putting aside input or syntax errors) is how you described what you wanted.

In other words, the place to look to correct the problem is the expression where you described the result you wanted. Either the expression is incomplete or it is improperly formulated. For instance, if a program evaluates this expression:

```
PAY = WEEKLY_SALARY * 52
```

---

[*] The Pentium family of microprocessors breaks our simple pattern-matching experiment, spoiling the fun. Not to mention the original 8086.

and knows the values of these variables, it will calculate the correct result. But someone might object that the formula did not account for salespeople, who also receive a commission. To describe this instance, the expression would need to be reformulated as:

```
PAY = WEEKLY_SALARY * 52 + COMMISSION
```

You could say that whoever wrote the first expression did not fully understand the scope of the problem and thus did not describe it well. It is important to know just how detailed a description must be. If you ask someone to bring you a book, and there are multiple books in view, you need to describe more specifically the book that you want (or be content with an indeterminate selection process).

The same is true with regular expressions. A program such as **grep** is simple and easy to use. Understanding the elements of regular expressions is not so hard, either. Regular expressions allow you to write simple or complex descriptions of patterns. However, what makes writing regular expressions difficult (and interesting) is the complexity of the application: the variety of occurrences or contexts in which a pattern appears. This complexity is inherent in language itself, just as you can't always understand an expression by looking up each word in the dictionary.

The process of writing a regular expression involves three steps:

1. Knowing what it is you want to match and how it might appear in the text.
2. Writing a pattern to describe what you want to match.
3. Testing the pattern to see what it matches.

This process is virtually the same kind of process that a programmer follows to develop a program. Step 1 might be considered the specification, which should reflect an understanding of the problem to be solved as well as how to solve it. Step 2 is analogous to the actual coding of the program, and Step 3 involves running the program and testing it against the specification. Steps 2 and 3 form a loop that is repeated until the program works satisfactorily.

Testing your description of what you want to match ensures that the description works as expected. It usually uncovers a few surprises. Carefully examining the results of a test, comparing the output against the input, will greatly improve your understanding of regular expressions. You might consider evaluating the results of a pattern matching-operation as follows:

*Hits*

    The lines that I wanted to match.

*Misses*

    The lines that I didn't want to match.

*Omissions*

The lines that I didn't match but wanted to match.

*False alarms*

The lines that I matched but didn't want to match.

Trying to perfect your description of a pattern is something that you work at from opposite ends: you try to eliminate the false alarms by limiting the possible matches and you try to capture the omissions by expanding the possible matches.

The difficulty is especially apparent when you must describe patterns using fixed strings. Each character you remove from the fixed-string pattern increases the number of possible matches. For instance, while searching for the string "what," you determine that you'd like to match "What" as well. The only fixed-string pattern that will match "What" and "what" is "hat," the longest string common to both. It is obvious, though, that searching for "hat" will produce unwanted matches. Each character you add to a fixed-string pattern decreases the number of possible matches. The string "them" will usually produce fewer matches than the string "the."

Using metacharacters in patterns provides greater flexibility in extending or narrowing the range of matches. Metacharacters, used in combination with literals or other metacharacters, can be used to expand the range of matches while still eliminating the matches that you do not want.

## Character Classes

A character class is a refinement of the wildcard concept. Instead of matching *any* character at a specific position, we can list the characters to be matched. The square bracket metacharacters ([]) enclose the list of characters, any of which can occupy a single position.

Character classes are useful for dealing with uppercase and lowercase letters, for instance. If "what" might appear with either an initial capital letter or a lowercase letter, you can specify:

    [Ww]hat

This regular expression can match "what" or "What." It will match any line that contains this four-character string, the first character of which is either "W" or "w." Therefore, it could match "Whatever" or "somewhat."

If a file contained structured heading macros, such as .H1, .H2, .H3, etc., you could extract any of these lines with the regular expression:

    \.H[12345]

This pattern matches a three-character string, where the last character is any number from 1 to 5.

The same syntax is used by the UNIX shell. Thus, you can use character classes to specify filenames in UNIX commands. For example, to extract headings from a group of chapter files, you might enter:

```
$ grep '\.H[123]' ch0[12]
ch01:.H1 "Contents of Distribution Tape"
ch01:.H1 "Installing the Software"
ch01:.H1 "Configuring the System"
ch01:.H2 "Specifying Input Devices"
ch01:.H3 "Using the Touch Screen"
ch01:.H3 "Using the Mouse"
ch01:.H2 "Specifying Printers"
ch02:.H1 "Getting Started"
ch02:.H2 "A Quick Tour"
  .
  .
  .
```

Note that you have to quote the pattern so that it is passed on to **grep** rather than interpreted by the shell. The output produced by **grep** identifies the name of the file for each line printed. As another example of a character class, assume you want to specify the different punctuation marks that end a sentence:

```
.[!?;:,".]□□.
```

This expression matches "any character followed by an exclamation mark or question mark or semicolon or colon or comma or quotation mark or period and then followed by two spaces and any character." It could be used to find places where two spaces had been left between the end of a sentence and the beginning of the next sentence, when this occurs on one line. Notice that there are three dots in this expression. The first and last dots are wildcard metacharacters, but the second dot is interpreted literally. Inside square brackets, the standard metacharacters lose their meaning. Thus, the dot inside the square brackets indicates a period. Table 3-2 lists the characters that have a special meaning inside square brackets.

*Table 3-2: Special Characters in Character Classes*

| Character | Function |
|---|---|
| \ | Escapes any special character (**awk** only) |
| - | Indicates a range when not in the first or last position. |
| ^ | Indicates a reverse match only when in the first position. |

The backslash is special only in awk, making it possible to write "[a\]1]" for a character class that will match an **a**, a right bracket, or a **1**.

## *A range of characters*

The hyphen character (-) allows you to specify a range of characters. For instance, the range of all uppercase English letters[*] can be specified as:

    [A-Z]

A range of single-digit numbers can be specified as:

    [0-9]

This character class helps solve an earlier problem of matching chapter references. Look at the following regular expression:

    [cC]hapter [1-9]

It matches the string "chapter" or "Chapter" followed by a space and then followed by any single-digit number from 1 to 9. Each of the following lines match the pattern:

    you will find the information in chapter 9
    and chapter 12.
    Chapter 4 contains a summary at the end.

Depending upon the task, the second line in this example might be considered a false alarm. You might add a space following "[1-9]" to avoid matching two-digit numbers. You could also specify a class of characters not to be matched at that position, as we'll see in the next section. Multiple ranges can be specified as well as intermixed with literal characters:

    [0-9a-z?,.;:'"]

This expression will match "any single character that is numeric, lowercase alphabetic, or a question mark, comma, period, semicolon, colon, single quote, or quotation mark." Remember that each character class matches a single character. If you specify multiple classes, you are describing multiple consecutive characters such as:

    [a-zA-Z][.?!]

This expression will match "any lowercase or uppercase letter followed by either a period, a question mark, or an exclamation mark."

The close bracket (]) is interpreted as a member of the class if it occurs as the first character in the class (or as the first character after a circumflex; see the next section). The hyphen loses its special meaning within a class if it is the first or last

---

[*] This can actually be very messy when working in non-ASCII character sets and/or languages other than English. The POSIX standard addresses this issue; the new POSIX features are presented below.

character. Therefore, to match arithmetic operators, we put the hyphen (-) first in the following example:

    [-+*/]

In awk, you could also use the backslash to escape the hyphen or close bracket wherever either one occurs in the range, but the syntax is messier.

Trying to match dates with a regular expression is an interesting problem. Here are two possible formats:

    MM-DD-YY
    MM/DD/YY

The following regular expression indicates the possible range of values for each character position:

    [0-1][0-9][-/][0-3][0-9][-/][0-9][0-9]

Either "-" or "/" could be the delimiter. Putting the hyphen in the first position ensures that it will be interpreted in a character class literally, as a hyphen, and not as indicating a range.[*]

## Excluding a class of characters

Normally, a character class includes all the characters that you want to match at that position. The circumflex (^) as the first character in the class excludes all of the characters in the class from being matched. Instead any character except newline[†] that is not listed in the square brackets will be matched. The following pattern will match any non-numeric character:

    [^0-9]

It matches all uppercase and lowercase letters of the alphabet and all special characters such as punctuation marks.

Excluding specific characters is sometimes more convenient than explicitly listing all the characters you want to match. For instance, if you wanted to match any consonant, you could simply exclude vowels:

    [^aeiou]

This expression would match any consonant, any vowel in uppercase, and any punctuation mark or special character.

---

[*] Note that the expression matches dates that mix their delimiters, as well as impossible dates like "15/32/78."

[†] In awk, newline can also be matched.

Look at the following regular expression:

```
\.DS "[^1]"
```

This expression matches the string ".DS" followed by a space, a quote followed by any character other than the number "1," followed by a quote.[*] It is designed to avoid matching the following line:

```
.DS "1"
```

while matching lines such as:

```
.DS "I"
.DS "2"
```

This syntax can also be used to limit the extent of a match, as we'll see up ahead.

### POSIX character class additions

The POSIX standard formalizes the meaning of regular expression characters and operators. The standard defines two classes of regular expressions: Basic Regular Expressions (BREs), which are the kind used by **grep** and sed, and Extended Regular Expressions, which are the kind used by **egrep** and awk.

In order to accommodate non-English environments, the POSIX standard enhanced the ability of character classes to match characters not in the English alphabet. For example, the French è is an alphabetic character, but the typical character class [a-z] would not match it. Additionally, the standard provides for sequences of characters that should be treated as a single unit when matching and collating (sorting) string data.

POSIX also changed what had been common terminology. What we've been calling a "character class" is called a "bracket expression" in the POSIX standard. Within bracket expressions, beside literal characters such as **a**, **!**, and so on, you can have additional components. These are:

- *Character classes.* A POSIX character class consists of keywords bracketed by [: and :]. The keywords describe different classes of characters such as alphabetic characters, control characters, and so on (see "SEDAWK-CH-3-TAB-3").

- *Collating symbols.* A collating symbol is a multicharacter sequence that should be treated as a unit. It consists of the characters bracketed by [. and .].

- *Equivalence classes.* An equivalence class lists a set of characters that should be considered equivalent, such as **e** and **è**. It consists of a named element from the locale, bracketed by [= and =].

---

[*] When typing this pattern at the command line, be sure to enclose it in single quotes. The ^ is special to the original Bourne shell.

All three of these constructs must appear inside the square brackets of a bracket expression. For example [[:alpha:]!] matches any single alphabetic character or the exclamation point, [[.ch.]] matches the collating element **ch**, but does not match just the letter **c** or the letter **h**. In a French locale, [[=e=]] might match any of **e**, **è**, or **é**. Classes and matching characters are shown in Table 3-3.

*Table 3-3: POSIX Character Classes*

| Class | Matching Characters |
| --- | --- |
| [:alnum:] | Alphanumeric characters |
| [:alpha:] | Alphabetic characters |
| [:blank:] | Space and tab characters |
| [:cntrl:] | Control characters |
| [:digit:] | Numeric characters |
| [:graph:] | Printable and visible (non-space) characters |
| [:lower:] | Lowercase characters |
| [:print:] | Alphanumeric characters |
| [:punct:] | Punctuation characters |
| [:space:] | Whitespace characters |
| [:upper:] | Uppercase characters |
| [:xdigit:] | Hexadecimal digits |

These features are slowly making their way into commercial versions of sed and awk, as vendors fully implement the POSIX standard. GNU awk and GNU sed support the character class notation, but not the other two bracket notations. Check your local system documentation to see if they are available to you.

Because these features are not widely available yet, the scripts in this book will not rely on them, and we will continue to use the term "character class" to refer to lists of characters in square brackets.

## *Repeated Occurrences of a Character*

The asterisk (*) metacharacter indicates that the preceding regular expression may occur zero or more times. That is, if it modifies a single character, the character may be there or not, and if it is, there may be more than one of them. You could use the asterisk metacharacter to match a word that might appear in quotes.

```
□"*hypertext"*□
```

The word "hypertext" will be matched regardless of whether it appears in quotes or not.

Also, if the literal character modified by the asterisk does exist, there could be more than one occurrence. For instance, let's examine a series of numbers:

```
1
5
10
50
100
500
1000
5000
```

The regular expression

```
[15]0*
```

would match all lines, whereas the regular expression

```
[15]00*
```

would match all but the first two lines. The first zero is a literal, but the second is modified by the asterisk, meaning it might or might not be present. A similar technique is used to match consecutive spaces because you usually want to match one or more, not zero or more, spaces. You can use the following to do that:

```
  *
```

When preceded by a dot metacharacter, the asterisk metacharacter matches any number of characters. It can be used to identify a span of characters between two fixed strings. If you wanted to match any string inside of quotation marks, you could specify:

```
".*"
```

This would match all characters between the first and last quotation marks on the line plus the quotation marks. The span matched by ".*" is always the longest possible. This may not seem important now but it will be once you learn about replacing the string that was matched.

As another example, a pair of angle brackets is a common notation for enclosing formatting instructions used in markup languages, such as SGML, HTML, and Ventura Publisher.

You could print all lines with these marks by specifying:

```
$ grep '<.*>' sample
```

When used to modify a character class, the asterisk can match any number of a character in that class. For instance, look at the following five-line sample file:

```
I can do it
I cannot do it
I can not do it
I can't do it
I cant do it
```

If we wanted to match each form of the negative statement, but not the positive statement, the following regular expression would do it:

```
can[□no']*t
```

The asterisk causes any of the characters in the class to be matched in any order and for any number of occurrences. Here it is:

```
$ grep "can[□no']*t" sample
I cannot do it
I can not do it
I can't do it
I cant do it
```

There are four hits and one miss, the positive statement. Notice that had the regular expression tried to match any number of characters between the string "can" and "t," as in the following example:

```
can.*t
```

it would have matched all lines.

The ability to match "zero or more" of something is known by the technical term "closure." The extended set of metacharacters used by **egrep** and awk provides several variations of closure that can be quite useful. The plus sign (+) matches one or more occurrences of the preceding regular expression. Our earlier example of matching one or more spaces can be simplified as such:

```
□+
```

The plus sign metacharacter can be thought of as "at least one" of the preceding character. In fact, it better corresponds to how many people think * works.

The question mark (?) matches zero or one occurrences. For instance, in a previous example, we used a regular expression to match "80286," "80386," and "80486." If we wanted to also match the string "8086," we could write a regular expression that could be used with **egrep** or awk:

```
80[234]?86
```

It matches the string "80" followed by a "2," a "3," a "4," or no character followed by the string "86." Don't confuse the ? in a regular expression with the ? wildcard in the shell. The shell's ? represents a single character, equivalent to . in a regular expression.

## *What's the Word? Part I*

As you have probably figured out, it is sometimes difficult to match a complete word. For instance, if we wanted to match the pattern "book," our search would hit lines containing the word "book" and "books" but also the words "bookish," "handbook," and "booky." The obvious thing to do to limit the matching is to surround "book" with spaces.

    □book□

However, this expression would only match the word "book"; it would miss the plural "books". To match either the singular or plural word, you could use the asterisk metacharacter:

    □books*□

This will match "book" or "books". However, it will not match "book" if it is followed by a period, a comma, a question mark, or a quotation mark.

When you combine the asterisk with the wildcard metacharacter (.), you can match zero or more occurrences of any character. In the previous example, we might write a fuller regular expression as:

    □book.*□

This expression matches the string "book" followed by "any number of characters or none followed by a space." Here are a few lines that would match:

```
Here are the books that you requested
Yes, it is a good book for children
It is amazing to think that it was called a "harmful book" when
once you get to the end of the book, you can't believe
```

(Note that only the second line would be matched by the fixed string "□book□".) The expression· "□book.*□" matches lines containing words such as "booky," "bookworm," and "bookish." We could eliminate two of these matches by using a different modifier. The question mark (?), which is part of the extended set of metacharacters, matches 0 or 1 occurrences of the preceding character. Thus, the expression:

    □book.?□

would match "book," "books," and "booky" but not "bookish" and "bookworm." To eliminate a word like "booky," we would have to use character classes to specify all the characters in that position that we want to match. Furthermore, since the question mark metacharacter is not available with sed, we would have to resort to character classes anyway, as you'll see later on.

Trying to be all-inclusive is not always practical with a regular expression, especially when using **grep**. Sometimes it is best to keep the expression simple and allow for the misses. However, as you use regular expressions in sed for making replacements, you will need to be more careful that your regular expression is complete. We will look at a more comprehensive regular expression for searching for words in Part II of "What's the Word?" later in this chapter.

## Positional Metacharacters

There are two metacharacters that allow you to specify the context in which a string appears, either at the beginning of a line or at the end of a line. The circumflex (^) metacharacter is a single-character regular expression indicating the beginning of a line. The dollar sign ($) metacharacter is a single-character regular expression indicating the end of a line. These are often referred to as "anchors," since they anchor, or restrict, the match to a specific position. You could print lines that begin with a tab:

    ^•

(The • represents a literal tab character, which is normally invisible.) Without the ^ metacharacter, this expression would print any line containing a tab.

Normally, using **vi** to input text to be processed by **troff**, you do not want spaces appearing at the end of lines. If you want to find (and remove) them, this regular expression will match lines with one or more spaces at the end of a line:

    ⊏⊏*$

**troff** requests and macros must be input at the beginning of a line. They are two-character strings, preceded by a dot. If a request or macro has an argument, it is usually followed by a space. The regular expression used to search for such requests is:

    ^\...⊏

This expression matches "a dot at the beginning of a line followed by any two-character string, and then followed by a space."

You can use both positional metacharacters together to match blank lines:

    ^$

You might use this pattern to count the number of blank lines in a file using the count option, -c, to **grep**:

```
$ grep -c '^$' ch04
5
```

This regular expression is useful if you want to delete blank lines using sed. The following regular expression can be used to match a blank line even if it contains spaces:

```
^□*$
```

Similarly, you can match the entire line:

```
^.*$
```

which is something you might possibly want to do with sed.

In sed (and **grep**), "^" and "$" are only special when they occur at the beginning or end of a regular expression, respectively. Thus "^abc" means "match the letters a, b, and c only at the beginning of the line," while "ab^c" means "match a, b, a literal ^, and then c, anywhere on the line." The same is true for the "$."

In awk, it's different; "^" and "$" are always special, even though it then becomes possible to write regular expressions that don't match anything. Suffice it to say that in awk, when you want to match either a literal "^" or "$," you should always escape it with a backslash, no matter what its position in the regular expression.

### Phrases

A pattern-matching program such as **grep** does not match a string if it extends over two lines. For all practical purposes, it is difficult to match phrases with assurance. Remember that text files are basically unstructured and line breaks are quite random. If you are looking for any sequence of words, it is possible that they might appear on one line but they may be split up over two.

You can write a series of regular expression to capture a phrase:

```
Almond Joy
Almond$
^Joy
```

This is not perfect, as the second regular expression will match "Almond" at the end of a line, regardless of whether or not the next line begins with "Joy". A similar problem exists with the third regular expression.

Later, when we look at sed, you'll learn how to match patterns over multiple lines and you'll see a shell script incorporating sed that makes this capability available in a general way.

## A Span of Characters

The metacharacters that allow you to specify repeated occurrences of a character (*+?) indicate a span of undetermined length. Consider the following expression:

```
11*0
```

It will match each of the following lines:

```
10
110
111110
1111111111111111111111111110
```

These metacharacters give elasticity to a regular expression.

Now let's look at a pair of metacharacters that allow you to indicate a span and also determine the length of the span. So, you can specify the minimum and maximum number of occurrences of a literal character or regular expression.

\{ and \} are available in **grep** and sed.[*] POSIX **egrep** and POSIX awk use { and }. In any case, the braces enclose one or two arguments.

```
\{n,m\}
```

$n$ and $m$ are integers between 0 and 255. If you specify \{$n$\} by itself, then exactly $n$ occurrences of the preceding character or regular expression will be matched. If you specify \{$n$,\}, then at least $n$ occurrences will be matched. If you specify \{$n,m$\}, then any number of occurrences between $n$ and $m$ will be matched.[†]

For example, the following expression will match "1001," "10001," and "100001" but not "101" or "1000001":

```
10\{2,4\}1
```

This metacharacter pair can be useful for matching data in fixed-length fields, data that perhaps was extracted from a database. It can also be used to match formatted data such as phone numbers, U.S. social security numbers, inventory part IDs, etc. For instance, the format of a social security number is three digits, a hyphen, followed by two digits, a hyphen, and then four digits. That pattern could be described as follows:

```
[0-9]\{3\}-[0-9]\{2\}-[0-9]\{4\}
```

---

[*] Very old versions may not have them; Caveat emptor.

[†] Note that "?" is equivalent to "\{0,1\}", "*" is equivalent to "\{0,\}", "+" is equivalent to "\{1,\}", and no modifier is equivalent to "\{1\}".

Similarly, a North American local phone number could be described with the following regular expression:

```
[0-9]\{3\}-[0-9]\{4\}
```

If you are using pre-POSIX awk, where you do not have braces available, you can simply repeat the character classes the appropriate number of times:

```
[0-9][0-9][0-9]-[0-9][0-9][0-9][0-9]
```

## *Alternative Operations*

The vertical bar ( | ) metacharacter, part of the extended set of metacharacters, allows you to specify a union of regular expressions. A line will match the pattern if it matches one of the regular expressions. For instance, this regular expression:

```
UNIX|LINUX
```

will match lines containing either the string "UNIX" or the string "LINUX". More than one alternative can be specified:

```
UNIX|LINUX|NETBSD
```

A line matching any of these three patterns will be printed by **egrep**.

In sed, lacking the union metacharacter, you would specify each pattern separately. In the next section, where we look at grouping operations, we will see additional examples of this metacharacter.

## *Grouping Operations*

Parentheses, (), are used to group regular expressions and establish precedence. They are part of the extended set of metacharacters. Let's say that a company's name in a text file is referred to as "BigOne" or "BigOne Computer":

```
BigOne(□Computer)?
```

This expression will match the string "BigOne" by itself or followed by a single occurrence of the string "□Computer". Similarly, if a term is sometime spelled out and at other times abbreviated:

```
$ egrep "Lab(oratorie)?s" mail.list
Bell Laboratories, Lucent Technologies
Bell Labs
```

You can use parentheses with a vertical bar to group alternative operations. In the following example, we use it to specify a match of the singular or plural of the word "company."

```
compan(y|ies)
```

It is important to note that applying a quantifier to a parenthesized group of characters can't be done in most versions of sed and **grep**, but is available in all versions of **egrep** and awk.

## What's the Word? Part II

Let's reevaluate the regular expression for searching for a single word in light of the new metacharacters we've discussed. Our first attempt at writing a regular expression to search for a word concluded with the following expression:

```
□book.*□
```

This expression is fairly simple, matching a space followed by the string "book" followed by any number of characters followed by a space. However, it does not match all possible occurrences and it does match a few nuisance words.

The following test file contains numerous occurrences of "book." We've added a notation, which is not part of the file, to indicate whether the input line should be a "hit" (>) and included in the output or a "miss" (<). We've tried to include as many different examples as possible.

```
$ cat bookwords
> This file tests for book in various places, such as
> book at the beginning of a line or
> at the end of a line book
> as well as the plural books and
< handbooks.  Here are some
< phrases that use the word in different ways:
> "book of the year award"
> to look for a line with the word "book"
> A GREAT book!
> A great book? No.
> told them about (the books) until it
> Here are the books that you requested
> Yes, it is a good book for children
> amazing that it was called a "harmful book" when
> once you get to the end of the book, you can't believe
< A well-written regular expression should
< avoid matching unrelated words,
< such as booky (is that a word?)
< and bookish and
< bookworm and so on.
```

As we search for occurrences of the word "book," there are 13 lines that should be matched and 7 lines that should not be matched. First, let's run the previous regular expression on the sample file and check the results.

```
$ grep '□book.*□' bookwords
This file tests for book in various places, such as
as well as the plural books and
A great book? No.
```

```
told them about (the books) until it
Here are the books that you requested
Yes, it is a good book for children
amazing that it was called a "harmful book" when
once you get to the end of the book, you can't believe
such as booky (is that a word?)
and bookish and
```

It only prints 8 of the 13 lines that we want to match and it prints 2 of the lines that we don't want to match. The expression matches lines containing the words "booky" and "bookish." It ignores "book" at the beginning of a line and at the end of a line. It ignores "book" when there are certain punctuation marks involved.

To restrict the search even more, we must use character classes. Generally, the list of characters that might end a word are punctuation marks, such as:

```
? . , ! ; : '
```

In addition, quotation marks, parentheses, braces, and brackets might surround a word or open or close with a word:

```
" () {} []
```

You would also have to accommodate the plural or possessive forms of the word.

Thus, you would have two different character classes: before and after the word. Remember that all we have to do is list the members of the class inside square brackets. Before the word, we now have:

```
["[{(]
```

and after the word:

```
[]})"?!.,;:'s]
```

Note that putting the closing square bracket as the first character in the class makes it a member of the class rather than closing the set. Putting the two classes together, we get the expression:

```
□["[{(]*book[]})"?!.,;:'s]*□
```

Show this to the uninitiated, and they'll throw up their hands in despair! But now that you know the principles involved, you can not only understand this expression, but could easily reconstruct it. Let's see how it does on the sample file (we use double quotes to enclose the single quote character, and then a backslash in front of the embedded double quotes):

```
$ grep " [\"[{(]*book[]})\"?!.,;:'s]* " bookwords
This file tests for book in various places, such as
as well as the plural books and
A great book? No.
told them about (the books) until it
```

```
Here are the books that you requested
Yes, it is a good book for children
amazing that it was called a "harmful book" when
once you get to the end of the book, you can't believe
```

We eliminated the lines that we don't want but there are four lines that we're not getting. Let's examine the four lines:

```
book at the beginning of a line or
at the end of a line book
"book of the year award"
A GREAT book!
```

All of these are problems caused by the string appearing at the beginning or end of a line. Because there is no space at the beginning or end of a line, the pattern is not matched. We can use the positional metacharacters, ^ and $. Since we want to match either a space or beginning or end of a line, we can use **egrep** and specify the "or" metacharacter along with parentheses for grouping. For instance, to match either the beginning of a line or a space, you could write the expression:

```
(^| )
```

(Because | and () are part of the extended set of metacharacters, if you were using sed, you'd have to write different expressions to handle each case.)

Here's the revised regular expression:

```
(^| )["[{(]*book[]})"?\!.,;:'s]*( |$)
```

Now let's see how it works:

```
$ egrep "(^| )[\"[{(]*book[]})\"?\!.,;:'s]*( |$)" bookwords
This file tests for book in various places, such as
book at the beginning of a line or
at the end of a line book
as well as the plural books and
"book of the year award"
to look for a line with the word "book"
A GREAT book!
A great book? No.
told them about (the books) until it
Here are the books that you requested
Yes, it is a good book for children
amazing that it was called a "harmful book" when
once you get to the end of the book, you can't believe
```

This is certainly a complex regular expression; however, it can be broken down into parts. This expression may not match every single instance, but it can be easily adapted to handle other occurrences that you may find.

You could also create a simple shell script to replace "book" with a command-line argument. The only problem might be that the plural of some words is not simply "s." By sleight of hand, you could handle the "es" plural by adding "e" to the character class following the word; it would work in many cases.

As a further note, the **ex** and **vi** text editors have a special metacharacter for matching a string at the beginning of a word, \<, and one for matching a string at the end of a word, \>. Used as a pair, they can match a string only when it is a complete word. (For these operators, a word is a string of non-whitespace characters with whitespace on both sides, or at the beginning or end of a line.) Matching a word is such a common case that these metacharacters would be widely used, if they were available for all regular expressions.[*]

## *Your Replacement Is Here*

When using **grep**, it seldom matters how you match the line as long as you match it. When you want to make a replacement, however, you have to consider the extent of the match. So, what characters on the line did you actually match?

In this section, we're going to look at several examples that demonstrate the extent of a match. Then we'll use a program that works like **grep** but also allows you to specify a replacement string. Lastly, we will look at several metacharacters used to describe the replacement string.

### *The extent of the match*

Let's look at the following regular expression:

```
A*Z
```

This matches "zero or more occurrences of A followed by Z." It will produce the same result as simply specifying "Z". The letter "A" could be there or not; in fact, the letter "Z" is the only character matched. Here's a sample two-line file:

```
All of us, including Zippy, our dog
Some of us, including Zippy, our dog
```

If we try to match the previous regular expression, both lines would print out. Interestingly enough, the actual match in both cases is made on the "Z" and only the "Z". We can use the **gres** command (see the sidebar, "A Program for Making Single Replacements") to demonstrate the extent of the match.

```
$ gres "A*Z" "00" test
All of us, including 00ippy, our dog
Some of us, including 00ippy, our dog
```

---

[*] GNU programs, such as the GNU versions of awk, sed, and **grep**, also support \< and \>.

---

## *A Program for Making Single Replacements*

The MKS Toolkit, a set of UNIX utilities for DOS by Mortice Kern Systems, Inc., contains a very useful program called **gres** (*g*lobal *r*egular *e*xpression *s*ubstitution). Just like **grep**, it searches for a pattern in a file; however, it allows you to specify a replacement for the string that you match. This program is in fact a simplified version of sed, and like sed, it prints all lines regardless of whether or not a replacement was made. It does not make the replacement in the file itself. You have to redirect the output from the program into a file if you want to save the changes.

**gres** is not part of standard UNIX but it would be a nice tool to have. It can be created using a simple shell script that invokes sed to do the work.

```
$ cat gres
if [ $# -lt "3" ]
then
        echo Usage: gres pattern replacement file
        exit 1
fi
pattern=$1
replacement=$2
if [ -f $3 ]
then
        file=$3
else
        echo $3 is not a file.
        exit 1
fi
A="`echo | tr '\012' '\001' `" # See footnote*

sed -e "s$A$pattern$A$replacement$A" $file
```

Throughout the rest of the chapter, we will use **gres** to demonstrate the use of replacement metacharacters. Remember that whatever applies to **gres** applies to sed as well. Here we replace the string matched by the regular expression "A.*Z" with double zero (00).

```
$ gres "A.*Z" "00" sample
00ippy, our dog
00iggy
00elda
```

---

* The **echo | tr** ... line is a complicated but portable way to generate a Control-A character to use as the separator for the sed substitute command. Doing this greatly decreases the chance of having the separator character appear in the pattern or replacement texts.

We would have expected the extent of the match on the first line to be from the "A" to the "Z" but only the "Z" is actually matched. This result may be more apparent if we change the regular expression slightly:

```
A.*Z
```

".*" can be interpreted as "zero or more occurrences of any character," which means that "any number of characters" can be found, including none at all. The entire expression can be evaluated as "an A followed by any number of characters followed by a Z." An "A" is the initial character in the pattern and "Z" is the last character; anything or nothing might occur in between. Running **grep** on the same two-line file produces one line of output. We've added a line of carets (^) underneath to mark what was matched.

```
All of us, including Zippy, our dog
^^^^^^^^^^^^^^^^^^^^^^^^^
```

The extent of the match is from "A" to "Z". The same regular expression would also match the following line:

```
I heard it on radio station WVAZ 1060.
                            ^^
```

The string "A.*Z" matches "A followed by any number of characters (including zero) followed by Z." Now, let's look at a similar set of sample lines that contain multiple occurrences of "A" and "Z".

```
All of us, including Zippy, our dog
All of us, including Zippy and Ziggy
All of us, including Zippy and Ziggy and Zelda
```

The regular expression "A.*Z" will match the longest possible extent in each case.

```
All of us, including Zippy, our dog
^^^^^^^^^^^^^^^^^^^^^^^^^

All of us, including Zippy and Ziggy
^^^^^^^^^^^^^^^^^^^^^^^^^^^^^^^

All of us, including Zippy and Ziggy and Zelda
^^^^^^^^^^^^^^^^^^^^^^^^^^^^^^^^^^^^^^^^^^
```

This can cause problems if what you want is to match the shortest extent possible.

## *Limiting the Extent*

Earlier we said that a regular expression tries to match the longest string possible and that can cause unexpected problems. For instance, look at the regular expression to match any number of characters inside of quotation marks:

```
".*"
```

Let's look at a **troff** macro that has two quoted arguments, as shown below:

```
.Se "Appendix" "Full Program Listings"
```

To match the first argument, we might describe the pattern with the following regular expression:

```
\.Se ".*"
```

However, it ends up matching the whole line because the second quotation mark in the pattern matches the last quotation mark on the line. If you know how many arguments there are, you can specify each of them:

```
\.Se ".*" ".*"
```

Although this works as you'd expect, each line might not have the same number of arguments, causing omissions—you simply want the first argument. Here's a different regular expression that matches the shortest possible extent between two quotation marks:

```
"[^"]*"
```

It matches "a quote followed by any number of characters that do not match a quote followed by a quote":

```
$ gres '"[^"]*"' '00' sampleLine
.Se 00 "Appendix"
```

Now let's look at a few lines with a dot character (.) used as a leader between two columns of numbers:

```
1........5
5........10
10.......20
100......200
```

The difficulty in matching the leader characters is that their number is variable. Let's say that you wanted to replace all of the leaders with a single tab. You might write a regular expression to match the line as follows:

```
[0-9][0-9]*\.\.*[0-9][0-9]*
```

This expression might unexpectedly match the line:

```
see Section 2.3
```

To restrict matching, you could specify the minimum number of dots that are common to all lines:

```
[0-9][0-9]*\.\{5,\}[0-9][0-9]*
```

This expression uses braces available in sed to match "a single number followed by at least five dots and then followed by a single number." To see this in action, we'll show a sed command that replaces the leader dots with a hyphen. However, we have not covered the syntax of sed's replacement metacharacters— \( and \) to save a part of a regular expression and \1 and \2 to recall the saved portion. This command, therefore, may look rather complex (it is!) but it does the job.

```
$ sed 's/\([0-9][0-9]*\)\.\{5,\}\([0-9][0-9]*\)/\1-\2/' sample
1-5
5-10
10-20
100-200
```

A similar expression can be written to match one or more leading tabs or tabs between columns of data. You could change the order of columns as well as replacing the tab with another delimiter. You should experiment on your own by making simple and complex replacements, using sed or **gres**.

# I Never Metacharacter I Didn't Like

Table 3-4 lists interesting examples of regular expressions, many of which have been described in this chapter.

*Table 3-4: Useful Regular Expressions*

| Item | Regular Expression |
|------|-------------------|
| Postal Abbreviation for State | □[A-Z][A-Z]□ |
| City, State | ^.*,□[A-Z][A-Z] |
| City, State, Zip (POSIX **egrep**) | ^.*,□[A-Z][A-Z]□[0-9]{5}(-[0-9]{4})? |
| Month, Day, Year | [A-Z][a-z]\{3,9\}□[0-9]\{1,2\},□[0-9]\{4\} |
| U.S. Social Security Number | [0-9]\{3\}-[0-9]\{2\}-[0-9]\{4\} |
| North-American Local Telephone | [0-9]\{3\}-[0-9]\{4\} |
| Formatted Dollar Amounts | \$[□0-9]*\.[0-9][0-9] |
| **troff** In-line Font Requests | \\f(BIRP]C*[BW]* |
| **troff** Requests | ^\.[a-z]\{2\} |
| **troff** Macros | ^\.[A-Z12]. |
| **troff** Macro with arguments | ^\.[A-Z12].□".*" |
| HTML In-line Codes | <[^>]*> |
| Ventura Publisher Style Codes | ^@.*□=□.* |
| Match blank lines | ^$ |
| Match entire line | ^.*$ |
| Match one or more spaces | □□* |

# 4

# *Writing sed Scripts*

To use sed, you write a script that contains a series of editing actions and then you run the script on an input file. Sed allows you to take what would be a *hands-on* procedure in an editor such as **vi** and transform it into a *look-no-hands* procedure that is executed from a script.

When performing edits manually, you come to trust the cause-and-effect relationship of entering an editing command and seeing the immediate result. There is usually an "undo" command that allows you to reverse the effect of a command and return the text file to its previous state. Once you learn an interactive text editor, you experience the feeling of making changes in a safe and controlled manner, one step at a time.

Most people new to sed will feel there is greater risk in writing a script to perform a series of edits than in making those changes manually. The fear is that by automating the task, something will happen that cannot be reversed. The object of learning sed is to understand it well enough to see that your results are predictable. In other words, you come to understand the cause-and-effect relationship between your editing script and the output that you get.

This requires using sed in a controlled, methodical way. In writing a script, you should follow these steps:

1. Think through what you want to do before you do it.

2. Describe, unambiguously, a procedure to do it.

3. Test the procedure repeatedly before committing to any final changes.

These steps are simply a restatement of the same process we described for writing regular expressions in Chapter 3, *Understanding Regular Expression Syntax.* They describe a methodology for writing programs of any kind. The best way to see if your script works is to run tests on different input samples and observe the results.

With practice, you can come to rely upon your sed scripts working just as you want them to. (There is something analogous in the management of one's own time, learning to trust that certain tasks can be delegated to others. You begin testing people on small tasks, and if they succeed, you give them larger tasks.)

This chapter, then, is about making you comfortable writing scripts that do your editing work for you. This involves understanding three basic principles of how sed works:

- All editing commands in a script are applied in order to each line of input.

- Commands are applied to all lines (globally) unless line addressing restricts the lines affected by editing commands.

- The original input file is unchanged; the editing commands modify a copy of original input line and the copy is sent to standard output.

After covering these basic principles, we'll look at four types of scripts that demonstrate different sed applications. These scripts provide the basic models for the scripts that you will write. Although there are a number of commands available for use in sed, the scripts in this chapter purposely use only a few commands. Nonetheless, you may be surprised at how much you can do with so few. (Chapter 5, *Basic sed Commands*, and Chapter 6, *Advanced sed Commands*, present the basic and advanced sed commands, respectively.) The idea is to concentrate from the outset on understanding how a script works and how to use a script before exploring all the commands that can be used in scripts.

## Applying Commands in a Script

Combining a series of edits in a script can have unexpected results. You might not think of the consequences one edit can have on another. New users typically think that sed applies an individual editing command to all lines of input before applying the next editing command. But the opposite is true. Sed applies the entire script to the first input line before reading the second input line and applying the editing script to it. Because sed is always working with the latest version of the original line, any edit that is made changes the line for subsequent commands. Sed doesn't retain the original. This means that a pattern that might have matched the original input line may no longer match the line after an edit has been made.

Let's look at an example that uses the substitute command. Suppose someone quickly wrote the following script to change "pig" to "cow" and "cow" to "horse":

```
s/pig/cow/
s/cow/horse/
```

What do you think happened? Try it on a sample file. We'll discuss what happened later, after we look at how sed works.

## The Pattern Space

Sed maintains a *pattern space*, a workspace or temporary buffer where a single line of input is held while the editing commands are applied.* The transformation of the pattern space by a two-line script is shown in Figure 4-1. It changes "The Unix System" to "The UNIX Operating System."

Initially, the pattern space contains a copy of a single input line. In Figure 4-1, that line is "The Unix System." The normal flow through the script is to execute each command on that line until the end of the script is reached. The first command in the script is applied to that line, changing "Unix" to "UNIX." Then the second command is applied, changing "UNIX System" to "UNIX Operating System."[†] Note that the pattern for the second substitute command does not match the original input line; it matches the current line as it has changed in the pattern space.

When all the instructions have been applied, the current line is output and the next line of input is read into the pattern space. Then all the commands in the script are applied to that line.

As a consequence, any sed command might change the contents of the pattern space for the next command. The contents of the pattern space are dynamic and do not always match the original input line. That was the problem with the sample script at the beginning of this chapter. The first command would change "pig" to "cow" as expected. However, when the second command changed "cow" to "horse" on the same line, it also changed the "cow" that had been a "pig." So, where the input file contained pigs and cows, the output file has only horses!

This mistake is simply a problem of the order of the commands in the script. Reversing the order of the commands—changing "cow" into "horse" before changing "pig" into "cow"—does the trick.

```
s/cow/horse/
s/pig/cow/
```

---

\* One advantage of the one-line-at-a-time design is that sed can read very large files without any problems. Screen editors that have to read the entire file into memory, or some large portion of it, can run out of memory or be extremely slow to use in dealing with large files.

† Yes, we could have changed "Unix System" to "UNIX Operating System" in one step. However, the input file might have instances of "UNIX System" as well as "Unix System." So by changing "Unix" to "UNIX" we make both instances consistent before changing them to "UNIX Operating System."

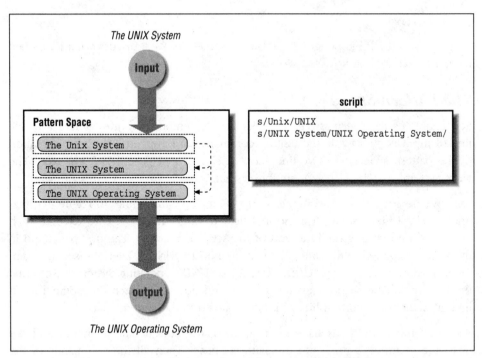

*Figure 4–1: The commands in the script change the contents of the pattern space.*

Some sed commands change the flow through the script, as we will see in subsequent chapters. For example, the **N** command reads another line into the pattern space without removing the current line, so you can test for patterns across multiple lines. Other commands tell sed to exit before reaching the bottom of the script or to go to a labeled command. Sed also maintains a second temporary buffer called the *hold space.* You can copy the contents of the pattern space to the hold space and retrieve them later. The commands that make use of the hold space are discussed in Chapter 6.

## A Global Perspective on Addressing

One of the first things you'll notice about sed commands is that sed will apply them to every input line. Sed is implicitly global, unlike **ed**, **ex**, or **vi**. The following substitute command will change every "CA" into "California."

```
s/CA/California/g
```

If the same command were entered from the **ex** command prompt in **vi**, it would make the replacement for all occurrences on the current line only. In sed, it is as though each line has a turn at becoming the current line and so the command is applied to every line. Line addresses are used to supply context for, or *restrict*, an operation. (In short: Nothing gets done in **vi** unless you tell it which lines to work on, while sed will work on every line unless you tell it not to.) For instance, by supplying the address "Sebastopol" to the previous substitute command, we can limit the replacement of "CA" by "California" to just lines containing "Sebastopol."

```
/Sebastopol/s/CA/California/g
```

An input line consisting of "Sebastopol, CA" would match the address and the substitute command would be applied, changing it to "Sebastopol, California." A line consisting of "San Francisco, CA" would not be matched and the substitution would not be applied.

A sed command can specify zero, one, or two addresses. An address can be a regular expression describing a pattern, a line number, or a line addressing symbol.

- If no address is specified, then the command is applied to each line.
- If there is only one address, the command is applied to any line matching the address.
- If two comma-separated addresses are specified, the command is performed on the first line matching the first address and all succeeding lines up to and including a line matching the second address.
- If an address is followed by an exclamation mark (!), the command is applied to all lines that do *not* match the address.

To illustrate how addressing works, let's look at examples using the delete command, **d**. A script consisting of simply the **d** command and no address produces no output since it deletes *all* lines:

```
d
```

When a line number is supplied as an address, the command affects only that line. For instance, the following example deletes only the first line:

```
1d
```

The line number refers to an internal line count maintained by sed. This counter is not reset for multiple input files. Thus, no matter how many files were specified as input, there is only one line 1 in the input stream.

Similarly, the input stream has only one last line. It can be specified using the addressing symbol **$**. The following example deletes the last line of input:

```
$d
```

The $ symbol should not be confused with the $ used in regular expressions, which means the end of the line.

When a regular expression is supplied as an address, the command affects only the lines matching that pattern. The regular expression must be enclosed by slashes (/). The following delete command

```
/^$/d
```

deletes only blank lines. All other lines are passed through untouched.

If you supply two addresses, then you specify a range of lines over which the command is executed. The following example shows hows to delete all lines blocked by a pair of macros, in this case, .TS and .TE, that mark **tbl** input.

```
/^\.TS/,/^\.TE/d
```

It deletes all lines beginning with the line matched by the first pattern and up to and including the line matched by the second pattern. Lines outside this range are not affected. The following command deletes from line 50 to the last line in the file:

```
50,$d
```

You can mix a line address and a pattern address:

```
1,/^$/d
```

This example deletes from the first line up to the first blank line, which, for instance, will delete a mailer header from an Internet mail message that you have saved in a file.

You can think of the first address as enabling the action and the second address as disabling it. Sed has no way of looking ahead to determine if the second match will be made. The action will be applied to lines once the first match is made. The command will be applied to *all* subsequent lines until the second match is made. In the previous example, if the file did not contain a blank line, then all lines would be deleted.

An exclamation mark (!) following an address reverses the sense of the match. For instance, the following script deletes all lines *except* those inside **tbl** input:

```
/^\.TS/,/^\.TE/!d
```

This script, in effect, extracts **tbl** input from a source file.

### *Grouping Commands*

Braces ({}) are used in sed to nest one address inside another or to apply multiple commands at the same address. You can nest addresses if you want to specify a range of lines and then, within that range, specify another address. For example, to delete blank lines only inside blocks of **tbl** input, use the following command:

```
/^\.TS/,/^\.TE/{
     /^$/d
}
```

The opening curly brace must end a line and the closing curly brace must be on a line by itself. Be sure there are no spaces after the braces.

You can apply multiple commands to the same range of lines by enclosing the editing commands within braces, as shown below.

```
/^\.TS/,/^\.TE/{
     /^$/d
     s/^\.ps 10/.ps 8/
     s/^\.vs 12/.vs 10/
}
```

This example not only deletes blank lines in **tbl** input but it also uses the substitute command, **s**, to change several **troff** requests. These commands are applied only to lines within the .TS/.TE block.

# *Testing and Saving Output*

In our previous discussion of the pattern space, you saw that sed:

1.  Makes a copy of the input line.

2.  Modifies that copy in the pattern space.

3.  Outputs the copy to standard output.

What this means is that sed has a built-in safeguard so that you don't make changes to the original file. Thus, the following command line:

```
$ sed -f sedscr testfile
```

does not make the change in *testfile*. It sends all lines to standard ouput (typically the screen)—the lines that were modified as well as the lines that are unchanged. You have to capture this output in a new file if you want to save it.

```
$ sed -f sedscr testfile > newfile
```

The redirection symbol ">" directs the output from sed to the file *newfile*. Don't redirect the output from the command back to the input file or you will overwrite the input file. This will happen *before* sed even gets a chance to process the file, effectively destroying your data.

One important reason to redirect the output to a file is to verify your results. You can examine the contents of *newfile* and compare it to *testfile*. If you want to be very methodical about checking your results (and you should be), use the **diff** program to point out the differences between the two files.

```
$ diff testfile newfile
```

This command will display lines that are unique to *testfile* preceded by a "<" and lines unique to *newfile* preceded by a ">". When you have verified your results, make a backup copy of the original input file and then use the **mv** command to overwrite the original with the new version. Be sure that the editing script is working properly before abandoning the original version.

Because these steps are repeated so frequently, you will find it helpful to put them into a shell script. While we can't go into much depth about the workings of shell scripts, these scripts are fairly simple to understand and use. Writing a shell script involves using a text editor to enter one or more command lines in a file, saving the file and then using the **chmod** command to make the file executable. The name of the file is the name of the command, and it can be entered at the system prompt. If you are unfamiliar with shell scripts, follow the shell scripts presented in this book as recipes in which you make your own substitutions.

The following two shell scripts are useful for testing sed scripts and then making the changes permanently in a file. They are particularly useful when the same script needs to be run on multiple files.

## *testsed*

The shell script **testsed** automates the process of saving the output of sed in a temporary file. It expects to find the script file, *sedscr*, in the current directory and applies these instructions to the input file named on the command line. The output is placed in a temporary file.

```
for x
do
        sed -f sedscr $x > tmp.$x
done
```

The name of a file must be specified on the command line. As a result, this shell script saves the output in a temporary file with the prefix "*tmp.*". You can examine the temporary file to determine if your edits were made correctly. If you approve of the results, you can use **mv** to overwrite the original file with the temporary file.

You might also incorporate the **diff** command into the shell script. (Add **diff $x tmp.$x** after the sed command.)

If you find that your script did not produce the results you expected, remember that the easiest "fix" is usually to perfect the editing script and run it again on the original input file. Don't write a new script to "undo" or improve upon changes made in the temporary file.

## *runsed*

The shell script **runsed** was developed to make changes to an input file permanently. In other words, it is used in cases when you would want the input file and the output file to be the same. Like **testsed**, it creates a temporary file, but then it takes the next step: copying the file over the original.

```
#! /bin/sh

for x
do
    echo "editing $x: \c"
    if test "$x" = sedscr; then
        echo "not editing sedscript!"
    elif test -s $x; then
        sed -f sedscr $x > /tmp/$x$$
        if test -s /tmp/$x$$
        then
            if cmp -s $x /tmp/$x$$
            then
                echo "file not changed: \c"
            else
                mv $x $x.bak  # save original, just in case
                cp /tmp/$x$$ $x
            fi
            echo "done"
        else
            echo "Sed produced an empty file\c"
            echo " - check your sedscript."
        fi
        rm -f /tmp/$x$$
    else
        echo "original file is empty."
    fi
done
echo "all done"
```

To use **runsed**, create a sed script named *sedscr* in the directory where you want to make the edits. Supply the name or names of the files to edit on the command line. Shell metacharacters can be used to specify a set of files.

```
$ runsed ch0?
```

**runsed** simply invokes **sed -f sedscr** on the named files, one at a time, and redirects the output to a temporary file. **runsed** then tests this temporary file to make sure that output was produced before copying it over the original.

The muscle of this shell script (line 9) is essentially the same as **testsed**. The additional lines are intended to test for unsuccessful runs—for instance, when no output is produced. It compares the two files to see if changes were actually made or to see if an empty output file was produced before overwriting the original.

However, **runsed** does not protect you from imperfect editing scripts. You should use **testsed** first to verify your changes before actually making them permanent with **runsed**.

# Four Types of sed Scripts

In this section, we are going to look at four types of scripts, each one illustrating a typical sed application.

## Multiple Edits to the Same File

The first type of sed script demonstrates making a series of edits in a file. The example we use is a script that converts a file created by a word processing program into a file coded for **troff**.

One of the authors once did a writing project for a computer company, here referred to as BigOne Computer. The document had to include a product bulletin for "Horsefeathers Software." The company promised that the product bulletin was online and that they would send it. Unfortunately, when the file arrived, it contained the formatted output for a line printer, the only way they could provide it. A portion of that file (saved for testing in a file named *horsefeathers*) follows.

```
            HORSEFEATHERS SOFTWARE PRODUCT BULLETIN

     DESCRIPTION
+      ------------

     BigOne Computer  offers three   software packages from the   suite
     of Horsefeathers  software products  --  Horsefeathers  Business
     BASIC, BASIC Librarian, and LIDO.  These software products can
     fill your    requirements    for    powerful,    sophisticated,
     general-purpose business   software providing you with a base for
     software customization or development.

     Horsefeathers BASIC is  BASIC optimized for use on  the  BigOne
     machine with UNIX  or MS-DOS operating systems.  BASIC Librarian
     is a full screen program editor, which also provides the ability
```

Note that the text has been justified with spaces added between words. There are also spaces added to create a left margin.

We find that when we begin to tackle a problem using sed, we do best if we make a mental list of all the things we want to do. When we begin coding, we write a script containing a single command that does one thing. We test that it works, then we add another command, repeating this cycle until we've done all that's obvious to do. ("All that's obvious" because the list is not always complete, and the cycle of implement-and-test often adds other items to the list.)

It may seem to be a rather tedious process to work this way and indeed there are a number of scripts where it's fine to take a crack at writing the whole script in one pass and then begin testing it. However, the one-step-at-a-time technique is highly recommended for beginners because you isolate each command and get to easily see what is working and what is not. When you try to do several commands at once, you might find that when problems arise you end up recreating the recommended process in reverse; that is, removing commands one by one until you locate the problem.

Here is a list of the obvious edits that need to be made to the Horsefeathers Software bulletin:

1. Replace all blank lines with a paragraph macro (.LP).

2. Remove all leading spaces from each line.

3. Remove the printer underscore line, the one that begins with a "+".

4. Remove multiple blank spaces that were added between words.

The first edit requires that we match blank lines. However, in looking at the input file, it wasn't obvious whether the blank lines had leading spaces or not. As it turns out, they do not, so blank lines can be matched using the pattern "^$". (If there were spaces on the line, the pattern could be written "^□*$".) Thus, the first edit is fairly straightforward to accomplish:

```
s/^$/.LP/
```

It replaces each blank line with ".LP". Note that you do not escape the literal period in the replacement section of the substitute command. We can put this command in a file named *sedscr* and test the command as follows:

```
$ sed -f sedscr horsefeathers
                HORSEFEATHERS SOFTWARE PRODUCT BULLETIN
.LP
   DESCRIPTION
+    _____
.LP
   BigOne Computer  offers three  software packages from the  suite
   of Horsefeathers  software products  --  Horsefeathers  Business
```

```
BASIC, BASIC Librarian,  and LIDO.  These software products can
fill  your  requirements  for  powerful,  sophisticated,
general-purpose business  software providing you with a base for
software customization or development.
.LP
Horsefeathers BASIC is  BASIC optimized for use on  the  BigOne
machine with UNIX  or MS-DOS operating systems.  BASIC Librarian
is a full screen program editor, which also provides the ability
```

It is pretty obvious which lines have changed. (It is frequently helpful to cut out a portion of a file to use for testing. It works best if the portion is small enough to fit on the screen yet is large enough to include different examples of what you want to change. After all edits have been applied successfully to the test file, a second level of testing occurs when you apply them to the complete, original file.)

The next edit that we make is to remove the line that begins with a "+" and contains a line-printer underscore. We can simply delete this line using the delete command, **d**. In writing a pattern to match this line, we have a number of choices. Each of the following would match that line:

```
/^+/
/^+□/
/^+□□*/
/^+□□*__*/
```

As you can see, each successive regular expression matches a greater number of characters. Only through testing can you determine how complex the expression needs to be to match a specific line and not others. The longer the pattern that you define in a regular expression, the more comfort you have in knowing that it won't produce unwanted matches. For this script, we'll choose the third expression:

```
/^+□□*/d
```

This command will delete any line that begins with a plus sign and is followed by at least one space. The pattern specifies two spaces, but the second is modified by "*", which means that the second space might or might not be there.

This command was added to the sed script and tested but since it only affects one line, we'll omit showing the results and move on. The next edit needs to remove the spaces that pad the beginning of a line. The pattern for matching that sequence is very similar to the address for the previous command.

```
s/^□□*//
```

This command removes any sequence of spaces found at the beginning of a line. The replacement portion of the substitute command is empty, meaning that the matched string is removed.

We can add this command to the script and test it.

```
$ sed -f sedscr horsefeathers
HORSEFEATHERS SOFTWARE PRODUCT BULLETIN
.LP
DESCRIPTION
.LP
BigOne Computer  offers three  software packages from the  suite
of Horsefeathers  software products  -- Horsefeathers  Business
BASIC, BASIC  Librarian,  and LIDO.  These software products can
fill  your    requirements   for    powerful,    sophisticated,
general-purpose business  software providing you with a base for
software customization or development.
.LP
Horsefeathers  BASIC is  BASIC optimized for use on  the  BigOne
machine with UNIX  or MS-DOS operating systems.  BASIC Librarian
is a full screen program editor, which also provides the ability
```

The next edit attempts to deal with the extra spaces added to justify each line. We can write a substitute command to match any string of consecutive spaces and replace it with a single space.

```
s/□□*/□/g
```

We add the global flag at the end of the command so that all occurrences, not just the first, are replaced. Note that, like previous regular expressions, we are not specifying how many spaces are there, just that one or more be found. There might be two, three, or four consecutive spaces. No matter how many, we want to reduce them to one.[*]

Let's test the new script:

```
$ sed -f sedscr horsefeathers
HORSEFEATHERS SOFTWARE PRODUCT BULLETIN
.LP
DESCRIPTION
.LP
BigOne Computer offers three software packages from the suite
of Horsefeathers software products -- Horsefeathers Business
BASIC, BASIC Librarian, and LIDO. These software products can
fill your requirements for powerful, sophisticated,
general-purpose business software providing you with a base for
software customization or development.
.LP
Horsefeathers BASIC is BASIC optimized for use on the BigOne
machine with UNIX or MS-DOS operating systems. BASIC Librarian
is a full screen program editor, which also provides the ability
```

---

* This command will also match just a single space. But since the replacement is also a single space, such a case is effectively a "no-op."

It works as advertised, reducing two or more spaces to one. On closer inspection, though, you might notice that the script removes a sequence of two spaces following a period, a place where they might belong.

We could perfect our substitute command such that it does not make the replacement for spaces following a period. The problem is that there are cases when three spaces follow a period and we'd like to reduce that to two. The best way seems to be to write a separate command that deals with the special case of a period followed by spaces.

```
s/\.□□*/.□□/g
```

This command replaces a period followed by any number of spaces with a period followed by two spaces. It should be noted that the previous command reduces multiple spaces to one, so that only one space will be found following a period.[*] Nonetheless, this pattern works regardless of how many spaces follow the period, as long as there is at least one. (It would not, for instance, affect a filename of the form *test.ext* if it appeared in the document.) This command is placed at the end of the script and tested:

```
$ sed -f sedscr horsefeathers
HORSEFEATHERS SOFTWARE PRODUCT BULLETIN
.LP
DESCRIPTION
.LP
BigOne Computer offers three software packages from the suite
of Horsefeathers software products -- Horsefeathers Business
BASIC, BASIC Librarian, and LIDO.  These software products can
fill your requirements for powerful, sophisticated,
general-purpose business software providing you with a base for
software customization or development.
.LP
Horsefeathers BASIC is BASIC optimized for use on the BigOne
machine with UNIX or MS-DOS operating systems.  BASIC Librarian
is a full screen program editor, which also provides the ability
```

It works. Here's the completed script:

```
s/^$/.LP/
/^+□□*/d
s/^□□*//
s/□□*/□/g
s/\.□□*/.□□/g
```

---

[*] The command could therefore be simplified to:

```
s/\.□/.□□/g
```

As we said earlier, the next stage would be to test the script on the complete file (*hf.product.bulletin*), using **testsed**, and examine the results thoroughly. When we are satisfied with the results, we can use **runsed** to make the changes permanent:

```
$ runsed hf.product.bulletin
done
```

By executing **runsed**, we have overwritten the original file.

Before leaving this script, it is instructive to point out that although the script was written to process a specific file, each of the commands in the script is one that you might expect to use again, even if you don't use the entire script again. In other words, you may well write other scripts that delete blank lines or check for two spaces following a period. Recognizing how commands can be reused in other situations reduces the time it takes to develop and test new scripts. It's like a singer learning a song and adding it to his or her repertoire.

## Making Changes Across a Set of Files

The most common use of sed is in making a set of search-and-replacement edits across a set of files. Many times these scripts aren't very unusual or interesting, just a list of substitute commands that change one word or phrase to another. Of course, such scripts don't need to be interesting as long as they are useful and save doing the work manually.

The example we look at in this section is a conversion script, designed to modify various "machine-specific" terms in a UNIX documentation set. One person went through the documentation set and made a list of things that needed to be changed. Another person worked from the list to create the following list of substitutions.

```
s/ON switch/START switch/g
s/ON button/START switch/g
s/STANDBY switch/STOP switch/g
s/STANDBY button/STOP switch/g
s/STANDBY/STOP/g
s/[cC]abinet [Ll]ight/control panel light/g
s/core system diskettes/core system tape/g
s/TERM=542[05] /TERM=PT200 /g
s/Teletype 542[05]/BigOne PT200/g
s/542[05] terminal/PT200 terminal/g
s/Documentation Road Map/Documentation Directory/g
s/Owner\/Operator Guide/Installation and Operation Guide/g
s/AT&T 3B20 [cC]omputer/BigOne XL Computer/g
s/AT&T 3B2 [cC]omputer/BigOne XL Computer/g
s/3B2 [cC]omputer/BigOne XL Computer/g
s/3B2/BigOne XL Computer/g
```

The script is straightforward. The beauty is not in the script itself but in sed's ability to apply this script to the hundreds of files comprising the documentation set. Once this script is tested, it can be executed using **runsed** to process as many files as there are at once.

Such a script can be a tremendous time-saver, but it can also be an opportunity to make big-time mistakes. What sometimes happens is that a person writes the script, tests it on one or two out of the hundreds of files and concludes from that test that the script works fine. While it may not be practical to test each file, it is important that the test files you do choose be both representative and exceptional. Remember that text is extremely variable and you cannot typically trust that what is true for a particular occurrence is true for all occurrences.

Using **grep** to examine large amounts of input can be very helpful. For instance, if you wanted to determine how "core system diskettes" appears in the documents, you could **grep** for it everywhere and pore over the listing. To be thorough, you should also **grep** for "core," "core system," "system diskettes," and "diskettes" to look for occurrences split over multiple lines. (You could also use the **phrase** script in Chapter 6 to look for occurrences of multiple words over consecutive lines.) Examining the input is the best way to know what your script must do.

In some ways, writing a script is like devising a hypothesis, given a certain set of facts. You try to prove the validity of the hypothesis by increasing the amount of data that you test it against. If you are going to be running a script on multiple files, use **testsed** to run the script on several dozen files after you've tested it on a smaller sample. Then compare the temporary files to the originals to see if your assumptions were correct. The script might be off slightly and you can revise it. The more time you spend testing, which is actually rather interesting work, the less chance you will spend your time unraveling problems caused by a botched script.

## *Extracting Contents of a File*

One type of sed application is used for extracting relevant material from a file. In this way, sed functions like **grep**, with the additional advantage that the input can be modified prior to output. This type of script is a good candidate for a shell script.

Here are two examples: extracting a macro definition from a macro package and displaying the outline of a document.

## *Extracting a macro definition*

**troff** macros are defined in a macro package, often a single file that's located in a directory such as */usr/lib/macros*. A **troff** macro definition always begins with the string ".de", followed by an optional space and the one- or two-letter name of the macro. The definition ends with a line beginning with two dots (..). The script we show in this section extracts a particular macro definition from a macro package. (It saves you from having to locate and open the file with an editor and search for the lines that you want to examine.)

The first step in designing this script is to write one that extracts a specific macro, in this case, the BL (Bulleted List) macro in the **-mm** package.[*]

```
$ sed -n  "/^\.deBL/,/^\.\.$/p" /usr/lib/macros/mmt
.deBL
.if\\n(.$<1 .)L \\n(Pin 0 1n 0 \\*(BU
.if\\n(.$=1 .LB 0\\$1 0 1 0 \\*(BU
.if\\n(.$>1 \{.ie !\w^G\\$1^G .)L \\n(Pin 0 1n 0 \\*(BU 0 1
.el.LB 0\\$1 0 1 0 \\*(BU 0 1 \}
..
```

Sed is invoked with the *-n* option to keep it from printing out the entire file. With this option, sed will print only the lines it is explicitly told to print via the print command. The sed script contains two addresses: the first matches the start of the macro definition ".deBL" and the second matches its termination, ".." on a line by itself. Note that dots appear literally in the two patterns and are escaped using the backslash.

The two addresses specify a range of lines for the print command, **p**. It is this capability that distinguishes this kind of search script from **grep**, which cannot match a range of lines.

We can take this command line and make it more general by placing it in a shell script. One obvious advantage of creating a shell script is that it saves typing. Another advantage is that a shell script can be designed for more general usage. For instance, we can allow the user to supply information from the command line. In this case, rather than hard-code the name of the macro in the sed script, we can use a command-line argument to supply it. You can refer to each argument on the command line in a shell script by positional notation: the first argument is $1, the second is $2, and so on. Here's the **getmac** script:

```
#! /bin/sh
# getmac -- print mm macro definition for $1
sed -n "/^\.de$1/,/^\.\.$/p" /usr/lib/macros/mmt
```

---

[*] We happen to know that the -mm macros don't have a space after the ".de" command.

The first line of the shell script forces interpretation of the script by the Bourne shell, using the "#!" executable interpreter mechanism available on all modern UNIX systems. The second line is a comment that describes the name and purpose of the script. The sed command, on the third line, is identical to the previous example, except that "BL" is replaced by "$1", a variable representing the first command-line argument. Note that the double quotes surrounding the sed script are necessary. Single quotes would not allow interpretation of "$1" by the shell.

This script, **getmac**, can be executed as follows:

```
$ getmac BL
```

where "BL" is the first command-line argument. It produces the same output as the previous example.

This script can be adapted to work with any of several macro packages. The following version of **getmac** allows the user to specify the name of a macro package as the second command-line argument.

```
#! /bin/sh
# getmac - read macro definition for $1 from package $2
file=/usr/lib/macros/mmt
mac="$1"
case $2 in
 -ms) file="/work/macros/current/tmac.s";;
 -mm) file="/usr/lib/macros/mmt";;
 -man) file="/usr/lib/macros/an";;
esac
sed -n "/^\.de *$mac/,/^\.\.$/p" $file
```

What is new here is a **case** statement that tests the value of $2 and then assigns a value to the variable **file**. Notice that we assign a default value to **file** so if the user does not designate a macro package, the **-mm** macro package is searched. Also, for clarity and readability, the value of $1 is assigned to the variable **mac**.

In creating this script, we discovered a difference among macro packages in the first line of the macro definition. The **-ms** macros include a space between ".de" and the name of the macro, while **-mm** and **-man** do not. Fortunately, we are able to modify the pattern to accommodate both cases.

```
/^\.de *$mac/
```

Following ".de", we specify a space followed by an asterisk, which means the space is optional.

The script prints the result on standard output, but it can easily be redirected into a file, where it can become the basis for the redefinition of a macro.

### Generating an outline

Our next example not only extracts information; it modifies it to make it easier to read. We create a shell script named **do.outline** that uses sed to give an outline view of a document. It processes lines containing coded section headings, such as the following:

```
.Ah "Shell Programming"
```

The macro package we use has a chapter heading macro named "Se" and hierarchical headings named "Ah", "Bh", and "Ch". In the **-mm** macro package, these macros might be "H", "H1", "H2", "H3", etc. You can adapt the script to whatever macros or tags identify the structure of a document. The purpose of the do.**outline** script is to make the structure more apparent by printing the headings in an indented outline format.

The result of **do.outline** is shown below:

```
$ do.outline ch13/sect1
CHAPTER  13 Let the Computer Do the Dirty Work
       A.   Shell Programming
            B.   Stored Commands
            B.   Passing Arguments to Shell Scripts
            B.   Conditional Execution
            B.   Discarding Used Arguments
            B.   Repetitive Execution
            B.   Setting Default Values
            B.   What We've Accomplished
```

It prints the result to standard output (without, of course, making any changes within the files themselves).

Let's look at how to put together this script. The script needs to match lines that begin with the macros for:

- Chapter title (.Se)
- Section heading (.Ah)
- Subsection heading (.Bh)

We need to make substitutions on those lines, replacing macros with a text marker (A, B, for instance) and adding the appropriate amount of spacing (using tabs) to indent each heading. (Remember, the "•" denotes a tab character.)

Here's the basic script:

```
sed -n '
s/^\.Se /Chapter /p
s/^\.Ah /•A. /p
s/^\.Bh /••B.  /p' $*
```

**do.outline** operates on all files specified on the command line ("$*"). The *-n* option suppresses the default output of the program. The sed script contains three substitute commands that replace the codes with the letters and indent each line. Each substitute command is modified by the **p** flag that indicates the line should be printed.

When we test this script, the following results are produced:

```
CHAPTER  "13" "Let the Computer Do the Dirty Work"
      A.  "Shell Programming"
         B.  "Stored Commands"
         B.  "Passing Arguments to Shell Scripts"
```

The quotation marks that surround the arguments to a macro are passed through. We can write a substitute command to remove the quotation marks.

```
s/"//g
```

It is necessary to specify the global flag, **g**, to catch all occurrences on a single line. However, the key decision is where to put this command in the script. If we put it at the end of the script, it will remove the quotation marks after the line has already been output. We have to put it at the top of the script and perform this edit for all lines, regardless of whether or not they are output later in the script.

```
sed -n '
s/"//g
s/^\.Se /Chapter /p
s/^\.Ah /•A.  /p
s/^\.Bh /••B.  /p' $*
```

This script now produces the results that were shown earlier.

You can modify this script to search for almost any kind of coded format. For instance, here's a rough version for a TeX file:

```
sed -n '
s/[{}]//g
s/\\section/•A.  /p
s/\\subsection/••B.  /p' $*
```

## *Edits To Go*

Let's consider an application that shows sed in its role as a true stream editor, making edits in a pipeline—edits that are never written back into a file.

On a typewriter-like device (including a CRT), an em-dash is typed as a pair of hyphens (--). In typesetting, it is printed as a single, long dash (—). **troff** provides a special character name for the em-dash, but it is inconvenient to type "\(em".

The following command changes two consecutive dashes into an em-dash.

```
s/--/\\(em/g
```

We double the backslashes in the replacement string for \(em, since the backslash has a special meaning to sed.

Perhaps there are cases in which we don't want this substitute command to be applied. What if someone is using hyphens to draw a horizontal line? We can refine this command to exclude lines containing three or more consecutive hyphens. To do this, we use the ! address modifier:

```
/---/!s/--/\\(em/g
```

It may take a moment to penetrate this syntax. What's different is that we use a pattern address to restrict the lines that are affected by the substitute command, and we use ! to reverse the sense of the pattern match. It says, simply, "If you find a line containing three consecutive hyphens, don't apply the edit." On all other lines, the substitute command will be applied.

We can use this command in a script that automatically inserts em-dashes for us. To do that, we will use sed as a preprocessor for a **troff** file. The file will be processed by sed and then piped to **troff**.

```
sed '/---/!s/--/\\(em/g' file | troff
```

In other words, sed changes the input file and passes the output directly to **troff**, without creating an intermediate file. The edits are made on-the-go, and do not affect the input file. You might wonder why not just make the changes permanently in the original file? One reason is simply that it's not necessary—the input remains consistent with what the user typed but **troff** still produces what looks best for typeset-quality output. Furthermore, because it is embedded in a larger shell script, the transformation of hyphens to em-dashes is invisible to the user, and not an additional step in the formatting process.

We use a shell script named **format** that uses sed for this purpose. Here's what the shell script looks like:

```
#! /bin/sh
eqn= pic= col=
files= options= roff="ditroff -Tps"
sed="| sed '/---/!s/--/\\(em/g'"
while [ $# -gt 0 ]
do
    case $1 in
      -E) eqn="| eqn";;
      -P) pic="| pic";;
      -N) roff="nroff" col="| col" sed= ;;
      -*) options="$options $1";;
```

```
      *) if [ -f $1 ]
         then files="$files $1"
         else echo "format: $1: file not found"; exit 1
         fi;;
   esac
   shift
done
eval "cat $files $sed | tbl $eqn $pic | $roff $options $col | lp"
```

This script assigns and evaluates a number of variables (prefixed by a dollar sign)
that construct the command line that is submitted to format and print a document.
(Notice that we've set up the *-N* option for **nroff** so that it sets the sed variable to
the empty string, since we only want to make this change if we are using **troff**.
Even though **nroff** understands the \(em special character, making this change
would have no actual effect on the output.)

Changing hyphens to em-dashes is not the only "prettying up" edit we might want
to make when typesetting a document. For example, most keyboards do not allow
you to type open and close quotation marks (" and " as opposed to "and"). In
**troff**, you can indicate a open quotation mark by typing two consecutive grave
accents, or "backquotes" (``), and a close quotation mark by typing two consecutive single quotes (''). We can use sed to change each doublequote character to a
pair of single open-quotes or close-quotes (depending on context), which, when
typeset, will produce the appearance of a proper "double quote."

This is a considerably more difficult edit to make, since there are many separate
cases involving punctuation marks, space, and tabs. Our script might look like this:

```
s/^"/''/
s/"$/''/
s/"?□/''?□/g
s/"?$/''?/g
s/□"/□''/g
s/"□/''□/g
s/•"/•''/g
s/"•/''•/g
s/")/'')/g
s/"]/'']/g
s/("/(''/g
s/\["/\[''/g
s/";/'';/g
s/":/'':/g
s/,"/,''/g
s/",/'',/g
s/\."/.\\\&''/g
s/"\./''.\\\&/g
s/\\(em\\^"/\\(em''/g
s/"\\(em/''\\(em/g
s/\\(em"/\\(em''/g
s/@DQ@/"/g
```

The first substitute command looks for a quotation mark at the beginning of a line and changes it to an open-quote. The second command looks for a quotation mark at the end of a line and changes it to a close-quote. The remaining commands look for the quotation mark in different contexts, before or after a punctuation mark, a space, a tab, or an em-dash. The last command allows us to get a real doublequote (") into the **troff** input if we need it. We put these commands in a "cleanup" script, along with the command changing hyphens to dashes, and invoke it in the pipeline that formats and prints documents using **troff**.

# *Getting to the PromiSed Land*

You have now seen four different types of sed scripts, as well as how they are embedded inside shell scripts to create easy-to-use applications. More and more, as you work with sed, you will develop methods for creating and testing sed scripts. You will come to rely upon these methods and gain confidence that you know what your script is doing and why.

Here are a few tips:

1. *Know Thy Input!* Carefully examine your input file, using **grep**, before designing your script.

2. *Sample Before Buying.* Start with a small sample of occurrences in a test file. Run your script on the sample and make sure the script is working. Remember, it's just as important to make sure the script *doesn't* work where you *don't* want it to. Then increase the size of the sample. Try to increase the complexity of the input.

3. *Think Before Doing.* Work carefully, testing each command that you add to a script. Compare the output against the input file to see what has changed. Prove to yourself that your script is complete. Your script may work perfectly, based on your assumptions of what is in the input file, but your assumptions may be wrong.

4. *Be Pragmatic!* Try to accomplish what you can with your sed script, but it doesn't have to do 100 percent of the job. If you encounter difficult situations, check and see how frequently they occur. Sometimes it's better to do a few remaining edits manually.

As you gain experience, add your own "scripting tips" to this list. You will also find that these tips apply equally well when working with awk.

# 5

# Basic sed Commands

The sed command set consists of 25 commands. In this chapter, we introduce four new editing commands: **d** (delete), **a** (append), **i** (insert), and **c** (change). We also look at ways to change the flow control (i.e., determine which command is executed next) within a script.

## About the Syntax of sed Commands

Before looking at individual commands, there are a couple of points to review about the syntax of all sed commands. We covered most of this material in the previous chapter.

A line address is optional with any command. It can be a pattern described as a regular expression surrounded by slashes, a line number, or a line-addressing symbol. Most sed commands can accept two comma-separated addresses that indicate a range of lines. For these commands, our convention is to specify:

> [*address*]command

A few commands accept only a single line address. They cannot be applied to a range of lines. The convention for them is:

> [*line-address*]command

Remember also that commands can be grouped at the same address by surrounding the list of commands in braces:

```
address {
                command1
                command2
                command3
    }
```

The first command can be placed on the same line with the opening brace but the closing brace must appear on its own line. Each command can have its own address and multiple levels of grouping are permitted. Also, as you can see from the indentation of the commands inside the braces, spaces, and tabs at the beginning of lines are permitted.

When sed is unable to understand a command, it prints the message "Command garbled." One subtle syntax error is adding a space after a command. This is not allowed; the end of a command must be at the end of the line.

Proof of this restriction is offered by an "undocumented" feature: multiple sed commands can be placed on the same line if each one is separated by a semicolon.[*] The following example is syntactically correct:

```
n;d
```

However, putting a space after the **n** command causes a syntax error. Putting a space *before* the **d** command is okay.

Placing multiple commands on the same line is highly discouraged because sed scripts are difficult enough to read even when each command is written on its own line. (Note that the change, insert, and append commands must be specified over multiple lines and cannot be specified on the same line.)

## *Comment*

You can use a comment to document a script by describing its purpose. Starting in this chapter, our full script examples begin with a comment line. A comment line can appear as the first line of a script. In System V's version of sed, a comment is permitted only on the first line. In some versions, including sed running under SunOS 4.1.x and with GNU sed, you can place comments anywhere in the script, even on a line following a command. The examples in this book will follow the more restrictive case of System V sed, limiting comments to the first line of the script. However, the ability to use comments to document your script is valuable and you should make use of it if your version of sed permits it.

---

[*] Surprisingly, the use of semicolons to separate commands is not documented in the POSIX standard.

An octothorpe (#) must be the first character on the line. The syntax of a comment line is:

    #[n]

The following example shows the first line of a script:

    # wstar.sed: convert WordStar files

If necessary, the comment can be continued on multiple lines by ending the pre-ceding line with a backslash.[*] For consistency, you might begin the continuation line with an # so that the line's purpose is obvious.

If the next character following # is **n**, the script will not automatically produce out-put. It is equivalent to specifying the command-line option *-n*. The rest of the line following the **n** is treated as a comment. Under the POSIX standard, **#n** used this way must be the first two characters in the file.

# *Substitution*

We have already demonstrated many uses of the substitute command. Let's look carefully at its syntax:

    [*address*]s/*pattern*/*replacement*/*flags*

where the *flags* that modify the substitution are:

**n**   A number (1 to 512) indicating that a replacement should be made for only the *n*th occurrence of the *pattern*.

**g**   Make changes globally on all occurrences in the pattern space. Normally only the first occurrence is replaced.

**p**   Print the contents of the pattern space.

**w** *file*
       Write the contents of the pattern space to *file*.

The substitute command is applied to the lines matching the *address*. If no address is specified, it is applied to all lines that match the *pattern*, a regular expression. If a regular expression is supplied as an address, and no *pattern* is specified, the substitute command matches what is matched by the address. This can be useful when the substitute command is one of multiple commands applied at the same address. For an example, see the section "Checking Out Reference Pages" later in this chapter.

---

* This does not work with GNU sed (version 2.05), though.

Unlike addresses, which require a slash (/) as a delimiter, the regular expression can be delimited by any character except a blank or a newline. Thus, if the pattern contained slashes, you could choose another character, such as an exclamation mark, as the delimiter.

```
s!/usr/mail!/usr2/mail!
```

Note that the delimiter appears three times and is required after the *replacement*. Regardless of which delimiter you use, if it does appear in the regular expression, or in the replacement text, use a backslash (\) to escape it.

Once upon a time, computers stored text in fixed-length records. A line ended after so many characters (typically 80), and then the next line started. There was no explicit character in the data to mark the end of one line and the beginning of the next; every line had the same (fixed) number of characters. Modern systems are more flexible; they use a special character (referred to as *newline*) to mark the end of the line. This allows lines to be of arbitrary[*] length.

Since newline is just another character when stored internally, a regular expression can use "\n" to match an *embedded* newline. This occurs, as you will see in the next chapter, in the special case when another line is appended to the current line in the pattern space. (See Chapter 2, *Understanding Basic Operations*, for a discussion of line addressing and Chapter 3, *Understanding Regular Expression Syntax*, for a discussion of regular expression syntax.)

The *replacement* is a string of characters that will replace what is matched by the regular expression. (See the section "The Extent of the Match" in Chapter 3.) In the `replacement` section, only the following characters have special meaning:

& Replaced by the string matched by the regular expression.

\n Matches the *n*th substring (*n* is a single digit) previously specified in the `pattern` using "\(" and "\)".

\ Used to escape the ampersand (&), the backslash (\), and the substitution command's delimiter when they are used literally in the replacement section. In addition, it can be used to escape the newline and create a multiline *replacement* string.

Thus, besides metacharacters in regular expressions, sed also has metacharacters in the replacement. See the next section, "Replacement Metacharacters," for examples of using them.

*Flags* can be used in combination where it makes sense. For instance, **gp** makes the substitution globally on the line and prints the line. The global flag is by far

---

[*] Well, more or less. Many UNIX programs have internal limits on the length of the lines that they will process. Most GNU programs, though, do not have such limits.

the most commonly used. Without it, the replacement is made only for the first occurrence on the line. The print flag and the write flag both provide the same functionality as the print and write commands (which are discussed later in this chapter) with one important difference. These actions are contingent upon a successful substitution occurring. In other words, if the replacement is made, the line is printed or written to file. Because the default action is to pass through all lines, regardless of whether any action is taken, the print and write flags are typically used when the default output is suppressed (the *-n* option). In addition, if a script contains multiple substitute commands that match the same line, multiple copies of that line will be printed or written to file.

The numeric flag can be used in the rare instances where the regular expression repeats itself on a line and the replacement must be made for only one of those occurrences by position. For instance, a line, perhaps containing **tbl** input, might contain multiple tabs. Let's say that there are three tabs per line, and you'd like to replace the second tab with ">". The following substitute command would do it:

```
s/•/>/2
```

"•" represents an actual tab character, which is otherwise invisible on the screen. If the input is a one-line file such as the following:

```
Column1•Column2•Column3•Column4
```

the output produced by running the script on this file will be:

```
Column1•Column2>Column3•Column4
```

Note that without the numeric flag, the substitute command would replace only the first tab. (Therefore "1" can be considered the default numeric flag.)

## Replacement Metacharacters

The replacement metacharacters are backslash (\), ampersand (&), and \\*n*. The backslash is generally used to escape the other metacharacters but it is also used to include a newline in a replacement string.

We can do a variation on the previous example to replace the second tab on each line with a newline.

```
s/•/\
/2
```

Note that no spaces are permitted after the backslash. This script produces the following result:

```
Column1•Column2
Column3•Column4
```

Another example comes from the conversion of a file for **troff** to an ASCII input format for Ventura Publisher. It converts the following line for **troff**:

```
.Ah "Major Heading"
```

to a similar line for Ventura Publisher:

```
@A HEAD = Major Heading
```

The twist in this problem is that the line needs to be preceded and followed by a blank line. It is an example of writing a multiline replacement string.

```
/^.Ah/{
s/.Ah */\
\
@A HEAD = /
s/""//g
s/$/\
/
}
```

The first substitute command replaces ".Ah" with two newlines and "@A HEAD =". A backslash at the end of the line is necessary to escape the newline. The second substitution removes the quotation marks. The last command matches the end of line in the pattern space (not the embedded newlines) and adds a newline after it.

In the next example, the backslash is used to escape the ampersand, which appears literally in the replacement section.

```
s/ORA/O'Reilly \& Associates, Inc./g
```

It's easy to forget about the ampersand appearing literally in the replacement string. If we had not escaped it in this example, the output would have been "O'Reilly ORA Associates, Inc."

As a metacharacter, the ampersand (&) represents the extent of the pattern match, not the line that was matched. You might use the ampersand to match a word and surround it by **troff** requests. The following example surrounds a word with point-size requests:

```
s/UNIX/\\s-2&\\s0/g
```

Because backslashes are also replacement metacharacters, two backslashes are necessary to output a single backslash. The "&" in the replacement string refers to "UNIX." If the input line is:

```
on the UNIX Operating System.
```

then the substitute command produces:

```
on the \s-2UNIX\s0 Operating System.
```

The ampersand is particularly useful when the regular expression matches variations of a word. It allows you to specify a variable replacement string that corresponds to what was actually matched. For instance, let's say that you wanted to surround with parentheses any cross reference to a numbered section in a document. In other words, any reference such as "See Section 1.4" or "See Section 12.9" should appear in parentheses, as "(See Section 12.9)." A regular expression can match the different combination of numbers, so we use "&" in the replacement string and surround whatever was matched.

```
s/See Section [1-9][0-9]*\.[1-9][0-9]*/(&)/
```

The ampersand makes it possible to reference the entire match in the replacement string.

Now let's look at the metacharacters that allow us to select any individual portion of a string that is matched and recall it in the replacement string. A pair of escaped parentheses are used in sed to enclose any part of a regular expression and save it for recall. Up to nine "saves" are permitted for a single line. "\*n*" is used to recall the portion of the match that was saved, where *n* is a number from 1 to 9 referencing a particular "saved" string in order of use.

For example, to put the section numbers in boldface when they appeared as a cross reference, we could write the following substitution:

```
s/\(See Section \)\([1-9][0-9]*\.[1-9][0-9]*\)/\1\\fB\2\\fP/
```

Two pairs of escaped parentheses are specified. The first captures "See Section□" (because this is a fixed string, it could have been simply retyped in the replacement string). The second captures the section number. The replacement string recalls the first saved substring as "\1" and the second as "\2," which is surrounded by bold-font requests.

We can use a similar technique to match parts of a line and swap them. For instance, let's say there are two parts of a line separated by a colon. We can match each part, putting them within escaped parentheses and swapping them in the replacement.

```
$ cat test1
first:second
one:two
$ sed 's/\(.*\):\(.*\)/\2:\1/' test1
second:first
two:one
```

The larger point is that you can recall a saved substring in any order, and multiple times, as you'll see in the next example.

## Correcting index entries

Later, in the awk section of this book, we will present a program for formatting an index, such as the one for this book. The first step in creating an index is to place index codes in the document files. We use an index macro named .XX, which takes a single argument, the index entry. A sample index entry might be:

```
.XX "sed, substitution command"
```

Each index entry appears on a line by itself. When you run an index, you get a collection of index entries with page numbers that are then sorted and merged in a list. An editor poring over that list will typically find errors and inconsistencies that need to be corrected. It is, in short, a pain to have to track down the file where an index entry resides and then make the correction, particularly when there are dozens of entries to be corrected.

Sed can be a great help in making these edits across a group of files. One can simply create a list of edits in a sed script and then run it on all the files. A key point is that the substitute command needs an address that limits it to lines beginning ".XX". Your script should not make changes in the text itself.

Let's say that we wanted to change the index entry above to "sed, substitute command." The following command would do it:

```
/^\.XX/ /s/sed, substitution command/sed, substitute command/
```

The address matches all lines that begin with ".XX " and only on those lines does it attempt to make the replacement. You might wonder, why not specify a shorter regular expression? For example:

```
/^\.XX/ /s/substitution/substitute/
```

The answer is simply that there could be other entries which use the word "substitution" correctly and which we would not want to change.

We can go a step further and provide a shell script that creates a list of index entries prepared for editing as a series of sed substitute commands.

```
#! /bin/sh
# index.edit -- compile list of index entries for editing.
grep "^\.XX" $* | sort -u |
sed '
s/^\.XX \(.*\)$/\/^\\.XX \/s\/\1\/\1\///'
```

The **index.edit** shell script uses **grep** to extract all lines containing index entries from any number of files specified on the command line. It passes this list through **sort** which, with the -*u* option, sorts and removes duplicate entries. The list is then piped to sed, and the one-line sed script builds a substitution command.

Let's look at it more closely. Here's just the regular expression:

```
^\.XX \(.*\)$
```

It matches the entire line, saving the index entry for recall. Here's just the replacement string:

```
\/^\\.XX \/s\/\1\/\1\/
```

It generates a substitute command beginning with an address: a slash, followed by two backslashes—to output one backslash to protect the dot in the ".XX" that follows—then comes a space, then another slash to complete the address. Next we output an "s" followed by a slash, and then recall the saved portion to be used as a regular expression. That is followed by another slash and again we recall the saved substring as the replacement string. A slash finally ends the command.

When the **index.edit** script is run on a file, it creates a listing similar to this:

```
$ index.edit ch05
/^\.XX /s/"append command(a)"/"append command(a)"/
/^\.XX /s/"change command"/"change command"/
/^\.XX /s/"change command(c)"/"change command(c)"/
/^\.XX /s/"commands:sed, summary of"/"commands:sed, summary of"/
/^\.XX /s/"delete command(d)"/"delete command(d)"/
/^\.XX /s/"insert command(i)"/"insert command(i)"/
/^\.XX /s/"line numbers:printing"/"line numbers:printing"/
/^\.XX /s/"list command(l)"/"list command(l)"/
```

This output could be captured in a file. Then you can delete the entries that don't need to change and you can make changes by editing the replacement string. At that point, you can use this file as a sed script to correct the index entries in all document files.

When doing a large book with lots of entries, you might use **grep** again to extract particular entries from the output of **index.edit** and direct them into their own file for editing. This saves you from having to wade through numerous entries.

There is one small failing in this program. It should look for metacharacters that might appear literally in index entries and protect them in regular expressions. For instance, if an index entry contains an asterisk, it will not be interpreted as such, but as a metacharacter. To make that change effectively requires the use of several advanced commands, so we'll put off improving this script until the next chapter.

# *Delete*

We previously showed examples of the delete command (**d**). It takes an address and deletes the contents of the pattern space if the line matches the address.

The delete command is also a command that can change the flow of control in a script. That is because once it is executed, no further commands are executed on the "empty" pattern space.[*] The delete command causes a new line of input to be read and a new pass on the editing script to begin from the top. (In this behavior, it is the same as the **next** command, which you'll encounter later in this chapter.)

The important thing to remember is: if the line matches the address, the entire line is deleted, not just the portion of the line that is matched. (To delete a portion of a line, use the substitute command and specify an empty replacement.) In the previous chapter, we showed a command to delete blank lines:

```
/^$/d
```

Another use of the delete command could be to strip out certain **troff** requests, such as those that add spacing, break the page, and turn fill mode off and on:

```
/^\.sp/d
/^\.bp/d
/^\.nf/d
/^\.fi/d
```

These commands delete an entire line. For instance, the first command will delete the line ".sp 1" or ".sp .03v".

The delete command can be used to delete a range of lines. In the previous chapter, there is an example of deleting all tables from a file by deleting the lines between the .TS and .TE macros. There is also a delete command (**D**) used to delete a portion of a multiline pattern space. This advanced command is presented in the next chapter.

## *Append, Insert, and Change*

The append (**a**), insert (**i**), and change (**c**) commands provide editing functions that are commonly performed with an interactive editor, such as **vi**. You may find it strange to use these same commands to "enter" text using a noninteractive editor. The syntax of these commands is unusual for sed because they must be specified over multiple lines. The syntax follows:

```
append  [line-address]a\
        text
insert  [line-address]i\
        text
change  [address]c\
        text
```

---

[*] UNIX documentation reads "no further commands are attempted on the corpse of a deleted line." R.I.P.

The insert command places the supplied text before the current line in the pattern space. The append command places it after the current line. The change command replaces the contents of the pattern space with the supplied text.

Each of these commands requires a backslash following it to escape the first end-of-line. The *text* must begin on the next line. To input multiple lines of text, each successive line must end with a backslash, with the exception of the very last line. For example, the following insert command inserts two lines of text at a line matching "<Larry's Address>":

```
/<Larry's Address>/i\
4700 Cross Court\
French Lick, IN
```

Also, if the text contains a literal backslash, add an extra backslash to escape it.*

The append and insert commands can be applied only to a single line address, not a range of lines. The change command, however, can address a range of lines. In this case, it replaces *all* addressed lines with a single copy of the text. In other words, it deletes each line in the range but the supplied text is output only once. For example, the following script, when run on a file containing a mail message:

```
/^From /,/^$/c\
<Mail Header Removed>
```

removes the entire mail-message header and replaces it with the line "<Mail Header Removed>." Note that you will see the opposite behavior when the change command is one of a group of commands, enclosed in braces, that act on a range of lines. For instance, the following script:

```
/^From /,/^$/{
        s/^From //p
        c\
<Mail Header Removed>
}
```

will output "<Mail Header Removed>" for each line in the range. So, while the former example outputs the text once, this example will output it 10 times if there are 10 lines in the range.

The change command clears the pattern space, having the same effect on the pattern space as the delete command. No command following the change command in the script is applied.

---

* UNIX documentation says that any leading tabs or spaces in the supplied text will disappear on output. This appears to work on System V and GNU sed, but not older versions, such as SunOS 4.1.x. If they disappear on your system, the solution is to put a backslash at the beginning of the line, preceding the first tab or space. The backslash is not output.

The insert and append commands do not affect the contents of the pattern space. The supplied text will not match any address in subsequent commands in the script, nor can those commands affect the text. No matter what changes occur to alter the pattern space, the supplied text will still be output appropriately. This is also true when the default output is suppressed—the supplied text will be output even if the pattern space is not. Also, the supplied text does not affect sed's internal line counter.

Let's look at an example of the insert command. Suppose we wanted to source a local file of macros in all the files of a particular document. In addition, we'd like to define a page header string that identifies the document as a draft. The following script inserts two new lines of text before the first line of a file:

```
1i\
.so macros\
.ds CH First Draft
```

After sed executes this command, the pattern space remains unchanged. The new text is output before the current line. A subsequent command could not successfully match "macros" or "First Draft."

A variation of the previous example shows the append command adding a line to the end of a file:

```
$a\
End of file
```

The $ is a line-addressing symbol that matches the last line of a file. The supplied text will be output after the current line, so it becomes the last line in the output. Note that even though only one line is output, the supplied text must start on a line by itself and cannot be on the same line as the append command.

The next example shows the insert and append commands used in the same script. The task here is to add a few **troff** requests before the macro that initializes a list, and several after the macro that closes the list.

```
/^\.Ls/i\
.in 5n\
.sp .3
/^\.Le/a\
.in 0\
.sp .3
```

The insert command puts two lines before the .Ls macro and the append command puts two lines after the .Le macro.

The insert command can be used to put a blank line before the current line, or the append command to put one after, by leaving the line following it blank.

The change command replaces the contents of the pattern space with the text you provide. In effect, it deletes the current line and puts the supplied text in its place. It can be used when you want to match a line and replace it entirely. Let's say for instance that a file contains a lot of explicit **troff** spacing requests with different amounts of spacing. Look at the following series:

```
.sp 1.5
.sp
.sp 1
.sp 1.5v
.sp .3v
.sp 3
```

If you wanted to change all the arguments to ".5", it is probably easier to use the change command than try to match all the individual arguments and make the proper substitution.

```
/^\.sp/c\
.sp .5
```

This command allows us to ignore the arguments and replace them regardless of what they are.

## *List*

The list command (l) displays the contents of the pattern space, showing non-printing characters as two-digit ASCII codes. It is similar in function to the list (:l) command in **vi**. You can use this command to detect "invisible" characters in the input.[*]

```
$ cat test/spchar
Here is a string of special characters: ^A  ^B
^M ^G

$ sed -n -e "l" test/spchar
Here is a string of special characters: \01 \02
\15 \07

$ # test with GNU sed too
$ gsed -n -e "l" test/spchar
Here is a string of special characters: \01  \02
\r \a
```

Because the list command causes immediate output, we suppress the default output or we would get duplicate copies of the lines.

---

\* GNU sed displays certain characters, such as carriage return, using the ANSI C escape sequences, instead of straight octal. Presumably, this is easier to comprehend for those who are familiar with C (or awk, as we'll see later in the book).

You cannot match a character by ASCII value (nor can you match octal values) in sed.[*] Instead, you have to find a key combination in **vi** to produce it. Use CTRL-V to quote the character. For instance, you can match an ESC character (^[). Look at the following script:

```
# list line and replace ^[ with "Escape"
l
s/^[/Escape/
```

Here's a one-line test file:

```
The Great ^[ is a movie starring Steve McQueen.
```

Running the script produces the following output:

```
The Great \33 is a movie starring Steve McQueen.
The Great Escape is a movie starring Steve McQueen.
```

GNU sed produces this:

```
The Great \1b is a movie starring Steve McQueen.
The Great Escape is a movie starring Steve McQueen.
```

The ^[ character was made in **vi** by entering CTRL-V, then pressing the ESC key.

## *Stripping Out Non-Printable Characters from nroff Files*

The UNIX formatter **nroff** produces output for line printers and CRT displays. To achieve such special effects as bolding, it outputs the character followed by a backspace and then outputs the same character again. A sample of it viewed with a text editor might look like:

```
N^HN^HN^HNA^HA^HA^HAM^HM^HM^HME^HE^HE^HE
```

which bolds the word "NAME." There are three overstrikes for each character output. Similarly, underlining is achieved by outputting an underscore, a backspace and then the character to be underlined. The following example is the word "file" surrounded by a sequence for underscoring it.

```
_^Hf_^Hi_^Hl_^He
```

It might be necessary at times to strip these printing "special-effects"; perhaps if you are given this type of output as a source file. The following line removes the sequences for emboldening and underscoring:

```
s/.^H//g
```

---

[*] You can do this in awk, however.

It removes any character preceding the backspace along with the backspace itself. In the case of underlining, "." matches the underscore; for emboldening, it matches the overstrike character. Because it is applied repeatedly, multiple occurrences of the overstrike character are removed, leaving a single character for each sequence. Note that ^H is entered in **vi** by pressing CTRL-V followed by CTRL-H.

A sample application is "de-formatting" an nroff-produced **man** page found on an older System V UNIX system.[*] If you should want to access the formatted pages with a text editor, you'd want to get a clean version. (In many ways, this is a similar problem to one we solved in converting a word processing file in the previous chapter.) A formatted **man** page captured in a file looks like this:

```
^[9     who(1)                                                    who(1)
^[9 N^HN^HN^HNA^HA^HA^HAM^HM^HM^HME^HE^HE^HE
      who - who is on the system?
S^HS^HS^HSY^HY^HY^HYN^HN^HN^HNO^HO^HO^HOP^HP^HP^HPS^HS^HS^HSI^HI
      who [-a] [-b] [-d] [-H] [-l] [-p] [-q] [-r] [-s] [-t] [-T]
      [-u] [_^Hf_^Hi_^Hl_^He]
          who am i
          who am I
D^HD^HD^HDE^HE^HE^HES^HS^HS^HSC^HC^HC^HCR^HR^HR^HRI^HI^HI^HIP^HP
      who can list the user's name, terminal line, login time,
      elapsed time since activity occurred on the line, and the
...
```

In addition to stripping out the bolding and underlining sequences, there are strange escape sequences that produce form feeds or various other printer functions. You can see the sequence "^[9" at the top of the formatted manpage. This escape sequence can simply be removed:

```
s/^[9//g
```

Once again, the ESC character is entered in **vi** by typing CTRL-V followed by pressing the ESC key. The number 9 is literal. There are also what look to be leading spaces that supply the left margin and indentation. On further examination, it turns out that leading spaces precede the heading such as "NAME" but a single tab precedes each line of text. Also, there are tabs that unexpectedly appear in the text, which have to do with how **nroff** optimizes for display on a CRT screen.

To eliminate the left margin and the unwanted tabs, we add two commands to our previous two:

---

* For a while, many System V UNIX vendors only provided preformatted manpages. This allowed the **man** command to show information quickly, instead of having to format it, but the lack of **troff** source to the manpages made it difficult to fix documentation errors. Fortunately, most vendors of modern UNIX systems supply source for their manuals.

```
# sedman -- deformat nroff-formatted manpage
s/.^H//g
s/^[9//g
s/^[□•]*//g
s/•/ /g
```

The third command looks for any number of tabs or spaces at the beginning of a line. (A tab is represented by "•" and a space by "□".) The last command looks for a tab and replaces it with a single space. Running this script on our sample **man** page output produces a file that looks like this:

```
who(1)                                                          who(1)
NAME
who - who is on the system?
SYNOPSIS
who [-a] [-b] [-d] [-H] [-l] [-p] [-q] [-r] [-s] [-t] [-T]
[-u] [file]
who am i
who am I
DESCRIPTION
who can list the user's name, terminal line, login time,
elapsed time since activity occurred on the line, and the
...
```

This script does not eliminate the unnecessary blank lines caused by paging. We will look at how to do that in the next chapter, as it requires a multiline operation.

# Transform

The transform command is peculiar, not only because it is the least mnemonic of all sed commands. This command transforms each character by position in string *abc* to its equivalent in string *xyz*.[*] Its syntax follows:

[*address*]y/*abc*/*xyz*/

The replacement is made by character position. Therefore, it has no idea of a "word." Thus, "a" is replaced by "x" anywhere on the line, regardless of whether or not it is followed by a "b". One possible use of this command is to replace lowercase letters with their uppercase counterparts.

y/abcdefghijklmnopqrstuvwxyz/ABCDEFGHIJKLMNOPQRSTUVWXYZ/

This command affects the entire contents of the pattern space. If you want to convert a single word on the input line, you could do it by using the hold space. See Chapter 6 for more details on how to use the hold space. (The process is not

---

* This command is patterned after the UNIX **tr** command, which translates characters. This is a useful command in its own right; see your local documentation for details. Undoubtedly sed's **y** command would have been named **t**, if **t** had not already been taken (by the **test** command, see Chapter 6, *Advanced sed Commands*).

trivial: you output the line up to the word you want to change, delete that portion of the line, copy the line after the word to the hold space, transform the word, and then append the contents of the hold space back to the pattern space.)

# *Print*

The print command (**p**) causes the contents of the pattern space to be output. It does not clear the pattern space nor does it change the flow of control in the script. However, it is frequently used before commands (**d**, **N**, **b**) that do change flow control. Unless the default output is suppressed (*-n*), the print command will cause duplicate copies of a line to be output. It can be used when default output is suppressed or when the flow control through the program avoids reaching the bottom of the script.

Let's look at a script that shows how the print command might be used for debugging purposes. It is used to show what the line looked like before you made any changes.

```
#n Print line before and after changes.
/^\.Ah/{
p
s/"//g
s/^\.Ah //p
}
```

Note that the print flag is supplied to the substitute command. The substitute command's print flag differs from the print command in that it is conditional upon a successful substitution.

Here's a sample run of the above script:

```
$ sed -f sed.debug ch05
.Ah "Comment"
Comment
.Ah "Substitution"
Substitution
.Ah "Delete"
Delete
.Ah "Append, Insert and Change"
Append, Insert and Change
.Ah "List"
List
```

Each affected line is printed twice.

We'll see additional examples of the print command in the next chapter. See also the multiline print command (**P**) in the next chapter.

# Print Line Number

An equal sign (=) following an address prints the line number of the matched line. Unless you suppress the automatic output of lines, both the line number and the line itself will be printed. Its syntax is:

[*line-address*]=

This command cannot operate on a range of lines.

A programmer might use this to print certain lines in a source file. For instance, the following script prints the line number followed by the line itself for each line containing a tab followed by the string "if". Here's the script:

```
#n print line number and line with if statement
/	if/{
=
p
}
```

Note that **#n** suppresses the default output of lines. Now let's see how it works on a sample program, **random.c**:

```
$ sed -f sedscr.= random.c
192
	if(  rand_type  ==  TYPE_0  )  {
234
	if(  rand_type  ==  TYPE_0  )  state[ -1 ] = rand_type;
236
	if(  n  <  BREAK_1  )  {
252
		if(  n  <  BREAK_3  )  {
274
	if(  rand_type  ==  TYPE_0  )  state[ -1 ] = rand_type;
303
	if(  rand_type  ==  TYPE_0  )  state[ -1 ] = rand_type;
```

The line numbers might be useful in finding problems reported by the compiler, which typically lists the line number.

# Next

The next command (**n**) outputs the contents of the pattern space and then reads the next line of input *without* returning to the top of the script. Its syntax is:

[*address*]n

The next command changes the normal flow control, which doesn't output the contents of the pattern space until the bottom of the script is reached and which always begins at the top of the script after reading in a new line. In effect, the next command causes the next line of input to replace the current line in the pattern space. Subsequent commands in the script are applied to the replacement line, not the current line. If the default output has not been suppressed, the current line is printed before the replacement takes place.

Let's look at an example of the next command in which we delete a blank line only when it follows a pattern matched on the previous line. In this case, a writer has inserted a blank line after a section heading macro (.**H1**). We want to remove that blank line without removing all blank lines in the file. Here's the sample file:

```
.H1 "On Egypt"

Napoleon, pointing to the Pyramids, said to his troops:
"Soldiers, forty centuries have their eyes upon you."
```

The following script removes that blank line:

```
/^\.H1/{
n
/^$/d
}
```

You can read this script as follows: "Match any line beginning with the string '.H1', then print that line and read in the next line. If that line is blank, delete it." The braces are used to apply multiple commands at the same address.

In a longer script, you must remember that commands occurring before the next command will not be applied to the new input line, nor will commands occuring after it be applied to the old input line.

You'll see additional examples of the **n** command in Chapter 6, along with a multi-line version of this command.

## Reading and Writing Files

The read (**r**) and write (**w**) commands allow you to work directly with files. Both take a single argument, the name of a file. The syntax follows:

```
[line-address]r file
[address]w file
```

The read command reads the contents of *file* into the pattern space after the addressed line. It cannot operate on a range of lines. The write command writes the contents of the pattern space to the *file*.

You must have a single space between the command and the filename. (Everything after that space and up to the newline is taken to be the filename. Thus, leading or embedded spaces will become part of the filename.) The read command will not complain if the file does not exist. The write command will create a file if it does not exist; if the file already exists, the write command will overwrite it each time the script is invoked. If there are multiple instructions writing to the same file in one script, then each write command appends to the file. Also, be aware that you can only open up to 10 files per script.

The read command can be useful for inserting the contents of one file at a particular place in another file. For instance, let's say that there is a set of files and each file should close with the same one- or two-paragraph statement. A sed script would allow you to maintain the closing separately while inserting it as needed, for instance, when sending the file to the printer.

```
sed '$r closing' $* | pr | lp
```

The $ is an addressing symbol specifying the last line of the file. The contents of the file named *closing* are placed after the contents of pattern space and output with it. This example does not specify a pathname, assuming the file to be in the same directory as the command. A more general-purpose command should use the full pathname.

You may want to test out a few quirks of the read command. Let's look at the following command:

```
/^<Company-list>/r company.list
```

That is, when sed matches a line beginning with the string "<Company-list>", it is going to append the contents of the file *company.list* to the end of the matched line. No subsequent command will affect the lines read from the file. For instance, you can't make any changes to the list of companies that you've read into the file. However, commands that address the original line will work. The previous command could be followed by a second command:

```
/^<Company-list>/d
```

to delete the original line. So that if the input file was as follows:

```
For service, contact any of the following companies:
<Company-list>
Thank you.
```

running the two-line script would produce:

```
For service, contact any of the following companies:
        Allied
        Mayflower
        United
Thank you.
```

Suppressing the automatic output, using the *-n* option or **#n** script syntax, prevents the original line in the pattern space from being output, but the result of a read command still goes to standard output.

Now let's look at examples of the write command. One use is to extract information from one file and place it in its own file. For instance, imagine that we had a file listing the names of salespeople alphabetically. For each person, the listing designates which of four regions the person is assigned to. Here's a sample:

```
Adams, Henrietta      Northeast
Banks, Freda          South
Dennis, Jim           Midwest
Garvey, Bill          Northeast
Jeffries, Jane        West
Madison, Sylvia       Midwest
Sommes, Tom           South
```

Writing a script for a seven-line file, of course, is ridiculous. Yet such a script can potentially handle as many names as you can put together, and is reusable.

If all we wanted was to extract the names for a particular region, we could easily use **grep** to do it. The advantage with sed is that we can break up the file into four separate files in a single step. The following four-line script does it:

```
/Northeast$/w region.northeast
/South$/w region.south
/Midwest$/w region.midwest
/West$/w region.west
```

All of the names of salespeople that are assigned to the Northeast region will be placed in a file named *region.northeast*.

The write command writes out the contents of the pattern space when the command is invoked, not when end of the script is reached. In the previous example, we might want to remove the name of the region before writing it to file. For each case, we could handle it as we show for the Northeast region:

```
/Northeast$/{
        s///
        w region.northeast
        }
```

The substitute command matches the same pattern as the address and removes it. There are many different uses for the write command; for example, you could use it in a script to generate several customized versions of the same source file.

## Checking Out Reference Pages

Like many programs, a sed script often starts out small, and is simple to write and simple to read. In testing the script, you may discover specific cases for which the general rules do not apply. To account for these, you add lines to your script, making it longer, more complex, and more complete. While the amount of time you spend refining your script may cancel out the time saved by not doing the editing manually, at least during that time your mind has been engaged by your own seeming sleight-of-hand: "See! The computer did it."

We encountered one such problem in preparing a formatted copy of command pages that the writer had typed as a text file without any formatting information. Although the files had no formatting codes, headings were used consistently to identify the format of the command pages. A sample file is shown below.

```
*****************************************************************

NAME:    DBclose - closes a database

SYNTAX:
         void    DBclose(fdesc)
                 DBFILE *fdesc;

USAGE:
         fdesc    - pointer to database file descriptor

DESC:
DBclose() closes a file when given its database file descriptor.
Your pending writes to that file will be completed before the
file is closed.  All of your update locks are removed.
*fdesc becomes invalid.

Other users are not affected when you call DBclose().  Their update
locks and pending writes are not changed.

Note that there is no default file as there is in BASIC.
*fdesc must specify an open file.

DBclose() is analogous to the CLOSE statement in BASIC.

RETURNS:
         There is no return value


*****************************************************************
```

The task was to format this document for the laser printer, using the reference header macros we had developed. Because there were perhaps forty of these command pages, it would have been utter drudgery to go through and add codes by hand. However, because there were that many, and even though the writer was generally consistent in entering them, there would be enough differences from command to command to have required several passes.

We'll examine the process of building this sed script. In a sense, this is a process of looking carefully at each line of a sample input file and determining whether or not an edit must be made on that line. Then we look at the rest of the file for similar occurrences. We try to find specific patterns that mark the lines or range of lines that need editing.

For instance, by looking at the first line, we know we need to eliminate the row of asterisks separating each command. We specify an address for any line beginning and ending with an asterisk and look for zero or more asterisks in between. The regular expression uses an asterisk as a literal and as a metacharacter:

```
/^\*\**\*$/d
```

This command deletes entire lines of asterisks anywhere they occur in the file. We saw that blank lines were used to separate paragraphs, but replacing every blank line with a paragraph macro would cause other problems. In many cases, the blank lines can be removed because spacing has been provided in the macro. This is a case where we put off deleting or replacing blank lines on a global basis until we have dealt with specific cases. For instance, some blank lines separate labeled sections, and we can use them to define the end of a range of lines. The script, then, is designed to delete unwanted blank lines as the last operation.

Tabs were a similar problem. Tabs were used to indent syntax lines and in some cases after the colon following a label, such as "NAME". Our first thought was to remove all tabs by replacing them with eight spaces, but there were tabs we wanted to keep, such as those inside the syntax line. So we removed only specific cases, tabs at the beginning of lines and tabs following a colon.

```
/^•/s///
/:•/s//:/
```

The next line we come across has the name of the command and a description.

```
NAME:    DBclose - closes a database
```

We need to replace it with the macro .Rh 0. Its syntax is:

**.Rh 0** *"command"* *"description"*

We insert the macro at the beginning of the line, remove the hyphen, and surround the arguments with quotation marks.

```
/NAME:/ {
        s//.Rh 0 "/
        s/ - /" "/
```

```
        s/$/"/
        }
```

We can jump ahead of ourselves a bit here and look at what this portion of our script does to the sample line:

```
.Rh 0 "DBclose" "Closes a database file"
```

The next part that we examine begins with "SYNTAX." What we need to do here is put in the .Rh macro, plus some additional **troff** requests for indentation, a font change, and no-fill and no-adjust. (The indentation is required because we stripped the tabs at the beginning of the line.) These requests must go in before and after the syntax lines, turning the capabilities on and off. To do this, we define an address that specifies the range of lines between two patterns, the label and a blank line. Then, using the change command, we replace the label and the blank line with a series of formatting requests.

```
/SYNTAX:/,/^$/ {
        /SYNTAX:/c\
.Rh Syntax\
.in +5n\
.ft B\
.nf\
.na
        /^$/c\
.in -5n\
.ft R\
.fi\
.ad b
        }
```

Following the change command, each line of input ends with a backslash except the last line. As a side effect of the change command, the current line is deleted from the pattern space.

The USAGE portion is next, consisting of one or more descriptions of variable items. Here we want to format each item as an indented paragraph with a hanging italicized label. First, we output the .Rh macro; then we search for lines having two parts separated by a tab and a hyphen. Each part is saved, using backslash-parentheses, and recalled during the substitution.

```
/USAGE:/,/^$/ {
        /USAGE:/c\
.Rh Usage
        /\(.*\)•- \(.*\)/s//.IP "\\fI\1\\fR" 15n\
\2./
        }
```

This is a good example of the power of regular expressions. Let's look ahead, once again, and preview the output for the sample.

```
.Rh Usage
.IP "\fIfdesc\fR" 15n
pointer to database file descriptor.
```

The next part we come across is the description. We notice that blank lines are used in this portion to separate paragraphs. In specifying the address for this portion, we use the next label, "RETURNS."

```
/DESC:/,/RETURNS/ {
        /DESC:/i\
.LP
        s/DESC: *$/.Rh Description/
        s/^$/.LP/
}
```

The first thing we do is insert a paragraph macro because the preceding USAGE section consisted of indented paragraphs. (We could have used the variable-list macros from the **-mm** package in the USAGE section; if so, we would insert the .LE at this point.) This is done only once, which is why it is keyed to the "DESC" label. Then we substitute the label "DESC" with the .Rh macro and replace all blank lines in this section with a paragraph macro.

When we tested this portion of the sed script on our sample file, it didn't work because there was a single space following the DESC label. We changed the regular expression to look for zero or more spaces following the label. Although this worked for the sample file, there were other problems when we used a larger sample. The writer was inconsistent in his use of the "DESC" label. Mostly, it occurred on a line by itself; sometimes, though, it was included at the start of the second paragraph. So we had to add another pattern to deal with this case. It searches for the label followed by a space and one or more characters.

```
s/DESC: *$/.Rh Description/
s/DESC: \(.*\)/.Rh Description\
\\1/
```

In the second case, the reference header macro is output followed by a newline.

The next section, labeled "RETURNS," is handled in the same way as the SYNTAX section.

We do make minor content changes, replacing the label "RETURNS" with "Return Value" and consequently adding this substitution:

```
s/There is no return value\.*/None./
```

The very last thing we do is delete remaining blank lines.

```
/^$/d
```

Our script is put in a file named *refsed*. Here it is in full:

```
# refsed -- add formatting codes to reference pages
/^\*\**\*$/d
/^•/s///
/:•/s//:/
/NAME:/ {
        s//.Rh 0 "/
        s/ - /" "/
        s/$/"/
}
/SYNTAX:/,/^$/ {
        /SYNTAX:/c\
.Rh Syntax\
.in +5n\
.ft B\
.nf\
.na
        /^$/c\
.in -5n\
.ft R\
.fi\
.ad b
}
/USAGE:/,/^$/ {
        /USAGE:/c\
.Rh Usage
        /\(.*\)•- \(.*\)/s//.IP "\\fI\1\\fR" 15n\
\2./
}
/DESC:/,/RETURNS/ {
        /DESC:/i\
.LP
        s/DESC: *$/.Rh Description/
        s/DESC: \(.*\)/.Rh Description\
\1/
        s/^$/.LP/
}
/RETURNS:/,/^$/ {
        /RETURNS:/c\
.Rh "Return Value"
        s/There is no return value\.*/None./
}
/^$/d
```

As we have remarked, you should not have sed overwrite the original. It is best to redirect the output of sed to another file or let it go to the screen. If the sed script does not work properly, you will find that it is generally easier to change the script and re-run it on the original file than to write a new script to correct the problems caused by a previous run.

```
$ sed -f refsed refpage
.Rh 0 "DBclose" "closes a database"
.Rh Syntax
```

```
.in +5n
.ft B
.nf
.na
void      DBclose(fdesc)
          DBFILE *fdesc;
.in -5n
.ft R
.fi
.ad b
.Rh Usage
.IP "\fIfdesc\fR" 15n
pointer to database file descriptor.
.LP
.Rh Description
DBclose() closes a file when given its database file descriptor.
Your pending writes to that file will be completed before the
file is closed.  All of your update locks are removed.
*fdesc becomes invalid.
.LP
Other users are not effected when you call DBclose().  Their update
locks and pending writes are not changed.
.LP
Note that there is no default file as there is in BASIC.
*fdesc must specify an open file.
.LP
DBclose() is analogous to the CLOSE statement in BASIC.
.LP
.Rh "Return Value"
None.
```

# *Quit*

The quit command (q) causes sed to stop reading new input lines (and stop sending them to the output). Its syntax is:

[*line-address*]q

It can take only a single-line address. Once the line matching *address* is reached, the script will be terminated.[*] For instance, the following one-liner uses the quit command to print the first 100 lines from a file:

```
$ sed '100q' test
. . .
```

It prints each line until it gets to line 100 and quits. In this regard, this command functions similarly to the UNIX **head** command.

---

* You need to be very careful not to use **q** in any program that writes its edits back to the original file. After **q** is executed, no further output is produced. It should not be used in any case where you want to edit the front of the file and pass the remainder through unchanged. Using **q** in this case is a very dangerous beginner's mistake.

Another possible use of **quit** is to quit the script after you've extracted what you want from a file. For instance, in an application like **getmac** (presented in Chapter 4, *Writing sed Scripts*, there is some inefficiency in continuing to scan through a large file after sed has found what it is looking for.

So, for example, we could revise the sed script in the **getmac** shell script as follows:

```
sed -n "
/^\.de *$mac/,/^\.\./{
p
/^\.\./q
}" $file
```

The grouping of commands keeps the line:

```
/^\.\./q
```

from being executed until sed reaches the end of the macro we're looking for. (This line by itself would terminate the script at the conclusion of the first macro definition.) The sed program quits on the spot, and doesn't continue through the rest of the file looking for other possible matches.

Because the macro definition files are not that long, and the script itself not that complex, the actual time saved from this version of the script is negligible. However, with a very large file, or a complex, multiline script that needs to be applied to only a small part of the file, this version of the script could be a significant time-saver.

If you compare the following two shell scripts, you should find that the first one performs better than the second. The following simple shell program prints out the top 10 lines of a file and then quits:

```
for file
do
        sed 10q $file
done
```

The next example also prints the first 10 lines using the print command and suppressing default output:

```
for file
do
        sed -n 1,10p $file
done
```

If you haven't already done so, you should practice using the commands presented in this chapter before going on to the advanced commands in the next chapter.

# 6

# Advanced sed Commands

In this chapter, we cover the remaining sed commands. These commands require more determination to master and are more difficult to learn from the standard documentation than any of the basic commands. You can consider yourself a true sed-master once you understand the commands presented here.

The advanced commands fall into three groupings:

1.  Working with a multiline pattern space (**N,D,P**).

2.  Using the *hold space* to preserve the contents of the pattern space and make it available for subsequent commands (**H,h,G,g,x**).

3.  Writing scripts that use branching and conditional instructions to change the flow of control (**:,b,t**).

If the advanced scripts in this chapter have one thing in common, it is that they alter the sequential flow of execution or control. Normally, a line is read into the pattern space and each command in the script, one right after the other, is applied to that line. When the bottom of the script is reached, the line is output and the pattern space is cleared. Then a new line is read into the pattern space and control passes back to the top of the script. That is the normal flow of control in a sed script.

The scripts in this chapter interrupt or break the normal flow of control for various reasons. They might want to prevent commands in the script from executing except under certain circumstances, or to prevent the contents of the pattern space from being cleared out. Altering the flow of control makes a script much more difficult to read and understand. In fact, the scripts may be easier to write than they are to read. When you are writing a difficult script, you have the benefit of testing it to see how and why commands work.

We'd recommend that you test the scripts presented in this chapter and experiment by adding or removing commands to understand how the script is working. Seeing the results for yourself will help you understand the script much better than simply reading about it.

# Multiline Pattern Space

We have emphasized in previous discussions of regular expressions that pattern matching is line-oriented. A program like **grep** attempts to match a pattern on a single line of input. This makes it difficult to match a phrase, for instance, which can start at the end of one line and finish at the beginning of the next line. Other patterns might be significant only when repeated on multiple lines.

Sed has the ability to look at more than one line in the pattern space. This allows you to match patterns that extend over multiple lines. In this section, we will look at commands that create a multiline pattern space and manipulate its contents. The three multiline commands (**N,D,P**) all correspond to lowercase basic commands (**n,d,p**) that were presented in the previous chapter. The Delete (**D**) command, for instance, is a multiline version of the delete command (**d**). The difference is that while **d** deletes the contents of the pattern space, **D** deletes only the first line of a multiline pattern space.

## Append Next Line

The multiline Next (**N**) command creates a multiline pattern space by reading a new line of input and appending it to the contents of the pattern space. The original contents of pattern space and the new input line are separated by a newline. The embedded newline character can be matched in patterns by the escape sequence "\n". In a multiline pattern space, the metacharacter "^" matches the very first character of the pattern space, and not the character(s) following any embedded newline(s). Similarly, "$" matches only the final newline in the pattern space, and not any embedded newline(s). After the Next command is executed, control is then passed to subsequent commands in the script.

The Next command differs from the next command, which outputs the contents of the pattern space and then reads a new line of input. The next command does not create a multiline pattern space.

For our first example, let's suppose that we wanted to change "Owner and Operator Guide" to "Installation Guide" but we found that it appears in the file on two lines, splitting between "Operator" and "Guide."

For instance, here are a few lines of sample text:

```
Consult Section 3.1 in the Owner and Operator
Guide for a description of the tape drives
available on your system.
```

The following script looks for "Operator" at the end of a line, reads the next line of input and then makes the replacement.

```
/Operator$/{
N
s/Owner and Operator\nGuide/Installation Guide/
}
```

In this example, we know where the two lines split and where to specify the embedded newline. When the script is run on the sample file, it produces the two lines of output, one of which combines the first and second lines and is too long to show here. This happens because the substitute command matches the embedded newline but does not replace it. Unfortunately, you cannot use "\n" to insert a newline in the replacement string. You must use a backslash to escape the newline, as follows:

```
s/Owner and Operator\nGuide /Installation Guide\
/
```

This command restores the newline after "Installation Guide". It is also necessary to match a space following "Guide" so the new line won't begin with a space. Now we can show the output:

```
Consult Section 3.1 in the Installation Guide
for a description of the tape drives
available on your system.
```

Remember, you don't have to replace the newline but if you don't it can make for some long lines.

What if there are other occurrences of "Owner and Operator Guide" that break over multiple lines in different places? You could modify the regular expression to look for a space or a newline between words, as shown below:

```
/Owner/{
N
s/Owner *\n*and *\n*Operator *\n*Guide/Installation Guide/
}
```

The asterisk indicates that the space or newline is optional. This seems like hard work, though, and indeed there is a more general way. We have also changed the address to match "Owner," the first word in the pattern instead of the last. We can read the newline into the pattern space and then use a substitute command to remove the embedded newline, wherever it is.

```
s/Owner and Operator Guide/Installation Guide/
/Owner/{
N
s/ *\n/ /
s/Owner and Operator Guide */Installation Guide\
/
}
```

The first line matches "Owner and Operator Guide" when it appears on a line by itself. (See the discussion after the example about why this is necessary.) If we match the string "Owner," we read the next line into the pattern space, and replace the embedded newline with a space. Then we attempt to match the whole pattern and make the replacement followed by a newline. This script will match "Owner and Operator Guide" regardless of how it is broken across two lines. Here's our expanded test file:

```
Consult Section 3.1 in the Owner and Operator
Guide for a description of the tape drives
available on your system.

Look in the Owner and Operator Guide shipped with your system.

Two manuals are provided including the Owner and
Operator Guide and the User Guide.

The Owner and Operator Guide is shipped with your system.
```

Running the above script on the sample file produces the following result:

```
$ sed -f sedscr sample
Consult Section 3.1 in the Installation Guide
for a description of the tape drives
available on your system.

Look in the Installation Guide shipped with your system.

Two manuals are provided including the Installation Guide
and the User Guide.

The Installation Guide is shipped with your system.
```

In this sample script, it might seem redundant to have two substitute commands that match the pattern. The first one matches it when the pattern is found already on one line and the second matches the pattern after two lines have been read into the pattern space. Why the first command is necessary is perhaps best demonstrated by removing that command from the script and running it on the sample file:

```
$ sed -f sedscr2 sample
Consult Section 3.1 in the Installation Guide
for a description of the tape drives
available on your system.
```

```
Look in the Installation Guide
shipped with your system.
Two manuals are provided including the Installation Guide
and the User Guide.
```

Do you see the two problems? The most obvious problem is that the last line did not print. The last line matches "Owner" and when **N** is executed, there is not another input line to read, so sed quits (immediately, without even outputting the line). To fix this, the Next command should be used as follows to be safe:

```
$!N
```

It excludes the last line ($) from the Next command. As it is in our script, by matching "Owner and Operator Guide" on the last line, we avoid matching "Owner" and applying the **N** command. However, if the word "Owner" appeared on the last line we'd have the same problem unless we use the "$!N" syntax.

The second problem is a little less conspicuous. It has to do with the occurrence of "Owner and Operator Guide" in the second paragraph. In the input file, it is found on a line by itself:

```
Look in the Owner and Operator Guide shipped with your system.
```

In the output shown above, the blank line following "shipped with your system." is missing. The reason for this is that this line matches "Owner" and the next line, a blank line, is appended to the pattern space. The substitute command removes the embedded newline and the blank line has in effect vanished. (If the line were not blank, the newline would still be removed but the text would appear on the same line with "shipped with your system.") The best solution seems to be to avoid reading the next line when the pattern can be matched on one line. So, that is why the first instruction attempts to match the case where the string appears all on one line.

### Converting an Interleaf file

FrameMaker and Interleaf make WYSIWYG technical publishing packages. Both of them have the ability to read and save the contents of a document in an ASCII-coded format as opposed to their normal binary file format. In this example, we convert an Interleaf file into **troff**; however, the same kind of script could be applied to convert a **troff**-coded file to Interleaf format. The same is true of FrameMaker. Both place coding tags in the file, surrounded by angle brackets.

In this example, our conversion demonstrates the effect of the change command on a multiline pattern space. In the Interleaf file, "<para>" marks a paragraph. Before and after the tag are blank lines. Look at the sample file:

```
<para>

This is a test paragraph in Interleaf style ASCII.  Another line
in a paragraph.  Yet another.

<Figure Begin>

v.11111111111111111111111000000000000000000001111111111111000000
10000100010010001000100001000000000000000000000000000000000000000
000000

<Figure End>

<para>

More lines of text to be found after the figure.
These lines should print.
```

This file also contains a bitmap figure, printed as a series of 1s and 0s. To convert this file to **troff** macros, we must replace the "<para>" code with a macro (.LP). However, there's a bit more to do because we need to remove the blank line that follows the code. There are several ways to do it, but we will use the Next command to create a multiline pattern space, consisting of "<para>" and the blank line, and then use the change command to replace what's in the pattern space with a paragraph macro. Here's the part of the script that does it:

```
/<para>/{
        N
        c\
.LP
}
```

The address matches lines with the paragraph tag. The Next command appends the next line, which should be blank, to the pattern space. We use the Next command (**N**) instead of next (**n**) because we don't want to output the contents of the pattern space. The change command overwrites the previous contents ("<para>" followed by a newline) of the pattern space, even when it contains multiple lines.

In this conversion script, we'd like to extract the bitmapped figure data and write it to a separate file. In its place, we insert figure macros that mark the figure in the file.

```
/<Figure Begin>/,/<Figure End>/{
        w fig.interleaf
        /<Figure End>/i\
.FG\
<insert figure here>\
.FE
        d
}
```

This procedure matches the lines between "<Figure Begin>" and "<Figure End>" and writes them to the file named *fig.interleaf*. Each time this instruction is matched, the delete command will be executed, deleting the lines that have been written to file. When "<Figure End>" is matched, a pair of macros are inserted in place of the figure in the output. Notice that the subsequent delete command does not affect the text output by the insert command. It does, however, delete "<Figure End>" from the pattern space.

Here's the entire script:

```
/<para>/{
        N
        c\
.LP
}
/<Figure Begin>/,/<Figure End>/{
        w fig.interleaf
        /<Figure End>/i\
.FG\
<insert figure here>\
.FE
        d
}
/^$/d
```

The third instruction simply removes unnecessary blank lines. (Note that this instruction could be depended upon to delete the blank line following the "<para>" tag; but you don't always want to remove all blank lines, and we wanted to demonstrate the change command across a multiline pattern space.)

The result of running this script on the test file produces:

```
$ sed -f sed.interleaf test.interleaf
.LP
This is a test paragraph in Interleaf style ASCII.  Another line
in a paragraph.  Yet another.
.FG
<insert figure here>
.FE
.LP
More lines of text to be found after the figure.
These lines should print.
```

## Multiline Delete

The delete command (d) deletes the contents of the pattern space and causes a new line of input to be read with editing resuming at the top of the script. The Delete command (D) works slightly differently: it deletes a portion of the pattern space, up to the first embedded newline. It does not cause a new line of input to be read; instead, it returns to the top of the script, applying these instructions to what remains in the pattern space. We can see the difference by writing a script that looks for a series of blank lines and outputs a single blank line. The version below uses the delete command:

```
# reduce multiple blank lines to one; version using d command
/^$/{
        N
        /^\n$/d
}
```

When a blank line is encountered, the next line is appended to the pattern space. Then we try to match the embedded newline. Note that the positional metacharacters, ˆ and $, match the beginning and the end of the pattern space, respectively. Here's a test file:

```
This line is followed by 1 blank line.

This line is followed by 2 blank lines.


This line is followed by 3 blank lines.



This line is followed by 4 blank lines.




This is the end.
```

Running the script on the test file produces the following result:

```
$ sed -f sed.blank test.blank
This line is followed by 1 blank line.

This line is followed by 2 blank lines.
This line is followed by 3 blank lines.

This line is followed by 4 blank lines.
This is the end.
```

Where there was an even number of blank lines, all the blank lines were removed. Only when there was an odd number was a single blank line preserved. That is because the delete command clears the entire pattern space. Once the first blank line is encountered, the next line is read in, and both are deleted. If a third blank line is encountered, and the next line is not blank, the delete command is not applied, and thus a blank line is output. If we use the multiline Delete command (**D** rather than **d**), we get the result we want:

```
$ sed -f sed2.blank test.blank
This line is followed by 1 blank line.

This line is followed by 2 blank lines.

This line is followed by 3 blank lines.

This line is followed by 4 blank lines.

This is the end.
```

The reason the multiline Delete command gets the job done is that when we encounter two blank lines, the Delete command removes only the first of the two. The next time through the script, the blank line will cause another line to be read into the pattern space. If that line is not blank, then both lines are output, thus ensuring that a single blank line will be output. In other words, when there are two blank lines in the pattern space, only the first one is deleted. When there is a blank line followed by text, the pattern space is output normally.

## *Multiline Print*

The multiline Print command differs slightly from its lowercase cousin. This command outputs the first portion of a multiline pattern space, up to the first embedded newline. After the last command in a script is executed, the contents of the pattern space are automatically output. (The *-n* option or **#n** suppresses this default action.) Therefore, print commands (**P** or **p**) are used when the default output is suppressed or when flow of control in a script changes such that the bottom of the script is not reached. The Print command frequently appears after the Next command and before the Delete command. These three commands can set up an input/output loop that maintains a two-line pattern space yet outputs only one line at a time. The purpose of this loop is to output only the first line in the pattern space, then return to the top of the script to apply all commands to what had been the second line in the pattern space. Without this loop, when the last command in the script was executed, both lines in the pattern space would be output. The flow through a script that sets up an input/output loop using the Next, Print, and Delete commands is illustrated in Figure 6-1. A multiline pattern space is created to match "UNIX" at the end of the first line and "System" at the beginning of the second line. If "UNIX System" is found across two lines, we change it to "UNIX Operating System". The loop is set up to return to the top of the script and look for "UNIX" at the end of the second line.

The Next command appends a new input line to the current line in the pattern space. After the substitute command is applied to the multiline pattern space, the

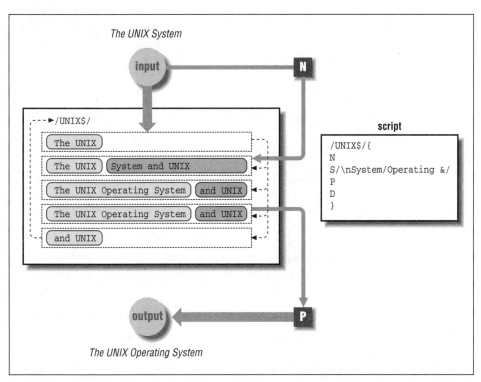

*Figure 6-1: The Next, Print, and Delete commands used to set up an input/output loop*

first part of the pattern space is output by the Print command and then removed by the Delete command. That means the current line is output and the new line becomes the current line. The Delete command prevents the script from reaching bottom, which would output both lines and clear the contents of the pattern space. The Delete command lets us preserve the second portion of the pattern space and pass control to the top of the script where all the editing commands can now be applied to that line. One of those commands is the Next command which reads another new line into the pattern space.

The following script implements the same loop:

```
/UNIX$/{
        N
        /\nSystem/{
        s// Operating &/
        P
        D
        }
   }
```

The substitute command matches "\nSystem" and replaces it with "Operating \nSystem." It is important that the newline be maintained, or else there will be only a single line in the pattern space. Note the order of the Print and Delete commands. Here's our test file:

```
Here are examples of the UNIX
System.  Where UNIX
System appears, it should be the UNIX
Operating System.
```

Running the script on the test file produces:

```
$ sed -f sed.Print test.Print
Here are examples of the UNIX Operating
System.  Where UNIX Operating
System appears, it should be the UNIX
Operating System.
```

The input/output loop lets us match the occurrence of UNIX at the end of the second line. It would be missed if the two-line pattern space was output normally.

If the relationship between the **P** and **D** commands remains unclear to you, we'll have another go at it in the next example. You can also experiment by removing either command from the above script, or try using their lowercase cousins.

## A Case for Study

Lenny, on our staff, was having difficulty converting a document coded for Scribe to our **troff** macro package, because of font changes. The problems he encountered are quite interesting, apart from the task he was trying to do.

The Scribe convention for putting text in a bold font is:

```
@f1(put this in bold)
```

This font change command can appear in-line and may begin on one line and end on a subsequent line. It can also appear more than once on a line. Here's a sample file that shows several different occurrences:

```
$ cat test
I want to see @f1(what will happen) if we put the
font change commands @f1(on a set of lines).  If I understand
things (correctly), the @f1(third) line causes problems. (No?).
Is this really the case, or is it (maybe) just something else?

Let's test having two on a line @f1(here) and @f1(there) as
well as one that begins on one line and ends @f1(somewhere
on another line).  What if @f1(it is here) on the line?
Another @f1(one).
```

The sample file shows the different contexts in which the font-change commands appear. The script must match "@f1(anything)" when it occurs on a single line or multiple times on the same line or when it extends across more than one line.

The easiest way to make a single match is:

```
s/@f1(\(.*\))/\\fB\1\\fR/g
```

The regular expression matches "@f1(.*)" and saves anything inside parentheses using \( and \). In the replacement section, the saved portion of the match is recalled as "\1".

Putting this command in a sed script, we will run it on our sample file.

```
$ sed -f sed.len test
I want to see \fBwhat will happen\fR if we put the
font change commands \fBon a set of lines\fR.  If I understand
things (correctly), the \fBthird) line causes problems. (No?\fR.
Is this really the case, or is it (maybe) just something else?

Let's test having two on a line \fBhere) and @f1(there\fR as
well as one that begins on one line and ends @f1(somewhere
on another line).  What if \fBit is here\fR on the line?
Another \fBone\fR.
```

The substitute command works properly in the first two lines. It fails on the third line. It also fails in the first line of the second paragraph where there are multiple occurrences on the same line.

Because a regular expression always makes the longest match possible, ".*" matches all the characters from "@f1(" to the *last* closing parenthesis on the line. In other words, the span indicated by ".*" ends with the last close parenthesis it finds, not the first.

We can fix this problem by modifying the regular expression ".*" to zero or more occurrences of any character except ")".

```
[^)]*
```

In a character class, the caret (^) reverses the sense of the operation so it matches all characters except those specified in the brackets. Here's how the revised command looks:

```
s/@f1(\(([^)]*\))/\\fB\1\\fR/g
```

Now we have a command that handles one or more occurrences on a single line.

```
I want to see \fBwhat will happen\fR if we put the
font change commands \fBon a set of lines\fR.  If I understand
things (correctly), the \fBthird\fR line causes problems. (No?).
Is this really the case, or is it (maybe) just something else?
```

```
Let's test having two on a line \fBhere\fR and \fBthere\fR as
well as one that begins on one line and ends @f1(somewhere
on another line).  What if \fBit is here\fR on the line?
Another \fBone\fR.
```

This command gets all instances except the one in the second paragraph that extends over two lines. Before solving this problem, it is interesting to look at Lenny's first solution to it and why it fails. Here's Lenny's first script:

```
/@f1(/,/)/{ ·
        s/@f1(/\\fB/g
        s/)/\\fR/g
}
```

He tried to attack the problem of matching an occurrence over multiple lines by specifying a range of lines. Here's the result of running the script on the test file:

```
$ sed -f sed.len test.len
I want to see \fBwhat will happen\fR if we put the
font change commands \fBon a set of lines\fR.  If I understand
things (correctly, the \fBthird) line causes problems. (No?\fR.
Is this really the case, or is it (maybe) just something else?

Let's test having two on a line \fBhere) and (there\fR as
well as one that begins on one line and ends \fBsomewhere
on another line\fR.  What if \fBit is here\fR on the line?
Another \fBone\fR.
```

Matching lines containing ")" makes unwanted matches on lines containing only parentheses. The solution to matching the pattern over more than one line is to create a multiline pattern space. If we match "@f1(" and no closing parenthesis is found, we need to read (**N**) another line into the buffer and try to make the same kind of match as the first case (the \n represents the newline).

```
s/@f1(\(([^)]*\))/\\fB\1\\fR/g
/@f1(.*/{
        N
        s/@f1(\(.*\n[^)]*\))/\\fB\1\\fR/g
}
```

We can test it out:

```
$ sed -f sednew test
I want to see \fBwhat will happen\fR if we put the
font change commands \fBon a set of lines\fR.  If I understand
things (correctly), the \fBthird\fR line causes problems. (No?).
Is this really the case, or is it (maybe) just something else?

Let's test having two on a line \fBhere\fR and \fBthere\fR as
well as one that begins on one line and ends \fBsomewhere
on another line\fR.  What if @f1(it is here) on the line?
Another \fBone\fR.
```

As you can see, we have caught all but the next to last font change. The **N** command reads a second line into the pattern space. The script matches the pattern across two lines and then outputs *both* lines from the pattern space. What about the second line? It needs a chance to have all the commands in the script applied to it from top to bottom. Now, perhaps you understand why we need to set up a multiline input/output loop like the one discussed in the previous section. We add the multiline Print and multiline Delete to the script.

```
# Scribe font change script.
s/@f1(\([^)]*\))/\\fB\1\\fR/g
/@f1(.*/{
        N
        s/@f1(\(.*\n[^)]*\))/\\fB\1\\fR/g
        P
        D
}
```

This can be translated as: Once making a substitution across two lines, print the first line and then delete it from the pattern space. With the second portion remaining in the pattern space, control passes to the top of the script where we see if there is an "@f1(" remaining on the line.

The revised script matches all occurrences in the sample file. However, it's not perfect, so we'll hear from Lenny again.

# Hold That Line

The pattern space is a buffer that contains the current input line. There is also a set-aside buffer called the *hold space*. The contents of the pattern space can be copied to the hold space and the contents of the hold space can be copied to the pattern space. A group of commands allows you to move data between the hold space and the pattern space. The hold space is used for temporary storage, and that's it. Individual commands can't address the hold space or alter its contents.

The most frequent use of the hold space is to have it retain a duplicate of the current input line while you change the original in the pattern space. The commands that affect the pattern space are:

| Command | Abbreviation | Function |
|---------|--------------|----------|
| Hold | h or H | Copy or append contents of pattern space to hold space. |
| Get | g or G | Copy or append contents of hold space to pattern space. |
| Exchange | x | Swap contents of hold space and pattern space. |

Each of these commands can take an address that specifies a single line or a range of lines. The hold (**h,H**) commands move data into the hold space and the get (**g,G**) commands move data from the hold space back into the pattern space. The difference between the lowercase and uppercase versions of the same command is that the lowercase command overwrites the contents of the target buffer, while the uppercase command appends to the buffer's existing contents.

The hold command replaces the contents of the hold space with the contents of the pattern space. The get command replaces the contents of the pattern space with the contents of the hold space.

The Hold command puts a newline followed by the contents of the pattern space after the contents of the hold space. (The newline is appended to the hold space even if the hold space is empty.) The Get command puts a newline followed by the contents of the hold space after the contents of the pattern space.

The exchange command swaps the contents of the two buffers. It has no side effects on either buffer.

Let's use a trivial example to illustrate putting lines into the hold space and retrieving them later. We are going to write a script that reverses pairs of lines. For a sample file, we'll use a list of numbers:

```
1
2
11
22
111
222
```

The object is to reverse the order of the lines beginning with 1 and the lines beginning with 2. Here's how we use the hold space: we copy the first line to the hold space—and hold on to it—while we clear the pattern space. Then sed reads the second line into the pattern space and we append the line from the hold space to the end of the pattern space. Look at the script:

```
# Reverse flip
/1/{
h
d
}
/2/{
G
}
```

Any line matching a "1" is copied to the hold space and deleted from the pattern space. Control passes to the top of the script and the line is not printed. When the next line is read, it matches the pattern "2" and the line that had been copied to the hold space is now appended to the pattern space. Then both lines are printed. In other words, we save the first line of the pair and don't output it until we match the second line.

Here's the result of running the script on the sample file:

```
$ sed -f sed.flip test.flip
2
1
22
11
222
111
```

The hold command followed by the delete command is a fairly common pairing. Without the delete command, control would reach the bottom of the script and the contents of the pattern space would be output. If the script used the next (**n**) command instead of the delete command, the contents of the pattern space would also be output. You can experiment with this script by removing the delete command altogether or by putting a next command in its place. You could also see what happens if you use **g** instead of **G**.

Note that the logic of this script is poor, though the script is useful for demonstration purposes. If a line matches the first instruction and the next line fails to match the second instruction, the first line will not be output. This is a hole down which lines disappear.

## A Capital Transformation

In the previous chapter, we introduced the transform command (**y**) and described how it can exchange lowercase letters for uppercase letters on a line. Since this command acts on the entire contents of the pattern space, it is something of a chore to do a letter-by-letter transformation of a portion of the line. But it is possible, though convoluted, as the following example will demonstrate.

While working on a programming guide, we found that the names of statements were entered inconsistently. They needed to be uppercase, but some were lowercase while others had an initial capital letter. While the task was simple—to capitalize the name of the statement—there were nearly 100 statements and it seemed a tedious project to write that many explicit substitutions of the form:

```
s/find the Match statement/find the MATCH statement/g
```

The transform command could do the lowercase-to-uppercase conversion but it applies the conversion to the entire line. The hold space makes this task possible because we use it to store a copy of the input line while we isolate and convert the statement name in the pattern space. Look at the script first:

```
# capitalize statement names
/the .* statement/{
h
s/.*the \(.*\) statement.*/\1/
```

```
y/abcdefghijklmnopqrstuvwxyz/ABCDEFGHIJKLMNOPQRSTUVWXYZ/
G
s/\(.*\)\n\(.*the \).*\( statement.*\)/\2\1\3/
}
```

The address limits the procedure to lines that match "the .* statement". Let's look at what each command does:

h    The hold command copies the current input line into the hold space. Using the sample line "find the Match statement," we'll show the contents of the pattern space and of the hold space. After the **h** command, both the pattern space and the hold space are identical.

> *Pattern Space:*     find the Match statement
> *Hold Space:*       find the Match statement

```
s/.*the \(.*\) statement.*/\1/
```
The substitute command extracts the name of the statement from the line and replaces the entire line with it.

> *Pattern Space:*     Match
> *Hold Space:*       find the Match statement

```
y/abcdefghijklmnopqrstuvwxyz/ABCDEFGHIJKLMNOPQRSTUVWXYZ/
```
The transform command changes each lowercase letter to an uppercase letter.

> *Pattern Space:*     MATCH
> *Hold Space:*       find the Match statement

G    The Get command appends the line saved in the hold space to the pattern space.

> *Pattern Space:*     MATCH\nfind the Match statement
> *Hold Space:*       find the Match statement

```
s/\(.*\)\n\(.*the \).*\( statement.*\)/\2\1\3/
```
The substitute command matches three different parts of the pattern space: 1) all characters up to the embedded newline, 2) all characters following the embedded newline and up to and including "the" followed by a space, and 3) all characters beginning with a space and followed by "statement" up to the end of the pattern space. The name of the statement as it appeared in the original line is matched but not saved. The replacement section of this command recalls the saved portions and reassembles them in a different order, putting the capitalized name of the command in between "the" and "statement."

```
Pattern Space:    find the MATCH statement
Hold Space:       find the Match statement
```

Let's look at a test run. Here's our sample file:

```
find the Match statement
Consult the Get statement.
using the Read statement to retrieve data
```

Running the script on the sample file produces:

```
find the MATCH statement
Consult the GET statement.
using the READ statement to retrieve data
```

As you can see from this script, skillful use of the hold space can aid in isolating and manipulating portions of the input line.

## *Correcting Index Entries (Part II)*

In the previous chapter, we looked at a shell script named **index.edit**. This script extracts index entries from one or more files and automatically generates a sed script consisting of a substitute command for each index entry. We mentioned that a small failing of the script was that it did not look out for regular expression metacharacters that appeared as literals in an index entry, such as the following:

```
.XX "asterisk (*) metacharacter"
```

After processing this entry, the original **index.edit** generated the following substitute command:

```
/^\.XX /s/asterisk (*) metacharacter/asterisk (*) metacharacter/
```

While it "knows" to escape the period before ".XX", it doesn't protect the metacharacter "*". The problem is that the pattern "(*)" does not match "(*)" and the substitute command would fail to be applied. The solution is to modify **index.edit** so it looks for metacharacters and escapes them. There's one more twist: a different set of metacharacters is recognized in the replacement string.

We have to maintain two copies of the index entry. The first copy we edit to escape regular expression metacharacters and then use for the pattern. The second copy we edit to escape the metacharacters special to the replacement string. The hold space keeps the second copy while we edit the first copy, then we swap the two and edit the second copy. Here's the script:

```
#! /bin/sh
# index.edit -- compile list of index entries for editing
#               new version that matches metacharacters
grep "^\.XX" $* | sort -u |
```

```
sed '
h
s/[][\\*.]/\\&/g
x
s/[\\&]/\\&/g
s/^\.XX //
s/$/\//
x
s/^\\\.XX \(.*\)$/\/^\\.XX \/s\/\1\//
G
s/\n//'
```

The hold command puts a copy of the current index entry into the hold space.
Then the substitute command looks for any of the following metacharacters: "]",
"[", "\", "*" or ".". This regular expression is rather interesting: 1) if the close
bracket is the first character in a character class, it is interpreted literally, not as the
closing delimiter of the class; and 2) of the metacharacters specified, only the
backslash has a special meaning in a character class and must be escaped. Also,
there is no need to escape the metacharacters "^" and "$" because they only have
special meaning if in the first or last positions in a regular expression, respectively,
which is impossible given the structure of the index entry. After escaping the
metacharacters, the exchange command swaps the contents of the pattern space
and the hold space.

Starting with a new copy of the line, the substitute command adds a backslash to
escape either a backslash or an ampersand for the replacement string. Then
another substitute command removes the ".XX" from the line and the one after
that appends a slash (/) to the end of the line, preparing a replacement string that
looks like:

```
"asterisk (*) metacharacter"/
```

Once again, the exchange command swaps the pattern space and the hold space.
With the first copy in the pattern space, we need to prepare the pattern address
and the substitute pattern. The substitute command saves the index entry, and
replaces the line with the first part of the syntax for the substitute command:

```
\/^\\.XX \/s\/\1\//
```

Using the sample entry, the pattern space would have the following contents:

```
/^\.XX /s/"asterisk (\*) metacharacter"/
```

Then the Get command takes the replacement string in the hold space and
appends it to the pattern space. Because Get also inserts a newline, the substitute
command is necessary to remove it. The following line is output at the end:

```
/^\.XX /s/"asterisk (\*) metacharacter"/"asterisk (*) metacharacter"/
```

## Building Blocks of Text

The hold space can be used to collect a block of lines before outputting them. Some **troff** requests and macros are block-oriented, in that commands must surround a block of text. Usually a code at the beginning enables the format and one at the end disables the format. HTML-coded documents also contain many block-oriented constructs. For instance, "<p>" begins a paragraph and "</p>" ends it. In the next example, we'll look at placing HTML-style paragraph tags in a plain text file. For this example, the input is a file containing variable-length lines that form paragraphs; each paragraph is separated from the next one by a blank line. Therefore, the script must collect all lines in the hold space until a blank line is encountered. The contents of the hold space are retrieved and surrounded with the paragraph tags.

Here's the script:

```
/^$/!{
    H
    d
    }
/^$/{
    x
    s/^\n/<p>/
    s/$/<\/p>/
    G
    }
```

Running the script on a sample file produces:

```
<p>My wife won't let me buy a power saw.  She is afraid of an
accident if I use one.
So I rely on a hand saw for a variety of weekend projects like
building shelves.
However, if I made my living as a carpenter, I would
have to use a power
saw.  The speed and efficiency provided by power tools
would be essential to being productive.</p>

<p>For people who create and modify text files,
sed and awk are power tools for editing.</p>

<p>Most of the things that you can do with these programs
can be done interactively with a text editor.  However,
using these programs can save many hours of repetitive
work in achieving the same result.</p>
```

The script has basically two parts, corresponding to each address. Either we do one thing if the input line is *not* blank or a different thing if it is. If the input line is not blank, it is appended to the hold space (with **H**), and then deleted from the pattern space. The delete command prevents the line from being output and clears the pattern space. Control passes back to the top of the script and a new line is read. The general idea is that we don't output any line of text; it is collected in the hold space.

If the input line is blank, we process the contents of the hold space. To illustrate what the second procedure does, let's use the second paragraph in the previous sample file and show what happens. After a blank line has been read, the pattern space and the hold space have the following contents:

```
Pattern Space:      ^$
Hold Space:         \nFor people who create and
                    modify text files, \nsed and
                    awk are power tools for
                    editing.
```

A blank line in the pattern space is represented as "^$", the regular expression that matches it. The embedded newlines are represented in the hold space by "\n". Note that the Hold command puts a newline in the hold space and then appends the current line to the hold space. Even when the hold space is empty, the Hold command places a newline before the contents of the pattern space.

The exchange command (**x**) swaps the contents of the hold space and the pattern space. The blank line is saved in the hold space so we can retrieve it at the end of the procedure. (We could insert a newline in other ways, also.)

```
Pattern Space:      \nFor people who create and
                    modify text files, \nsed and
                    awk are power tools for
                    editing.
Hold Space:         ^$
```

Now we make two substitutions: placing "<p>" at the beginning of the pattern space and "</p>" at the end. The first substitute command matches "^\n" because a newline is at the beginning of the line as a consequence of the Hold command. The second substitute command matches the end of the pattern space ("$" does not match any embedded newlines but only the terminal newline.)

```
Pattern Space:      <p>For people who create and
                    modify text files, \nsed and
                    awk are power tools for
                    editing.</p>
Hold Space:         ^$
```

Note that the embedded newline is preserved in the pattern space. The last command, **G**, appends the blank line in the hold space to the pattern space. Upon reaching the bottom of the script, sed outputs the paragraph we had collected in the hold space and coded in the pattern space.

This script illustrates the mechanics of collecting input and holding on to it until another pattern is matched. It's important to pay attention to flow control in the script. The first procedure in the script does not reach bottom because we don't want any output *yet*. The second procedure does reach bottom, clearing the pattern space and the hold space before we begin collecting lines for the next paragraph.

This script also illustrates how to use addressing to set up exclusive addresses, in which a line must match one or the other address. You can also set up addresses to handle various exceptions in the input and thereby improve the reliability of a script. For instance, in the previous script, what happens if the last line in the input file is *not* blank? All the lines collected since the last blank line will not be output. There are several ways to handle this, but a rather clever one is to manufacture a blank line that the blank-line procedure will match later in the script. In other words, if the last line contains a line of text, we will copy the text to the hold space and clear the contents of the pattern space with the substitute command. We make the current line blank so that it matches the procedure that outputs what has been collected in the hold space. Here's the procedure:

```
${
/^$/!{
    H
    s/.*//
    }
}
```

This procedure must be placed in the script *before* the two procedures shown earlier. The addressing symbol "$" matches only the last line in the file. Inside this procedure, we test for lines that are not blank. If the line is blank, we don't have to do anything with it. If the current line is not blank, then we append it to the hold space. This is what we do in the other procedure that matches a non-blank line. Then we use the substitute command to create a blank line in the pattern space.

Upon exiting this procedure, there is a blank line in the pattern space. It matches the subsequent procedure for blank lines that adds the HTML paragraph codes and outputs the paragraph.

## *Advanced Flow Control Commands*

You have already seen several examples of changes in sed's normal flow control. In this section, we'll look at two commands that allow you to direct which portions of the script get executed and when. The branch (**b**) and test (**t**) commands transfer control in a script to a line containing a specified label. If no label is specified, control passes to the end of the script. The branch command transfers control unconditionally while the test command is a conditional transfer, occurring only if a substitute command has changed the current line.

A label is any sequence of up to seven characters.[*] A label is put on a line by itself that begins with a colon:

```
:mylabel
```

There are no spaces permitted between the colon and the label. Spaces at the end of the line will be considered part of the label. When you specify the label in a branch or test command, a space is permitted between the command and the label itself:

```
b mylabel
```

Be sure you don't put a space after the label.

## Branching

The branch command allows you to transfer control to another line in the script.

```
[address]b[label]
```

The *label* is optional, and if not supplied, control is transferred to the end of the script. If a label is supplied, execution resumes at the line following the label.

In Chapter 4, *Writing sed Scripts*, we looked at a typesetting script that transformed quotation marks and hyphens into their typesetting counterparts. If we wanted to avoid making these changes on certain lines, then we could use the branch command to skip that portion of the script. For instance, text inside computer-generated examples marked by the .ES and .EE macros should not be changed. Thus, we could write the previous script like this:

```
/^\.ES/,/^\.EE/b
s/^"/'`/
s/"$/''/
s/"?□/''?□/g
    :
    :
s/\\(em\\^"/\\(em'`/g
s/"\\(em/''\\(em/g
s/\\(em"/\\(em'`/g
s/@DQ@/"/g
```

---

[*] The POSIX standard says that an implementation can allow longer labels if it wishes to. GNU sed allows labels to be of any length.

Because no label is supplied, the branch command branches to the end of the script, skipping all subsequent commands.

The branch command can be used to execute a set of commands as a procedure, one that can be called repeatedly from the main body of the script. As in the case above, it also allows you to avoid executing the procedure at all based on matching a pattern in the input.

You can have a similar effect by using ! and grouping a set of commands. The advantage of the branch command over ! for our application is that we can more easily specify multiple conditions to avoid. The ! symbol can apply to a single command, or it can apply to a set of commands enclosed in braces that immediately follows. The branch command, on the other hand, gives you almost unlimited control over movement around the script.

For example, if we are using multiple macro packages, there may be other macro pairs besides .ES and .EE that define a range of lines that we want to avoid altogether. So, for example, we can write:

```
/^\.ES/,/^\.EE/b
/^\.PS/,/^\.PE/b
/^\.G1/,/^\.G2/b
```

To get a good idea of the types of flow control possible in a sed script, let's look at some simple but abstract examples. The first example shows you how to use the branch command to create a loop. Once an input line is read, command1 and command2 will be applied to the line; afterwards, if the contents of the pattern space match the pattern, then control will be passed to the line following the label "top," which means command1 then command2 will be executed again.

```
:top
command1
command2
/pattern/b top
command3
```

The script executes command3 only if the pattern doesn't match. All three commands will be executed, although the first two may be executed multiple times.

In the next example, command1 is executed. If the pattern is matched, control passes to the line following the label "end." This means command2 is skipped.

```
command1
/pattern/b end
command2
:end
command3
```

In all cases, command1 and command3 are executed.

Now let's look at how to specify that either command2 or command3 are executed, but not both. In the next script, there are two branch commands.

```
command1
/pattern/b dothree
command2
b
:dothree
command3
```

The first branch command transfers control to command3. If that pattern is not matched, then command2 is executed. The branch command following command2 sends control to the end of the script, bypassing command3. The first of the branch commands is conditional upon matching the pattern; the second is not. We will look at a "real-world" example after looking at the test command.

## *The Test Command*

The test command branches to a label (or the end of the script) if a successful substitution has been made on the currently addressed line. Thus, it implies a conditional branch. Its syntax follows:

[*address*]t[*label*]

If no *label* is supplied, control falls through to the end of the script. If the label is supplied, then execution resumes at the line following the label.

Let's look at an example from Tim O'Reilly. He was trying to generate automatic index entries based on evaluating the arguments in a macro that produced the top of a command reference page. If there were three quoted arguments, he wanted to do something different than if there were two or only one. The task was to try to match each of these cases in succession (3,2,1) and when a successful substitution was made, avoid making any further matches. Here's Tim's script:

```
/\.Rh 0/{
s/"\(.*\)" "\(.*\)" "\(.*\)"/"\1" "\2" "\3"/
t
s/"\(.*\)" "\(.*\)"/"\1" "\2"/
t
s/"\(.*\)"/"\1"/
}
```

The test command allows us to drop to the end of the script once a substitution has been made. If there are three arguments on the .Rh line, the test command after the first substitute command will be true, and sed will go on to the next input line. If there are fewer than three arguments, no substitution will be made, the test command will be evaluated false, and the next substitute command will be tried. This will be repeated until all the possibilities are used up.

The test command provides functionality similar to a case statement in the C programming language or the shell programming languages. You can test each case and when a case proves true, then you exit the construct.

If the above script were part of a larger script, we could use a label, perhaps tellingly named "break," to drop to the end of the command grouping where additional commands can be applied.

```
/\.Rh 0/{
s/"\(.*\)" "\(.*\)" "\(.*\)"/"\1" "\2" "\3"/
t break
:
:
}
:break
more commands
```

The next section gives a full example of the test command and the use of labels.

## One More Case

Remember Lenny? He was the fellow given the task of converting Scribe documents to **troff**. We had sent him the following script:

```
# Scribe font change script.
s/@f1(\([^)]*\))/\\fB\1\\fR/g
/@f1(.*/{
N
s/@f1(\(.*\n[^)]*\))/\\fB\1\\fR/g
P
D
}
```

He sent the following mail after using the script:

Thank you so much!  You've not only fixed the script but shown me
where I was confused about the way it works.  I can repair the
conversion script so that it works with what you've done, but to be
optimal it should do two more things that I can't seem to get working
at all—maybe it's hopeless and I should be content with what's
there.

First, I'd like to reduce multiple blank lines down to one.
Second, I'd like to make sed match the pattern over more than two
(say, even only three) lines.

Thanks again.

Lenny

The first request to reduce a series of blank lines to one has already been shown in this chapter. The following four lines perform this function:

```
/^$/{
N
/^\n$/D
}
```

We want to look mainly at accomplishing the second request. Our previous font-change script created a two-line pattern space, tried to make the match across those lines, and then output the first line. The second line became the first line in the pattern space and control passed to the top of the script where another line was read in.

We can use labels to set up a loop that reads multiple lines and makes it possible to match a pattern across multiple lines. The following script sets up two labels: **begin** at the top of the script and **again** near the bottom. Look at the improved script:

```
# Scribe font change script.  New and Improved.
:begin
/@f1(\([^)]*\))/{
s//\\fB\1\\fR/g
b begin
}
/@f1(.*/{
N
s/@f1(\([^)]*\n[^)]*\))/\\fB\1\\fR/g
t again
b begin
}
:again
P
D
```

Let's look more closely at this script, which has three parts. Beginning with the line that follows :**begin**, the first part attempts to match the font change syntax if it is found completely on one line. After making the substitution, the branch command transfers control back to the label **begin**. In other words, once we have made a match, we want to go back to the top and look for other possible matches, including the instruction that has already been applied—there could be multiple occurrences on the line.

The second part attempts to match the pattern over multiple lines. The Next command builds a multiple line pattern space. The substitution command attempts to locate the pattern with an embedded newline. If it succeeds, the test command passes control to the line following the **again** label. If no substitution is made, control is passed to the line following the label **begin** so that we can read in another line. This is a loop that goes into effect when we've matched the beginning sequence of a font change request but have not yet found the ending sequence. Sed will loop back and keep appending lines into the pattern space until a match has been found.

The third part is the procedure following the label **again**. The first line in the pattern space is output and then deleted. Like the previous version of this script, we deal with multiple lines in succession. Control never reaches the bottom of the script but is redirected by the Delete command to the top of the script.

## *To Join a Phrase*

We have covered all the advanced constructs of sed and are now ready to look at a shell script named **phrase** that uses nearly all of them. This script is a general-purpose, **grep**-like program that allows you to look for a series of multiple words that might appear across two lines.

An essential element of this program is that, like **grep**, it prints out only the lines that match the pattern. You might think we'd use the *-n* option to suppress the default output of lines. However, what is unusual about this sed script is that it creates an input/output loop, controlling when a line is output or not.

The logic of this script is to first look for the pattern on one line and print the line if it matches. If no match is found, we read another line into the pattern space (as in previous multiline scripts). Then we copy the two-line pattern space to the hold space for safekeeping. Now the new line that was read into the pattern space previously could match the search pattern on its own, so the next match we attempt is on the second line only. Once we've determined that the pattern is not found on either the first or second lines, we remove the newline between the two lines and look for it spanning those lines.

The script is designed to accept arguments from the command line. The first argument is the search pattern. All other command-line arguments will be interpreted as filenames. Let's look at the entire script before analyzing it:

```
#! /bin/sh
# phrase -- search for words across lines
# $1 = search string; remaining args = filenames
search=$1
shift
for file
do
sed '
/'"$search"'/b
N
h
```

```
s/.*\n//
/'"$search"'/b
g
s/ *\n/ /
/'"$search"'/{
g
b
}
g
D' $file
done
```

A shell variable named **search** is assigned the first argument on the command line, which should be the search pattern. This script shows another method of passing a shell variable into a script. Here we surround the variable reference with a pair of double quotes and then single quotes. Notice the script itself is enclosed in single quotes, which protect characters that are normally special to the shell from being interpreted. The sequence of a double-quote pair inside a single-quote pair[*] makes sure the enclosed argument is evaluated first by the shell before the sed script is evaluated by sed.[†]

The sed script tries to match the search string at three different points, each marked by the address that looks for the search pattern. The first line of the script looks for the search pattern on a line by itself:

```
/'"$search"'/b
```

If the search pattern matches the line, the branch command, without a label, transfers control to the bottom of the script where the line is printed. This makes use of sed's normal control-flow so that the next input line is read into the pattern space and control then returns to the top of the script. The branch command is used in the same way each time we try to match the pattern.

If a single input line does not match the pattern, we begin our next procedure to create a multiline pattern space. It is possible that the new line, by itself, will match the search string. It may not be apparent why this step is necessary—why not just immediately look for the pattern anywhere across two lines? The reason is that if the pattern is actually matched on the second line, we'd still output the pair of lines. In other words, the user would see the line preceding the matched line and might be confused by it. This way we output the second line by itself if that is what matches the pattern.

---

[*] Actually, this is the concatenation of single-quoted text with double-quoted text with more single-quoted text (and so on, whew!) to produce one large quoted string. Being a shell wizard helps here.

[†] You can also use shell variables to pass a series of commands into a sed script. This somewhat simulates a procedure call but it makes the script more difficult to read.

```
N
h
s/.*\n//
/'"$search"'/b
```

The Next command appends the next input line to the pattern space. The hold command places a copy of the two-line pattern space into the hold space. The next action will change the pattern space and we want to preserve the original intact. Before looking for the pattern, we use the substitute command to remove the previous line, up to and including the embedded newline. There are several reasons for doing it this way and not another way, so let's consider some of the alternatives. You could write a pattern that matches the search pattern only if it occurs after the embedded newline:

```
/\n.*'"$search"'/b
```

However, if a match is found, we don't want to print the entire pattern space, just the second portion of it. Using the above construct would print both lines when only the second line matches.

You might want to use the Delete command to remove the first line in the pattern space before trying to match the pattern. A side effect of the Delete command is a change in flow control that would resume execution at the top of the script. (The Delete command could conceivably be used but not without changing the logic of this script.)

So, we try to match the pattern on the second line, and if that is unsuccessful, then we try to match it across two lines:

```
g
s/ *\n/ /
/'"$search"'/{
g
b
}
```

The get command retrieves a copy of the original two-line pair from the hold space, overwriting the line we had worked with in the pattern space. The substitute command replaces the embedded newline and any spaces preceding it with a single space. Then we attempt to match the pattern. If the match is made, we don't want to print the contents of the pattern space, but rather get the duplicate from the hold space (which preserves the newline) and print it. Thus, before branching to the end of the script, the get command retrieves the copy from the hold space.

The last part of the script is executed only if the pattern has not been matched.

```
g
D
```

The get command retrieves the duplicate, that preserves the newline, from the hold space. The Delete command removes the first line in the pattern space and passes control back to the top of the script. We delete only the first part of the pattern space, instead of clearing it, because after reading another input line, it is possible to match the pattern spanning across both lines.

Here's the result when the program is run on a sample file:

```
$ phrase "the procedure is followed" sect3
If a pattern is followed by a \f(CW!\fP, then the procedure
is followed for all lines that do not match the pattern.
so that the procedure is followed only if there is no match.
```

As we mentioned at the outset, writing sed scripts is a good primer for programming. In the chapters that follow, we will be looking at the awk programming language. You will see many similarities to sed to make you comfortable but you will see a broader range of constructs for writing useful programs. As you begin trying to do more complicated tasks with sed, the scripts get so convoluted as to make them difficult to understand. One of the advantages of awk is that it handles complexity better, and once you learn the basics, awk scripts are easier to write and understand.

7

# Writing Scripts for awk

As mentioned in the preface, this book describes POSIX awk; that is, the awk language as specified by the POSIX standard. Before diving into the details, we'll provide a bit of history.

The original awk was a nice little language. It first saw the light of day with Version 7 UNIX, around 1978. It caught on, and people used it for significant programming.

In 1985, the original authors, seeing that awk was being used for more serious programming than they had ever intended, decided to beef up the language. (See Chapter 11, *A Flock of awks*, for a description of the original awk, and all the things it did not have when compared to the new one.) The new version was finally released to the world at large in 1987, and it is this version that is still found on SunOS 4.1.x systems.

In 1989, for System V Release 4, awk was updated in some minor ways.[*] This version became the basis for the awk feature list in the POSIX standard. POSIX clarified a number of things about awk, and added the **CONVFMT** variable (to be discussed later in this chapter).

As you read the rest of this book, bear in mind that the term **awk** refers to POSIX awk, and not to any particular implementation, whether the original one from Bell

---

[*] The *-v* option and **tolower()** and **toupper()** functions were added, and **srand()** and **printf** were cleaned up. The details will be presented in this and the following chapters.

Labs, or any of the others discussed in Chapter 11. However, in the few cases where different versions have fundamental differences of behavior, that will be pointed out in the main body of the discussion.

## Playing the Game

To write an awk script, you must become familiar with the rules of the game. The rules can be stated plainly and you will find them described in Appendix B, *Quick Reference for awk*, rather than in this chapter. The goal of this chapter is not to describe the rules but to show you how to play the game. In this way, you will become acquainted with many of the features of the language and see examples that illustrate how scripts actually work. Some people prefer to begin by reading the rules, which is roughly equivalent to learning to use a program from its manual page or learning to speak a language by scanning its rules of grammar—not an easy task. Having a good grasp of the rules, however, is essential once you begin to use awk regularly. But the more you use awk, the faster the rules of the game become second nature. You learn them through trial and error—spending a long time trying to fix a silly syntax error such as a missing space or brace has a magical effect upon long-term memory. Thus, the best way to learn to write scripts is to begin writing them. As you make progress writing scripts, you will no doubt benefit from reading the rules (and rereading them) in Appendix B or the awk manpage or *The AWK Programming Language* book. You can do that later—let's get started now.

## Hello, World

It has become a convention to introduce a programming language by demonstrating the "Hello, world" program. Showing how this program works in awk will demonstrate just how unconventional awk is. In fact, it's necessary to show several different approaches to printing "Hello, world."

In the first example, we create a file named *test* that contains a single line. This example shows a script that contains the **print** statement:

```
$ echo 'this line of data is ignored' > test
$ awk '{ print "Hello, world" }' test
Hello, world
```

This script has only a single action, which is enclosed in braces. That action is to execute the **print** statement for each line of input. In this case, the *test* file contains only a single line; thus, the action occurs once. Note that the input line is read but never output.

Now let's look at another example. Here, we use a file that contains the line "Hello, world."

```
$ cat test2
Hello, world
$ awk '{ print }' test2
Hello, world
```

In this example, "Hello, world" appears in the input file. The same result is achieved because the **print** statement, without arguments, simply outputs each line of input. If there were additional lines of input, they would be output as well.

Both of these examples illustrate that awk is usually input-driven. That is, nothing happens unless there are lines of input on which to act. When you invoke the awk program, it reads the script that you supply, checking the syntax of your instructions. Then awk attempts to execute the instructions for each line of input. Thus, the **print** statement will not be executed unless there is input from the file.

To verify this for yourself, try entering the command line in the first example but omit the filename. You'll find that because awk expects input to come from the keyboard, it will wait until you give it input to process: press RETURN several times, then type an EOF (CTRL-D on most systems) to signal the end of input. For each time that you pressed RETURN, the action that prints "Hello, world" will be executed.

There is yet another way to write the "Hello, world" message and not have awk wait for input. This method associates the action with the **BEGIN** pattern. The **BEGIN** pattern specifies actions that are performed *before* the first line of input is read.

```
$ awk 'BEGIN { print "Hello, world" }'
Hello, world
```

Awk prints the message, and then exits. If a program has only a **BEGIN** pattern, and no other statements, awk will not process any input files.

# Awk's Programming Model

It's important to understand the basic model that awk offers the programmer. Part of the reason why awk is easier to learn than many programming languages is that it offers such a well-defined and useful model to the programmer.

An awk program consists of what we will call a *main input loop*. A *loop* is a routine that is executed over and over again until some condition exists that terminates it. You don't write this loop, it is given—it exists as the framework within which the code that you do write will be executed. The main input loop in awk is a routine that reads one line of input from a file and makes it available for processing. The actions you write to do the processing assume that there is a line of input available. In another programming language, you would have to create the main input loop as part of your program. It would have to open the input file and read one line at a time. This is not necessarily a lot of work, but it illustrates a basic awk shortcut that makes it easier for you to write your program.

The main input loop is executed as many times as there are lines of input. As you saw in the "Hello, world" examples, this loop does not execute until there is a line of input. It terminates when there is no more input to be read.

Awk allows you to write two special routines that can be executed *before* any input is read and *after* all input is read. These are the procedures associated with the **BEGIN** and **END** rules, respectively. In other words, you can do some preprocessing before the main input loop is ever executed and you can do some postprocessing after the main input loop has terminated. The **BEGIN** and **END** procedures are optional.

You can think of an awk script as having potentially three major parts: what happens before, what happens during, and what happens after processing the input. Figure 7-1 shows the relationship of these parts in the flow of control of an awk script.

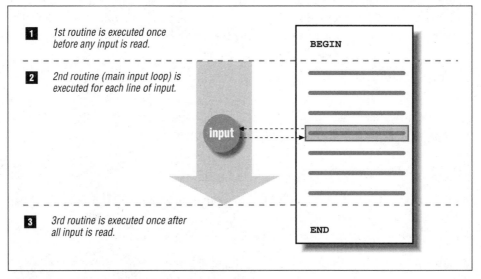

*Figure 7-1: Flow and control in awk scripts*

Of these three parts, the main input loop or "what happens during processing" is where most of the work gets done. Inside the main input loop, your instructions are written as a series of pattern/action procedures. A pattern is a rule for testing the input line to determine whether or not the action should be applied to it. The actions, as we shall see, can be quite complex, consisting of statements, functions, and expressions.

The main thing to remember is that each pattern/action procedure sits in the main input loop, which takes care of reading the input line. The procedures that you write will be applied to each input line, one line at a time.

# Pattern Matching

The "Hello, world" program does not demonstrate the power of pattern-matching rules. In this section, we look at a number of small, even trivial examples that nonetheless demonstrate this central feature of awk scripts.

When awk reads an input line, it attempts to match each pattern-matching rule in a script. Only the lines matching the particular pattern are the object of an action. If no action is specified, the line that matches the pattern is printed (executing the **print** statement is the default action). Consider the following script:

```
/^$/ { print "This is a blank line." }
```

This script reads: *if the input line is blank, then print "This is a blank line."* The pattern is written as a regular expression that identifies a blank line. The action, like most of those we've seen so far, contains a single **print** statement.

If we place this script in a file named *awkscr* and use an input file named *test* that contains three blank lines, then the following command executes the script:

```
$ awk -f awkscr test
This is a blank line.
This is a blank line.
This is a blank line.
```

(From this point on, we'll assume that our scripts are placed in a separate file and invoked using the *-f* command-line option.) The result tells us that there are three blank lines in *test*. This script ignores lines that are not blank.

Let's add several new rules to the script. This script is now going to analyze the input and classify it as an integer, a string, or a blank line.

```
# test for integer, string or empty line.
/[0-9]+/    { print "That is an integer" }
/[A-Za-z]+/ { print "This is a string" }
/^$/        { print "This is a blank line." }
```

The general idea is that if a line of input matches any of these patterns, the associated **print** statement will be executed. The + metacharacter is part of the extended set of regular expression metacharacters and means "one or more." Therefore, a line containing a sequence of one or more digits will be considered an integer. Here's a sample run, taking input from standard input:

```
$ awk -f awkscr
4
That is an integer
t
This is a string
4T
That is an integer
This is a string
RETURN
This is a blank line.
44
That is an integer
CTRL-D
$
```

Note that input "4T" was identified as both an integer and a string. A line can match more than one rule. You can write a stricter rule set to prevent a line from matching more than one rule. You can also write actions that are designed to skip other parts of the script.

We will be exploring the use of pattern-matching rules throughout this chapter.

## Describing Your Script

Adding comments as you write the script is a good practice. A comment begins with the "#" character and ends at a newline. Unlike sed, awk allows comments anywhere in the script.

---

*NOTE*          If you are supplying your awk program on the command line, rather than putting it in a file, do not use a single quote anywhere in your program. The shell would interpret it and become confused.

---

As we begin writing scripts, we'll use comments to describe the action:

```
#  blank.awk -- Print message for each blank line.
/^$/ { print "This is a blank line." }
```

This comment offers the name of the script, **blank.awk**, and briefly describes what the script does. A particularly useful comment for longer scripts is one that identifies the expected structure of the input file. For instance, in the next section, we are going to look at writing a script that reads a file containing names and phone numbers. The introductory comments for this program should be:

```
# blocklist.awk -- print name and address in block form.
# fields: name, company, street, city, state and zip, phone
```

It is useful to embed this information in the script because the script won't work unless the structure of the input file corresponds to that expected by the person who wrote the script.

# Records and Fields

Awk makes the assumption that its input is structured and not just an endless string of characters. In the simplest case, it takes each input line as a record and each word, separated by spaces or tabs, as a field. (The characters separating the fields are often referred to as *delimiters.*) The following record in the file *names* has three fields, separated by either a space or a tab.

```
John Robinson      666-555-1111
```

Two or more consecutive spaces and/or tabs count as a single delimiter.

## Referencing and Separating Fields

Awk allows you to refer to fields in actions using the field operator $. This operator is followed by a number or a variable that identifies the position of a field by number. "$1" refers to the first field, "$2" to the second field, and so on. "$0" refers to the entire input record. The following example displays the last name first and the first name second, followed by the phone number.

```
$ awk '{ print $2, $1, $3 }' names
Robinson John 666-555-1111
```

$1 refers to the first name, $2 to the last name, and $3 to the phone number. The commas that separate each argument in the **print** statement cause a space to be output between the values. (Later on, we'll discuss the output field separator (**OFS**), whose value the comma outputs and which is by default a space.) In this example, a single input line forms one record containing three fields: there is a space between the first and last names and a tab between the last name and the phone number. If you wanted to grab the first and last name as a single field, you could set the field separator explicitly so that only tabs are recognized. Then, awk would recognize only two fields in this record.

You can use any expression that evaluates to an integer to refer to a field, not just numbers and variables.

```
$ echo a b c d | awk 'BEGIN { one = 1; two = 2 }
> { print $(one + two) }'
c
```

You can change the field separator with the *-F* option on the command line. It is followed by the delimiter character (either immediately, or separated by white-space). In the following example, the field separator is changed to a tab.

```
$ awk -F"\t" '{ print $2 }' names
666-555-1111
```

"\t" is an *escape sequence* (discussed below) that represents an actual tab character. It should be surrounded by single or double quotes.

Commas delimit fields in the following two address records.

```
John Robinson,Koren Inc.,978 4th Ave.,Boston,MA 01760,696-0987
Phyllis Chapman,GVE Corp.,34 Sea Drive,Amesbury,MA 01881,879-0900
```

An awk program can print the name and address in block format.

```
# blocklist.awk -- print name and address in block form.
# input file -- name, company, street, city, state and zip, phone
{       print "" # output blank line
        print $1 # name
        print $2 # company
        print $3 # street
        print $4, $5    # city, state zip
}
```

The first **print** statement specifies an empty string ("") (remember, **print** by itself outputs the current line). This arranges for the records in the report to be separated by blank lines. We can invoke this script and specify that the field separator is a comma using the following command:

```
awk -F, -f blocklist.awk names
```

The following report is produced:

```
John Robinson
Koren Inc.
978 4th Ave.
Boston  MA 01760

Phyllis Chapman
GVE Corp.
34 Sea Drive
Amesbury  MA 01881
```

It is usually a better practice, and more convenient, to specify the field separator in the script itself. The system variable **FS** can be defined to change the field separator. Because this must be done before the first input line is read, we must assign this variable in an action controlled by the **BEGIN** rule.

```
BEGIN { FS = "," }
```

Now let's use it in a script to print out the names and phone numbers.

```
# phonelist.awk -- print name and phone number.
# input file -- name, company, street, city, state and zip, phone

BEGIN { FS = "," }  # comma-delimited fields

{ print $1 ", " $6 }
```

Notice that we use blank lines in the script itself to improve readability. The **print** statement puts a comma followed by a space between the two output fields. This script can be invoked from the command line:

```
$ awk -f phonelist.awk names
John Robinson, 696-0987
Phyllis Chapman, 879-0900
```

This gives you a basic idea of how awk can be used to work with data that has a recognizable structure. This script is designed to print all lines of input, but we could modify the single action by writing a pattern-matching rule that selected only certain names or addresses. So, if we had a large listing of names, we could select only the names of people residing in a particular state. We could write:

```
/MA/ { print $1 ", " $6 }
```

where MA would match the postal state abbreviation for Massachusetts. However, we could possibly match a company name or some other field in which the letters "MA" appeared. We can test a specific field for a match. The tilde (~) operator allows you to test a regular expression against a field.

```
$5 ~ /MA/   { print $1 ", " $6 }
```

You can reverse the meaning of the rule by using bang-tilde (!~).

```
$5 !~ /MA/   { print $1 ", " $6 }
```

This rule would match all those records whose fifth field did not have "MA" in it. A more challenging pattern-matching rule would be one that matches only long-distance phone numbers. The following regular expression looks for an area code.

```
$6 ~ /1?(-|□)?\(?(?[0-9]+\)?(□|-)?[0-9]+-[0-9]+/
```

This rule matches any of the following forms:

```
707-724-0000
(707) 724-0000
(707)724-0000
1-707-724-0000
1 707-724-0000
1(707)724-0000
```

The regular expression can be deciphered by breaking down its parts. "1?" means zero or one occurrences of "1". "(-|□)?" looks for either a hyphen or a space in the next position, or nothing at all. "\(?" looks for zero or one left parenthesis; the backslash prevents the interpretation of "(" as the grouping metacharacter. "[0-9]+"

looks for one or more digits; note that we took the lazy way out and specified one or more digits rather than exactly three. In the next position, we are looking for an optional right parenthesis, and again, either a space or a hyphen, or nothing at all. Then we look for one or more digits "[0-9]+" followed by a hyphen followed by one or more digits "[0-9]+".

## Field Splitting: The Full Story

There are three distinct ways you can have awk separate fields. The first method is to have fields separated by whitespace. To do this, set **FS** equal to a single space. In this case, leading and trailing whitespace (spaces and/or tabs) are stripped from the record, and fields are separated by runs of spaces and/or tabs. Since the default value of **FS** is a single space, this is the way awk normally splits each record into fields.

The second method is to have some other single character separate fields. For example, awk programs for processing the UNIX */etc/passwd* file usually use a ":" as the field separator. When **FS** is any single character, *each* occurrence of that character separates another field. If there are two successive occurrences, the field between them simply has the empty string as its value.

Finally, if you specify more than a single character as the field separator, it will be interpreted as a regular expression. That is, the field separator will be the "leftmost longest non-null and nonoverlapping" substring[*] that matches the regular expression. (The phrase "null string" is technical jargon for what we've been calling the "empty string.") You can see the difference between specifying:

```
FS = "\t"
```

which causes each tab to be interpreted as a field separator, and:

```
FS = "\t+"
```

which specifies that one or more consecutive tabs separate a field. Using the first specification, the following line would have three fields:

```
abc\t\tdef
```

whereas the second specification would only recognize two fields. Using a regular expression allows you to specify several characters to be used as delimiters:

```
FS = "[':\t]"
```

Any of the three characters in brackets will be interpreted as the field separator.

---

[*] *The AWK Programming Language* [Aho], p. 60.

# *Expressions*

The use of expressions in which you can store, manipulate, and retrieve data is quite different from anything you can do in sed, yet it is a common feature of most programming languages.

An expression is evaluated and returns a value. An expression consists of any combination of numeric and string constants, variables, operators, functions, and regular expressions. We covered regular expressions in detail in Chapter 2, *Understanding Basic Operations*, and they are summarized in Appendix B. Functions will be discussed fully in Chapter 9, *Functions*. In this section, we will look at expressions consisting of constants, variables, and operators.

There are two types of constants: string or numeric (**"red"** or **1**). A string must be quoted in an expression. Strings can make use of the escape sequences listed in Table 7-1.

*Table 7–1: Escape Sequences*

| Sequence | Description |
| --- | --- |
| \a | Alert character, usually ASCII BEL character |
| \b | Backspace |
| \f | Formfeed |
| \n | Newline |
| \r | Carriage return |
| \t | Horizontal tab |
| \v | Vertical tab |
| \\*ddd* | Character represented as 1 to 3 digit octal value |
| \x*hex* | Character represented as hexadecimal value[a] |
| \\*c* | Any literal character *c* (e.g., \" for ")[b] |

[a] POSIX does not provide "\x", but it is commonly available.
[b] Like ANSI C, POSIX leaves purposely undefined what you get when you put a backslash before any character not listed in the table. In most awks, you just get that character.

A *variable* is an identifier that references a value. To define a variable, you only have to name it and assign it a value. The name can only contain letters, digits, and underscores, and may not start with a digit. Case distinctions in variable names are important: **Salary** and **salary** are two different variables. Variables are not declared; you do not have to tell awk what *type* of value will be stored in a variable. Each variable has a string value and a numeric value, and awk uses the appropriate value based on the context of the expression. (Strings that do not consist of numbers have a numeric value of 0.) Variables do not have to be initialized;

awk automatically initializes them to the empty string, which acts like 0 if used as a number. The following expression assigns a value to **x**:

```
x = 1
```

**x** is the name of the variable, = is an assignment operator, and 1 is a numeric constant.

The following expression assigns the string "Hello" to the variable **z**:

```
z = "Hello"
```

A space is the string concatenation operator. The expression:

```
z = "Hello" "World"
```

concatenates the two strings and assigns "HelloWorld" to the variable **z**.

The dollar sign ($) operator is used to reference fields. The following expression assigns the value of the first field of the current input record to the variable **w**:

```
w = $1
```

A variety of operators can be used in expressions. Arithmetic operators are listed in Table 7-2.

*Table 7-2: Arithmetic Operators*

| Operator | Description |
|----------|-------------|
| + | Addition |
| - | Subtraction |
| * | Multiplication |
| / | Division |
| % | Modulo |
| ^ | Exponentiation |
| ** | Exponentiation[a] |

[a] This is a common extension. It is not in the POSIX standard, and often not in the system documentation, either. Its use is thus nonportable.

Once a variable has been assigned a value, that value can be referenced using the name of the variable. The following expression adds 1 to the value of **x** and assigns it to the variable **y**:

```
y = x + 1
```

So, evaluate **x**, add 1 to it, and put the result into the variable **y**. The statement:

```
print y
```

prints the value of **y**. If the following sequence of statements appears in a script:

```
x = 1
y = x + 1
print y
```

then the value of **y** is 2.

We could reduce these three statements to two:

```
x = 1
print x + 1
```

Notice, however, that after the **print** statement the value of **x** is still 1. We didn't change the value of **x**; we simply added 1 to it and printed that value. In other words, if a third statement **print x** followed, it would output 1. If, in fact, we wished to accumulate the value in **x**, we could use an assignment operator +=. This operator combines two operations; it adds 1 to **x** and assigns the new value to **x**. Table 7-3 lists the assignment operators used in awk expressions.

*Table 7-3: Assignment Operators*

| Operator | Description |
|----------|-------------|
| ++ | Add 1 to variable. |
| -- | Subtract 1 from variable. |
| += | Assign result of addition. |
| -= | Assign result of subtraction. |
| *= | Assign result of multiplication. |
| /= | Assign result of division. |
| %= | Assign result of modulo. |
| ^= | Assign result of exponentiation. |
| **= | Assign result of exponentiation.[a] |

[a] As with "**", this is a common extension, which is also nonportable.

Look at the following example, which counts each blank line in a file.

```
# Count blank lines.
/^$/ {
        print x += 1
    }
```

Although we didn't initialize the value of **x**, we can safely assume that its value is 0 up until the first blank line is encountered. The expression "x += 1" is evaluated each time a blank line is matched and the value of **x** is incremented by 1. The **print** statement prints the value returned by the expression. Because we execute the **print** statement for every blank line, we get a running count of blank lines.

There are different ways to write expressions, some more terse than others. The expression "x += 1" is more concise than the following equivalent expression:

```
x = x + 1
```

But neither of these expressions is as terse as the following expression:

```
++x
```

"++" is the increment operator. ("--" is the decrement operator.) Each time the expression is evaluated the value of the variable is incremented by one. The increment and decrement operators can appear on either side of the operand, as *prefix* or *postfix* operators. The position has a different effect.

```
++x        Increment x before returning value (prefix)
x++        Increment x after returning value (postfix)
```

For instance, if our example was written:

```
/^$/ {
        print x++
    }
```

When the first blank line is matched, the expression returns the value "0"; the second blank line returns "1", and so on. If we put the increment operator before **x**, then the first time the expression is evaluated, it will return "1."

Let's implement that expression in our example. In addition, instead of printing a count each time a blank line is matched, we'll accumulate the count as the value of **x** and print only the total number of blank lines. The **END** pattern is the place to put the **print** that displays the value of **x** after the last input line is read.

```
# Count blank lines.
/^$/ {
        ++x
}
END {
        print x
}
```

Let's try it on the sample file that has three blank lines in it.

```
$ awk -f awkscr test
3
```

The script outputs the number of blank lines.

## *Averaging Student Grades*

Let's look at another example, one in which we sum a series of student grades and then calculate the average. Here's what the input file looks like:

```
john 85 92 78 94 88
andrea 89 90 75 90 86
jasper 84 88 80 92 84
```

There are five grades following the student's name. Here is the script that will give us each student's average:

```
# average five grades
{ total = $2 + $3 + $4 + $5 + $6
  avg = total / 5
  print $1, avg }
```

This script adds together fields 2 through 6 to get the sum total of the five grades. The value of **total** is divided by 5 and assigned to the variable **avg**. ("/" is the operator for division.) The **print** statement outputs the student's name and average. Note that we could have skipped the assignment of **avg** and instead calculated the average as part of the **print** statement, as follows:

```
print $1, total / 5
```

This script shows how easy it is to write programs in awk. Awk parses the input into fields and records. You are spared having to read individual characters and declaring data types. Awk does this for you, automatically.

Let's see a sample run of the script that calculates student averages:

```
$ awk -f grades.awk grades
john 87.4
andrea 86
jasper 85.6
```

# *System Variables*

There are a number of system or built-in variables defined by awk. Awk has two types of system variables. The first type defines values whose default can be changed, such as the default field and record separators. The second type defines values that can be used in reports or processing, such as the number of fields found in the current record, the count of the current record, and others. These are *automatically* updated by awk; for example, the current record number and input file name.

There are a set of default values that affect the recognition of records and fields on input and their display on output. The system variable **FS** defines the field separator. By default, its value is a single space, which tells awk that any number of spaces and/or tabs separate fields. **FS** can also be set to any single character, or to a regular expression. Earlier, we changed the field separator to a comma in order to read a list of names and addresses.

The output equivalent of **FS** is **OFS**, which is a space by default. We'll see an example of redefining **OFS** shortly.

Awk defines the variable **NF** to be the number of fields for the current input record. Changing the value of **NF** actually has side effects. The interactions that occur when $0, the fields, and **NF** are changed is a murky area, particularly when **NF** is decreased.[*] Increasing it creates new (empty) fields, and rebuilds $0, with the fields separated by the value of **OFS**. In the case where **NF** is decreased, gawk and mawk rebuild the record, and the fields that were above the new value of **NF** are set equal to the empty string. The Bell Labs awk does not change $0.

Awk also defines **RS**, the record separator, as a newline. **RS** is a bit unusual; it's the only variable where awk only pays attention to the first character of the value.

The output equivalent to **RS** is **ORS**, which is also a newline by default. In the next section, "Working with Multiline Records," we'll show how to change the default record separator. Awk sets the variable **NR** to the number of the current input record. It can be used to number records in a list. The variable **FILENAME** contains the name of the current input file. The variable **FNR** is useful when multiple input files are used as it provides the number of the current record relative to the current input file.

Typically, the field and record separators are defined in the **BEGIN** procedure because you want these values set before the first input line is read. However, you can redefine these values anywhere in the script. In POSIX awk, assigning a new value to **FS** has no effect on the current input line; it only affects the next input line.

---

*NOTE*     Prior to the June 1996 release of Bell Labs awk, versions of awk for UNIX did not follow the POSIX standard in this regard. In those versions, if you have not yet referenced an individual field, and you set the field separator to a different value, the current input line is split into fields using the new value of **FS**. Thus, you should test how your awk behaves, and if at all possible, upgrade to a correct version of awk.

---

* Unfortunately, the POSIX standard isn't as helpful here as it should be.

Finally, POSIX added a new variable, **CONVFMT**, which is used to control number-to-string conversions. For example,

```
str = (5.5 + 3.2) " is a nice value"
```

Here, the result of the numeric expression **5.5 + 3.2** (which is 8.7) must be converted to a string before it can be used in the string concatenation. **CONVFMT** controls this conversion. Its default value is "%.6g", which is a **printf**-style format specification for floating-point numbers. Changing **CONVFMT** to "%d", for instance, would cause all numbers to be converted to strings as integers. Prior to the POSIX standard, awk used **OFMT** for this purpose. **OFMT** does the same job, but controlling the conversion of numeric values when using the **print** statement. The POSIX committee wanted to separate the tasks of output conversion from simple string conversion. Note that numbers that are integers are always converted to strings as integers, no matter what the values of **CONVFMT** and **OFMT** may be.

Now let's look at some examples, beginning with the **NR** variable. Here's a revised **print** statement for the script that calculates student averages:

```
print NR ".", $1, avg
```

Running the revised script produces the following output:

```
1. john 87.4
2. andrea 86
3. jasper 85.6
```

After the last line of input is read, **NR** contains the number of input records that were read. It can be used in the **END** action to provide a report summary. Here's a revised version of the **phonelist.awk** script.

```
# phonelist.awk -- print name and phone number.
# input file -- name, company, street, city, state and zip, phone
BEGIN { FS = ", *" }  # comma-delimited fields
{ print $1 ", " $6 }
END {    print ""
         print NR, "records processed." }
```

This program changes the default field separator and uses **NR** to print the total number of records printed. Note that this program uses a regular expression for the value of **FS**. This program produces the following output:

```
John Robinson, 696-0987
Phyllis Chapman, 879-0900
2 records processed.
```

The output field separator (**OFS**) is generated when a comma is used to separate the arguments in a **print** statement. You may have wondered what effect the comma has in the following expression:

```
print NR ".", $1, avg
```

By default, the comma causes a space (the default value of **OFS**) to be output. For instance, you could redefine **OFS** to be a tab in a **BEGIN** action. Then the preceding **print** statement would produce the following output:

```
1.      john    87.4
2.      andrea  86
3.      jasper  85.6
```

This is especially useful if the input consists of tab-separated fields and you want to generate the same kind of output. **OFS** can be redefined to be a sequence of characters, such as a comma followed by a space.

Another commonly used system variable is **NF**, which is set to the number of fields for the current record. As we'll see in the next section, you can use **NF** to check that a record has the same number of fields that you expect. You can also use **NF** to reference the last field of each record. Using the "$" field operator and **NF** produces that reference. If there are six fields, then "$NF" is the same as "$6." Given a list of names, such as the following:

```
John Kennedy
Lyndon B. Johnson
Richard Milhouse Nixon
Gerald R. Ford
Jimmy Carter
Ronald Reagan
George Bush
Bill Clinton
```

you will note that the last name is not the same field number for each record. You could print the last name of each President using "$NF."[*]

These are the basic system variables, the ones most commonly used. There are more of them, as listed in Appendix B, and we'll introduce new system variables as needed in the chapters that follow.

## *Working with Multiline Records*

All of our examples have used input files whose records consisted of a single line. In this section, we show how to read a record where each field consists of a single line.

Earlier, we looked at an example of processing a file of names and addresses. Let's suppose that the same data is stored on file in block format. Instead of having all the information on one line, the person's name is on one line, followed by the company's name on the next line and so on. Here's a sample record:

---

[*] This scheme breaks down for Martin Van Buren; fortunately, our list contains only recent U.S. presidents.

```
John Robinson
Koren Inc.
978 Commonwealth Ave.
Boston
MA 01760
696-0987
```

This record has six fields. A blank line separates each record.

To process this data, we can specify a multiline record by defining the field separator to be a newline, represented as "\n", and set the record separator to the empty string, which stands for a blank line.

```
BEGIN { FS = "\n"; RS = "" }
```

We can print the first and last fields using the following script:

```
# block.awk - print first and last fields
# $1 = name; $NF = phone number

BEGIN { FS = "\n"; RS = "" }

{ print $1, $NF }
```

Here's a sample run:

```
$ awk -f block.awk phones.block
John Robinson 696-0987
Phyllis Chapman 879-0900
Jeffrey Willis 914-636-0000
Alice Gold (707) 724-0000
Bill Gold 1-707-724-0000
```

The two fields are printed on the same line because the default output separator (**OFS**) remains a single space. If you want the fields to be output on separate lines, change **OFS** to a newline. While you're at it, you probably want to preserve the blank line between records, so you must specify the output record separator **ORS** to be two newlines.

```
OFS = "\n"; ORS = "\n\n"
```

## *Balance the Checkbook*

This is a simple application that processes items in your check register. While not necessarily the easiest way to balance the checkbook, it is amazing how quickly you can build something useful with awk.

This program presumes you have entered in a file the following information:

```
1000
125     Market         125.45
126     Hardware Store  34.95
```

```
127      Video Store      7.45
128      Book Store       14.32
129      Gasoline         16.10
```

The first line contains the beginning balance. Each of the other lines represent information from a single check: the check number, a description of where it was spent, and the amount of the check. The three fields are separated by tabs.

The core task of the script is that it must get the beginning balance and then deduct the amount of each check from that balance. We can provide detail lines for each check to compare against the check register. Finally, we can print the ending balance. Here it is:

```
# checkbook.awk
BEGIN { FS = "\t" }

#1 Expect the first record to have the starting balance.
NR == 1 { print "Beginning Balance: \t" $1
        balance = $1
        next                # get next record and start over
}

#2 Apply to each check record, subtracting amount from balance.
{       print $1, $2, $3
        print balance -= $3
}
```

Let's run this program and look at the results:

```
$ awk -f checkbook.awk checkbook.test
Beginning Balance:        1000
125 Market 125.45
874.55
126 Hardware Store 34.95
839.6
127 Video Store 7.45
832.15
128 Book Store 14.32
817.83
129 Gasoline 16.10
801.73
```

The report is difficult to read, but later we will learn to fix the format using the **printf** statement. What's important is to confirm that the script is doing what we want. Notice, also, that getting this far takes only a few minutes in awk. In a programming language such as C, it would take you much longer to write this program; for one thing, you might have many more lines of code; and you'd be programming at a much lower level. There are any number of refinements that you'd want to make to this program to improve it, and refining a program takes much longer. The point is that with awk you are able to isolate and implement the basic functionality quite easily.

# *Relational and Boolean Operators*

Relational and Boolean operators allow you to make comparisons between two expressions. The relational operators are found in Table 7-4.

*Table 7-4: Relational Operators*

| Operator | Description |
|---|---|
| < | Less than |
| > | Greater than |
| <= | Less than or equal to |
| >= | Greater than or equal to |
| == | Equal to |
| != | Not equal to |
| ~ | Matches |
| !~ | Does not match |

A relational expression can be used in place of a pattern to control a particular action. For instance, if we wanted to limit the records selected for processing to those that have five fields, we could use the following expression:

```
NF == 5
```

This relational expression compares the value of **NF** (the number of fields for each input record) to five. If it is true, the action will be executed; otherwise, it will not.

---

*NOTE*        Make sure you notice that the relational operator "==" ("is equal to") is not the same as the assignment operator "=" ("equals"). It is a common error to use "=" instead of "==" to test for equality.

---

We can use a relational expression to validate the *phonelist* database before attempting to print out the record.

```
NF == 6 { print $1, $6 }
```

Then only lines with six fields will be printed.

The opposite of "==" is "!=" ("is not equal to"). Similarly, you can compare one expression to another to see if it is greater than (>) or less than (<) or greater than or equal to (>=) or less than or equal to (<=). The expression

```
NR > 1
```

tests whether the number of the current record is greater than 1. As we'll see in the next chapter, relational expressions are typically used in conditional (if) statements and are evaluated to determine whether or not a particular statement should be executed.

Regular expressions are usually written enclosed in slashes. These can be thought of as regular expression *constants*, much as **"hello"** is a string constant. We've seen many examples so far:

```
/^$/ { print "This is a blank line." }
```

However, you are not limited to regular expression constants. When used with the relational operators ˜ ("match") and !˜ ("no match"), the right-hand side of the expression can be any awk expression; awk treats it as a string that specifies a regular expression.[*] We've already seen an example of the ˜ operator used in a pattern-matching rule for the phone database:

```
$5 ˜ /MA/  { print $1 ", " $6 }
```

where the value of field 5 is compared against the regular expression "MA."

Since any expression can be used with ˜ and !˜, regular expressions can be supplied through variables. For instance, in the *phonelist* script, we could replace "/MA/" with **state** and have a procedure that defines the value of state.

```
$5 ˜ state { print $1 ", " $6 }
```

This makes the script much more general to use because *a pattern can change dynamically* during execution of the script. For instance, it allows us to get the value of **state** from a command-line parameter. We will talk about passing command-line parameters into a script later in this chapter.

Boolean operators allow you to combine a series of comparisons. They are listed in Table 7-5.

*Table 7-5: Boolean Operators*

| Operator | Description |
| --- | --- |
| \|\| | Logical OR |
| && | Logical AND |
| ! | Logical NOT |

Given two or more expressions, || specifies that one of them must evaluate to true (non-zero or non-empty) for the whole expression to be true. **&&** specifies that *both* of the expressions must be true to return true.

---

[*] You may also use strings instead of regular expression constants when calling the **match()**, **split()**, **sub()**, and **gsub()** functions.

The following expression:

```
NF == 6 && NR > 1
```

states that the number of fields must be equal to 6 *and* that the number of the record must be greater than 1.

**&&** has higher precedence than **||**. Can you tell how the following expression will be evaluated?

```
NR > 1 && NF >= 2 || $1 ~ /\t/
```

The parentheses in the next example show which expression would be evaluated first based on the rules of precedence.

```
(NR > 1 && NF >= 2) || $1 ~ /\t/
```

In other words, both of the expressions in parentheses must be true *or* the right hand side must be true. You can use parentheses to override the rules of precedence, as in the following example which specifies that two conditions must be true.

```
NR > 1 && (NF >= 2 || $1 ~ /\t/)
```

The first condition must be true *and* either of two other conditions must be true.

Given an expression that is either true or false, the ! operator inverts the sense of the expression.

```
! (NR > 1 && NF > 3)
```

This expression is true if the parenthesized expression is false. This operator is most useful with awk's **in** operator to see if an index is not in an array (as we shall see later), although it has other uses as well.

## Getting Information About Files

Now we are going to look at a couple of scripts that process the output of a UNIX command, **ls**. The following is a sample of the long listing produced by the command **ls -l**:[*]

```
$ ls -l
-rw-rw-rw-   1 dale     project   6041 Jan  1 12:31 com.tmp
-rwxrwxrwx   1 dale     project   1778 Jan  1 11:55 combine.idx
-rw-rw-rw-   1 dale     project   1446 Feb 15 22:32 dang
-rwxrwxrwx   1 dale     project   1202 Jan  2 23:06 format.idx
```

---

[*] Note that on a Berkeley 4.3BSD-derived UNIX system such as Ultrix or SunOS 4.1.x, **ls -l** produces an eight-column report; use **ls -lg** to get the same report format shown here.

This listing is a report in which data is presented in rows and columns. Each file is presented across a single row. The file listing consists of nine columns. The file's permissions appear in the first column, the size of the file in bytes in the fifth column, and the filename is found in the last column. Because one or more spaces separate the data in columns, we can treat each column as a field.

In our first example, we're going to pipe the output of this command to an awk script that prints selected fields from the file listing. To do this, we'll create a shell script so that we can make the pipe transparent to the user. Thus, the structure of the shell script is:

```
ls -l $* | awk 'script'
```

The $* variable is used by the shell and expands to all arguments passed from the command line. (We could use $1 here, which would pass the first argument, but passing *all* the arguments provides greater flexibility.) These arguments can be the names of files or directories or additional options to the **ls** command. If no arguments are specified, the "$*" will be empty and the current directory will be listed. Thus, the output of the **ls** command will be directed to awk, which will automatically read standard input, since no filenames have been given.

We'd like our awk script to print the size and name of the file. That is, print field 5 ($5) and field 9 ($9).

```
ls -l $* | awk '{
        print $5, "\t", $9
}'
```

If we put the above lines in a file named *fls* and make that file executable, we can enter **fls** as a command.

```
$ fls
6041      com.tmp
1778      combine.idx
1446      dang
1202      format.idx
$ fls com*
6041      com.tmp
1778      combine.idx
```

So what our program does is take the long listing and reduce it to two fields. Now, let's add new functionality to our report by producing some information that the **ls -l** listing does not provide. We add each file's size to a running total, to produce the total number of bytes used by all files in the listing. We can also keep track of the number of files and produce that total. There are two parts to adding this functionality. The first is to accumulate the totals for each input line. We create the variable **sum** to accumulate the size of files and the variable **filenum** to accumulate the number of files in the listing.

```
{
        sum += $5
        ++filenum
        print $5, "\t", $9
}
```

The first expression uses the assignment operator **+=**. It adds the value of field 5 to the present value of the variable **sum**. The second expression increments the present value of the variable **filenum**. This variable is used as a *counter*, and each time the expression is evaluated, 1 is added to the count.

The action we've written will be applied to all input lines. The totals that are accumulated in this action must be printed after awk has read all the input lines. Therefore, we write an action that is controlled by the **END** rule.

```
END { print "Total: ", sum, "bytes (" filenum " files)" }
```

We can also use the **BEGIN** rule to add column headings to the report.

```
BEGIN { print "BYTES", "\t", "FILE" }
```

Now we can put this script in an executable file named *filesum* and execute it as a single-word command.

```
$ filesum c*
BYTES   FILE
882     ch01
1771    ch03
1987    ch04
6041    com.tmp
1778    combine.idx
Total:  12459 bytes (5 files)
```

What's nice about this command is that it allows you to determine the size of all files in a directory or any group of files.

While the basic mechanism works, there are a few problems to be taken care of. The first problem occurs when you list the entire directory using the **ls -l** command. The listing contains a line that specifies the total number of blocks in the directory. The partial listing (all files beginning with "c") in the previous example does not have this line. But the following line would be included in the output if the full directory was listed:

```
total 555
```

The block total does not interest us because the program displays the total file size in bytes. Currently, **filesum** does not print this line; however, it does read this line and cause the **filenum** counter to be incremented.

There is also a problem with this script in how it handles subdirectories. Look at the following line from an **ls -l**:

```
drwxrwxrwx   3 dale     project         960 Feb  1 15:47 sed
```

A "d" as the first character in column 1 (file permissions) indicates that the file is a subdirectory. The size of this file (960 bytes) does not indicate the size of files in that subdirectory and therefore, it is slightly misleading to add it to the file size totals. Also, it might be helpful to indicate that it is a directory.

If you want to list the files in subdirectories, supply the *-R* (recursive) option on the command line. It will be passed to the **ls** command. However, the listing is slightly different as it identifies each directory. For instance, to identify the subdirectory *old*, the **ls -lR** listing produces a blank line followed by:

```
./old:
```

Our script ignores that line and a blank line preceding it but nonetheless they increment the file counter. Fortunately, we can devise rules to handle these cases. Let's look at the revised, commented script:

```
ls -l $* | awk '
# filesum: list files and total size in bytes
# input: long listing produced by "ls -l"

#1 output column headers
BEGIN { print "BYTES", "\t", "FILE" }

#2 test for 9 fields; files begin with "-"
NF == 9 && /^-/ {
        sum += $5        # accumulate size of file
        ++filenum        # count number of files
        print $5, "\t", $9       # print size and filename
}

#3 test for 9 fields; directory begins with "d"
NF == 9 && /^d/ {
        print "<dir>", "\t", $9 # print <dir> and name
}

#4 test for ls -lR line ./dir:
$1 ~ /^\..*:$/ {
        print "\t" $0 # print that line preceded by tab
}

#5 once all is done,
END {
        # print total file size and number of files
        print "Total: ", sum, "bytes (" filenum " files)"
}'
```

The rules and their associated actions have been numbered to make it easier to discuss them. The listing produced by ls -l contains nine fields for a file. Awk supplies the number of fields for a record in the system variable **NF**. Therefore, rules 2 and 3 test that **NF** is equal to 9. This helps us avoid matching odd blank lines or the line stating the block total. Because we want to handle directories and files differently, we use another pattern to match the first character of the line. In rule 2 we test for "-" in the first position on the line, which indicates a file. The associated action increments the file counter and adds the file size to the previous total. In rule 3, we test for a directory, indicated by "d" as the first character. The associated action prints "<dir>" in place of the file size. Rules 2 and 3 are *compound* expressions, specifying two patterns that are combined using the **&&** operator. Both patterns must be matched for the expression to be true.

Rule 4 tests for the special case produced by the ls -lR listing ("./old:"). There are a number of patterns that we can write to match that line, using regular expressions or relational expressions:

| | |
|---|---|
| NF == 1 | *If the number of fields equals 1 ...* |
| /^\..*:$/ | *If the line begins with a period followed by any number of characters and ends in a colon...* |
| $1 ~ /^\..*:$/ | *If field 1 matches the regular expression...* |

We used the latter expression because it seems to be the most specific. It employs the match operator (~) to test the first field against a regular expression. The associated action consists of only a **print** statement.

Rule 5 is the **END** pattern and its action is only executed once, printing the sum of file sizes as well as the number of files.

The **filesum** program demonstrates many of the basic constructs used in awk. What's more, it gives you a pretty good idea of the process of developing a program (although syntax errors produced by typos and hasty thinking have been gracefully omitted). If you wish to tinker with this program, you might add a counter for a directories, or a rule that handles symbolic links.

# *Formatted Printing*

Many of the scripts that we've written so far perform the data processing tasks just fine, but the output has not been formatted properly. That is because there is only so much you can do with the basic **print** statement. And since one of awk's most common functions is to produce reports, it is crucial that we be able to format our reports in an orderly fashion. The **filesum** program performs the arithmetic tasks well but the report lacks an orderly format.

Awk offers an alternative to the **print** statement, **printf**, which is borrowed from the C programming language. The **printf** statement can output a simple string just like the **print** statement.

```
awk 'BEGIN { printf ("Hello, world\n") }'
```

The main difference that you will notice at the outset is that, unlike **print**, **printf** does not automatically supply a newline. You must specify it explicitly as "\n".

The full syntax of the **printf** statement has two parts:

> **printf** ( *format-expression* [, *arguments*] )

The parentheses are optional. The first part is an expression that describes the format specifications; usually this is supplied as a string constant in quotes. The second part is an argument list, such as a list of variable names, that correspond to the format specifications. A format specification is preceded by a percent sign (%) and the specifier is one of the characters shown in Table 7-6. The two main format specifiers are **s** for strings and **d** for decimal integers.[*]

*Table 7–6: Format Specifiers Used in printf*

| Character | Description |
|---|---|
| c | ASCII character |
| d | Decimal integer |
| i | Decimal integer. (Added in POSIX) |
| e | Floating-point format ([-]$d.precision$e[+-]$dd$) |
| E | Floating-point format ([-]$d.precision$E[+-]$dd$) |
| f | Floating-point format ([-]$ddd.precision$) |
| g | **e** or **f** conversion, whichever is shortest, with trailing zeros removed |
| G | **E** or **f** conversion, whichever is shortest, with trailing zeros removed |
| o | Unsigned octal value |
| s | String |
| x | Unsigned hexadecimal number. Uses **a-f** for 10 to 15 |
| X | Unsigned hexadecimal number. Uses **A-F** for 10 to 15 |
| % | Literal % |

This example uses the **printf** statement to produce the output for rule 2 in the **filesum** program. It outputs a string and a decimal value found in two different fields:

```
printf("%d\t%s\n", $5, $9)
```

---

[*] The way **printf** does rounding is discussed in Appendix B.

The value of **$5** is to be output, followed by a tab (\t) and **$9** and then a newline (\n).[*] For each format specification, you must supply a corresponding argument.

This **printf** statement can be used to specify the width and alignment of output fields. A format expression can take three optional modifiers following "%" and preceding the format specifier:

```
%-width.precision format-specifier
```

The *width* of the output field is a numeric value. When you specify a field width, the contents of the field will be right-justified by default. You must specify "-" to get left-justification. Thus, "%-20s" outputs a string left-justified in a field 20 characters wide. If the string is less than 20 characters, the field will be padded with whitespace to fill. In the following examples, a " | " is output to indicate the actual width of the field. The first example right-justifies the text:

```
printf("|%10s|\n", "hello")
```

It produces:

```
|     hello|
```

The next example left-justifies the text:

```
printf("|%-10s|\n", "hello")
```

It produces:

```
|hello     |
```

The *precision* modifier, used for decimal or floating-point values, controls the number of digits that appear to the right of the decimal point. For string values, it controls the maximum number of characters from the string that will be printed. Note that the default precision for the output of numeric values is "%.6g".

You can specify both the *width* and *precision* dynamically, via values in the **printf** or **sprintf** argument list. You do this by specifying asterisks, instead of literal values.

```
printf("%*.*g\n", 5, 3, myvar);
```

In this example, the width is 5, the precision is 3, and the value to print will come from **myvar**.

The default precision used by the **print** statement when outputting numbers can be changed by setting the system variable **OFMT**. For instance, if you are using

---

[*] Compare this statement with the **print** statement in the **filesum** program that prints the header line. The **print** statement automatically supplies a newline (the value of **ORS**); when using **printf**, you must supply the newline, it is never automatically provided for you.

awk to write reports that contain dollar values, you might prefer to change **OFMT** to "%.2f".

Using the full syntax of the format expression can solve the problem with **filesum** of getting fields and headings properly aligned. One reason we output the file size before the filename was that the fields had a greater chance of aligning themselves if they were output in that order. The solution that **printf** offers us is the ability to fix the width of output fields; therefore, each field begins in the same column.

Let's rearrange the output fields in the **filesum** report. We want a minimum field width so that the second field begins at the same position. You specify the field width place between the % and the conversion specification. "%-15s" specifies a minimum field width of 15 characters in which the value is left-justified. "%10d", without the hyphen, is right-justified, which is what we want for a decimal value.

```
printf("%-15s\t%10d\n", $9, $5)        # print filename and size
```

This will produce a report in which the data is aligned in columns and the numbers are right-justified. Look at how the **printf** statement is used in the **END** action:

```
printf("Total: %d bytes  (%d files)\n", sum, filenum)
```

The column header in the **BEGIN** rule is also changed appropriately. With the use of the **printf** statement, **filesum** now produces the following output:

```
$ filesum g*
FILE              BYTES
g                    23
gawk               2237
gawk.mail          1171
gawk.test            74
gawkro              264
gfilesum            610
grades               64
grades.awk          231
grepscript            6
Total: 4680 bytes  (9 files)
```

# Passing Parameters Into a Script

One of the more confusing subtleties of programming in awk is passing parameters into a script. A parameter assigns a value to a variable that can be accessed within the awk script. The variable can be set on the command line, after the script and before the filename.

```
awk 'script' var=value inputfile
```

Each parameter must be interpreted as a single argument. Therefore, spaces are not permitted on either side of the equal sign. Multiple parameters can be passed this way. For instance, if you wanted to define the variables **high** and **low** from the command line, you could invoke awk as follows:

```
$ awk -f scriptfile high=100 low=60 datafile
```

Inside the script, these two variables are available and can be accessed as any awk variable. If you were to put this script in a shell script wrapper, then you could pass the shell's command-line arguments as values. (The shell makes available command-line arguments in the positional variables—$1 for the first parameter, $2 for the second, and so on.)[*] For instance, look at the shell script version of the previous command:

```
awk -f scriptfile "high=$1" "low=$2" datafile
```

If this shell script were named **awket**, it could be invoked as:

```
$ awket 100 60
```

"100" would be $1 and passed as the value assigned to the variable **high**.

In addition, environment variables or the output of a command can be passed as the value of a variable. Here are two examples:

```
awk '{ ... }' directory=$cwd file1 ...
awk '{ ... }' directory=`pwd` file1 ...
```

"$cwd" returns the value of the variable **cwd**, the current working directory (**csh** only). The second example uses backquotes to execute the **pwd** command and assign its result to the variable **directory** (this is more portable).

You can also use command-line parameters to define system variables, as in the following example:

```
$ awk '{ print NR, $0 }' OFS='. ' names
1. Tom 656-5789
2. Dale 653-2133
3. Mary 543-1122
4. Joe 543-2211
```

The output field separator is redefined to be a period followed by a space.

An important restriction on command-line parameters is that they are not available in the **BEGIN** procedure. That is, they are not available until *after* the first line of input is read. Why? Well, here's the confusing part. A parameter passed from the command line is treated as though it were a filename. The assignment does not occur until the parameter, if it were a filename, is actually evaluated.

---

[*] Careful! Don't confuse the shell's parameters with awk's field variables.

Look at the following script that sets a variable *n* as a command-line parameter.

```
awk 'BEGIN { print n }
{
if (n == 1) print "Reading the first file"
if (n == 2) print "Reading the second file"
}' n=1 test n=2 test2
```

There are four command-line parameters: "n=1," "test," "n=2," and "test2". Now, if you remember that a **BEGIN** procedure is "what we do before processing input," you'll understand why the reference to *n* in the **BEGIN** procedure returns nothing. So the **print** statement will print a blank line. If the first parameter were a file and not a variable assignment, the file would not be opened until the **BEGIN** procedure had been executed.

The variable *n* is given an initial value of 1 from the first parameter. The second parameter supplies the name of the file. Thus, for each line in *test*, the conditional "n == 1" will be true. After the input is exhausted from *test*, the third parameter is evaluated, and it sets **n** to 2. Finally, the fourth parameter supplies the name of a second file. Now the conditional "n == 2" in the main procedure will be true.

One consequence of the way parameters are evaluated is that you cannot use the **BEGIN** procedure to test or verify parameters that are supplied on the command line. They are available only after a line of input has been read. You can get around this limitation by composing the rule "NR == 1" and using its procedure to verify the assignment. Another way is to test the command-line parameters in the shell script before invoking awk.

POSIX awk provides a solution to the problem of defining parameters before any input is read. The *-v* option[*] specifies variable assignments that you want to take place before executing the **BEGIN** procedure (i.e., before the first line of input is read.) The *-v* option must be specified before a command-line script. For instance, the following command uses the *-v* option to set the record separator for multiline records.

```
$ awk -F"\n" -v RS="" '{ print }' phones.block
```

A separate *-v* option is required for each variable assignment that is passed to the program.

Awk also provides the system variables **ARGC** and **ARGV**, which will be familiar to C programmers. Because this requires an understanding of arrays, we will discuss this feature in Chapter 8, *Conditionals, Loops, and Arrays*.

---

[*] The *-v* option was not part of the original (1987) version of nawk (still used on SunOS 4.1.x systems and some System V Release 3.x systems). It was added in 1989 after Brian Kernighan of Bell Labs, the GNU awk authors, and the authors of MKS awk agreed on a way to set variables on the command line that would be available inside the **BEGIN** block. It is now part of the POSIX specification for awk.

# *Information Retrieval*

An awk program can be used to retrieve information from a database, the database basically being any kind of text file. The more structured the text file, the easier it is to work with, although the structure might be no more than a line consisting of individual words.

The list of acronyms below is a simple database.

```
$ cat acronyms
BASIC    Beginner's All-Purpose Symbolic Instruction Code
CICS     Customer Information Control System
COBOL    Common Business Oriented Language
DBMS     Data Base Management System
GIGO     Garbage In, Garbage Out
GIRL     Generalized Information Retrieval Language
```

A tab is used as the field separator. We're going to look at a program that takes an acronym as input and displays the appropriate line from the database as output. (In the next chapter, we're going to look at two other programs that use the acronym database. One program reads the list of acronyms and then finds occurrences of these acronyms in another file. The other program locates the first occurrence of these acronyms in a text file and inserts the description of the acronym.)

The shell script that we develop is named **acro**. It takes the first argument from the command line (the name of the acronym) and passes it to the awk script. The **acro** script follows:

```
$ cat acro
#! /bin/sh
# assign shell's $1 to awk search variable
awk '$1 == search' search=$1 acronyms
```

The first argument specified on the shell command line ($1) is assigned to the variable named **search**; this variable is passed as a parameter into the awk program. Parameters passed to an awk program are specified *after* the script section. (This gets somewhat confusing, because **$1** inside the awk program represents the first field of each input line, while **$1** in the shell represents the first argument supplied on the command line.)

The example below demonstrates how this program can be used to find a particular acronym on our list.

```
$ acro CICS
CICS Customer Information Control System
```

Notice that we tested the parameter as a string (**$1 == search**). We could also have written this as a regular expression match (**$1 ˜ search**).

## Finding a Glitch

A net posting was once forwarded to one of us because it contained a problem that could be solved using awk. Here's the original posting by Emmett Hogan:

> I have been trying to rewrite a sed/tr/fgrep script that we use quite
> a bit here in Perl, but have thus far been unsuccessful...hence this
> posting.  Having never written anything in perl, and not wishing to
> wait for the Nutshell Perl Book, I figured I'd tap the knowledge of this
> group.
>
> Basically, we have several files which have the format:
>
> item      info line 1
>           info line 2
>             .
>             .
>             .
>           info line n
>
> Where each info line refers to the item and is indented by either
> spaces or tabs.  Each item "block" is separated by a blank line.
>
> What I need to do, is to be able to type:
>
> info glitch filename
>
> Where info is the name of the perl script, glitch is what I want to
> find out about, and filename is the name of the file with the
> information in it.  The catch is that I need it to print the entire
> "block" if it finds glitch anywhere in the file, i.e.:
>
> machine           Sun 3/75
>                   8 meg memory
>                   Prone to memory glitches
>                   more info
>                   more info
>
> would get printed if you looked for "glitch" along with any other
> "blocks" which contained the word glitch.
>
> Currently we are using the following script:
>
> ```
> #!/bin/csh -f
> #
> sed '/^ /\!s/^/@/' $2 | tr '\012@' '@\012' | fgrep -i $1 | tr '@' '\012'
> ```
>
> Which is in a word....SLOW.
>
> I am sure Perl can do it faster, better, etc...but I cannot figure it out.
>
> Any, and all, help is greatly appreciated.

```
Thanks in advance,
Emmett


-------------------------------------------------------------------
Emmett Hogan              Computer Science Lab, SRI International
```

The problem yielded a solution based on awk. You may want to try to tackle the problem yourself before reading any further. The solution relies on awk's multiline record capability and requires that you be able to pass the search string as a command-line parameter.

Here's the **info** script using awk:

```
awk 'BEGIN { FS = "\n"; RS = "" }
$0 ~ search { print $0 }' search=$1 $2
```

Given a test file with multiple entries, **info** was tested to see if it could find the word "glitch."

```
$ info glitch glitch.test
machine          Sun 3/75
                 8 meg memory
                 Prone to memory glitches
                 more info
                 more info
```

In the next chapter, we look at conditional and looping constructs, and arrays.

# 8

# *Conditionals, Loops, and Arrays*

This chapter covers some fundamental programming constructs. It covers all the control statements in the awk programming language. It also covers arrays, variables that allow you to store a series of values. If this is your first exposure to such constructs, you'll recognize that even sed provided conditional and looping capabilities. In awk, these capabilities are much more generalized and the syntax is much easier to use. In fact, the syntax of awk's conditional and looping constructs is borrowed from the C programming language. Thus, by learning awk and the constructs in this chapter, you are also on the way to learning the C language.

## *Conditional Statements*

A conditional statement allows you to make a test before performing an action. In the previous chapter, we saw examples of pattern matching rules that were essentially conditional expressions affecting the main input loop. In this section, we look at conditional statements used primarily within actions.

A conditional statement is introduced by **if** and evaluates an expression placed in parentheses. The syntax is:

```
if ( expression )
    action1
[else
    action2]
```

If *expression* evaluates as true (non-zero or non-empty), *action1* is performed. When an **else** clause is specified, *action2* is performed if *expression* evaluates to false (zero or empty). An expression might contain the arithmetic, relational, or Boolean operators discussed in Chapter 7, *Writing Scripts for awk.*

Perhaps the simplest conditional expression that you could write is one that tests whether a variable contains a non-zero value.

```
if ( x ) print x
```

If **x** is zero, the **print** statement will not be executed. If **x** has a non-zero value, that value will be printed. You can also test whether **x** equals another value:

```
if ( x == y ) print x
```

Remember that "==" is a relational operator and "=" is an assignment operator. We can also test whether **x** matches a pattern using the pattern-matching operator "~":

```
if ( x ~ /[yY](es)?/ ) print x
```

Here are a few additional syntactical points:

- If any action consists of more than one statement, the action is enclosed within a pair of braces.

  ```
  if ( expression ) {
      statement1
      statement2
  }
  ```

  Awk is not very particular about the placement of braces and statements (unlike sed). The opening brace is placed after the conditional expression, either on the same line or on the next line. The first statement can follow the opening brace or be placed on the line following it. The closing brace is put after the last statement, either on the same line or after it. Spaces or tabs are allowed before or after the braces. The indentation of statements is not required but is recommended to improve readability.

- A newline is optional after the close parenthesis, and after **else**.

  ```
  if ( expression ) action1
  [else action2]
  ```

- A newline is also optional after *action1*, providing that a semicolon ends *action1*.

  ```
  if ( expression ) action1; [else action2]
  ```

- You cannot avoid using braces by using semicolons to separate multiple statements on a single line.

In the previous chapter, we saw a script that averaged student grades. We could use a conditional statement to tell us whether the student passed or failed.

Presuming that an average of 65 or above is a passing grade, we could write the following conditional:

```
if ( avg >= 65 )
        grade = "Pass"
else
        grade = "Fail"
```

The value assigned to **grade** depends upon whether the expression "avg >= 65" evaluates to true or false.

Multiple conditional statements can be used to test whether one of several possible conditions is true. For example, perhaps the students are given a letter grade instead of a pass-fail mark. Here's a conditional that assigns a letter grade based on a student's average:

```
if (avg >= 90)  grade = "A"
else if (avg >= 80) grade = "B"
else if (avg >= 70) grade = "C"
else if (avg >= 60) grade = "D"
else grade = "F"
```

The important thing to recognize is that successive conditionals like this are evaluated until one of them returns true; once that occurs, the rest of the conditionals are skipped. If none of the conditional expressions evaluates to true, the last **else** is accepted, constituting the default action; in this case, it assigns "F" to **grade**.

### Conditional Operator

Awk provides a conditional operator that is found in the C programming language. Its form is:

> *expr* ? *action1* : *action2*

The previous simple **if/else** condition can be written using a conditional operator:

```
grade = (avg >= 65) ? "Pass" : "Fail"
```

This form has the advantage of brevity and is appropriate for simple conditionals such as the one shown here. While the ?: operator can be nested, doing so leads to programs that quickly become unreadable. For clarity, we recommend parenthesizing the conditional, as shown above.

# Looping

A loop is a construct that allows us to perform one or more actions again and again. In awk, a loop can be specified using a **while**, **do**, or **for** statement.

## While Loop

The syntax of a **while** loop is:

> **while** (*condition*)
>     *action*

The newline is optional after the right parenthesis. The conditional expression is evaluated at the top of the loop and, if true, the action is performed. If the expression is never true, the action is not performed. Typically, the conditional expression evaluates to true and the action changes a value such that the conditional expression eventually returns false and the loop is exited. For instance, if you wanted to perform an action four times, you could write the following loop:

```
i = 1
while ( i <= 4 ) {
        print $i
        ++i
}
```

As in an **if** statement, an action consisting of more than one statement must be enclosed in braces. Note the role of each statement. The first statement assigns an initial value to i. The expression "i <= 4" compares i to 4 to determine if the action should be executed. The action consists of two statements, one that simply prints the value of a field referenced as "$i" and another that increments i. i is a counter variable and is used to keep track of how many times we go through the loop. If we did not increment the counter variable or if the comparison would never evaluate to false (e.g., i > 0), then the action would be repeated without end.

## Do Loop

The **do** loop is a variation of the **while** loop. The syntax of a **do** loop is:

> **do**
>     *action*
> **while** (*condition*)

The newline is optional after **do**. It is also optional after *action* providing the statement is terminated by a semicolon. The main feature of this loop is that the conditional expression appears *after* the action. Thus, the action is performed at least once. Look at the following **do** loop.

```
BEGIN {
        do {
                ++x
                print x
        } while ( x <= 4 )
}
```

In this example, the value of **x** is set in the body of the loop using the auto-increment operator. The body of the loop is executed once and the expression is evaluated. In the previous example of a **while** loop, the initial value of **i** was set before the loop. The expression was evaluated first, then the body of the loop was executed once. Note the value of **x** when we run this example:

```
$ awk -f do.awk
1
2
3
4
5
```

Before the conditional expression is first evaluated, **x** is incremented to 1. (This relies on the fact that all awk variables are initialized to zero.) The body of the loop is executed five times, not four; when **x** equals 4, the conditional expression is true and the body of the loop is executed again, incrementing **x** to 5 and printing its value. Only then is the conditional expression evaluated to false and the loop exited. By changing the operator from "<=" to "<", or less than, the body of the loop will be executed four times.

To keep in mind the difference between the **do** loop and the **while** loop, remember that the **do** loop always executes the body of the loop *at least once*. At the bottom of the procedure, you decide if you need to execute it again.

For an example, let's look at a program that loops through the fields of a record, referencing as many fields as necessary until their cumulative value exceeds 100. The reason we use a **do** loop is that we will reference at least one of the fields. We add the value of the field to the total, and if the total exceeds 100 we don't reference any other fields. We reference the second field only if the first field is less than 100. Its value is added to the total and if the total exceeds 100 then we exit the loop. If it is still less than 100, we execute the loop once again.

```
{
        total = i = 0
        do {
                ++i
                total += $i
        } while ( total <= 100 )
        print i, ":", total
}
```

The first line of the script initializes the values of two variables: **total** and **i**. The loop increments the value of **i** and uses the field operator to reference a particular field. Each time through the loop, it refers to a different field. When the loop is executed for the first time, the field reference gets the value of field one and assigns it to the variable **total**. The conditional expression at the end of the loop evaluates whether **total** exceeds 100. If it does, the loop is exited. Then the value of i, the number of fields that we've referred to, and the total are printed. (This script assumes that each record totals at least 100; otherwise, we'd have to check that i does not exceed the number of fields for the record. We construct such a test in the example presented in next section to show the **for** loop.)

Here's a test file containing a series of numbers:

```
$ cat test.do
45 25 60 20
10 105 50 40
33 5 9 67
108 3 5 4
```

Running the script on the test file produces the following:

```
$ awk -f do.awk test.do
3 : 130
2 : 115
4 : 114
1 : 108
```

For each record, only as many fields are referenced as needed for the total to exceed 100.

## For Loop

The **for** statement offers a more compact syntax that achieves the same result as a **while** loop. Although it looks more difficult, this syntax is much easier to use and makes sure that you provide all the required elements of a loop. The syntax of a **for** loop is:

> **for** ( *set_counter* ; *test_counter* ; *increment_counter* )
>     *action*

The newline after the right parenthesis is optional. The **for** loop consists of three expressions:

*set_counter*
> Sets the initial value for a counter variable.

*test_counter*
> States a condition that is tested at the top of the loop.

*increment_counter*
> Increments the counter each time at the bottom of the loop, right before testing the *test_counter* again.

Look at this rather common **for** loop that prints each field on the input line.

```
for ( i = 1; i <= NF; i++ )
        print $i
```

As in the previous example, i is a variable that is used to reference a field using the field operator. The system variable **NF** contains the number of fields for the current input record, and we test it to determine if i has reached the last field on the line. The value of **NF** is the maximum number of times to go through the loop. Inside the loop, the **print** statement is executed, printing each field on its own line. A script using this construct can print each word on a line by itself, which can then be run through **sort | uniq -c** to get word distribution statistics for a file.

You can also write a loop to print from the last field to the first.

```
for ( i = NF; i >= 1; i-- )
        print $i
```

Each time through the loop the counter is decremented. You could use this to reverse the order of fields.

The **grades.awk** script that we showed earlier determined the average of five grades. We can make the script much more useful by averaging any number of grades. That is, if you were to run this script throughout the school year, the number of grades to average would increase. Rather than revising the script to accommodate the specific number of fields, we can write a generalized script that loops to read however many fields there are. Our earlier version of the program calculated the average of 5 grades using these two statements:

```
total = $2 + $3 + $4 + $5 + $6
avg = total / 5
```

We can revise that using a **for** loop to sum each field in the record.

```
total = 0
for (i = 2; i <= NF; ++i)
        total += $i
avg = total / (NF - 1)
```

We initialize the variable **total** each time because we don't want its value to accumulate from one record to the next. At the beginning of the **for** loop, the counter i is initialized to 2 because the first numeric field is field 2. Each time through the loop the value of the current field is added to **total**. When the last field has been referenced (i is greater than **NF**), we break out of the loop and calculate the average. For instance, if the record consists of 4 fields, the first time through the loop, we assign the value of $2 to **total**. At the bottom of the loop, i is incremented by 1, then compared to **NF**, which is 4. The expression evaluates to true and **total** is incremented by the value of $3.

Notice how we divide the total by the number of fields minus 1 to remove the student name from the count. The parentheses are required around "NF - 1" because the precedence of operators would otherwise divide **total** by **NF** and then subtract 1, instead of subtracting 1 from **NF** first.

## *Deriving Factorials*

The factorial of a number is the product of successively multiplying that number by one less than that number. The factorial of 4 is $4 \times 3 \times 2 \times 1$, or 24. The factorial of 5 is 5 times the factorial of 4 or $5 \times 24$, or 120. Deriving a factorial for a given number can be expressed using a loop as follows:

```
fact = number
for (x = number - 1 ; x > 1; x--)
        fact *= x
```

where **number** is the number for which we will derive the factorial **fact**. Let's say that **number** equals 5. The first time through the loop **x** is equal to 4. The action evaluates "5 * 4" and assigns the value to **fact**. The next time through the loop, **x** is 3 and 20 is multiplied by it. We go through the loop until **x** equals 1.

Here is the above fragment incorporated into a standalone script that prompts the user for a number and then prints the factorial of that number.

```
awk '# factorial: return factorial of user-supplied number
BEGIN {
        # prompt user; use printf, not print, to avoid the newline
        printf("Enter number: ")
}

# check that user enters a number
$1 ~ /^[0-9]+$/ {
        # assign value of $1 to number & fact
        number = $1
        if (number == 0)
                fact = 1
        else
                fact = number
        # loop to multiply fact*x until x = 1
        for (x = number - 1; x > 1; x--)
                fact *= x
        printf("The factorial of %d is %g\n", number, fact)
        # exit -- saves user from typing CRTL-D.
        exit
}

# if not a number, prompt again.
{ printf("\nInvalid entry. Enter a number: ")
}' -
```

This is an interesting example of a main input loop that prompts for input and reads the reply from standard input. The **BEGIN** rule is used to prompt the user to enter a number. Because we have specified that input is to come not from a file but from standard input, the program will halt after putting out the prompt and then wait for the user to type a number. The first rule checks that a number has been entered. If not, the second rule will be applied, prompting the user again to re-enter a number. We set up an input loop that will continue to read from standard input until a valid entry is found. See the **lookup** program in the next section for another example of constructing an input loop.

Here's an example of how the **factorial** program works:

```
$ factorial
Enter number: 5
The factorial of 5 is 120
```

Note that the result uses "%g" as the conversion specification format in the **printf** statement. This permits floating point notation to be used to express very large numbers. Look at the following example:

```
$ factorial
Enter number: 33
The factorial of 33 is 8.68332e+36
```

# *Other Statements That Affect Flow Control*

The **if**, **while**, **for**, and **do** statements allow you to change the normal flow through a procedure. In this section, we look at several other statements that also affect a change in flow control.

There are two statements that affect the flow control of a loop, **break** and **continue**. The **break** statement, as you'd expect, breaks out of the loop, such that no more iterations of the loop are performed. The **continue** statement stops the current iteration before reaching the bottom of the loop and starts a new iteration at the top.

Consider what happens in the following program fragment:

```
for ( x = 1; x <= NF; ++x )
        if ( y == $x ) {
                print x, $x
                break
        }
print
```

A loop is set up to examine each field of the current input record. Each time through the loop, the value of **y** is compared to the value of a field referenced as

**$x**. If the result is true, we print the field number and its value and then break from the loop. The next statement to be executed is **print**. The use of **break** means that we are interested only in the first match on a line and that we don't want to loop through the rest of the fields.

Here's a similar example using the **continue** statement:

```
for ( x = 1; x <= NF; ++x ) {
        if ( x == 3 )
                continue
        print x, $x
}
```

This example loops through the fields of the current input record, printing the field number and its value. However (for some reason), we want to avoid printing the third field. The conditional statement tests the counter variable and if it is equal to 3, the **continue** statement is executed. The **continue** statement passes control back to the top of the loop where the counter variable is incremented again. It avoids executing the **print** statement for that iteration. The same result could be achieved by simply re-writing the conditional to execute **print** as long as **x** is not equal to 3. The point is that you can use the **continue** statement to avoid hitting the bottom of the loop on a particular iteration.

There are two statements that affect the main input loop, **next** and **exit**. The **next** statement causes the next line of input to be read and then resumes execution at the top of the script.[*] This allows you to avoid applying other procedures on the current input line. A typical use of the **next** statement is to continue reading input from a file, ignoring the other actions in the script until that file is exhausted. The system variable **FILENAME** provides the name of the current input file. Thus, a pattern can be written:

```
FILENAME == "acronyms" {
        action
        next
}
{ print }
```

This causes the action to be performed for each line in the file *acronyms*. After the action is performed, the next line of input is read. Control does not pass to the **print** statement until the input is taken from a different source.

The **exit** statement exits the main input loop and passes control to the END rule, if there is one. If the END rule is not defined, or the **exit** statement is used in the END rule, then the script terminates. We used the **exit** statement earlier in the **factorial** program to exit after reading one line of input.

---

[*] Some awks don't allow you to use **next** from within a user-defined function; Caveat emptor.

An **exit** statement can take an expression as an argument. The value of this expression will be returned as the exit status of awk. If the expression is not supplied, the exit status is 0. If you supply a value to an initial **exit** statement, and then call **exit** again from the **END** rule without a value, the first value is used. For example:

```
awk '{
        ...
        exit 5
}
END { exit }'
```

Here, the exit status from awk will be 5.

You will come across examples that use these flow-control statements in upcoming sections.

## *Arrays*

An array is a variable that can be used to store a set of values. Usually the values are related in some way. Individual elements are accessed by their *index* in the array. Each index is enclosed in square brackets. The following statement assigns a value to an element of an array:

```
array[subscript] = value
```

In awk, you don't have to declare the size of the array; you only have to use the identifier as an array. This is best done by assigning a value to an array element. For instance, the following example assigns the string **"cherry"** to an element of the array named **flavor**.

```
flavor[1] = "cherry"
```

The index or subscript of this element of the array is "1". The following statement prints the string "cherry":

```
print flavor[1]
```

Loops can be used to load and extract elements from arrays. For instance, if the array **flavor** has five elements, you can write a loop to print each element:

```
flavor_count = 5
for (x = 1; x <= flavor_count; ++x)
        print flavor[x]
```

One way that arrays are used in awk is to store a value from each record, using the record number as the index to the array. Let's suppose we wanted to keep track of the averages calculated for each student and come up with a class average. Each time a record is read we make the following assignment.

```
student_avg[NR] = avg
```

The system variable **NR** is used as the subscript for the array because it is incremented for each record. When the first record is read, the value of **avg** is placed in **student_avg[1]**; for the second record, the value is placed in **student_avg[2]**, and so on. After we have read all of the records, we have a list of averages in the array **student_avg**. In an **END** rule, we can average all of these grades by writing a loop to get the total of the grades and then dividing it by the value of **NR**. Then we can compare each student average to the class average to collect totals for the number of students at or above average and the number below.

```
END {
        for ( x = 1; x <= NR; x++ )
                class_avg_total += student_avg[x]

        class_average = class_avg_total / NR

        for ( x = 1; x <= NR; x++ )
                if (student_avg[x] >= class_average)
                        ++above_average
                else
                        ++below_average

        print "Class Average: ", class_average
        print "At or Above Average: ", above_average
        print "Below Average: ", below_average
}
```

There are two **for** loops for accessing the elements of the array. The first one totals the averages so that it can be divided by the number of student records. The next loop retrieves each student average so that it can be compared to the class average. If it is at or above average, we increment the variable **above_average**; otherwise, we increment **below_average**.

## Associative Arrays

In awk, all arrays are *associative* arrays. What makes an associative array unique is that its index can be a string or a number.

In most programming languages, the indices of arrays are exclusively numeric. In these implementations, an array is a sequence of locations where values are stored. The indices of the array are derived from the order in which the values are stored. There is no need to keep track of indices. For instance, the index of the first element of an array is "1" or the first location in the array.

An associative array makes an "association" between the indices and the elements of an array. For each element of the array, a pair of values is maintained: the index of the element and the value of the element. The elements are not stored in any particular order as in a conventional array. Thus, even though you can use numeric subscripts in awk, the numbers do not have the same meaning that they do in other programming languages—they do not necessarily refer to sequential locations. However, with numeric indices, you can still access all the elements of an array in sequence, as we did in previous examples. You can create a loop to increment a counter that references the elements of the array in order.

Sometimes, the distinction between numeric and string indices is important. For instance, if you use "04" as the index to an element of the array, you cannot reference that element using "4" as its subscript. You'll see how to handle this problem in a sample program **date-month**, shown later in this chapter.

Associative arrays are a distinctive feature of awk, and a very powerful one that allows you to use a string as an index to another value. For instance, you could use a word as the index to its definition. If you know the word, you can retrieve the definition.

For example, you could use the first field of the input line as the index to the second field with the following assignment:

```
array[$1] = $2
```

Using this technique, we could take our list of acronyms and load it into an array named **acro**.

```
acro[$1] = $2
```

Each element of the array would be the description of an acronym and the subscript used to retrieve the element would be the acronym itself. The following expression:

```
acro["BASIC"]
```

produces:

```
Beginner's All-Purpose Symbolic Instruction Code
```

There is a special looping syntax for accessing all the elements of an associative array. It is a version of the **for** loop.

```
for ( variable in array )
        do something with array[variable]
```

The *array* is the name of an array, as it was defined. The *variable* is any variable, which you can think of as a temporary variable similar to a counter that is incremented in a conventional **for** loop. This variable is set to a particular subscript each time through the loop. (Because *variable* is an arbitrary name, you often see **item** used, regardless of what variable name was used for the subscript when the array was loaded.) For example, the following **for** loop prints the name of the acronym **item** and the definition referenced by that name, **acro[item]**.

```
for ( item in acro )
        print item, acro[item]
```

In this example, the print statement prints the current subscript ("BASIC," for instance) followed by the element of the **acro** array referenced by the subscript ("Beginner's All-Purpose Symbolic Instruction Code").

This syntax can be applied to arrays with numeric subscripts. However, the order in which the items are retrieved is somewhat random.[*] The order is very likely to vary among awk implementations; be careful to write your programs so that they don't depend on any one version of awk.

It is important to remember that all array indices in awk are strings. Even when you use a number as an index, awk automatically converts it to a string first. You don't have to worry about this when you use integer indices, since they get converted to strings as integers, no matter what the value may be of **OFMT** (original awk and earlier versions of new awk) or **CONVFMT** (POSIX awk). But if you use a real number as an index, the number to string conversion might affect you. For instance:

```
$ gawk 'BEGIN { data[1.23] = "3.21"; CONVFMT = "%d"
> printf "<%s>\n", data[1.23] }'
<>
```

Here, nothing was printed between the angle brackets, since the second time, **1.23** was converted to just **1**, and **data["1"]** has the empty string as its value.

---

*NOTE*       Not all implementations of awk get the number to string conversion right when **CONVFMT** has changed between one use of a number and the next. Test the above example with your awk to be sure it works correctly.

---

Now let's return to our student grade program for an example. Let's say that we wanted to report how many students got an "A," how many got a "B," and so on. Once we determine the grade, we could increment a counter for that grade. We

---

[*] The technical term used in *The AWK Programming Language* is "implementation dependent."

could set up individual variables for each letter grade and then test which one to increment.

```
if ( grade == "A" )
        ++gradeA
else if (grade == "B" )
        ++gradeB
    .
    .
    .
```

However, an array makes this task much easier. We can define an array called **class_grade**, and simply use the letter grade (A through F) as the index to the array.

```
++class_grade[grade]
```

Thus, if the grade is an "A" then the value of **class_grade["A"]** is incremented by one. At the end of the program, we can print out these values in the **END** rule using the special **for** loop:

```
for (letter_grade in class_grade)
        print letter_grade ":", class_grade[letter_grade] | "sort"
```

The variable **letter_grade** references a single subscript of the array **class_grade** each time through the loop. The output is piped to **sort**, to make sure the grades come out in the proper order. (Piping output to programs is discussed in Chapter 10, *The Bottom Drawer.*) Since this is the last addition we make to the **grades.awk** script, we can look at the full listing.

```
# grades.awk -- average student grades and determine
# letter grade as well as class averages.
# $1 = student name; $2 - $NF = test scores.

# set output field separator to tab.
BEGIN { OFS = "\t" }

# action applied to all input lines
{
  # add up grades
        total = 0
        for (i = 2; i <= NF; ++i)
                total += $i
  # calculate average
        avg = total / (NF - 1)
  # assign student's average to element of array
        student_avg[NR] = avg
  # determine letter grade
        if (avg >= 90)  grade = "A"
        else if (avg >= 80) grade = "B"
        else if (avg >= 70) grade = "C"
        else if (avg >= 60) grade = "D"
        else grade = "F"
```

```
            # increment counter for letter grade array
                    ++class_grade[grade]
            # print student name, average and letter grade
                    print $1, avg, grade
        }
        # print out class statistics
        END {
            # calculate class average
                    for (x = 1; x <= NR; x++)
                            class_avg_total += student_avg[x]
                    class_average = class_avg_total / NR
            # determine how many above/below average
                    for (x = 1; x <= NR; x++)
                            if (student_avg[x] >= class_average)
                                    ++above_average
                            else
                                    ++below_average
            # print results
                    print ""
                    print "Class Average: ", class_average
                    print "At or Above Average: ", above_average
                    print "Below Average: ", below_average
            # print number of students per letter grade
                    for (letter_grade in class_grade)
                            print letter_grade ":", class_grade[letter_grade] | "sort"
        }
```

Here's a sample run:

```
$ cat grades.test
mona 70 77 85 83 70 89
john 85 92 78 94 88 91
andrea 89 90 85 94 90 95
jasper 84 88 80 92 84 82
dunce 64 80 60 60 61 62
ellis 90 98 89 96 96 92
$ awk -f grades.awk grades.test
mona     79      C
john     88      B
andrea   90.5    A
jasper   85      B
dunce    64.5    D
ellis    93.5    A

Class Average:  83.4167
At or Above Average:    4
Below Average: 2
A:      2
B:      2
C:      1
D:      1
```

## Testing for Membership in an Array

The keyword **in** is also an operator that can be used in a conditional expression to test that a subscript is a *member* of an array. The expression:

```
item in array
```

returns 1 if **array[item]** exists and 0 if it does not. For example, the following conditional statement is true if the string "BASIC" is a subscript of the array **acro**.

```
if ( "BASIC" in acro )
       print "Found BASIC"
```

This is true if "BASIC" is a subscript used to access an element of **acro**. This syntax cannot tell you whether "BASIC" is the value of an element of **acro**. This expression is the same as writing a loop to check that such a subscript exists, although the above expression is much easier to write, and much more efficient to execute.

## A Glossary Lookup Script

This program reads a series of glossary entries from a file named *glossary* and puts them into an array. The user is prompted to enter a glossary term and if it is found, the definition of the term is printed.

Here's the **lookup** program:

```
awk '# lookup -- reads local glossary file and prompts user for query

#0
BEGIN { FS = "\t"; OFS = "\t"
        # prompt user
        printf("Enter a glossary term: ")
}

#1 read local file named glossary
FILENAME == "glossary" {
        # load each glossary entry into an array
        entry[$1] = $2
        next
}

#2 scan for command to exit program
$0 ~ /^(quit|[qQ]|exit|[Xx])$/ { exit }

#3 process any non-empty line
$0 != "" {
        if ( $0 in entry ) {
                # it is there, print definition
                print entry[$0]
        } else
                print $0 " not found"
}
```

```
#4 prompt user again for another term
{
        printf("Enter another glossary term (q to quit): ")
}' glossary -
```

The pattern-matching rules are numbered to make this discussion easier. As we look at the individual rules, we'll discuss them in the order in which they are encountered in the flow of the script. Rule #0 is the **BEGIN** rule, which is performed only once before any input is read. It sets **FS** and **OFS** to a tab and then prompts the user to enter a glossary item. The response will come from standard input, but that is read after the *glossary* file.

Rule #1 tests to see if the current filename (the value of **FILENAME**) is "glossary" and is therefore only applied while reading input from this file. This rule loads the glossary entries into an array:

```
entry[term] = definition
```

where $1 is the term and $2 is the definition. The **next** statement at the end of rule #1 is used to skip other rules in the script and causes a new line of input to be read. So, until all the entries in the *glossary* file are read, no other rule is evaluated.

Once input from *glossary* is exhausted, awk reads from standard input because "-" is specified on the command line. Standard input is where the user's response comes from. Rule #3 tests that the input line ($0) is not empty. This rule should match whatever the user types. The action uses **in** to see if the input line is an index in the array. If it is, it simply prints out the corresponding value. Otherwise, we tell the user that no valid entry was found.

After rule #3, rule #4 will be evaluated. This rule simply prompts the user for another entry. Note that regardless of whether a valid entry was processed in rule #3, rule #4 is executed. The prompt also tells the user how to quit the program. After this rule, awk looks for the next line of input.

If the user chooses to quit by entering "q" as the next line of input, rule #2 will be matched. The pattern looks for a complete line consisting of alternative words or single letters that the user might enter to quit. The "^" and "$" are important, signifying that the input line contains no other characters but these; otherwise a "q" appearing in a glossary entry would be matched. Note that the placement of this rule in the sequence of rules is significant. It must appear before rules #3 and #4 because these rules will match anything, including the words "quit" and "exit."

Let's look at how the program works. For this example, we will make a copy of the *acronyms* file and use it as the *glossary* file.

```
$ cp acronyms glossary
$ lookup
Enter a glossary term: GIGO
Garbage in, garbage out
Enter another glossary term (q to quit): BASIC
Beginner's All-Purpose Symbolic Instruction Code
Enter another glossary term (q to quit): q
```

As you can see, the program is set up to prompt the user for additional items until the user enters "q".

Note that this program can be easily revised to read a glossary anywhere on the file system, including the user's home directory. The shell script that invokes awk could handle command-line options that allow the user to specify the glossary filename. You could also read a shared glossary file and then read a local one by writing separate rules to process the entries.

## Using split() to Create Arrays

The built-in function **split()** can parse any string into elements of an array. This function can be useful to extract "subfields" from a field. The syntax of the **split()** function is:

```
n = split(string, array, separator)
```

*string* is the input string to be parsed into elements of the named *array*. The array's indices start at 1 and go to *n*, the number of elements in the array. The elements will be split based on the specified *separator* character. If a separator is not specified, then the field separator (**FS**) is used. The *separator* can be a full regular expression, not just a single character. Array splitting behaves identically to field splitting; see the section "Referencing and Separating Fields" in Chapter 7.

For example, if you had a record in which the first field consisted of the person's full name, you could use the **split()** function to extract the person's first and last names. The following statement breaks up the first field into elements of the array **fullname**:

```
z = split($1, fullname, " ")
```

A space is specified as the delimiter. The person's first name can be referenced as:

```
fullname[1]
```

and the person's last name can be referenced as:

```
fullname[z]
```

because **z** contains the number of elements in the array. This works, regardless of whether the person's full name contains a middle name. If **z** is the value returned by **split()**, you can write a loop to read all the elements of this array.

```
z = split($1, array, " ")
for (i = 1; i <= z; ++i)
        print i, array[i]
```

The next section contains additional examples of using the **split( )** function.

## Making Conversions

This section looks at two examples that demonstrate similar methods of converting output from one format to another.

When working on the index program shown in Chapter 12, *Full-Featured Applications*, we needed a quick way to assign roman numerals to volume numbers. In other words, volume 4 needed to be identified as "IV" in the index. Since there was no immediate prospect of the number of volumes exceeding 10, we wrote a script that took as input a number between 1 and 10 and converted it to a roman numeral.

This shell script takes the first argument from the command line and echoes it as input to the awk program.

```
echo $1 |
awk '# romanum -- convert number 1-10 to roman numeral

# define numerals as list of roman numerals 1-10
BEGIN {
        # create array named numerals from list of roman numberals
        split("I,II,III,IV,V,VI,VII,VIII,IX,X", numerals, ",")
}

# look for number between 1 and 10
$1 > 0 && $1 <= 10 {
        # print specified element
        print numerals[$1]
        exit
}

{       print "invalid number"
        exit
}'
```

This script defines a list of 10 roman numerals, then uses **split( )** to load them into an array named **numerals**. This is done in the **BEGIN** action because it only needs to be done once.

The second rule checks that the first field of the input line contains a number between 1 and 10. If it does, this number is used as the index to the **numerals** array, retrieving the corresponding element. The **exit** statement terminates the program. The last rule is executed only if there is no valid entry.

Here's an example of how it works:

```
$ romanum 4
IV
```

Following along on the same idea, here's a script that converts dates in the form "mm-dd-yy" or "mm/dd/yy" to "month day, year."

```
awk '
# date-month -- convert mm/dd/yy or mm-dd-yy to month day, year

# build list of months and put in array.
BEGIN {
        # the 3-step assignment is done for printing in book
        listmonths = "January,February,March,April,May,June,"
        listmonths = listmonths "July,August,September,"
        listmonths = listmonths "October,November,December"
        split(listmonths, month, ",")
}

# check that there is input
$1 != "" {

# split on "/" the first input field into elements of array
        sizeOfArray = split($1, date, "/")

# check that only one field is returned
        if (sizeOfArray == 1)
                # try to split on "-"
                sizeOfArray = split($1, date, "-")

# must be invalid
        if (sizeOfArray == 1)
                exit

# add 0 to number of month to coerce numeric type
        date[1] += 0

# print month day, year
        print month[date[1]], (date[2] ", 19" date[3])
}'
```

This script reads from standard input. The **BEGIN** action creates an array named **month** whose elements are the names of the months of the year. The second rule verifies that we have a non-empty input line. The first statement in the associated action splits the first field of input looking for "/" as the delimiter. **sizeOfArray** contains the number of elements in the array. If awk was unable to parse the string, it creates the array with only one element. Thus, we can test the value of **sizeOfArray** to determine if we have several elements. If we do not, we assume that perhaps "-" was used as the delimiter. If that fails to produce an array with multiple elements, we assume the input is invalid, and exit. If we have successfully parsed the input, **date[1]** contains the number of the month. This value can be used as the index to the array **month**, nesting one array inside another. However, before using **date[1]**, we coerce the type of **date[1]** by adding 0 to it. While awk will correctly interpret "11" as a number, leading zeros may cause a number to be treated as a string. Thus, "06" might not be recognized properly without type coercion. The element referenced by **date[1]** is used as the subscript for **month**.

Here's a sample run:

```
$ echo "5/11/55" | date-month
May 11, 1955
```

## Deleting Elements of an Array

Awk provides a statement for deleting an element of an array. The syntax is:

delete *array*[*subscript*]

The brackets are required. This statement removes the element indexed by *subscript* from *array*. In particular, the **in** test for *subscript* will now return false. This is different than just assigning the empty string to that element; in that case **in** would still be true. See the **lotto** script in the next chapter for an example of using the **delete** statement.

# An Acronym Processor

Now let's look at a program that scans a file for acronyms. Each acronym is replaced with a full text description, and the acronym in parentheses. If a line refers to "BASIC," we'd like to replace it with the description "Beginner's All-Purpose Symbolic Instruction Code" and put the acronym in parentheses afterwards. (This is probably not a useful program in and of itself, but the techniques used in the program are general and have many such uses.)

We can design this program for use as a *filter* that prints all lines, regardless of whether a change has been made. We'll call it **awkro**.

```
awk '# awkro - expand acronyms
# load acronyms file into array "acro"
FILENAME == "acronyms" {
        split($0, entry, "\t")
        acro[entry[1]] = entry[2]
        next
}

# process any input line containing caps
/[A-Z][A-Z]+/ {
```

```
        # see if any field is an acronym
        for (i = 1; i <= NF; i++)
                if ( $i in acro ) {
                        # if it matches, add description
                        $i = acro[$i] " (" $i ")"
                }
}


{
        # print all lines
        print $0
}' acronyms  $*
```

Let's first see it in action. Here's a sample input file.

```
$ cat sample
The USGCRP is a comprehensive
research effort that includes applied
as well as basic research.
The NASA program Mission to Planet Earth
represents the principal space-based component
of the USGCRP and includes new initiatives
such as EOS and Earthprobes.
```

And here is the file *acronyms*:

```
$ cat acronyms
USGCRP   U.S. Global Change Research Program
NASA     National Aeronautic and Space Administration
EOS      Earth Observing System
```

Now we run the program on the sample file.

```
$ awkro sample
The U.S. Global Change Research Program (USGCRP) is a comprehensive
research effort that includes applied
as well as basic research.
The National Aeronautic and Space Administration (NASA) program
Mission to Planet Earth
represents the principal space-based component
of the U.S. Global Change Research Program (USGCRP) and includes new
initiatives
such as Earth Observing System (EOS) and Earthprobes.
```

We'll look at this program in two parts. The first part reads records from the *acronyms* file.

```
# load acronyms file into array "acro"
FILENAME == "acronyms" {
        split($0, entry, "\t")
        acro[entry[1]] = entry[2]
        next
}
```

The two fields from these records are loaded into an array using the first field as the subscript and assigning the second field to an element of the array. In other words, the acronym itself is the index to its description.

Note that we did not change the field separator, but instead used the split() function to create the array **entry**. This array is then used in creating an array named **acro**.

Here is the second half of the program:

```
# process any input line containing caps
/[A-Z][A-Z]+/ {
        # see if any field is an acronym
        for (i = 1; i <= NF; i++)
                if ( $i in acro ) {
                        # if it matches, add description
                        $i = acro[$i] " (" $i ")"
                }
}


{
        # print all lines
        print $0
}
```

Only lines that contain more than one consecutive capital letter are processed by the first of the two actions shown here. This action loops through each field of the record. At the heart of this section is the conditional statement that tests if the current field (**$i**) is a subscript of the array (**acro**). If the field is a subscript, we replace the original value of the field with the array element and the original value in parentheses. (Fields can be assigned new values, just like regular variables.) Note that the insertion of the description of the acronym results in lines that may be too long. See the next chapter for a discussion of the **length()** function, which can be used to determine the length of a string so you can divide it up if it is too long.

Now we're going to change the program so it makes a replacement only the first time an acronym appears. After we've found it, we don't want to search for that acronym any more. This is easy to do; we simply delete that acronym from the array.

```
if ( $i in acro ) {
        # if it matches, add description
        $i = acro[$i] " (" $i ")"
        # only expand the acronym once
        delete acro[acronym]
}
```

There are other changes that would be good to make. In running the **awkro** program, we soon discovered that it failed to match the acronym if it was followed by a punctuation mark. Our initial solution was not to handle it in awk at all. Instead, we used two sed scripts, one before processing:

```
sed 's/\([^.,;:!][^.,;:!]*\)\([.,;:!]\)/\1 @@@\2/g'
```

and one after:

```
sed 's/ @@@\([.,;:!]\)/\1/g'
```

A sed script, run prior to invoking awk, could simply insert a space before any punctuation mark, causing it to be interpreted as a separate field. A string of garbage characters (@@@) was also added so we'd be able to easily identify and restore the punctuation mark. (The complicated expression used in the first sed command makes sure that we catch the case of more than one punctuation mark on a line.)

This kind of solution, using another tool in the UNIX toolbox, demonstrates that not everything needs to be done as an awk procedure. Awk is all the more valuable because it is situated in the UNIX environment.

However, with POSIX awk, we can implement a different solution, one that uses a regular expression to match the acronym. Such a solution can be implemented with the **match()** and **sub()** functions described in the next chapter.

## *Multidimensional Arrays*

Awk supports linear arrays in which the index to each element of the array is a single subscript. If you imagine a linear array as a row of numbers, a two-dimensional array represents rows and columns of numbers. You might refer to the element in the second column of the third row as "array[3, 2]." Two- and three-dimensional arrays are examples of multidimensional arrays. Awk does not support multidimensional arrays but instead offers a syntax for subscripts that simulate a reference to a multidimensional array. For instance, you could write the following expression:

```
file_array[NR, i] = $i
```

where each field of an input record is indexed by its record number and field number. Thus, the following reference:

```
file_array[2, 4]
```

would produce the value of the fourth field of the second record.

This syntax does not create a multidimensional array. It is converted into a string that uniquely identifies the element in a linear array. The components of a multidimensional subscript are interpreted as individual strings ("2" and "4," for instance) and concatenated together separated by the value of the system variable **SUBSEP**.

The subscript-component separator is defined as "\034" by default, an unprintable character rarely found in ASCII text. Thus, awk maintains a one-dimensional array and the subscript for our previous example would actually be "2\0344" (the concatenation of "2," the value of **SUBSEP**, and "4"). The main consequence of this simulation of multidimensional arrays is that the larger the array, the slower it is to access individual elements. However, you should time this, using your own application, with different awk implementations (see Chapter 11, *A Flock of awks*).

Here is a sample awk script named **bitmap.awk** that shows how to load and output the elements of a multidimensional array. This array represents a two-dimensional bitmap that is 12 characters in width and height.

```
BEGIN { FS = ","   # comma-separated fields
        # assign width and height of bitmap
        WIDTH = 12
        HEIGHT = 12
        # loop to load entire array with "O"
        for (i = 1; i <= WIDTH; ++i)
                for (j = 1; j <= HEIGHT; ++j)
                        bitmap[i, j] = "O"
}
# read input of the form x,y.
{
        # assign "X" to that element of array
        bitmap[$1, $2] = "X"
}
# at end output multidimensional array
END {
        for (i = 1; i <= WIDTH; ++i){
                for (j = 1; j <= HEIGHT; ++j)
                        printf("%s", bitmap[i, j] )
                # after each row, print newline
                printf("\n")
        }
}
```

Before any input is read, the **bitmap** array is loaded with O's. This array has 144 elements. The input to this program is a series of coordinates, one per line.

```
$ cat bitmap.test
1,1
2,2
3,3
4,4
5,5
6,6
7,7
8,8
9,9
10,10
11,11
12,12
```

```
1,12
2,11
3,10
4,9
5,8
6,7
7,6
8,5
9,4
10,3
11,2
12,1
```

For each coordinate, the program will put an "X" in place of an "O" as that element of the array. At the end of the script, the same kind of loop that loaded the array, now outputs it. The following example reads the input from the file *bitmap.test*.

```
$ awk -f bitmap.awk bitmap.test
XOOOOOOOOOOX
OXOOOOOOOOXO
OOXOOOOOOXOO
OOOXOOOOXOOO
OOOOXOOXOOOO
OOOOOXXOOOOO
OOOOOXXOOOOO
OOOOXOOXOOOO
OOOXOOOOXOOO
OOXOOOOOOXOO
OXOOOOOOOOXO
XOOOOOOOOOOX
```

The multidimensional array syntax is also supported in testing for array membership. The subscripts must be placed inside parentheses.

```
if ((i, j) in array)
```

This tests whether the subscript **i,j** (actually, **i SUBSEP j**) exists in the specified array.

Looping over a multidimensional array is the same as with one-dimensional arrays.

```
for (item in array)
```

You must use the **split()** function to access individual subscript components. Thus:

```
split(item, subscr, SUBSEP)
```

creates the array **subscr** from the subscript **item**.

Note that we needed to use the loop-within-a-loop to output the two-dimensional bitmap array in the previous example because we needed to maintain rows and columns.

# System Variables That Are Arrays

Awk provides two system variables that are arrays:

**ARGV**

> An array of command-line arguments, excluding the script itself and any options specified with the invocation of awk. The number of elements in this array is available in **ARGC**. The index of the first element of the array is 0 (unlike all other arrays in awk but consistent with C) and the last is **ARGC - 1**.

**ENVIRON**

> An array of environment variables. Each element of the array is the value in the current environment and the index is the name of the environment variable.

## An Array of Command-Line Parameters

You can write a loop to reference all the elements of the **ARGV** array.

```
# argv.awk - print command-line parameters
BEGIN { for (x = 0; x < ARGC; ++x)
            print ARGV[x]
        print ARGC
}
```

This example also prints out the value of **ARGC**, the number of command-line arguments. Here's an example of how it works on a sample command line:

```
$ awk -f argv.awk 1234 "John Wayne" Westerns n=44 -
awk
1234
John Wayne
Westerns
n=44
-
6
```

As you can see, there are six elements in the array. The first element is the name of the command that invoked the script. The last argument, in this case, is the filename, "-", for standard input. Note the "-f argv.awk" does not appear in the parameter list.

Generally, the value of **ARGC** will be at least 2. If you don't want to refer to the program name or the filename, you can initialize the counter to 1 and then test against **ARGC - 1** to avoid referencing the last parameter (assuming that there is only one filename).

Remember that if you invoke awk from a shell script, the command-line parameters are passed to the shell script and not to awk. You have to pass the shell script's command-line parameters to the awk program inside the shell script. For instance, you can pass all command-line parameters from the shell script to awk, using "$*". Look at the following shell script:

```
awk '
# argv.sh - print command-line parameters
BEGIN {
        for (x = 0; x < ARGC; ++x)
                print ARGV[x]
        print ARGC
}' $*
```

This shell script works the same as the first example of invoking awk.

One practical use is to test the command-line parameters in the **BEGIN** rule using a regular expression. The following example tests that all the parameters, except the first, are integers.

```
# number.awk - test command-line parameters
BEGIN {
        for (x = 1; x < ARGC; ++x)
                if ( ARGV[x] !~ /^[0-9]+$/ ) {
                        print ARGV[x], "is not an integer."
                        exit 1
                }
}
```

If the parameters contain any character that is not a digit, the program will print the message and quit.

After testing the value, you can, of course, assign it to a variable. For instance, we could write a **BEGIN** procedure of a script that checks the command-line parameters before prompting the user. Let's look at the following shell script that uses the phone and address database from the previous chapter:

```
awk '# phone - find phone number for person
# supply name of person on command line or at prompt.
BEGIN { FS = ","
        # look for parameter
        if ( ARGC > 2 ){
                name = ARGV[1]
                delete ARGV[1]
        } else {
```

```
                        # loop until we get a name
                        while (! name) {
                                printf("Enter a name? ")
                                getline name < "-"
                        }
                }
        }
        $1 ~ name {
                print $1, $NF
        }' $* phones.data
```

We test the **ARGC** variable to see if there are more than two parameters. By specifying "$*", we can pass all the parameters from the shell command line inside to the awk command line. If this parameter has been supplied, we assume the second parameter, **ARGV[1]**, is the one we want and it is assigned to the variable **name**. Then that parameter is deleted from the array. This is very important if the parameter that is supplied on the command line is not of the form "*var=value*"; otherwise, it will later be interpreted as a filename. If additional parameters are supplied, they will be interpreted as filenames of alternative phone databases. If there are not more than two parameters, then we prompt for the name. The **getline** function is discussed in Chapter 10; using this syntax, it reads the next line from standard input.

Here are several examples of this script in action:

```
$ phone John
John Robinson 696-0987
$ phone
Enter a name? Alice
Alice Gold (707) 724-0000
$ phone Alice /usr/central/phonebase
Alice Watson (617) 555-0000
Alice Gold (707) 724-0000
```

The first example supplies the name on the command line, the second prompts the user, and the third takes two command-line parameters and uses the second as a filename. (The script will not allow you to supply a filename without supplying the person's name on the command line. You could devise a test that would permit this syntax, though.)

Because you can add to and delete from the **ARGV** array, there is the potential for doing a lot of interesting manipulation. You can place a filename at the end of the **ARGV** array, for instance, and it will be opened as though it were specified on the command line. Similarly, you can delete a filename from the array and it will never be opened. Note that if you add new elements to **ARGV**, you should also increment **ARGC**; awk uses the value of **ARGC** to know how many elements in **ARGV** it should process. Thus, simply decrementing **ARGC** will keep awk from examining the final element in **ARGV**.

As a special case, if the value of an **ARGV** element is the empty string (`""`), awk will skip over it and continue on to the next element.

## An Array of Environment Variables

The **ENVIRON** array was added independently to both gawk and MKS awk. It was then added to the System V Release 4 nawk, and is now included in the POSIX standard for awk. It allows you to access variables in the environment. The following script loops through the elements of the **ENVIRON** array and prints them.

```
# environ.awk - print environment variable
BEGIN {
        for (env in ENVIRON)
                print env "=" ENVIRON[env]
}
```

The index of the array is the variable name. The script generates the same output produced by the **env** command (**printenv** on some systems).

```
$ awk -f environ.awk
DISPLAY=scribe:0.0
FRAME=Shell 3
LOGNAME=dale
MAIL=/usr/mail/dale
PATH=:/bin:/usr/bin:/usr/ucb:/work/bin:/mac/bin:.
TERM=mac2cs
HOME=/work/dale
SHELL=/bin/csh
TZ=PST8PDT
EDITOR=/usr/bin/vi
```

You can reference any element, using the variable name as the index of the array:

```
ENVIRON["LOGNAME"]
```

You can also change any element of the **ENVIRON** array.

```
ENVIRON["LOGNAME"] = "Tom"
```

However, this change does not affect the user's actual environment (i.e., when awk is done, the value of **LOGNAME** will not be changed) nor does it affect the environment inherited by programs that are invoked from awk via the **getline** or **system()** functions, which are described in Chapter 10.

This chapter has covered many important programming constructs. You will continue to see examples in upcoming chapters that make use of these constructs. If programming is new to you, be sure you take the time to run and modify the programs in this chapter, and write small programs of your own. It is essential, like learning how to conjugate verbs, that these constructs become familiar and predictable to you.

# 9

# *Functions*

A function is a self-contained computation that accepts a number of arguments as input and returns some value. Awk has a number of built-in functions in two groups: arithmetic and string functions. Awk also provides user-defined functions, which allow you to expand upon the built-in functions by writing your own.

## *Arithmetic Functions*

Nine of the built-in functions can be classified as arithmetic functions. Most of them take a numeric argument and return a numeric value. Table 9-1 summarizes these arithmetic functions.

*Table 9-1: awk's Built-In Arithmetic Functions*

| Awk Function | Description |
|---|---|
| **cos**($x$) | Returns cosine of $x$ ($x$ is in radians). |
| **exp**($x$) | Returns $e$ to the power $x$. |
| **int**($x$) | Returns truncated value of $x$. |
| **log**($x$) | Returns natural logarithm (base-$e$) of $x$. |
| **sin**($x$) | Returns sine of $x$ ($x$ is in radians). |
| **sqrt**($x$) | Returns square root of $x$. |
| **atan2**($y$,$x$) | Returns arctangent of $y/x$ in the range $-\pi$ to $\pi$. |
| **rand**( ) | Returns pseudo-random number $r$, where $0 <= r < 1$. |
| **srand**($x$) | Establishes new seed for **rand**( ). If no seed is specified, uses time of day. Returns the old seed. |

## Trigonometric Functions

The trigonometric functions **cos()** and **sin()** work the same way, taking a single argument that is the size of an angle in radians and returning the cosine or sine for that angle. (To convert from degrees to radians, multiply the number by $\pi/180$.) The trigonometric function **atan2()** takes two arguments and returns the arctangent of their quotient. The expression

```
atan2(0, -1)
```

produces $\pi$.

The function **exp()** uses the natural exponential, which is also known as base-*e* exponentiation. The expression

```
exp(1)
```

returns the natural number 2.71828, the base of the natural logarithms, referred to as *e*. Thus, **exp($x$)** is *e* to the *x*-th power.

The **log()** function gives the inverse of the **exp()** function, the natural logarithm of *x*. The **sqrt()** function takes a single argument and returns the (positive) square root of that argument.

## Integer Function

The **int()** function truncates a numeric value by removing digits to the right of the decimal point. Look at the following two statements:

```
print 100/3
print int(100/3)
```

The output from these statements is shown below:

```
33.3333
33
```

The **int()** function simply truncates; it does not round up or down. (Use the **printf** format "%.0f" to perform rounding.)[*]

## Random Number Generation

The **rand()** function generates a pseudo-random floating-point number between 0 and 1. The **srand()** function sets the seed or starting point for random number generation. If **srand()** is called without an argument, it uses the time of day to generate the seed. With an argument *x*, **srand()** uses *x* as the seed.

---

[*] The way **printf** does rounding is discussed in Appendix B, *Quick Reference for awk*.

If you don't call **srand()** at all, awk acts as if **srand()** had been called with a constant argument before your program started, causing you to get the same starting point every time you run your program. This is useful if you want reproducible behavior for testing, but inappropriate if you really do want your program to behave differently every time. Look at the following script:

```
# rand.awk -- test random number generation
BEGIN {
        print rand()
        print rand()
        srand()
        print rand()
        print rand()
}
```

We print the result of the **rand()** function twice, and then call the **srand()** function before printing the result of the **rand()** function two more times. Let's run the script.

```
$ awk -f rand.awk
0.513871
0.175726
0.760277
0.263863
```

Four random numbers are generated. Now look what happens when we run the program again:

```
$ awk -f rand.awk
0.513871
0.175726
0.787988
0.305033
```

The first two "random" numbers are identical to the numbers generated in the previous run of the program while the last two numbers are different. The last two numbers are different because we provided the **rand()** function with a new seed.

The return value of the **srand()** function is the seed it was using. This can be used to keep track of sequences of random numbers, and re-run them if needed.

## Pick 'em

To show how to use **rand()**, we'll look at a script that implements a "quick-pick" for a lottery game. This script, named **lotto**, picks $x$ numbers from a series of numbers 1 to $y$. Two arguments can be supplied on the command line: how many numbers to pick (the default is 6) and the highest number in the series (the default is 30). Using the default values for *x* and *y*, the script generates six unique random numbers between 1 and 30. The numbers are sorted for readability from lowest to highest and output. Before looking at the script itself, let's run the program:

```
$ lotto
Pick 6 of 30
9 13 25 28 29 30
$ lotto 7 35
Pick 7 of 35
1 6 9 16 20 22 27
```

The first example uses the default values to print six random numbers from 1 to 30. The second example prints seven random numbers out of 35.

The full **lotto** script is fairly complicated, so before looking at the entire script, let's look at a smaller script that generates a single random number in a series:

```
awk -v TOPNUM=$1 '
# pick1 - pick one random number out of y
# main routine
BEGIN {
# seed random number using time of day
        srand()
# get a random number
        select = 1 + int(rand() * TOPNUM)
# print pick
        print select
}'
```

The shell script expects a single argument from the command line and this is passed into the program as "TOPNUM=$1," using the *-v* option. All the action happens in the **BEGIN** procedure. Since there are no other statements in the program, awk exits when the **BEGIN** procedure is done.

The main routine first calls the **srand()** function to seed the random number generator. Then we get a random number by calling the **rand()** function:

```
select = 1 + int(rand() * TOPNUM)
```

It might be helpful to see this expression broken up so each part of it is obvious.

| Statement | Result |
|---|---|
| `print r = rand()` | 0.467315 |
| `print r * TOPNUM` | 14.0195 |
| `print int(r * TOPNUM)` | 14 |
| `print 1 + int(r * TOPNUM)` | 15 |

Because the **rand()** function returns a number between 0 and 1, we multiply it by **TOPNUM** to get a number between 0 and **TOPNUM**. We then truncate the number to remove the fractional values and then add 1 to the number. The latter is necessary because **rand( )** could return 0. In this example, the random number that is generated is 15. You could use this program to print any single number, such as picking a number between 1 and 100.

```
$ pick1 100
83
```

The **lotto** script must "pick one" multiple times. Basically, we need to set up a **for** loop to execute the **rand( )** function as many times as needed. One of the reasons this is difficult is that we have to worry about duplicates. In other words, it is possible for a number to be picked again; therefore we have to keep track of the numbers already picked.

Here's the **lotto** script:

```
awk -v NUM=$1 -v TOPNUM=$2 '
# lotto - pick x random numbers out of y
# main routine
BEGIN {
# test command line args; NUM = $1, how many numbers to pick
#                        TOPNUM = $2, last number in series
        if (NUM <= 0)
                NUM = 6
        if (TOPNUM <= 0)
                TOPNUM = 30
# print "Pick x of y"
        printf("Pick %d of %d\n", NUM, TOPNUM)
# seed random number using time and date; do this once
        srand( )
# loop until we have NUM selections
        for (j = 1; j <= NUM; ++j) {
                # loop to find a not-yet-seen selection
                do {
                        select = 1 + int(rand( ) * TOPNUM)
                } while (select in pick)
                pick[select] = select
        }
# loop through array and print picks.
        for (j in pick)
                printf("%s ", pick[j])
        printf("\n")
}'
```

Unlike the previous program, this one looks for two command-line arguments, indicating *x* numbers out of *y*. The main routine looks to see if these numbers were supplied and if not, assigns default values.

There is only one array, **pick**, for holding the random numbers that are selected. Each number is guaranteed to be in the desired range, because the result of **rand( )**

(a value between 0 and 1) is multiplied by **TOPNUM** and then truncated. The heart of the script is a loop that occurs **NUM** times to assign **NUM** elements to the **pick** array.

To get a new non-duplicate random number, we use an inner loop that generates selections and tests to see if they are in the **pick** array. (Using the **in** operator is much faster than looping through the array comparing subscripts.) While (**select in pick**), the corresponding element has been found already, so the selection is a duplicate and we reject the selection. If it is not true that **select in pick**, then we assign **select** to an element of the **pick** array. This will make future **in** tests return true, causing the **do** loop to continue.

Finally, the program loops through the **pick** array and prints the elements. This version of the **lotto** script leaves one thing out. See if you can tell what it is if we run it again:

```
$ lotto 7 35
Pick 7 of 35
5 21 9 30 29 20 2
```

That's right, the numbers are not sorted. We'll defer showing the code for the sort routine until we discuss user-defined functions. While it's not necessary to have written the sorting code as a function, it makes a lot of sense. One reason is that you can tackle a more generalized problem and retain the solution for use in other programs. Later on, we will write a function that sorts the elements of an array.

Note that the **pick** array isn't ready for sorting, since its indices are the same as its values, not numbers in order. We would have to set up a separate array for sorting by our sort function:

```
# create a numerically indexed array for sorting
i = 1
for (j in pick)
        sortedpick[i++] = pick[j]
```

The **lotto** program is set up to do everything in the **BEGIN** block. No input is processed. You could, however, revise this script to read a list of names from a file and for each name generate a "quick-pick."

## *String Functions*

The built-in string functions are much more significant and interesting than the numeric functions. Because awk is essentially designed as a string-processing language, a lot of its power derives from these functions. Table 9-2 lists the string functions found in awk.

*Table 9–2: Awk's Built-In String Functions*

| Awk Function | Description |
|---|---|
| gsub(*r,s,t*) | Globally substitutes *s* for each match of the regular expression *r* in the string *t*. Returns the number of substitutions. If *t* is not supplied, defaults to **$0**. |
| index(*s, t*) | Returns position of substring *t* in string *s* or zero if not present. |
| length(*s*) | Returns length of string *s* or length of **$0** if no string is supplied. |
| match(*s,r*) | Returns either the position in *s* where the regular expression *r* begins, or 0 if no occurrences are found. Sets the values of **RSTART** and **RLENGTH**. |
| split(*s, a, sep*) | Parses string *s* into elements of array *a* using field separator *sep*; returns number of elements. If *sep* is not supplied, **FS** is used. Array splitting works the same way as field splitting. |
| sprintf(*"fmt", expr*) | Uses **printf** format specification for **expr**. |
| sub(*r,s,t*) | Substitutes *s* for first match of the regular expression *r* in the string *t*. Returns 1 if successful; 0 otherwise. If *t* is not supplied, defaults to **$0**. |
| substr(*s, p, n*) | Returns substring of string *s* at beginning position *p* up to a maximum length of *n*. If *n* is not supplied, the rest of the string from *p* is used. |
| tolower(*s*) | Translates all uppercase characters in string *s* to lowercase and returns the new string. |
| toupper(*s*) | Translates all lowercase characters in string *s* to uppercase and returns the new string. |

The **split()** function was introduced in the previous chapter in the discussion on arrays.

The **sprintf()** function uses the same format specifications as **printf()**, which is discussed in Chapter 7, *Writing Scripts for awk*. It allows you to apply the format specifications on a string. Instead of printing the result, **sprintf()** returns a string that can be assigned to a variable. It can do specialized processing of input records or fields, such as performing character conversions. For instance, the following example uses the **sprintf()** function to convert a number into an ASCII character.

```
for (i = 97; i <= 122; ++i) {
        nextletter = sprintf("%c", i)
        ...
}
```

A loop supplies numbers from 97 to 122, which produce ASCII characters from **a** to **z**.

That leaves us with three basic built-in string functions to discuss: **index()**, **substr()**, and **length()**.

## *Substrings*

The **index()** and **substr()** functions both deal with substrings. Given a string *s*, **index**(*s, t*) returns the leftmost position where string *t* is found in *s*. The beginning of the string is position 1 (which is different from the C language, where the first character in a string is at position 0). Look at the following example:

```
pos = index("Mississippi", "is")
```

The value of **pos** is 2. If the substring is not found, the **index()** function returns 0.

Given a string *s*, **substr**(*s, p*) returns the characters beginning at position *p*. The following example creates a phone number without an area code.

```
phone = substr("707-555-1111", 5)
```

You can also supply a third argument which is the number of characters to return. The next example returns just the area code:

```
area_code = substr("707-555-1111", 1, 3)
```

The two functions can be and often are used together, as in the next example. This example capitalizes the first letter of the first word for each input record.

```
awk '# caps - capitalize 1st letter of 1st word
# initialize strings
BEGIN { upper = "ABCDEFGHIJKLMNOPQRSTUVWXYZ"
        lower = "abcdefghijklmnopqrstuvwxyz"
}

# for each input line
{
# get first character of first word
        FIRSTCHAR = substr($1, 1, 1)
# get position of FIRSTCHAR in lowercase array; if 0, ignore
        if (CHAR = index(lower, FIRSTCHAR))
                # change $1, using position to retrieve
                # uppercase character
                $1 = substr(upper, CHAR, 1) substr($1, 2)
# print record
        print $0
}'
```

This script creates two variables, **upper** and **lower**, consisting of uppercase and lowercase letters. Any character that we find in **lower** can be found at the same position in **upper**. The first statement of the main procedure extracts a single character, the first one, from the first field. The conditional statement tests to see if that character can be found in **lower** using the **index()** function. If **CHAR** is not 0, then **CHAR** can be used to extract the uppercase character from **upper**. There are two **substr()** function calls: the first one retrieves the capitalized letter and the second call gets the rest of the first field, extracting all characters, beginning with the second character. The values returned by both **substr()** functions are concatenated and assigned to $1. Making an assignment to a field as we do here is a new twist, but it has the added benefit that the record can be output normally. (If the assignment was made to a variable, you'd have to output the variable and then output the record's remaining fields.) The **print** statement prints the changed record. Let's see it in action:

```
$ caps
root user
Root user
dale
Dale
Tom
Tom
```

In a little bit, we'll see how to revise this program to change all characters in a string from lower- to uppercase or vice versa.

## *String Length*

When presenting the **awkro** program in the previous chapter, we noted that the program was likely to produce lines that exceed 80 characters. After all, the descriptions are quite long. We can find out how many characters are in a string using the built-in function **length()**. For instance, to evaluate the length of the current input record, we specify **length($0)**. (As it happens, if **length()** is called without an argument, it returns the length of $0.)

The **length()** function is often used to find the length of the current input record, in order to determine if we need to break the line.

One way to handle the line break, perhaps more efficiently, is to use the **length()** function to get the length of each field. By accumulating those lengths, we could specify a line break when a new field causes the total to exceed a certain number.

Chapter 13, *A Miscellany of Scripts*, contains a script that uses the **length()** function to break lines greater than 80 columns wide.

## Substitution Functions

Awk provides two substitution functions: **sub()** and **gsub()**. The difference between them is that **gsub()** performs its substitution globally on the input string whereas **sub()** makes only the first possible substitution. This makes **gsub()** equivalent to the sed substitution command with the **g** (global) flag.

Both functions take at least two arguments. The first is a regular expression (surrounded by slashes) that matches a pattern and the second argument is a string that replaces what the pattern matches. The regular expression can be supplied by a variable, in which case the slashes are omitted. An optional third argument specifies the string that is the target of the substitution. If there is no third argument, the substitution is made for the current input record ($0).

The substitution functions change the specified string directly. You might expect, given the way functions work, that the function returns the new string created when the substitution is made. The substitution functions actually return the *number* of substitutions made. **sub()** will always return 1 if successful; both return 0 if not successful. Thus, you can test the result to see if a substitution was made.

For example, the following example uses **gsub()** to replace all occurrences of "UNIX" with "POSIX".

```
if (gsub(/UNIX/, "POSIX"))
        print
```

The conditional statement tests the return value of **gsub()** such that the current input line is printed only if a change is made.

As with sed, if an "&" appears in the substitution string, it will be replaced by the string matched by the regular expression. Use "&" to output an ampersand. (Remember that to get a literal "\" into a string, you have to type two of them.) Also, note that awk does not "remember" the previous regular expression, as does sed, so you cannot use the syntax "//" to refer to the last regular expression.

The following example surrounds any occurrence of "UNIX" with the **troff** font-change escape sequences.

```
gsub(/UNIX/, "\\fB&\\fR")
```

If the input is "the UNIX operating system", the output is "the \fBUNIX\fR operating system".

In Chapter 4, *Writing sed Scripts*, we presented the following sed script named **do.outline**:

```
sed -n '
s/"//g
s/^\.Se /Chapter /p
```

```
s/^\.Ah /•A. /p
s/^\.Bh /••B.  /p' $*
```

Now here's that script rewritten using the substitution functions:

```
awk '
{
gsub(/"/, "")
if (sub(/^\.Se /, "Chapter ")) print
if (sub(/^\.Ah /, "\tA. ")) print
if (sub(/^\.Bh /, "\t\tB. ")) print
}' $*
```

The two scripts are exactly equivalent, printing out only those lines that are changed. For the first edition of this book, Dale compared the run-time of both scripts and, as he expected, the awk script was slower. For the second edition, new timings showed that performance varies by implementation, and in fact, all tested versions of new awk were faster than sed! This is nice, since we have the capabilities in awk to make the script do more things. For instance, instead of using letters of the alphabet, we could number the headings. Here's the revised awk script:

```
awk '# do.outline -- number headings in chapter.
{
gsub(/"/, "")
}
/^\.Se/ {
        sub(/^\.Se /, "Chapter ")
        ch = $2
        ah = 0
        bh = 0
        print
        next
}
/^\.Ah/ {
        sub(/^\.Ah /, "\t " ch "." ++ah " ")
        bh = 0
        print
        next
}
/^\.Bh/ {
        sub(/^\.Bh /, "\t\t " ch "."  ah "." ++bh " ")
        print
}' $*
```

In this version, we break out each heading into its own pattern-matching rule. This is not necessary but seems more efficient since we know that once a rule is applied, we don't need to look at the others. Note the use of the **next** statement to bypass further examination of a line that has already been identified.

The chapter number is read as the first argument to the ".Se" macro and is thus the second field on that line. The numbering scheme is done by incrementing a variable each time the substitution is made. The action associated with the chapter-level heading initializes the section-heading counters to zero. The action associated with the top-level heading ".Ah" zeroes the second-level heading counter. Obviously, you can create as many levels of heading as you need. Note how we can specify a concatenation of strings and variables as a single argument to the **sub**( ) function.

```
$ do.outline ch02
Chapter 2 Understanding Basic Operations
        2.1 Awk, by Sed and Grep, out of Ed
        2.2 Command-line Syntax
                2.2.1 Scripting
                2.2.2 Sample Mailing List
        2.3 Using Sed
                2.3.1 Specifying Simple Instructions
                2.3.2 Script Files
        2.4 Using Awk
        2.5 Using Sed and Awk Together
```

If you wanted the option of choosing either numbers or letters, you could maintain both programs and construct a shell wrapper that uses some flag to determine which program should be invoked.

## *Converting Case*

POSIX awk provides two functions for converting the case of characters within a string. The functions are **tolower**( ) and **toupper**( ). Each takes a single string argument, and returns a copy of that string, with all the characters of one case converted to the other (upper to lower and lower to upper, respectively). Their use is straightforward:

```
$ cat test
Hello, World!
Good-bye CRUEL world!
1, 2, 3, and away we GO!
$ awk '{ printf("<%s>, <%s>\n", tolower($0), toupper($0)) }' test
<hello, world!>, <HELLO, WORLD!>
<good-bye cruel world!>, <GOOD-BYE CRUEL WORLD!>
<1, 2, 3, and away we go!>, <1, 2, 3, AND AWAY WE GO!>
```

Note that nonalphabetic characters are left unchanged.

# *The match() Function*

The **match()** function allows you to determine if a regular expression matches a specified string. It takes two arguments, the string and the regular expression. (This function is confusing because the regular expression is in the second position, whereas it is in the first position for the substitution functions.)

The **match()** function returns the starting position of the substring that was matched by the regular expression. You might consider it a close relation to the **index()** function. In the following example, the regular expression matches any sequence of capital letters in the string "the UNIX operating system".

```
match("the UNIX operating system", /[A-Z]+/)
```

The value returned by this function is 5, the character position of "U," the first capital letter in the string.

The **match()** function also sets two system variables: **RSTART** and **RLENGTH**. **RSTART** contains the same value returned by the function, the starting position of the substring. **RLENGTH** contains the length of the string in characters (not the ending position of the substring). When the pattern does not match, **RSTART** is set to 0 and **RLENGTH** is set to -1. In the previous example, **RSTART** is equal to 5 and **RLENGTH** is equal to 4. (Adding them together gives you the position of the first character after the match.)

Let's look at a rather simple example that prints out a string matched by a specified regular expression, demonstrating the "extent of the match," as discussed in Chapter 3, *Understanding Regular Expression Syntax*. The following shell script takes two command-line arguments: the regular expression, which should be specified in quotes, and the name of the file to search.

```
awk '# match -- print string that matches line
# for lines match pattern
match($0, pattern) {
        # extract string matching pattern using
        # starting position and length of string in $0
        # print string
        print substr($0, RSTART, RLENGTH)
}' pattern="$1" $2
```

The first command-line parameter is passed as the value of **pattern**. Note that $1 is surrounded by quotes, necessary to protect any spaces that might appear in the regular expression. The **match()** function appears in a conditional expression that controls execution of the only procedure in this awk script. The **match()** function returns 0 if the pattern is not found, and a non-zero value (**RSTART**) if it is found, allowing the return value to be used as a condition. If the current record matches the pattern, then the string is extracted from $0, using the values of **RSTART** and **RLENGTH** in the **substr( )** function to specify the starting position of the substring to be extracted and its length. The substring is printed. This procedure only matches the first occurrence in $0.

Here's a trial run, given a regular expression that matches "emp" and any number of characters up to a blank space:

```
$ match "emp[^ ]*" personnel.txt
employees
employee
employee.
employment,
employer
employment
employee's
employee
```

The **match** script could be a useful tool in improving your understanding of regular expressions.

The next script uses the **match( )** function to locate any sequence of uppercase letters so that they can be converted to lowercase. Compare it to the **caps** program shown earlier in the chapter.

```
awk '# lower - change upper case to lower case
# initialize strings
BEGIN { upper = "ABCDEFGHIJKLMNOPQRSTUVWXYZ"
        lower = "abcdefghijklmnopqrstuvwxyz"
}

# for each input line
{
# see if there is a match for all caps
        while (match($0, /[A-Z]+/))
                # get each cap letter
                for (x = RSTART; x < RSTART+RLENGTH; ++x) {
                        CAP = substr($0, x, 1)
                        CHAR = index(upper, CAP)
                        # substitute lowercase for upper
                        gsub(CAP, substr(lower, CHAR, 1))
                }

# print record
        print $0
}' $*
```

In this script, the **match( )** function appears in a conditional expression that determines whether a **while** loop will be executed. By placing this function in a loop, we apply the body of the loop as many times as the pattern occurs in the current input record.

The regular expression matches any sequence of uppercase letters in $0. If a match is made, a **for** loop does the lookup of each character in the substring that was matched, similar to what we did in the **caps** sample program, shown earlier in this chapter. What's different here is how we use the system variables **RSTART** and **RLENGTH**. **RSTART** initializes the counter variable **x**. It is used in the **substr()** function to extract one character at a time from $0, beginning with the first character that matched the pattern. By adding **RLENGTH** to **RSTART**, we get the position of the first character after the ones that matched the pattern. That is why the loop uses "<" instead of "<=". At the end, we use **gsub()** to replace the uppercase letter with the corresponding lowercase letter.[*] Notice that we use **gsub()** instead of **sub()** because it offers us the advantage of making several substitutions if there are multiple instances of the same letter on the line.

```
$ cat test
Every NOW and then, a WORD I type appears in CAPS.
$ lower test
every now and then, a word i type appears in caps.
```

Note that you could change the regular expression to avoid matching individual capital letters by matching a sequence of two or more uppercase characters, by using: "/[A-Z][A-Z]+/." This would also require revising the way the lowercase conversion was made using **gsub()**, since it matches a single character on the line.

In our discussion of the sed substitution command, you saw how to save and recall a portion of a string matched by a pattern, using \( and \) to surround the pattern to be saved and \*n* to recall the saved string in the replacement pattern. Unfortunately, awk's standard substitution functions offer no equivalent syntax. The **match()** function can solve many such problems, though.

For instance, if you match a string using the **match()** function, you can single out characters or a substring at the head or tail of the string. Given the values of **RSTART** and **RLENGTH**, you can use the **substr()** function to extract the characters. In the following example, we replace the second of two colons with a semicolon. We can't use **gsub()** to make the replacement because "/:/" matches the first colon and "/:[^:]*:/" matches the whole string of characters. We can use **match()** to match the string of characters and to extract the last character of the string.

```
# replace 2nd colon with semicolon using match, substr
if (match($1, /:[^:]*:/)) {
        before = substr($1, 1, (RSTART + RLENGTH - 2))
        after = substr($1, (RSTART + RLENGTH))
        $1 = before ";" after
}
```

---

[*] You may be wondering, "why not just use **tolower()**?" Good question. Some early versions of **nawk**, including the one on SunOS 4.1.x systems, don't have **tolower()** and **toupper()**; thus it's useful to know how to do it yourself.

The **match( )** function is placed within a conditional statement that tests that a match was found. If there is a match, we use the **substr( )** function to extract the substring before the second colon as well as the substring after it. Then we concatenate **before**, the literal ";", and **after**, assigning it to $1.

You can see examples of the **match( )** function in use in Chapter 12, *Full-Featured Applications.*

# *Writing Your Own Functions*

With user-defined functions, awk allows the novice programmer to take another step toward C programming[*] by writing programs that make use of self-contained functions. When you write a function properly, you have defined a program component that can be reused in other programs. The real benefit of modularity becomes apparent as programs grow in size or in age, and as the number of programs you write increases significantly.

A function definition can be placed anywhere in a script that a pattern-action rule can appear. Typically, we put the function definitions at the top of the script before the pattern-action rules. A function is defined using the following syntax:

```
function name (parameter-list) {
        statements
}
```

The newlines after the left brace and before the right brace are optional. You can also have a newline after the close-parenthesis of the parameter list and before the left brace.

The *parameter-list* is a comma-separated list of variables that are passed as arguments into the function when it is called. The body of the function consists of one or more statements. The function typically contains a **return** statement that returns control to that point in the script where the function was called; it often has an expression that returns a value as well.

```
return expression
```

The following example shows the definition for an **insert( )** function:

```
function insert(STRING, POS, INS) {
        before_tmp = substr(STRING, 1, POS)
        after_tmp = substr(STRING, POS + 1)
        return before_tmp INS after_tmp
}
```

---

[*] Or programming in any other traditional high-level language.

This function takes three arguments, inserting one string **INS** in another string **STRING** after the character at position **POS**.* The body of this function uses the **substr()** function to divide the value of **STRING** into two parts. The **return** statement returns a string that is the result of concatenating the first part of **STRING**, the **INS** string, and the last part of **STRING**. A function call can appear anywhere that an expression can. Thus, the following statement:

```
print insert($1, 4, "XX")
```

If the value of $1 is "Hello," then this functions returns "HellXXo." Note that when *calling* a user-defined function, there can be no spaces between the function name and the left parenthesis. This is not true of built-in functions.

It is important to understand the notion of local and global variables. A local variable is a variable that is local to a function and cannot be accessed outside of it. A global variable, on the other hand, can be accessed or changed anywhere in the script. There can be potentially damaging side effects of global variables if a function changes a variable that is used elsewhere in the script. Therefore, it is usually a good idea to eliminate global variables in a function.

When we call the **insert()** function, and specify $1 as the first argument, then a copy of that variable is passed to the function, where it is manipulated as a local variable named **STRING**. All the variables in the function definition's parameter list are local variables and their values are not accessible outside the function. Similarly, the arguments in the function call are not changed by the function itself. When the **insert()** function returns, the value of $1 is not changed.

However, the variables defined in the body of the function are global variables, by default. Given the above definition of the **insert()** function, the temporary variables **before_tmp** and **after_tmp** are visible outside the function. Awk provides what its developers call an "inelegant" means of declaring variables local to a function, and that is by specifying those variables in the parameter list.

The local temporary variables are put at the end of the parameter list. This is *essential*; parameters in the parameter list receive their values, in order, from the values passed in the function call. Any extra parameters, like normal awk variables, are initialized to the empty string. By convention, the local variables are separated from the "real" parameters by several spaces. For instance, the following example shows how to define the **insert()** function with two local variables.

---

* We've used a convention of giving all uppercase names to our parameters. This is mostly to make the explanation easier to follow. In practice, this is probably not a good idea, since it becomes much easier to accidentally have a parameter conflict with a system variable.

```
function insert(STRING, POS, INS,   before_tmp, after_tmp) {
        body
}
```

If this seems confusing,[*] seeing how the following script works might help:

```
function insert(STRING, POS, INS,   before_tmp) {
        before_tmp = substr(STRING, 1, POS)
        after_tmp = substr(STRING, POS + 1)
        return before_tmp INS after_tmp
}

# main routine
{
print "Function returns", insert($1, 4, "XX")
print "The value of $1 after is:", $1
print "The value of STRING is:", STRING
print "The value of before_tmp:", before_tmp
print "The value of after_tmp:", after_tmp
}
```

Notice that we specify **before_tmp** in the parameter list. In the main routine, we call the **insert()** function and print its result. Then we print different variables to see what their value is, if any. Now let's run the above script and look at the output:

```
$ echo "Hello" | awk -f insert.awk -
Function returns HellXXo
The value of $1 after is: Hello
The value of STRING is:
The value of before_tmp:
The value of after_tmp: o
```

The **insert()** function returns "HellXXo," as expected. The value of $1 is the same after the function was called as it was before. The variable **STRING** is local to the function and it does not have a value when called from the main routine. The same is true for **before_tmp** because its name was placed in the parameter list for the function definition. The variable **after_tmp** which was not specified in the parameter list does have a value, the letter "o."

As this example shows, $1 is passed "by value" into the function. This means that a copy is made of the value when the function is called and the function manipulates the copy, not the original. Arrays, however, are passed "by reference." That is, the function does not work with a copy of the array but is passed the array itself. Thus, any changes that the function makes to the array are visible outside of the function. (This distinction between "scalar" variables and arrays also holds true for functions written in the C language.) The next section presents an example of a function that operates on an array.

---

[*] The documentation calls it a syntactical botch.

## *Writing a Sort Function*

Earlier in this chapter we presented the **lotto** script for picking *x* random numbers out of a series of *y* numbers. The script that we showed did not sort the list of numbers that were selected. In this section, we develop a **sort** function that sorts the elements of an array.

We define a function that takes two arguments, the name of the array and the number of elements in the array. This function can be called this way:

```
sort(sortedpick, NUM)
```

The function definition lists the two arguments and three local variables used in the function.

```
# sort numbers in ascending order
function sort(ARRAY, ELEMENTS,    temp, i, j) {
       for (i = 2; i <= ELEMENTS; ++i) {
              for (j = i; ARRAY[j-1] > ARRAY[j]; --j) {
                     temp = ARRAY[j]
                     ARRAY[j] = ARRAY[j-1]
                     ARRAY[j-1] = temp
              }
       }
       return
}
```

The body of the function implements an insertion sort. This sorting algorithm is very simple. We loop through each element of the array and compare it to the value preceding it. If the first element is greater than the second, the first and second elements are swapped. To actually swap the values, we use a temporary variable to hold a copy of the value while we overwrite the original. The loop continues swapping adjacent elements until all are in order. At the end of the function, we use the **return** statement to simply return control.[*] The function does not need to pass the array back to the main routine because the array itself is changed and it can be accessed directly.

Here's proof positive:

```
$ lotto 7 35
Pick 7 of 35
6 7 17 19 24 29 35
```

In fact, many of the scripts that we developed in this chapter could be turned into functions. For instance, if we only had the original, 1987, version of nawk, we might want to write our own **tolower()** and **toupper()** functions.

---

[*] In this case, the **return** is not strictly necessary; "falling off the end" of the function would have the same effect. Since functions can have return values, it's a good idea to always use a **return** statement, even when you are not returning a value. This helps make your programs more readable.

The value of writing the **sort()** function in a general fashion is that you can easily reuse it. To demonstrate this, we'll take the above sort function and use it to sort student grades. In the following script, we read all of the student grades into an array and then call **sort()** to put the grades in ascending order.

```
# grade.sort.awk -- script for sorting student grades
# input: student name followed by a series of grades

# sort function -- sort numbers in ascending order
function sort(ARRAY, ELEMENTS,    temp, i, j) {
        for (i = 2; i <= ELEMENTS; ++i)
                for (j = i; ARRAY[j-1] > ARRAY[j]; --j) {
                        temp = ARRAY[j]
                        ARRAY[j] = ARRAY[j-1]
                        ARRAY[j-1] = temp
                }
        return
}

# main routine
{
# loop through fields 2 through NF and assign values to
# array named grades
for (i = 2; i <= NF; ++i)
        grades[i-1] = $i

# call sort function to sort elements

sort(grades, NF-1)

# print student name
printf("%s: ", $1)

# output loop
for (j = 1; j <= NF-1; ++j)
        printf("%d ", grades[j])
printf("\n")
}
```

Note that the sort routine is identical to the previous version. In this example, once we've sorted the grades we simply output them:

```
$ awk -f grade.sort.awk grades.test
mona: 70 70 77 83 85 89
john: 78 85 88 91 92 94
andrea: 85 89 90 90 94 95
jasper: 80 82 84 84 88 92
dunce: 60 60 61 62 64 80
ellis: 89 90 92 96 96 98
```

However, you could, for instance, delete the first element of the sort array if you wanted to average the student grades after dropping the lowest grade.

As another exercise, you could write a version of the sort function that takes a third argument indicating an ascending or descending sort.

## Maintaining a Function Library

You might want to put a useful function in its own file and store it in a central directory. Awk permits multiple uses of the *-f* option to specify more than one program file.[*] For instance, we could have written the previous example such that the sort function was placed in a separate file from the main program **grade.awk**. The following command specifies both program files:

```
$ awk -f grade.awk -f /usr/local/share/awk/sort.awk grades.test
```

This command assumes that grade.awk is in the working directory and that the sort function is defined in sort.awk in the directory */usr/local/share/awk*.

---

*NOTE*        You cannot put a script on the command line and also use the *-f* option to specify a filename for a script.

---

Remember to document functions clearly so that you will understand how they work when you want to reuse them.

## Another Sorted Example

Lenny, our production editor, is back with another request.

```
Dale:

The last section of each Xlib manpage is called "Related Commands"
(that is the argument of a .SH) and it's followed by a list of commands
(often 10 or 20) that are now in random order.  It'd be more
useful and professional if they were alphabetized.  Currently, commands
are separated by a comma after each one except the last, which has a
period.

The question is: could awk alphabetize these lists?  We're talking
about a couple of hundred manpages.  Again, don't bother if this is a
bigger job than it seems to someone who doesn't know what's involved.

Best to you and yours,

Lenny
```

---

* The SunOS 4.1.x version of nawk does not support multiple script files.  This feature was not in the original 1987 version of nawk either. It was added in 1989 and is now part of POSIX awk.

To see what he is talking about, a simplified version of an Xlib manpage is shown below:

```
.SH "Name"
XSubImage — create a subimage from part of an image.
     .
     .
     .
.SH "Related Commands"
XDestroyImage, XPutImage, XGetImage,
XCreateImage, XGetSubImage, XAddPixel,
XPutPixel, XGetPixel, ImageByteOrder.
```

You can see that the names of related commands appear on several lines following the heading. You can also see that they are in no particular order.

To sort the list of related commands is actually fairly simple, given that we've already covered sorting. The structure of the program is somewhat interesting, as we must read several lines *after* matching the "Related Commands" heading.

Looking at the input, it is obvious that the list of related commands is the last section in the file. All other lines except these we want to print as is. The key is to match all lines from the heading "Related Commands" to the end of the file. Our script can consist of four rules, that match:

1.  The "Related Commands" heading

2.  The lines following that heading

3.  All other lines

4.  After all lines have been read (**END**)

Most of the "action" takes place in the **END** procedure. That's where we sort and output the list of commands. Here's the script:

```
# sorter.awk -- sort list of related commands
# requires sort.awk as function in separate file
BEGIN { relcmds = 0 }

#1 Match related commands; enable flag x
/\.SH "Related Commands"/ {
        print
        relcmds = 1
        next
}

#2 Apply to lines following "Related Commands"
(relcmds == 1) {
        commandList = commandList $0
}
```

```
#3 Print all other lines, as is.
(relcmds == 0) { print }

#4 now sort and output list of commands
END {
# remove leading spaces and final period.
        gsub(/, */, ",", commandList)
        gsub(/\. *$/, "", commandList)
# split list into array
        sizeOfArray = split(commandList, comArray, ",")
# sort
        sort(comArray, sizeOfArray)
# output elements
        for (i = 1; i < sizeOfArray; i++)
                printf("%s,\n", comArray[i])
        printf("%s.\n", comArray[i])
}
```

Once the "Related Commands" heading is matched, we print that line and then set a flag, the variable **relcmds**, which indicates that subsequent input lines are to be collected.[*] The second procedure actually collects each line into the variable **commandList**. The third procedure is executed for all other lines, simply printing them.

When all lines of input have been read, the **END** procedure is executed, and we know that our list of commands is complete. Before splitting up the commands into fields, we remove any number of spaces following a comma. Next we remove the final period and any trailing spaces. Finally, we create the array **comArray** using the **split()** function. We pass this array as an argument to the **sort()** function, and then we print the sorted values.

This program generates the following output:

```
$ awk -f sorter.awk test
.SH "Name"
XSubImage — create a subimage from part of an image.
.SH "Related Commands"
ImageByteOrder,
XAddPixel,
XCreateImage,
XDestroyImage,
XGetImage,
XGetPixel,
XGetSubImage,
XPutImage,
XPutPixel.
```

Once again, the virtue of calling a function to do the sort versus writing or copying the code to do the same task is that the function is a module that's been tested

---

[*] The **getline** function introduced in the next chapter provides a simpler way to control reading input lines.

previously and has a standard interface. That is, you know that it works and you know how it works. When you come upon the same sort code in the awk version, which uses different variable names, you have to scan it to verify that it works the same way as other versions. Even if you were to copy the lines into another program, you would have to make changes to accommodate the new circumstances. With a function, all you need to know is what kind of arguments it expects and their calling sequence. Using a function reduces the chance for error by reducing the complexity of the problem that you are solving.

Because this script presumes that the **sort( )** function exists in a separate file, it must be invoked using the multiple *-f* options:

```
$ awk -f sort.awk -f sorter.awk test
```

where the **sort( )** function is defined in the file *sort.awk*.

# 10

# *The Bottom Drawer*

This chapter is proof that not everything has its place. Some things just don't seem to fit, no matter how you organize them. This chapter is a collection of such things. It is tempting to label it "Advanced Topics," as if to explain its organization (or lack thereof), but some readers might feel they need to make more progress before reading it. We have therefore called it "The Bottom Drawer," thinking of the organization of a chest of drawers, with underwear, socks, and other day-to-day things in the top drawers and heavier things that are less frequently used, like sweaters, in the bottom drawers. All of it is equally accessible, but you have to bend over to get things in the bottom drawer. It requires a little more effort to get something, that's all.

In this chapter we cover a number of topics, including the following:

- The **getline** function

- The **system()** function

- Directing output to files and pipes

- Debugging awk scripts

## *The getline Function*

The **getline** function is used to read another line of input. Not only can **getline** read from the regular input data stream, it can also handle input from files and pipes.

The **getline** function is similar to awk's **next** statement. While both cause the next input line to be read, the **next** statement passes control back to the top of the script. The **getline** function gets the next line without changing control in the script. Possible return values are:

1    If it was able to read a line.
0    If it encounters the end-of-file.
-1   If it encounters an error.

---

*NOTE*          Although **getline** is called a function and it does return a value, its syntax resembles a statement. Do not write **getline()**; its syntax does not permit parentheses.

---

In the previous chapter, we used a manual page source file as an example. The **-man** macros typically place the text argument on the next line. Although the macro is the pattern that you use to find the line, it is actually the next line that you process. For instance, to extract the name of the command from the manpage, the following example matches the heading "Name," reads the next line, and prints the first field of it:

```
# getline.awk -- test getline function
/^\.SH "?Name"?/ {
        getline # get next line
        print $1 # print $1 of new line.
}
```

The pattern matches any line with ".SH" followed by "Name," which might be enclosed in quotes. Once this line is matched, we use **getline** to read the next input line. When the new line is read, **getline** assigns it $0 and parses it into fields. The system variables **NF**, **NR**, and **FNR** are also set. Thus, the new line becomes the current line, and we are able to refer to "$1" and retrieve the first field. Note that the previous line is no longer available as $0. However, if necessary, you can assign the line read by **getline** to a variable and avoid changing $0, as we'll see shortly.

Here's an example that shows how the previous script works, printing out the first field of the line following ".SH Name."

```
$ awk -f getline.awk test
XSubImage
```

The **sorter.awk** program that we demonstrated at the end of Chapter 9, *Functions*, could have used **getline** to read all the lines after the heading "Related Commands." We can test the return value of **getline** in a **while** loop to read a number of lines from the input. The following procedure replaces the first two procedures in the **sorter** program:

```
# Match "Related Commands" and collect them
/^\.SH "?Related Commands"?/ {
        print
        while (getline > 0)
                commandList = commandList $0
}
```

The expression "getline > 0" will be true as long as **getline** successfully reads an input line. When it gets to the end-of-file, **getline** returns 0 and the loop is exited.

## Reading Input from Files

Besides reading from the regular input stream, the **getline** function allows you to read input from a file or a pipe. For instance, the following statement reads the next line from the file *data*:

```
getline < "data"
```

Although the filename can be supplied through a variable, it is typically specified as a string constant, which must be enclosed in quotes. The symbol "<" is the same as the shell's input redirection symbol and will not be interpreted as the "less than" symbol. We can use a **while** loop to read all the lines from a file, testing for an end-of-file to exit the loop. The following example opens the file *data* and prints all of its lines:

```
while ( (getline < "data") > 0 )
        print
```

(We parenthesize to avoid confusion; the "<" is a redirection, while the ">" is a comparison of the return value.) The input can also come from standard input. You can use **getline** following a prompt for the user to enter information:

```
BEGIN { printf "Enter your name: "
        getline < "-"
        print
}
```

This sample code prints the prompt "Enter your name:" (**printf** is used because we don't want a carriage return after the prompt), and then calls **getline** to gather the user's response.[*] The response is assigned to $0, and the **print** statement outputs that value.

---

[*] At least at one time, SGI versions of nawk did not support the use of "-" with **getline** to read from standard input. Caveat emptor.

## Assigning the Input to a Variable

The **getline** function allows you to assign the input record to a variable. The name of the variable is supplied as an argument. Thus, the following statement reads the next line of input into the variable **input**:

```
getline input
```

Assigning the input to a variable does not affect the current input line; that is, $0 is not affected. The new input line is not split into fields, and thus the variable **NF** is also unaffected. It does increment the record counters, **NR** and **FNR**.

The previous example demonstrated how to prompt the user. That example could be written as follows, assigning the user's response to the variable **name**.

```
BEGIN { printf "Enter your name: "
        getline name < "-"
        print name
}
```

Study the syntax for assigning the input data to a variable because it is a common mistake to instead write:

```
name = getline     # wrong
```

which assigns the return value of **getline** to the variable **name**.

## Reading Input from a Pipe

You can execute a command and pipe the output into **getline**. For example, look at the following expression:

```
"who am i" | getline
```

That expression sets "$0" to the output of the **who am i** command.

```
dale        ttyC3       Jul 18 13:37
```

The line is parsed into fields and the system variable **NF** is set. Similarly, you can assign the result to a variable:

```
"who am i" | getline me
```

By assigning the output to a variable, you avoid setting $0 and **NF**, but the line is not split into fields.

The following script is a fairly simple example of piping the output of a command to **getline**. It uses the output from the **who am i** command to get the user's name. It then looks up the name in */etc/passwd*, printing out the fifth field of that file, the user's full name:

```
awk '# getname - print users fullname from /etc/passwd
BEGIN { "who am i" | getline
        name = $1
        FS = ":"
}
name ~ $1 { print $5 }
' /etc/passwd
```

The command is executed from the **BEGIN** procedure, and it provides us with the name of the user that will be used to find the user's entry in */etc/passwd*. As explained above, **who am i** outputs a single line, which **getline** assigns to $0. $1, the first field of that output, is then assigned to **name**.

The field separator is set to a colon (:) to allow us to access individual fields in entries in the */etc/passwd* file. Notice that **FS** is set after **getline** or else the parsing of the command's output would be affected.

Finally, the main procedure is designed to test that the first field matches **name**. If it does, the fifth field of the entry is printed. For instance, when Dale runs this script, it prints "Dale Dougherty."

When the output of a command is piped to **getline** and it contains multiple lines, **getline** reads a line at a time. The first time **getline** is called it reads the first line of output. If you call it again, it reads the second line. To read all the lines of output, you must set up a loop that executes **getline** until there is no more output. For instance, the following example uses a **while** loop to read each line of output and assign it to the next element of the array, **who_out**:

```
while ("who" | getline)
      who_out[++i] = $0
```

Each time the **getline** function is called, it reads the next line of output. The **who** command, however, is executed only once.

The next example looks for "@date" in a document and replaces it with today's date:

```
# subdate.awk -- replace @date with todays date
/@date/ {
        "date +'%a., %h %d, %Y'" | getline today
        gsub(/@date/, today)
}
{ print }
```

The **date** command, using its formatting options,[*] provides the date and **getline** assigns it to the variable **today**. The **gsub()** function replaces each instance of "@date" with today's date.

---

[*] Older versions of **date** don't support formatting options. Particularly the one on SunOS 4.1.x systems; there you have to use */usr/5bin/date*. Check your local documentation.

This script might be used to insert the date in a form letter:

```
To: Peabody
From: Sherman
Date: @date

I am writing you on @date to
remind you about our special offer.
```

All lines of the input file would be passed through as is, except the lines containing "@date", which are replaced with today's date:

```
$ awk -f subdate.awk subdate.test
To: Peabody
From: Sherman
Date: Sun., May 05, 1996

I am writing you on Sun., May 05, 1996 to
remind you about our special offer.
```

## *The close() Function*

The **close**() function allows you to close open files and pipes. There are a number of reasons you should use it.

- You can only have so many pipes open at a time. (See the section "Limitations" below, which describes how such limitations can differ from system to system.) In order to open as many pipes in a program as you wish, you must use the **close**() function to close a pipe when you are done with it (ordinarily, when **getline** returns 0 or -1). It takes a single argument, the same expression used to create the pipe. Here's an example:

  ```
  close("who")
  ```

- Closing a pipe allows you to run the same command twice. For example, you can use **date** twice to time a command.

- Using **close**() may be necessary in order to get an output pipe to finish its work. For example:

  ```
  { some processing of $0 | "sort > tmpfile" }
  END {
          close("sort > tmpfile")
          while ((getline < "tmpfile") > 0) {
                  do more work
          }
  }
  ```

- Closing open files is necessary to keep you from exceeding your system's limit on simultaneously open files.

We will see an example of the **close()** function in the section "Working with Multiple Files" later in this chapter.

# The system() Function

The **system()** function executes a command supplied as an expression.[*] It does not, however, make the output of the command available within the program for processing. It returns the exit status of the command that was executed. The script waits for the command to finish before continuing execution. The following example executes the **mkdir** command:

```
BEGIN { if (system("mkdir dale") != 0)
                print "Command Failed" }
```

The **system()** function is called from an **if** statement that tests for a non-zero exit status. Running the program twice produces one success and one failure:

```
$ awk -f system.awk
$ ls dale
$ awk -f system.awk
mkdir: dale: File exists
Command Failed
```

The first run creates the new directory and **system()** returns an exit status of 0 (success). The second time the command is executed, the directory already exists, so **mkdir** fails and produces an error message. The "Command Failed" message is produced by awk.

The Berkeley UNIX command set has a small but useful command for **troff** users named **soelim**, named because it "eliminates" ".so" lines from a **troff** input file. (**.so** is a request to include or "source" the contents of the named file.) If you have an older System V system that does not have **soelim**, you can use the following awk script to create it:

```
/^\.so/ { gsub(/"/, "", $2)
                system("cat " $2)
                next
                }
        { print }
```

This script looks for ".so" at the beginning of a line, removes any quotation marks, and then uses **system()** to execute the **cat** command and output the contents of the file. This output merges with the rest of the lines in the file, which are simply printed to standard output, as in the following example.

---

[*] The **system()** function is modeled after the standard C library function of the same name.

```
$ cat soelim.test
This is a test
.so test1
This is a test
.so test2
This is a test.
$ awk -f soelim.awk soelim.test
This is a test
first:second
one:two
This is a test
three:four
five:six
This is a test.
```

We don't explicitly test the exit status of the command. Thus, if the file does not
exist, the error messages merge with the output:

```
$ awk -f soelim.awk soelim.test
This is a test
first:second
one:two
This is a test
cat: cannot open test2
This is a test.
```

We might want to test the return value of the **system()** function and generate an
error message for the user. This program is also very simplistic: it does not handle
instances of ".so" nested in the included file. Think about how you might implement a version of this program that did handle nested ".so" requests.

This example is a function prompting you to enter a filename. It uses the **system()**
function to execute the **test** command to verify the file exists and is readable:

```
# getFilename function -- prompts user for filename,
#    verifies that file exists and returns absolute pathname.
function getFilename(    file) {
    while (! file) {
        printf "Enter a filename: "
        getline < "-" # get response
        file = $0
        # check that file exists and is readable
        # test returns 1 if file does not exist.
        if (system("test -r " file)) {
                print file " not found"
                file = ""
        }
    }
    if (file !~ /^\//) {
        "pwd" | getline # get current directory
        close("pwd")
        file = $0 "/" file
    }
    return file
}
```

This function returns the absolute pathname of the file specified by the user. It places the prompting and verification sequence inside a **while** loop in order to allow the user to make a different entry if the previous one is invalid.

The **test -r** command returns 0 if the file exists and is readable, and 1 if not. Once it is determined that the filename is valid, then we test the filename to see if it begins with a "/", which would indicate that the user supplied an absolute pathname. If that test fails, we use the **getline** function to get the output of the **pwd** command and prepend it to the filename. (Admittedly, the script makes no attempt to deal with "./" or "../" entries, although tests can be easily devised to match them.) Note the two uses of the **getline** function: the first gets the user's response and the second executes the **pwd** command.

# A Menu-Based Command Generator

In this section, we look at a general use of the **system()** and **getline** functions to implement a menu-based command generator. The object of this program is to give unsophisticated users a simple way to execute long or complex UNIX commands. A menu is used to prompt the user with a description of the task to be performed, allowing the user to choose by number any selection of the menu to execute.

This program is designed as a kind of interpreter that reads from a file the descriptions that appear in the menu and the actual command lines that are executed. That way, multiple menu-command files can be used, and they can be easily modified by awk-less users without changing the program.

The format of a menu-command file contains the menu title as the first line in the file. Subsequent lines contain two fields: the first is the description of the action to be performed and the second is the command line that performs it. An example is shown below:

```
$ cat uucp_commands
UUCP Status Menu
Look at files in PUBDIR:find /var/spool/uucppublic -print
Look at recent status in LOGFILE:tail /var/spool/uucp/LOGFILE
Look for lock files:ls /var/spool/uucp/*.LCK
```

The first step in implementing the menu-based command generator is to read the menu-command file. We read the first line of this file and assign it to a variable named **title**. The rest of the lines contain two fields and are read into two arrays, one for the menu items and one for the commands to be executed. A **while** loop is used, along with **getline**, to read one line at a time from the file.

```
BEGIN { FS = ":"
if ((getline < CMDFILE) > 0)
        title = $1
else
        exit 1
while ((getline < CMDFILE) > 0) {
        # load array
        ++sizeOfArray
        # array of menu items
        menu[sizeOfArray] = $1
        # array of commands associated with items
        command[sizeOfArray] = $2
        }
...
}
```

Look carefully at the syntax of the expression tested by the **if** statement and the
**while** loop.

```
(getline < CMDFILE) > 0
```

The variable **CMDFILE** is the name of the menu-command file, which is passed as
a command-line parameter. The two angle-bracket symbols have completely different functions. The "<" symbol is interpreted by **getline** as the input redirection
operator. Then the value returned by **getline** is tested to see if it is greater than
(">") 0. It is parenthesized on purpose, in order to make this clear. In other words,
"getline < CMDFILE" is evaluated first and then its return value is compared to 0.

This procedure is placed in the **BEGIN** pattern. However, there is one catch.
Because we intended to pass the name of the menu file as a command-line param-
eter, the variable **CMDFILE** would not normally be defined and available in the
**BEGIN** pattern. In other words, the following command will *not* work:

```
awk script CMDFILE="uucp_commands" -
```

because **CMDFILE** variable won't be defined until the first line of input is read.

Fortunately, awk provides the *-v* option to handle just such a case. Using the *-v*
option makes sure that the variable is set immediately and thus available in the
**BEGIN** pattern.

```
awk -v CMDFILE="uucp_commands" script
```

If your version of awk doesn't have the *-v* option, you can pass the value of **CMD-
FILE** as a shell variable. Create a shell script to execute awk and in it define **CMD-
FILE**. Then change the line that reads **CMDFILE** in the **invoke** script (see below) as
follows:

```
while ((getline < '"$CMDFILE"') > 0 ) {
```

Once the menu-command file is loaded, the program must display the menu and prompt the user. This is implemented as a function because we need to call it in two places: from the **BEGIN** pattern to prompt the user initially, and after we have processed the user's response so that another choice can be made. Here's the **display_menu( )** function:

```
function display_menu() {
        # clear screen -- comment out if clear does not work
        system("clear")
        # print title, list of items, exit item, and prompt
        print "\t" title
        for (i = 1; i <= sizeOfArray; ++i)
                printf "\t%d. %s\n", i, menu[i]
        printf "\t%d. Exit\n", i
        printf("Choose one: ")
}
```

The first thing we do is use the **system( )** function to call a command to clear the screen. (On my system, **clear** does this; on others it may be **cls** or some other command. Comment out the line if you cannot find such a command.) Then we print the title and each of the items in a numbered list. The last item is always "Exit." Finally, we prompt the user for a choice.

The program will take standard input so that the user's answer to the prompt will be the first line of input. Our reading of the menu-command file was done within the program and not as part of the input stream. Thus, the main procedure of the program is to respond to the user's choice and execute a command. Here's that part of the program:

```
# Applies the user response to prompt
{
    # test value of user response
    if ($1 > 0 && $1 <= sizeOfArray) {
            # print command that is executed
            printf("Executing ... %s\n", command[$1])
            # then execute it.
            system(command[$1])
            printf("<Press RETURN to continue>")
            # wait for input before displaying menu again
            getline
    }
    else
            exit
    # re-display menu
    display_menu()
}
```

First, we test the range of the user's response. If the response falls outside the range, we simply exit the program. If it is a valid response, then we retrieve the command from the array **command**, display it, and then execute it using the system() function. The user sees the result of the command on the screen followed by the message "<Press RETURN to continue>." The purpose of this message is to wait for the user to finish before clearing the screen and redisplaying the menu. The **getline** function causes the program to wait for a response. Note that we don't do anything with the response. The **display_menu()** function is called at the end of this procedure to redisplay the menu and prompt for another line of input.

Here's the **invoke** program in full:

```
awk -v CMDFILE="uucp_commands"  '# invoke -- menu-based
                                 # command generator
# first line in CMDFILE is the title of the menu
# subsequent lines contain: $1 - Description;
# $2 Command to execute
BEGIN { FS = ":"
# process CMDFILE, reading items into menu array
   if ((getline < CMDFILE) > 0)
          title = $1
   else
          exit 1
   while ((getline < CMDFILE) > 0) {
          # load array
          ++sizeOfArray
          # array of menu items
          menu[sizeOfArray] = $1
          # array of commands associated with items
          command[sizeOfArray] = $2
   }
   # call function to display menu items and prompt
   display_menu()
}
# Applies the user response to prompt
{
   # test value of user response
   if ($1 > 0 && $1 <= sizeOfArray) {
          # print command that is executed
          printf("Executing ... %s\n", command[$1])
          # then execute it.
          system(command[$1])
          printf("<Press RETURN to continue>")
          # wait for input before displaying menu again
          getline
   }
   else
          exit
   # re-display menu
   display_menu()
}
```

```
function display_menu() {
        # clear screen -- if clear does not work, try "cls"
        system("clear")
        # print title, list of items, exit item, and prompt
        print "\t" title
        for (i = 1; i <= sizeOfArray; ++i)
                printf "\t%d. %s\n", i, menu[i]
        printf "\t%d. Exit\n", i
        printf("Choose one: ")
}' -
```

When a user runs the program, the following output is displayed:

```
UUCP Status Menu
        1. Look at files in PUBDIR
        2. Look at recent status in LOGFILE
        3. Look for lock files
        4. Exit
Choose one:
```

The user is prompted to enter the number of a menu selection. Anything other than a number between 1 and 3 exits the menu. For instance, if the user enters "1" to see a list of files in *uucp*'s public directory, then the following result is displayed on the screen:

```
Executing ...find /var/spool/uucppublic -print
/var/spool/uucppublic
/var/spool/uucppublic/dale
/var/spool/uucppublic/HyperBugs
<Press RETURN to continue>
```

When the user presses the RETURN key, the menu is redisplayed on the screen. The user can quit from the program by choosing "4".

This program is really a shell for executing commands. Any sequence of commands (even other awk programs) can be executed by modifying the menu-command file. In other words, the part of the program that might change the most is extracted from the program itself and maintained in a separate file. This allows the menu list to be changed and extended very easily by a nontechnical user.

## *Directing Output to Files and Pipes*

The output of any **print** or **printf** statement can be directed to a file, using the output redirection operators ">" or ">>". For example, the following statement writes the current record to the file *data.out*:

```
print > "data.out"
```

The filename can be any expression that evaluates to a valid filename. A file is opened by the first use of the redirection operator, and subsequent uses append data to the file. The difference between ">" and ">>" is the same as between the shell redirection operators. A right-angle bracket (">") truncates the file when opening it while ">>" preserves whatever the file contains and appends data to it.

Because the redirection operator ">" is the same as the relational operator, there is the potential for confusion when you specify an expression as an argument to the **print** command. The rule is that ">" will be interpreted as a redirection operator when it appears in an argument list for any of the print statements. To use ">" as a relational operator in an expression that appears in the argument list, put either the expression or the argument list in parentheses. For example, the following example uses parentheses around the conditional expression to make sure that the relational expression is evaluated properly:

```
print "a =", a, "b =", b, "max =", (a > b ? a : b) > "data.out"
```

The conditional expression evaluates whether **a** is greater than **b**; if it is, then the value of **a** is printed as the maximum value; otherwise, **b**'s value is used.

## Directing Output to a Pipe

You can also direct output to a pipe. The command

```
print | command
```

opens a pipe the first time it is executed and sends the current record as input to that command. In other words, the command is only invoked once, but each execution of the **print** command supplies another line of input.

The following script strips **troff** macros and requests from the current input line and then sends the line as input to **wc** to determine how many words are in the file:

```
{# words.awk - strip macros then get word count
sub(/^\.../,"")
print | "wc -w"
}
```

By removing formatting codes, we get a truer word count.

In most cases, we prefer to use a shell script to pipe the output of the awk command to another command rather than do it inside the awk script. For instance, we'd write the previous example as a shell script invoking awk and piping its output to **wc**:

```
awk '{ # words -- strip macros
sub(/^\.../,"")
print
}' $* |
# get word count
wc -w
```

This method seems simpler and easier to understand. Nonetheless, the other method has the advantage of accomplishing the same thing without creating a shell script.

Remember that you can only have so many pipes open at a time. Use the **close()** function to close the pipe when you are done with it.

## Working with Multiple Files

A file is opened whenever you read from or write to a file. Every operating system has some limit on the number of files a running program may have open. Furthermore, each implementation of awk may have an internal limit on the number of open files; this number could be smaller than the system's limit.[*] So that you don't run out of open files, awk provides a **close()** function that allows you to close an open file. Closing files that you have finished processing allows your program to open more files later on.

A common use for directing output to files is to split up a large file into a number of smaller files. Although UNIX provides utilities, **split** and **csplit**, that do a similar job, they do not have the ability to give the new file a useful filename.

Similarly, sed can be used to write to a file, but you must specify a fixed filename. With awk, you can use a variable to specify the filename and pick up the value from a pattern in the file. For instance, if $1 provided a string that could be used as a filename, you could write a script to output each record to its own file:

```
print $0 > $1
```

You should perhaps test the filename, either to determine its length or to look for characters that cannot be used in a filename.

If you don't close your files, such a program would eventually run out of available open files, and have to give up. The example we are going to look at works because it uses the **close()** function so that you will not run into any open-file limitations.

---

[*] Gawk will attempt to appear to have more files open than the system limit by closing and reopening files as needed. Even though gawk is "smart," it is still more efficient to close your files when you're done with them.

The following script was used to split up a large file containing dozens of man-pages. Each manual page began by setting a number register and ended with a blank line:

```
.nr X 0
```

(Although they used the **-man** macros for the most part, the beginning of a man-page was strangely coded, making things a little harder.) The line that provides the filename looks like this:

```
.if \nX=0 .ds x}  XDrawLine "" "Xlib - Drawing Primitives"
```

The fifth field on this line, "XDrawLine," contains the filename. Perhaps the only difficulty in writing the script is that the first line is not the one that provides the filename. Therefore, we collect the lines in an array until we get a filename. Once we get the filename, we output the array, and from that point on we simply write each input line to the new file. Here's the **man.split** script:

```
# man.split -- split up a file containing X manpages.
BEGIN { file = 0; i = 0; filename = "" }

# First line of new manpage is ".nr X 0"
# Last line is blank
/^\.nr X 0/,/^$/ {
        # this conditional collects lines until we get a filename.
        if (file == 0)
                line[++i] = $0
        else
                print $0 > filename

        # this matches the line that gives us the filename
        if ($4 == "x}") {
                # now we have a filename
                filename = $5
                file = 1
                # output name to screen
                print filename
                # print any lines collected
                for (x = 1; x <= i; ++x){
                        print line[x] > filename
                }
                i = 0
        }

        # close up and clean up for next one
        if ($0 ~ /^$/) {
                close(filename)
                filename = ""
                file = 0
                i = 0
        }
}
```

As you can see, we use the variable **file** as a flag to convey whether or not we have a valid filename and can write to the file. Initially, **file** is 0, and the current input line is stored in an array. The variable **i** is a counter used to index the array. When we encounter the line that sets the filename, then we set **file** to 1. The name of the new file is printed to the screen so that the user can get some feedback on the progress of the script. Then we loop through the array and output it to the new file. When the next input line is read, **file** will be set to 1 and the **print** statement will output it to the named file.

# *Generating Columnar Reports*

This section describes a small-scale business application that produces reports with dollar amounts. While this application doesn't introduce any new material, it does emphasize the data processing and reporting capabilities of awk. (Surprisingly, some people do use awk to write small business applications.)

It is presumed that a script exists for data entry. The data-entry script has two jobs: the first is to enter the customer's name and mailing address for later use in building a mailing list; the second is to record the customer's order of any of seven items, the number of items ordered, and the price per item. The data collected for the mailing list and the customer order were written to separate files.

Here are two sample customer records from the customer order file:

```
Charlotte Webb
P.O  N61331 97 Y 045      Date: 03/14/97
#1 3   7.50
#2 3   7.50
#3 1   7.50
#4 1   7.50
#7 1   7.50

Martin S. Rossi
P.O  NONE        Date: 03/14/97
#1 2   7.50
#2 5   6.75
```

Each order covers multiple lines, and a blank line separates one order from another. The first two lines supply the customer's name, purchase order number and the date of the order. Each subsequent line identifies an item by number, the number ordered, and the price of the item.

Let's write a simple program that multiplies the number of items by the price. The script can ignore the first two lines of each record. We only want to read the lines where an item is specified, as in the following example.

```
awk '/^#/ {
                amount = $2 * $3
                printf "%s %6.2f\n", $0, amount
                next
        }
{ print }' $*
```

The main procedure only affects lines that match the pattern. It multiplies the second field by the third field, assigning the value to the variable **amount**. The **printf** conversion %f is used to print a floating-point number; "6.2" specifies a minimum field width of six and a precision of two. Precision is the number of digits to the right of the decimal point; the default for %f is six. We print the current record along with the value of the variable **amount**. If a line is printed within this procedure, the next line is read from standard input. Lines not matching the pattern are simply passed through. Let's look at how **addem** works:

```
$ addem orders
Charlotte Webb
P.O  N61331 97 Y 045      Date: 03/14/97
#1 3  7.50  22.50
#2 3  7.50  22.50
#3 1  7.50   7.50
#4 1  7.50   7.50
#7 1  7.50   7.50


Martin S. Rossi
P.O  NONE        Date: 03/14/97
#1 2  7.50  15.00
#2 5  6.75  33.75
```

This program did not need to access the customer record as a whole; it simply acted on the individual item lines. Now, let's design a program that reads multiline records and accumulates order information for display in a report. This report should display for each item the total number of copies and the total amount. We also want totals reflecting all copies ordered and the sum of all orders.

Our new script will begin by setting the field and record separators:

```
BEGIN { FS = "\n"; RS = "" }
```

Each record has a variable number of fields, depending upon how many items have been ordered. First, we check that the input record has at least three fields. Then a **for** loop is built to read all of the fields beginning with the third field.

```
NF >= 3 {
for (i = 3; i <= NF; ++i) {
```

In database terms, each field has a value and each value can be further broken up as subvalues. That is, if the value of a field in a multiline record is a single line, subvalues are the words that are on that line. We can use the **split()** function to divide a field into subvalues.

The following part of the script splits each field into subvalues. **$i** will supply the value of the current field that will be divided into elements of the array **order**:

```
sv = split($i, order, " ")
if (sv == 3) {
        procedure
} else
        print "Incomplete Record"
} # end for loop
```

The number of elements returned by the function is saved in a variable **sv**. This allows us to test that there are three subvalues. If there are not, the **else** statement is executed, printing the error message to the screen.

Next we assign each individual element of the array to a specific variable. This is mainly to make it easier to remember what each element represents:

```
title = order[1]
copies = order[2]
price = order[3]
```

Then we perform a group of arithmetic operations on these values:

```
amount = copies * price
total_vol += copies
total_amt += amount
vol[title] += copies
amt[title] += amount
```

We accumulate these values until the last input record is read. The **END** procedure prints the report.

Here's the complete program:

```
$ cat addemup
#! /bin/sh
# addemup -- total customer orders
awk 'BEGIN { FS = "\n"; RS = "" }
NF >= 3 {
        for (i = 3; i <= NF; ++i) {
                sv = split($i, order, " ")
                if (sv == 3) {
                        title = order[1]
                        copies = order[2]
                        price = order[3]
                        amount = copies * price
                        total_vol += copies
                        total_amt += amount
                        vol[title] += copies
                        amt[title] += amount
                } else
                        print "Incomplete Record"
        }
}
```

```
END {
    printf "%5s\t%10s\t%6s\n\n", "TITLE", "COPIES SOLD", "TOTAL"
    for (title in vol)
        printf "%5s\t%10d\t$%7.2f\n", title, vol[title], amt[title]
    printf "%s\n", "-------------"
    printf "\t%s%4d\t$%7.2f\n", "Total ", total_vol, total_amt
}' $*
```

We have defined two arrays that have the same subscript. We only need to have one **for** loop to read both arrays.

**addemup**, an order report generator, produces the following output:

```
$ addemup orders.today
TITLE       COPIES SOLD      TOTAL

  #1              5       $  37.50
  #2              8       $  56.25
  #3              1       $   7.50
  #4              1       $   7.50
  #7              1       $   7.50
-------------
      Total      16       $ 116.25
```

# *Debugging*

No aspect of programming is more frustrating or more essential than debugging. In this section, we'll look at ways to debug awk scripts and offer advice on how to correct an awk program that fails to do what it is supposed to do.

Modern versions of awk do a pretty good job of reporting syntax errors. But even with good error detection, it is often difficult to isolate the problem. The techniques for discovering the source of the problem are a modest few and are fairly obvious. Unfortunately, most awk implementations come with no debugging tools or extensions.

There are two classes of problems with a program. The first is really a bug in the program's logic. The program runs—that is, it finishes without reporting any error messages, but it does not produce the result you wanted. For instance, perhaps it does not create any output. This bug could be caused by failing to use a **print** statement to output the result of a calculation. Program errors are mental errors, if you will.

The second class of error is one in which the program fails to execute or complete execution. This could result from a syntax error and cause awk to spit code at you that it is unable to interpret. Many syntax errors are the result of a typo or a missing brace or parenthesis. Syntax errors usually generate error messages that help direct you to the problem. Sometimes, however, a program may cause awk to fail (or "core dump") without producing any reasonable error message.* This may also be caused by a syntax error, but there could be problems specific to the machine. We have had a few larger scripts that dumped core on one machine while they ran without a problem on another. You could, for instance, be running up against limitations set for awk for that particular implementation. See the section "Limitations", later in this chapter.

You should be clear in your mind which type of program bug you are trying to find: an error in the script's logic or an error in its syntax.

## *Make a Copy*

Before you begin debugging a program, make a copy of it. This is extremely important. To debug an awk script, you have to change it. These modifications may point you to the error but many changes will have no effect or may introduce new problems. It's good to be able to restore changes that you make. However, it is bothersome to restore each change that you make, so I like to continue making changes until I have found the problem. When I know what it is, I go back to the original and make the change. In effect, that restores all the other inconsequential changes that were made in the copy.

It is also helpful to view the process of creating a program as a series of stages. Look at a core set of features as a single stage. Once you have implemented these features and tested them, make a copy of the program before going to the next stage to develop new features. That way, you can always return to the previous stage if you have problems with the code that you add.

We would recommend that you formalize this process, and go so far as to use a source code management system, such as SCCS (Source Code Control System), RCS (Revision Control System), or CVS (Concurrent Versioning System, which is compatible with RCS). The latter two are freely available from any GNU FTP mirror site.

## *Before and After Photos*

What is difficult in debugging awk is that you don't always know what is happening during the course of the program. You can inspect the input and the output, but there is no way to stop the program in mid-course and examine its state. Thus, it is difficult to know which part of the program is causing a problem.

---

* This indicates that the awk implementation is poor. Core dumps are very rare in modern versions of awk.

A common problem is determining when or where in the program the assignment of a variable takes place. The first method of attack is to use the **print** statement to print the value of the variable at various points in the program. For instance, it is common to use a variable as a flag to determine that a certain condition has occurred. At the beginning of the program, the flag might be set to 0. At one or more points in the program, the value of this flag might be set to 1. The problem is to find where the change actually occurs. If you want to check the flag at a particular part of the program, use **print** statements before and after the assignment. For instance:

```
print flag, "before"
if (! $1) {
        .
        .
        .
        flag = 1
}
print flag, "after"
```

If you are unsure about the result of a substitution command or any function, print the string before and after the function is called:

```
print $2
sub(/ *\(/, "(", $2)
print $2
```

The value of printing the value before the substitution command is to make sure that the command sees the value that you think should be there. A previous command might have changed that variable. The problem may turn out to be that the format of the input record is not as you thought. Checking the input carefully is a very important step in debugging. In particular, use **print** statements to verify that the sequence of fields is as you expect. When you find that input is causing the problem, you can either fix the input or write new code to accommodate it.

## Finding Out Where the Problem Is

The more modular a script is—that is, the more it can be broken down into separate parts—the easier it is to test and debug the program. One of the advantages of writing functions is that you can isolate what is going on inside the function and test it without affecting other parts of the program. You can omit an entire action and see what happens.

If a program has a number of branching constructs, you might find that an input line falls through one of branches. Test that the input reaches part of a program. For instance, when debugging the **masterindex** program, described in Chapter 12,

*Full-Featured Applications*, we wanted to know if an entry containing the word "retrieving" was being handled in a particular part of the program. We inserted the following line in the part of the program where we thought it should be encountered:

```
if ($0 ~ /retrieving/) print ">> retrieving" > "/dev/tty"
```

When the program runs, if it encounters the string "retrieving," it will print the message. ("`>>`" is used as a pair of characters that will instantly call attention to the output; "`!!`" is also a good one.)

Sometimes you might not be sure which of several **print** statements are causing a problem. Insert identifiers into the **print** statement that will alert you to the **print** statement being executed. In the following example, we simply use the variable name to identify what is printed with a label:

```
if (PRIMARY)
        print (">>PRIMARY:", PRIMARY)
else
        if (SECONDARY)
                print (">>SECONDARY:", SECONDARY)
        else
                print (">>TERTIARY:", TERTIARY)
```

This technique is also useful for investigating whether or not parts of the program are executed at all. Some programs get to be like remodeled homes: a room is added here, a wall is taken down there. Trying to understand the basic structure can be difficult. You might wonder if each of the parts is truly needed or indeed if it is ever executed at all.

If an awk program is part of a pipeline of several programs, even other awk programs, you can use the **tee** command to redirect output to a file, while also piping the output to the next command. For instance, look at the shell script for running the **masterindex** program, as shown in Chapter 12:

```
$INDEXDIR/input.idx $FILES |
sort -bdf -t:  +0 -1 +1 -2 +3 -4 +2n -3n | uniq |
$INDEXDIR/pagenums.idx | tee page.tmp |
$INDEXDIR/combine.idx |
$INDEXDIR/format.idx
```

By adding "tee page.tmp", we are able to capture the output of the **pagenums.idx** program in a file named *page.tmp*. The same output is also piped to **combine.idx**.

## Commenting Out Loud

Another technique is simply commenting out a series of lines that may be causing problems to see whether they really are. We recommend developing a consistent two-character symbol such as "#%" to comment out lines temporarily. Then you will notice them on subsequent editing and remember to deal with them. It also becomes easier to remove the symbols and restore the lines with a single editing command that does not affect program comments:

```
#% if ( thisFails )
        print "I give up"
```

Using the comment here eliminates the conditional, so the **print** statement is executed unconditionally.

## Slash and Burn

When all else fails, arm yourself with your editor's delete command and begin deleting portions of the program until the error disappears. Of course, make a copy of the program and delete lines from the temporary copy. This is a very crude technique, but an effective one to use before giving up altogether or starting over from scratch. It is sometimes the only way to discover what is wrong when the only result you get is that the program dumps core. The idea is the same as above, to isolate the problem code. Remove a function, for instance, or a **for** loop to see if it is the cause of the problem. Be sure to cut out complete units: for instance, all the statements within braces and the matching braces. If the problem persists—the program continues to break—then cut out another large section of the program. Sooner or later, you will find the part that is causing the problem.

You can use "slash and burn" to learn how a program works. First, run the original program on sample input, saving the output. Begin by removing a part of the program that you don't understand. Then run the modified program on sample input and compare the output to the original. Look to see what changed.

## Getting Defensive About Your Script

There are all types of input errors and inconsistencies that will turn up bugs in your script. You probably didn't consider that *user* errors will be pointed to as problems with *your* program. Therefore, it is a good idea to surround your core program with "defensive" procedures designed to trap inconsistent input records and prevent the program from failing unexpectedly. For instance, you might want to verify each input record before processing it, making sure that the proper number of fields exist or that the kind of data that you expect is found in a particular field.

Another aspect of incorporating defensive techniques is error handling. In other words, what do you want to have happen once the program detects an error? While in some cases you can have the program continue, in other cases it may be preferable that the program print an error message and/or halt.

It is also appropriate to recognize that awk scripts are typically confined to the realm of quick fixes, programs that solve a particular problem rather than solving a class of problems encountered by many different users. Because of the nature of these programs, it is not really necessary that they be professional quality. Thus, it is not necessary to write 100% user-proof programs. For one thing, defensive programming is quite time-consuming and frequently tedious. Secondly, as amateurs, we are at liberty to write programs that perform the way we expect them to; a professional has to write for an audience and must account for their expectations. In brief, if you are writing the script for others to use, consider how it may be used and what problems its users may encounter before considering the program complete. If not, maybe the fact that the script works—even for a very narrow set of circumstances—is good enough and all there is time for.

# *Limitations*

There are fixed limits within any awk implementation. The only trouble is that the documentation seldom reports them. Table 10-1 lists the limitations as described in *The AWK Programming Language*. These limitations are implementation-specific but they are good ballpark figures for most systems.

*Table 10–1: Limitations*

| Item | Limit |
|---|---|
| Number of fields per record | 100 |
| Characters per input record | 3000 |
| Characters per output record | 3000 |
| Characters per field | 1024 |
| Characters per printf string | 3000 |
| | |
| Characters in literal string | 400 |
| Characters in character class | 400 |
| Files open | 15 |
| Pipes open | 1 |

---

*NOTE*     Despite the number in Table 10-1, experience has shown that most awks allow you to have more than one open pipe.

---

In terms of numeric values, awk uses double-precision, floating-point numbers that are limited in size by the machine's architecture.

Running into these limits can cause unanticipated problems with scripts. In developing examples for the first edition of this book, Dale thought he'd write a search program that could look for a word or sequence of words in a single paragraph. The idea was to read a document as a series of multiline records and if any of the fields contained the search term, print the record, which was a paragraph. It could be used to search through mail files where blank lines delimit paragraphs. The resulting program worked for small test files. However, when tried on larger files, the program dumped core because it encountered a paragraph that was longer than the maximum input record size, which is 3000 characters. (Actually, the file contained an included mail message where blank lines within the message were prefixed by ">".) Thus, when reading multiple lines as a single record, you better be sure that you don't anticipate records longer than 3000 characters. By the way, there is no particular error message that alerts you to the fact that the problem is the size of the current record.

Fortunately, gawk and mawk (see Chapter 11, *A Flock of awks*) don't have such small limits; for example, the number of fields in a record is limited in gawk to the maximum value that can be held in a C **long**, and certainly records can be longer than 3000 characters. These versions allow you to have more open files and pipes.

Recent versions of the Bell Labs awk have two options, *-mf N* and *-mr N*, that allow you to set the maximum number of fields and the maximum record size on the command line, as an emergency way to get around the default limits.

(Sed implementations also have their own limits, which aren't documented. Experience has shown that most UNIX versions of sed have a limit of 99 or 100 substitute (**s**) commands.)

# *Invoking awk Using the #! Syntax*

The "#!" syntax is an alternative syntax for invoking awk from a shell script. It has the advantage of allowing you to specify awk parameters and filenames on the shell-script command line. The "#!" syntax is recognized on modern UNIX systems, but is not typically found in older System V systems. The best way to use this syntax is to put the following line as the first line[*] of the shell script:

```
#!/bin/awk -f
```

"#!" is followed by the pathname that locates your version of awk and then the *-f* option. After this line, you specify the awk script:

---

* Note that the pathname to use is system-specific.

```
#!/bin/awk -f
{ print $1 }
```

Note that no quotes are necessary around the script. All lines in the file after the first one will be executed as though they were specified in a separate script file.

A few years ago, there was an interesting discussion on the Net about the use of the "#!" syntax that clarified how it works. The discussion was prompted by a 4.2BSD user's observation that the shell script below fails:

```
#!/bin/awk
{ print $1 }
```

while the one below works:

```
#!/bin/sh
/bin/awk '{ print $1 }'
```

The two responses that we saw were by Chris Torek and Guy Harris and we will try to summarize their explanation. The first script fails because it passes the file-name of the script as the first parameter (**argv[1]** in C) and awk interprets it as the input file and not the script file. Because no script has been supplied, awk produces a syntax error message. In other words, if the name of the shell script is "myscript," then the first script executes as:

```
/bin/awk myscript
```

If the script was changed to add the *-f* option, it looks like this:

```
#!/bin/awk -f
{ print $1 }
```

Then you enter the following command:

```
$ myscript myfile
```

It then executes as though you had typed:

```
/bin/awk -f myscript myfile
```

---

*NOTE*    You can put only one parameter on the "#!" line. This line is pro-
          cessed directly by the UNIX kernel; it is not processed by the shell
          and thus cannot contain arbitrary shell constructs.

---

The "#!" syntax allows you to create shell scripts that pass command-line parameters transparently to awk. In other words, you can pass awk parameters from the command line that invokes the shell script.

For instance, we demonstrate passing parameters by changing our sample awk script to expect a parameter **n**:

```
{ print $1*n }
```

Assuming that we have a test file in which the first field contains a number that can be multiplied by **n**, we can invoke the program, as follows:

```
$ myscript n=4 myfile
```

This spares us from having to pass "$1" as a shell variable and assigning it to **n** as an awk parameter inside the shell script.

The **masterindex**, described in Chapter 12, uses the "#!" syntax to invoke awk. If your system does not support this syntax, you can change the script by removing the "#!", placing single quotes around the entire script, and ending the script with "$*", which expands to all shell command-line parameters.

Well, we've quite nearly cleaned out this bottom drawer. The material in this chapter has a lot to do with how awk interfaces with the UNIX operating system, invoking other utilities, opening and closing files, and using pipes. And, we have discussed some of the admittedly crude techniques for debugging awk scripts.

We have covered all of the features of the awk programming language. We have concentrated on the POSIX specification for awk, with only an occasional mention of actual awk implementations. The next chapter covers the differences among various awk versions. Chapter 12 is devoted to breaking down two large, complex applications: a document spellchecker and an indexing program. Chapter 13, *A Miscellany of Scripts*, presents a variety of user-contributed programs that provide additional examples of how to write programs.

# 11

# *A Flock of awks*

In the previous four chapters, we have looked at POSIX awk, with only occasional reference to actual awk implementations that you would run. In this chapter, we focus on the different versions of awk that are available, what features they do or do not have, and how you can get them.

First, we'll look at the original V7 version of awk. The original awk lacks many of the features we've described, so this section mostly describes what's not there. Next, we'll look at the three versions whose source code is freely available. All of them have extensions to the POSIX standard. Those that are common to all three versions are discussed first. Finally, we look at three commercial versions of awk.

## Original awk

In each of the sections that follow, we'll take a brief look at how the original awk differs from POSIX awk. Over the years, UNIX vendors have enhanced their versions of original awk; you may need to write small test programs to see exactly what features your old awk has or doesn't have.

### Escape Sequences

The original V7 awk only had "\t", "\n", "\"", and, of course, "\\". Most UNIX vendors have added some or all of "\b" and "\r" and "\f".

### Exponentiation

Exponentiation (using the ^, ^=, **, and **= operators) is not in old awk.

## The C Conditional Expression

The three-argument conditional expression found in C, "*expr1 ? expr2 : expr3*" is not in old awk. You must resort to a plain old **if-else** statement.

## Variables as Boolean Patterns

You cannot use the value of a variable as a Boolean pattern.

```
flag { print "..." }
```

You must instead use a comparison expression.

```
flag != 0 { print "..." }
```

## Faking Dynamic Regular Expressions

The original awk made it difficult to use patterns dynamically because they had to be fixed when the script was interpreted. You can get around the problem of not being able to use a variable as a regular expression by importing a shell variable inside an awk program. The value of the shell variable will be interpreted by awk as a constant. Here's an example:

```
$ cat awkro2
#! /bin/sh
# assign shell's $1 to awk search variable
search=$1
awk '$1 ~ /'"$search"'/' acronyms
```

The first line of the script makes the variable assignment before awk is invoked. To get the shell to expand the variable inside the awk procedure, we enclose it within single, then double, quotation marks.[*] Thus, awk never sees the shell variable and evaluates it as a constant string.

Here's another version that makes use of the Bourne shell variable substitution feature. Using this feature gives us an easy way to specify a default value for the variable if, for instance, the user does not supply a command-line argument.

```
search=$1
awk '$1 ~ /'"${search:-.*}"'/' acronyms
```

The expression "${search:-.*}" tells the shell to use the value of **search** if it is defined; if not, use ".*" as the value. Here, ".*" is regular-expression syntax specifying any string of characters; therefore, all entries are printed if no entry is supplied on the command line. Because the whole thing is inside double quotes, the shell does not perform a wildcard expansion on ".*".

---

[*] Actually, this is the concatenation of single-quoted text with double-quoted text with more single-quoted text to produce one large quoted string. This trick was used earlier, in Chapter 6.

## Control Flow

In POSIX awk, if a program has just a **BEGIN** procedure, and nothing else, awk will exit after executing that procedure. The original awk is different; it will execute the **BEGIN** procedure and then go on to process input, even if there are no pattern-action statements. You can force awk to exit by supplying */dev/null* on the command line as a data file argument, or by using **exit**.

In addition, the **BEGIN** and **END** procedures, if present, have to be at the beginning and end of program, respectively. Furthermore, you can only have one of each.

## Field Separating

Field separating works the same in old awk as it does in modern awk, except that you can't use regular expressions.

## Arrays

There is no way in the original awk to delete an element from an array. The best thing you can do is assign the empty string to the unwanted array element, and then code your program to ignore array elements whose values are empty.

Along the same lines, **in** is not an operator in original awk; you cannot use **if (item in array)** to see if an item is present. Unfortunately, this forces you to loop through every item in an array to see if the index you want is present.

```
for (item in array) {
        if (item == searchkey) {
                process array[item]
                break
        }
}
```

## The getline Function

The original V7 awk did not have **getline**. If your awk is really ancient, then **getline** may not work for you. Some vendors have the simplest form of **getline**, which reads the next record from the regular input stream, and sets $0, **NF** and **NR** (there is no **FNR**, see below). All of the other forms of **getline** are not available.

## Functions

The original awk had only a limited number of built-in string functions. (See Table 11-1.)

*Table 11-1: Original awk's Built-In String Functions*

| Awk Function | Description |
|---|---|
| **index**(*s, t*) | Returns position of substring *t* in string *s* or zero if not present. |
| **length**(*s*) | Returns length of string *s* or length of **$0** if no string is supplied. |
| **split**(*s, a, sep*) | Parses string *s* into elements of array *a* using field separator *sep*; returns number of elements. If *sep* is not supplied, **FS** is used. Array splitting works the same way as field splitting. |
| **sprintf**("*fmt*", *expr*) | Uses **printf** format specification for *expr*. |
| **substr**(*s, p, n*) | Returns substring of string *s* at beginning position *p* up to maximum length of *n*. If *n* isn't supplied, the rest of the string from *p* is used. |

Some built-in functions can be classified as arithmetic functions. Most of them take a numeric argument and return a numeric value. Table 11-2 summarizes these arithmetic functions.

*Table 11-2: Original awk's Built-In Arithmetic Functions*

| Awk Function | Description |
|---|---|
| **exp**(*x*) | Returns *e* to the power *x*. |
| **int**(*x*) | Returns truncated value of *x*. |
| **log**(*x*) | Returns natural logarithm (base-*e*) of *x*. |
| **sqrt**(*x*) | Returns square root of *x*. |

One of the nicest facilities in awk, the ability to define your own functions, is also not available in original awk.

## Built-In Variables

In original awk only the variables shown in Table 11-3 are built in.

*Table 11-3: Original awk System Variables*

| Variable | Description |
|---|---|
| **FILENAME** | Current filename |
| **FS** | Field separator (a blank) |
| **NF** | Number of fields in current record |
| **NR** | Number of the current record |
| **OFMT** | Output format for numbers (%.6g) |
| **OFS** | Output field separator (a blank) |
| **ORS** | Output record separator (a newline) |
| **RS** | Record separator (a newline) |

**OFMT** does double duty, serving as the conversion format for the **print** statement, as well as for converting numbers to strings.

# *Freely Available awks*

There are three versions of awk whose source code is freely available. They are the Bell Labs awk, GNU awk, and mawk, by Michael Brennan. This section discusses the extensions that are common to two or more of them, and then looks at each version in detail and describes how to obtain it.

## *Common Extensions*

This section discusses extensions to the awk language that are available in two or more of the freely available awks.[*]

### *Deleting all elements of an array*

All three free awks extend the **delete** statement, making it possible to delete all the elements of an array at one time. The syntax is:

> **delete** *array*

Normally, to delete every element from an array, you have to use a loop, like this.

```
for (i in data)
        delete data[i]
```

With the extended version of the **delete** statement, you can simply use

```
delete data
```

This is particularly useful for arrays with lots of subscripts; this version is considerably faster than the one using a loop.

Even though it no longer has any elements, you cannot use the array name as a simple variable. Once an array, always an array.

This extension appeared first in gawk, then in mawk and the Bell Labs awk.

### *Obtaining individual characters*

All three awks extend field splitting and array splitting as follows. If the value of **FS** is the empty string, then each character of the input record becomes a separate field. This greatly simplifies cases where it's necessary to work with individual characters.

---

[*] As the maintainer of gawk and the author of many of the extensions described here and in the section below on gawk, my opinion about the usefulness of these extensions may be biased. ☺ You should make your own evaluation. [A.R.]

Similarly, if the third argument to the **split()** function is the empty string, each character in the original string will become a separate element of the target array.

Without these extensions, you have to use repeated calls to the **substr()** function to obtain individual characters.

This extension appeared first in mawk, then in gawk and the Bell Labs awk.

### Flushing buffered output

The 1993 version of the Bell Labs awk introduced a new function that is not in the POSIX standard, **fflush()**. Like **close()**, the argument to **fflush()** is the name of an open file or pipe. Unlike **close()**, the **fflush()** function only works on *output* files and pipes.

Most programs *buffer* their output, storing data to be written to a file or pipe in an internal chunk of memory until there's enough to send on to the destination. Occasionally, it's useful for the programmer to be able to explicitly *flush* the buffer, that is, force all buffered data to actually be delivered. This is the purpose of the **fflush()** function.

This function appeared first in the Bell Labs awk, then in gawk and mawk.

### Special filenames

With any version of awk, you can write directly to the special UNIX file, */dev/tty*, that is a name for the user's terminal. This can be used to direct prompts or messages to the user's attention when the output of the program is directed to a file:

```
printf "Enter your name:" >"/dev/tty"
```

This prints "Enter your name:" directly on the terminal, no matter where the standard output and the standard error are directed.

The three free awks support several special filenames, as listed in Table 11-4.

*Table 11-4: Special Filenames*

| Filename | Description |
| --- | --- |
| */dev/stdin* | Standard input (not mawk)[a] |
| */dev/stdout* | Standard output |
| */dev/stderr* | Standard error |

[a] The mawk manpage recommends using "-" for the standard input, which is most portable.

Note that a special filename, like any filename, must be quoted when specified as a string constant.

The */dev/stdin*, */dev/stdout*, and */dev/stderr* special files originated in V8 UNIX. Gawk was the first to build in special recognition of these files, followed by mawk and the Bell Labs awk.

---

# *A printerr() function*

Error messages inform users about problems often related to missing or incorrect input. You can simply inform the user with a **print** statement. However, if the output of the program is redirected to a file, the user won't see it. Therefore, it is good practice to specify explicitly that the error message be sent to the terminal.

The following **printerr()** function helps to create consistent user error messages. It prints the word "ERROR" followed by a supplied message, the record number, and the current record. The following example directs output to */dev/tty*:

```
function printerr (message) {
        # print message, record number and record
        printf("ERROR:%s (%d) %s\n", message, NR, $0) > "/dev/tty"
}
```

If the output of the program is sent to the terminal screen, then error messages will be mixed in with the output. Outputting "ERROR" will help the user recognize error messages.

In UNIX, the standard destination for error messages is standard error. The rationale for writing to standard error is the same as above. To write to standard error explicitly, you must use the convoluted syntax "cat 1>&2" as in the following example:

```
print "ERROR" | "cat 1>&2"
```

This directs the output of the **print** statement to a pipe which executes the **cat** command. You can also use the **system()** function to execute a UNIX command such as **cat** or **echo** and direct its output to standard error.

When the special file */dev/stderr* is available, this gets much simpler:

```
print "ERROR" > "/dev/stderr"  # recent awks only
```

---

## The nextfile statement

The **nextfile** statement is similar to **next**, but it operates at a higher level. When **nextfile** is executed, the current data file is abandoned, and processing starts over at the top of the script, using the first record of the following file. This is useful when you know that you only need to process part of a file; there's no need to then set up a loop to skip records using **next**.

The **nextfile** statement originated in gawk, and then was added to the Bell Labs awk. It will be available in mawk, starting with version 1.4.

### Regular expression record separators (gawk and mawk)

Gawk and mawk allow **RS** to be a full regular expression, not just a single character. In that case, the records are separated by the longest text in the input that matches the regular expression. Gawk also sets **RT** (the record terminator) to the actual input text that matched **RS**. An example of this is given below.

The ability to have **RS** be a regular expression first appeared in mawk, and was later added to gawk.

## Bell Labs awk

The Bell Labs awk is, of course, the direct descendant of the original V7 awk, and of the "new" awk that first became avaliable with System V Release 3.1. Source code is freely available via anonymous FTP to the host *netlib.bell-labs.com*. It is in the file */netlib/research/awk.bundle.Z*. This is a compressed shell archive file. Be sure to use "binary," or "image" mode to transfer the file. This version of awk requires an ANSI C compiler.

There have been several distinct versions; we will identify them here according to the year they became available.

The first version of new awk became available in late 1987. It had almost everything we've described in the previous four chapters (although there are footnotes that indicate those things that are not available). This version is still in use on SunOS 4.1.x systems and some System V Release 3 UNIX systems.

In 1989, for System V Release 4, several new things were added. The only difference between this version and POSIX awk is that POSIX uses **CONVFMT** for number-to-string conversions, while the 1989 version still used **OFMT**. The new features were:

- Escape characters in command-line assignments were now interpreted.

- The **tolower()** and **toupper()** functions were added.

- **printf** was improved: dynamic width and precision were added, and the behavior for "%c" was rationalized.

- The return value from the **srand()** function was defined to be the previous seed. (The awk book didn't state what **srand()** returned.)

- It became possible to use regular expressions as simple expressions. For example:

```
if (/cute/ || /sweet/)
        print "potential here!"
```

- The *-v* option was added to allow setting variables on the command line before execution of the **BEGIN** procedure.

- Multiple *-f* options could now be used to have multiple source files. (This originated in MKS awk, was adopted by gawk, and then added to the Bell Labs awk.)

- The **ENVIRON** array was added. (This was developed independently for both MKS awk and gawk, and then added to the Bell Labs awk.)

In 1993, Brian Kernighan of Bell Labs was able to release the source code to his awk. At this point, **CONVFMT** became available, and the **fflush()** function, described above, was added. A bug-fix release was made in August of 1994.

In June of 1996, Brian Kernighan made another release. It can be retrieved either from the FTP site given above, or via a World Wide Web browser from Dr. Kernighan's Web page (*http://cm.bell-labs.com/who/bwk*), which refers to this version as "the one true awk." ☺ This version adds several features that originated in gawk and mawk, described earlier in this chapter in the "Common Extensions" section.

## GNU awk (gawk)

The Free Software Foundation GNU project's version of awk, gawk, implements all the features of the POSIX awk, and many more. It is perhaps the most popular of the freely available implementations; gawk is used on Linux systems, as well as various other freely available UNIX-like systems, such as NetBSD and FreeBSD.

Source code for gawk is available via anonymous FTP[*] to the host *ftp.gnu.ai.mit.edu*. It is in the file */pub/gnu/gawk-3.0.3.tar.gz* (there may be a later version there by the time you read this). This is a tar file compressed with the **gzip** program, whose source code is available in the same directory. There are many sites worldwide that "mirror" the files from the main GNU distribution site; if you know of one close to you, you should get the files from there. Be sure to use "binary" or "image" mode to transfer the file(s).

Besides the common extensions listed earlier, gawk has a number of additional features. We examine them in this section.

---

[*] If you don't have Internet access and wish to get a copy of gawk, contact the Free Software Foundation, Inc., 59 Temple Place, Suite 330, Boston, MA 02111-1307 U.S.A. The telephone number is 617-542-5942, and the fax number is 617-542-2652.

## Command line options

Gawk has several very useful command-line options. Like most GNU programs, these options are spelled out and begin with two dashes, "--".

- *--lint* and *--lint-old* cause gawk to check your program, both at parse-time and at run-time, for constructs that are dubious or nonportable to other versions of awk. The *--lint-old* option warns about function calls that are not portable to the original version of awk. It is separate from *--lint*, since most systems now have some version of new awk.

- *--traditional* disables GNU-specific extensions, such as the time functions and **gensub( )** (see below). With this option, gawk is intended to behave the same as the Bell Labs awk.

- *--re-interval* enables full POSIX regular expression matching, by allowing gawk to recognize interval expressions (such as "/stuff{1,3}/").

- *--posix* disables *all* extensions that are not specified in the POSIX standard. This option also turns on recognition of interval expressions.

There are a number of other options that are less important for everyday programming and script portability; see the gawk documentation for details.

Although POSIX awk allows you to have multiple instances of the *-f* option, there is no easy way to use library functions from a command-line program. The *--source* option in gawk makes this possible.

```
gawk --source 'script' -f mylibs.awk file1 file2
```

This example runs the program in *script*, which can use awk functions from the file *mylibs.awk*. The input data comes from *file1* and *file2*.

## An awk program search path

Gawk allows you to specify an environment variable named **AWKPATH** that defines a search path for awk program files. By default, it is defined to be .:/usr/local/share/awk. Thus, when a filename is specified with the *-f* option, the two default directories will be searched, beginning with the current directory. Note that if the filename contains a "/", then no search is performed.

For example, if *mylibs.awk* was a file of awk functions in */usr/local/share/awk*, and *myprog.awk* was a program in the current directory, we run gawk like this:

```
gawk -f myprog.awk -f mylibs.awk datafile1
```

Gawk would find each file in the appropriate place. This makes it much easier to have and use awk library functions.

## Line continuation

Gawk allows you to break lines after either a "?" or ":". You can also continue strings across newlines using a backslash.

```
$ gawk 'BEGIN { print "hello, \
> world" }'
hello, world
```

## Extended regular expressions

Gawk provides several additional regular expression operators. These are common to most GNU programs that work with regular expressions. The extended operators are listed in Table 11-5.

*Table 11-5: Gawk Extended Regular Expressions*

| Special Operators | Usage |
|---|---|
| \w | Matches any *word-constituent* character (a letter, digit, or underscore). |
| \W | Matches any character that is not word-constituent. |
| \< | Matches the empty string at the beginning of a word. |
| \> | Matches the empty string at the end of a word. |
| \y | Matches the empty string at either the beginning or end of a word (the word boundary). Other GNU software uses "\b", but that was already taken. |
| \B | Matches the empty string within a word. |
| \` | Matches the empty string at the beginning of a buffer. This is the same as a string in awk, and thus is the same as ^. It is provided for compatibility with GNU Emacs and other GNU software. |
| \' | Matches the empty string at the end of a buffer. This is the same as a string in awk, and thus is the same as $. It is provided for compatibility with GNU Emacs and other GNU software. |

You can think of "\w" as a shorthand for the (POSIX) notation [[:alnum:]_] and "\W" as a shorthand for [^[:alnum:]_]. The following table gives examples of what the middle four operators match, borrowed from *Effective AWK Programming*.

*Table 11-6: Examples of gawk Extended Regular Expression Operators*

| Expression | Matches | Does Not Match |
|---|---|---|
| \<away | away | stowaway |
| stow\> | stow | stowaway |
| \yballs?\y | ball or balls | ballroom or baseball |
| \Brat\B | crate | dirty rat |

## Regular expression record terminators

Besides allowing **RS** to be a regular expression, gawk sets the variable **RT** (record terminator) to the actual input text that matched the value of **RS**.

Here is a simple example, due to Michael Brennan, that shows the power of gawk's **RS** and **RT** variables. As we have seen, one of the most common uses of sed is its substitute command (**s/old/new/g**). By setting **RS** to the pattern to match, and **ORS** to the replacement text, a simple **print** statement can print the unchanged text followed by the replacement text.

```
$ cat simplesed.awk
# simplesed.awk --- do s/old/new/g using just print
#    Thanks to Michael Brennan for the idea
#
# NOTE! RS and ORS must be set on the command line
{
    if (RT == " ")
        printf "%s", $0
    else
        print
}
```

There is one wrinkle; at end of file, **RT** will be empty, so we use a **printf** statement to print the record.[*] We could run the program like this.

```
$ cat simplesed.data
"This OLD house" is a great show.
I like shopping for old things at garage sales.
$ gawk -f simplesed.awk RS="old|OLD" ORS="brand new" simplesed.data
"This brand new house" is a great show.
I like shopping for brand new things at garage sales.
```

## Separating fields

Besides the regular way that awk lets you split the input into records and the record into fields, gawk gives you some additional capabilities.

First, as mentioned above, if the value of **FS** is the empty string, then each character of the input record becomes a separate field.

Second, the special variable **FIELDWIDTHS** can be used to split out data that occurs in fixed-width columns. Such data may or may not have whitespace separating the values of the fields.

```
FIELDWIDTHS = "5 6 8 3"
```

Here, the record has four fields: $1 is five characters wide, $2 is six characters wide, and so on. Assigning a value to **FIELDWIDTHS** causes gawk to start using it

---

[*] See *Effective AWK Programming* [Robbins], Section 16.2.8, for an elaborate version of this program.

for field splitting. Assigning a value to **FS** causes gawk to return to the regular field splitting mechanism. Use **FS** = **FS** to make this happen without having to save the value of **FS** in an extra variable.

This facility would be of most use when working with fixed-width field data, where there may not be any whitespace separating fields, or when intermediate fields may be all blank.

### Additional special files

Gawk has a number of additional special filenames that it interprets internally. All of the special filenames are listed in Table 11-7.

*Table 11-7: Gawk's Special Filenames*

| Filename | Description |
| --- | --- |
| */dev/stdin* | Standard input. |
| */dev/stdout* | Standard output. |
| */dev/stderr* | Standard error. |
| */dev/fd/n* | The file referenced as file descriptor *n*. |
| **Obsolete Filename** | **Description** |
| */dev/pid* | Returns a record containing the process ID number. |
| */dev/ppid* | Returns a record containing the parent process ID number. |
| */dev/pgrpid* | Returns a record containing the process group ID number. |
| */dev/user* | Returns a record with the real and effective user IDs, the real and effective group IDs, and if available, any secondary group IDs. |

The first three were described earlier. The fourth filename provides access to any open file descriptor that may have been inherited from gawk's parent process (usually the shell). You can use file descriptor 0 for standard input, 1 for standard output, and 2 for standard error.

The second group of special files, labeled "obsolete," have been in gawk for a while, but are being phased out. They will be replaced by a **PROCINFO** array, whose subscipts are the desired item and whose element value is the associated value.

For example, you would use **PROCINFO["pid"]** to get the current process ID, instead of using **getline pid** < "/dev/pid". Check the gawk documentation to see if **PROCINFO** is available and if these filenames are still supported.

## Additional variables

Gawk has several more system variables. They are listed in Table 11-8.

*Table 11–8: Additional gawk System Variables*

| Variable | Description |
|---|---|
| ARGIND | The index in **ARGV** of the current input file. |
| ERRNO | A message describing the error if **getline** or **close( )** fail. |
| FIELDWIDTHS | A space-separated list of numbers describing the widths of the input fields. |
| IGNORECASE | If non-zero, pattern matches and string comparisons are case-independent. |
| RT | The value of the input text that matched **RS**. |

We have already seen the record terminator variable, **RT**, so we'll proceed to the other variables that we haven't covered yet.

All pattern matching and string comparison in awk is case sensitive. Gawk introduced the **IGNORECASE** variable so that you can specify that regular expressions be interpreted without regard for upper- or lowercase characters. Beginning with version 3.0 of gawk, string comparisons can also be done without case sensitivity.

The default value of **IGNORECASE** is zero, which means that pattern matching and string comparison are performed the same as in traditional awk. If **IGNORECASE** is set to a non-zero value, then case distinctions are ignored. This applies to all places where regular expressions are used, including the field separator **FS**, the record separator **RS**, and all string comparisons. It does *not* apply to array subscripting.

Two more gawk variables are of interest. **ARGIND** is set automatically by gawk to be the index in **ARGV** of the current input file name. This variable gives you a way to track how far along you are in the list of filenames.

Finally, if an error occurs doing a redirection for **getline** or during a **close()**, gawk sets **ERRNO** to a string describing the error. This makes it possible to provide descriptive error messages when something goes wrong.

## Additional functions

Gawk has one additional string function, and two functions for dealing with the current date and time. They are listed in Table 11-9.

*Table 11-9: Additional gawk Functions*

| Gawk Function | Description |
|---|---|
| **gensub**(*r, s, h, t*) | If *h* is a string starting with **g** or **G**, globally substitutes *s* for *r* in *t*. Otherwise, *h* is a number: substitutes for the *h*'th occurrence. Returns the new value, *t* is unchanged. If *t* is not supplied, defaults to **$0**. |
| **systime**() | Returns the current time of day in seconds since the Epoch (00:00 a.m., January 1, 1970 UTC). |
| **strftime**(*format, timestamp*) | Formats *timestamp* (of the same form returned by **systime**()) according to *format*. If no *timestamp*, use current time. If no *format* either, use a default format whose output is similar to the **date** command. |

## A general substitution function

The 3.0 version of gawk introduced a new general substitution function, named **gensub**(). The **sub**() and **gsub**() functions have some problems.

- You can change either the first occurrence of a pattern or all the occurrences of a pattern. There is no way to change, say, only the third occurrence of a pattern but not the ones before it or after it.

- Both **sub**() and **gsub**() change the actual target string, which may be undesirable.

- It is impossible to get **sub**() and **gsub**() to emit a literal backslash followed by the matched text, because an ampersand preceded by a backslash is never replaced.[*]

- There is no way to get at parts of the matched text, analogous to the \(...\) construct in sed.

For all these reasons, gawk introduced the **gensub**() function. The function takes at least three arguments. The first is a regular expression to search for. The second is the replacement string. The third is a flag that controls how many substitutions should be performed. The fourth argument, if present, is the original string to change. If it is not provided, the current input record ($0) is used.

The pattern can have subpatterns delimited by parentheses. For example, it can have "/(part) (one|two|three)/". Within the replacement string, a backslash followed by a digit represents the text that matched the *n*th subpattern.

---

[*] A full discussion is given in *Effective AWK Programming* [Robbins], Section 12.3. The details are not for the faint of heart.

```
$ echo part two | gawk '{ print gensub(/(part) (one|two|three)/, "\\2", "g") }'
two
```

The flag is either a string beginning with **g** or **G**, in which case the substitution happens globally, or it is a number indicating that the *n*th occurrence should be replaced.

```
$ echo a b c a b c a b c | gawk '{ print gensub(/a/, "AA", 2) }'
a b c AA b c a b c
```

The fourth argument is the string in which to make the change. Unlike **sub()** and **gsub()**, the target string is not changed. Instead, the new string is the return value from **gensub()**.

```
$ gawk '
BEGIN { old = "hello, world"
        new = gensub(/hello/, "goodbye", 1, old)
        printf("<%s>, <%s>\n", old, new)
}'
<hello, world>, <goodbye, world>
```

## Time management for programmers

Awk programs are very often used for processing the log files produced by various programs. Often, each record in a log file contains a timestamp, indicating when the record was produced. For both conciseness and precision, the timestamp is written as the result of the UNIX *time*(2) system call, which is the number of seconds since midnight, January 1, 1970 UTC. (This date is often referred to as "the Epoch.") To make it easier to generate and process log file records with these kinds of timestamps in them, gawk has two functions, **systime()** and **strftime()**.

The **systime()** function is primarily intended for generating timestamps to go into log records. Suppose, for example, that we use an awk script to respond to CGI queries to our WWW server. We might log each query to a log file.

```
{
...
printf("%s:%s:%d\n", User, Host, systime()) >> "/var/log/cgi/querylog"
...
}
```

Such a record might look like

```
arnold:some.domain.com:831322007
```

The **strftime()** function[*] makes it easy to turn timestamps into human-readable dates. The format string is similar to the one used by **sprintf()**; it consists of literal text mixed with format specifications for different components of date and time.

---

[*] This function is patterned after the function of the same name in ANSI C.

```
$ gawk 'BEGIN { print strftime("Today is %A, %B %d, %Y") }'
Today is Sunday, May 05, 1996
```

The list of available formats is quite long. See your local *strftime*(3) manpage, and the gawk documentation for the full list. Our hypothetical CGI log file might be processed by this program:

```
# cgiformat --- process CGI logs
# data format is user:host:timestamp
#1
BEGIN { FS = ":"; SUBSEP = "@" }

#2
{
# make data more obvious
        user = $1; host = $2; time = $3
# store first contact by this user
        if (! ((user, host) in first))
                first[user, host] = time
# count contacts
        count[user, host]++
# save last contact
        last[user, host] = time
}

#3
END {
# print the results
        for (contact in count) {
                i = strftime("%y-%m-%d %H:%M", first[contact])
                j = strftime("%y-%m-%d %H:%M", last[contact])
                printf "%s -> %d times between %s and %s\n",
                        contact, count[contact], i, j
        }
}
```

The first step is to set **FS** to ":" to split the field correctly. We also use a neat trick and set the subscript separator to "@", so that the arrays become indexed by "user@host" strings.

In the second step, we look to see if this is the first time we've seen this user. If so (they're not in the **first** array), we add them. Then we increment the count of how many times they've connected. Finally we store this record's timestamp in the **last** array. This element keeps getting overwritten each time we see a new connection by the user. That's OK; what we will end up with is the last (most recent) connection stored in the array.

The **END** procedure formats the data for us. It loops through the **count** array, formatting the timestamps in the **first** and **last** arrays for printing. Consider a log file with the following records in it.

```
$ cat /var/log/cgi/querylog
arnold:some.domain.com:831322007
mary:another.domain.org:831312546
arnold:some.domain.com:831327215
mary:another.domain.org:831346231
arnold:some.domain.com:831324598
```

Here's what running the program produces:

```
$ gawk -f cgiformat.awk /var/log/cgi/querylog
mary@another.domain.org -> 2 times between 96-05-05 12:09 and 96-05-05 21:30
arnold@some.domain.com -> 3 times between 96-05-05 14:46 and 96-05-05 15:29
```

## *Michael's awk (mawk)*

The third freely available awk is mawk, written by Michael Brennan. This program is upwardly compatible with POSIX awk, and has a few extensions as well. It is solid and performs very well. Source code for mawk is freely available via anonymous FTP from *ftp.whidbey.net*. It is in */pub/brennan/mawk1.3.3.tar.gz*. (There may be a later version there by the time you read this.) This is also a tar file compressed with the **gzip** program. Be sure to use "binary," or "image" mode to transfer the file.

Mawk's primary advantages are its speed and robustness. Although it has fewer features than gawk, it almost always outperforms it.[*] Besides UNIX systems, mawk also runs under MS-DOS.

The common extensions described above are also available in mawk.

# *Commercial awks*

There are also several commercial versions of awk. In this section, we review the ones that we know about.

## *MKS awk*

Mortice Kern Systems (MKS) in Waterloo, Ontario (Canada)[†] supplies awk as part of the MKS Toolkit for MS-DOS/Windows, OS/2, Windows 95, and Windows NT.

The MKS version implements POSIX awk. It has the following extensions:

---

[*] Gawk's advantages are that it has a larger feature set, it has been ported to more non-UNIX kinds of systems, and it comes with much more extensive documentation.

[†] Mortice Kern Systems, 185 Columbia Street West, Waterloo, Ontario N2L 5Z5, Canada. Phone: 1-800-265-2797 in North America, 1-519-884-2251 elsewhere. URL is *http://www.mks.com/*.

- The **exp()**, **int()**, **log()**, **sqrt()**, **tolower()**, and **toupper()** functions use $0 if given no argument.

- An additional function **ord()** is available. This function takes a string argument, and returns the numeric value of the first character in the string. It is similar to the function of the same name in Pascal.

## Thompson Automation awk (tawk)

Thompson Automation Software[*] makes a version of awk (tawk)[†] for MS-DOS/Windows, Windows 95 and NT, and Solaris. Tawk is interesting on several counts. First, unlike other versions of awk, which are interpreters, tawk is a compiler. Second, tawk comes with a screen-oriented debugger, written in awk! The source for the debugger is included. Third, tawk allows you to link your compiled program with arbitrary functions written in C. Tawk has received rave reviews in the *comp.lang.awk* newsgroup.

Tawk comes with an **awk** interface that acts like POSIX awk, compiling and running your program. You can, however, compile your program into a standalone executable file. The tawk compiler actually compiles into a compact intermediate form. The intermediate representation is linked with a library that executes the program when it is run, and it is at link time that other C routines can be integrated with the awk program.

Tawk is a very full-featured implementation of awk. Besides implementing the features of POSIX awk (based on new awk), it extends the language in some fundamental ways, and also has a very large number of built-in functions.

### Tawk language extensions

This section provides a "laundry list" of the new features in tawk. A full treatment of them is beyond the scope of this book; the tawk documentation does a nice job of presenting them. Hopefully, by now you should be familiar enough with awk that the value of these features will be apparent. Where relevant, we'll contrast the tawk feature with a comparable feature in gawk.

- Additional special patterns, **INIT**, **BEGINFILE**, and **ENDFILE**. **INIT** is like **BEGIN**, but the actions in its procedure are run before[‡] those of the **BEGIN** procedure. **BEGINFILE** and **ENDFILE** provide you the ability to have per-file

---

[*] Thompson Automation Software, 5616 SW Jefferson, Portland OR 97221 U.S.A. Phone: 1-800-944-0139 within the U.S., 1-503-224-1639 elsewhere.

[†] Michael Brennan, in the *mawk(1)* manpage, makes the following statement: "Implementors of the AWK language have shown a consistent lack of imagination when naming their programs."

[‡] I confess that I don't see the real usefulness of this. [A.R.]

start-up and clean-up actions. Unlike using a rule based on **FNR == 1**, these actions are executed even when files are empty.

- Controlled regular expressions. You can add a flag to a regular expression ("/match me/") that tells tawk how to treat the regular expression. An **i** flag ("/match me/i") indicates that case should be ignored when doing matching. An **s** flag indicates that the shortest possible text should be matched, instead of the longest.

- An **abort** [*expr*] statement. This is similar to **exit**, except that tawk exits immediately, bypassing any **END** procedure. The *expr*, if provided, becomes the return value from tawk to its parent program.

- True multidimensional arrays. Conventional awk simulates multidimensional arrays by concatenating the values of the subscripts, separated by the value of **SUBSEP**, to generate a (hopefully) unique index in a regular associative array. While implementing this feature for compatibility, tawk also provides true multidimensional arrays.

```
a[1][1] = "hello"
       a[1][2] = "world"
       for (i in a[1])
               print a[1][i]
```

Multidimensional arrays guarantee that the indices will be unique, and also have the potential for greater performance when the number of elements gets to be very large.

- Automatic sorting of arrays. When looping over every element of an array using the **for (item in array)** construct, tawk will first sort the indices of the array, so that array elements are processed in order. You can control whether this sorting is turned on or off, and if on, whether the sorting is numeric or alphabetic, and in ascending or descending order. While the sorting incurs a performance penalty, it is likely to be less than the overhead of sorting the array yourself using awk code, or piping the results into an external invocation of **sort**.

- Scope control for functions and variables. You can declare that functions and variables are global to an entire program, global within a "module" (source file), local to a module, and local to a function. Regular awk only gives you global variables, global functions, and extra function parameters, which act as local variables. This feature is a very nice one, making it much easier to write libraries of awk functions without having to worry about variable names inadvertently conflicting with those in other library functions or in the user's main program.

- **RS** can be a regular expression. This is similar to gawk and mawk; however, the regular expression cannot be one that requires more than one character of look-ahead. The text that matched **RS** is saved in the variable **RSM** (record separator match), similar to gawk's **RT** variable.

- Describing fields, instead of the field separators. The variable **FPAT** can be a regular expression that describes the contents of the fields. Successive occurrences of text that matches **FPAT** become the contents of the fields.

- Controlling the implicit file processing loop. The variable **ARGI** tracks the position in **ARGV** of the current input data file. Unlike gawk's **ARGIND** variable, assigning a value to **ARGI** can be used to make tawk skip over input data files.

- Fixed-length records. By assigning a value to the **RECLEN** variable, you can make tawk read records in fixed-length chunks. If **RS** is not matched within **RECLEN** characters, then tawk returns a record that is **RECLEN** characters long.

- Hexadecimal constants. You can specify C-style hexadecimal constants (**0xDEAD** and **0xBEEF** being two rather famous ones) in tawk programs. This helps when using the built-in bit manipulation functions (see the next section).

Whew! That's a rather long list, but these features bring additional power to programming in awk.

## Additional built-in tawk functions

Besides extending the language, tawk provides a large number of additional built-in functions. Here is another "laundry list," this time of the different classes of functions available. Each class has two or more functions associated with it. We'll briefly describe the functionality of each class.

- Extended string functions. Extensions to the standard string functions and new string functions allow you to match and substitute for subpatterns within patterns (similar to gawk's **gensub( )** function), assign to substrings within strings, and split a string into an array based on a pattern that matches elements, instead of the separator. There are additional **printf** formats, and string translation functions. While undoubtedly some of these functions could be written as user-defined functions, having them built in provides greater performance.

- Bit manipulation functions. You can perform bitwise AND, OR, and XOR operations on (integer) values. These could also be written as user-defined functions, but with a loss of performance.

- More I/O functions. There is a suite of functions modeled after those in the *stdio*(3) library. In particular, the ability to seek within a file, and do I/O in fixed-size amounts, is quite useful.

- Directory operation functions. You can make, remove, and change directories, as well as remove and rename files.

- File information functions. You can retrieve file permissions, size, and modification times.

- Directory reading functions. You can get the current directory name, as well as read a list of all the filenames in a directory.

- Time functions. There are functions to retrieve the current time of day, and format it in various ways. These functions are not quite as flexible as gawk's **strftime( )** function.

- Execution functions. You can sleep for a specific amount of time, and start other functions running. Tawk's **spawn( )** function is interesting because it allows you to provide values for the new program's environment, and also indicate whether the program should or should not run asynchronously. This is particularly valuable on non-UNIX systems, where the command interpreters (such as MS-DOS's **command.com**) are quite limited.

- File locking. You can lock and unlock files and ranges within files.

- Screen functions. You can do screen-oriented I/O. Under UNIX, these functions are implemented on top of the *curses*(3) library.

- Packing and unpacking of binary data. You can specify how binary data structures are laid out. This, together with the new I/O functions, makes it possible to do binary I/O, something you would normally have to do in C or C++.

- Access to internal state. You can get or set the value of any awk variable through function calls.

- Access to MS-DOS low-level facilities. You can use system interrupts, and peek and poke values at memory addresses. These features are obviously for experts only.

From this list, it becomes clear that tawk provides a nice alternative to C and to Perl for serious programming tasks. As an example, the screen functions and internal state functions are used to implement the tawk debugger in awk.

## Videosoft VSAwk

Videosoft[*] sells software called VSAwk that brings awk-style programming into the Visual Basic environment. VSAwk is a Visual Basic control that works in an event driven fashion. Like awk, VSAwk gives you startup and cleanup actions, and splits

---

[*] Videosoft can be reached at 2625 Alcatraz Avenue, Suite 271, Berkeley CA 94705 U.S.A. Phone: 1-510-704-8200. Fax: 1-510-843-0174. Their site is *http://www.videosoft.com.*

the input record into fields, as well as the ability to write expressions and call the awk built-in functions.

VSAwk resembles UNIX awk mostly in its data processing model, not its syntax. Nevertheless, it's interesting to see how people apply the concepts from awk to the environment provided by a very different language.

# *Epilogue*

Well, we've pretty thoroughly covered the ins and outs of programming in awk, both the standard language, and the extensions available in different implementations. As you work with awk, you'll come to find it an easy and pleasant language to program in, since it does almost all of the drudgery for you, allowing you to concentrate on the actual problem to be solved.

# 12

# Full-Featured Applications

This chapter presents two complex applications that integrate most features of the awk programming language. The first program, **spellcheck**, provides an interactive interface to the UNIX **spell** program. The second application, **masterindex**, is a batch program for generating an index for a book or a set of books. Even if you are not interested in the particular application, you should study these larger programs to get a feel for the scope of the problems that an awk program can solve.

## An Interactive Spelling Checker

The UNIX **spell** program does an adequate job of catching spelling errors in a document. For most people, however, it only does half the job. It doesn't help you correct the misspelled words. First-time users of **spell** find themselves jotting down the misspelled words and then using the text editor to change the document. More skilled users build a sed script to make the changes automatically.

The **spellcheck** program offers another way—it shows you each word that **spell** has found and asks if you want to correct the word. You can change each occurrence of the word after seeing the line on which it occurs, or you can correct the spelling error globally. You can also choose to add any word that **spell** turns up to a local dictionary file.

Before describing the program, let's have a demonstration of how it works. The user enters **spellcheck**, a shell script that invokes awk, and the name of the document file.

```
$ spellcheck ch00
Use local dict file? (y/n)y
```

If a dictionary file is not specified on the command line, and a file named *dict* exists in the current directory, then the user is asked if the local dictionary should be used. **spellcheck** then runs **spell** using the local dictionary.

```
Running spell checker ...
```

Using the list of "misspelled" words turned up by **spell**, **spellcheck** prompts the user to correct them. Before the first word is displayed, a list of responses is shown that describes what actions are possible.

```
Responses:
        Change each occurrence,
        Global change,
        Add to Dict,
        Help,
        Quit
        CR to ignore:
1 - Found SparcStation (C/G/A/H/Q/):a
```

The first word found by **spell** is "SparcStation." A response of "a" (followed by a carriage return) adds this word to a list that will be used to update the dictionary. The second word is clearly a misspelling and a response of "g" is entered to make the change globally:

```
2 - Found languauge (C/G/A/H/Q/):g
Globally change to:language
Globally change languauge to language? (y/n):y
> and a full description of its scripting language.
1 lines changed. Save changes? (y/n)y
```

After prompting the user to enter the correct spelling and confirming the entry, the change is made and each line affected is displayed, preceded by a ">". The user is then asked to approve these changes before they are saved. The third word is also added to the dictionary:

```
3 - Found nawk (C/G/A/H/Q/):a
```

The fourth word is a misspelling of "utilities."

```
4 - Found utlities (C/G/A/H/Q/):c
These utlities have many things in common, including
      ^^^^^^^^^
Change to:utilities
Change utlities to utilities? (y/n):y
Two other utlities that are found on the UNIX system
          ^^^^^^^^^
Change utlities to utilities? (y/n):y
>These utilities have many things in common, including
>Two other utilities that are found on the UNIX system
2 lines changed. Save changes? (y/n)y
```

The user enters "c" to change each occurrence. This response allows the user to see the line containing the misspelling and then make the change. After the user has made each change, the changed lines are displayed and the user is asked to confirm saving the changes.

It is unclear whether the fifth word is a misspelling or not, so the user enters "c" to view the line.

```
5 - Found xvf (C/G/A/H/Q/):c
tar xvf filename
    ^^^
Change to:RETURN
```

After determining that it is not a misspelling, the user enters a carriage return to ignore the word. Generally, **spell** turns up a lot of words that are not misspellings so a carriage return means to ignore the word.

After all the words in the list have been processed, or if the user quits before then, the user is prompted to save the changes made to the document and the dictionary.

```
Save corrections in ch00 (y/n)? y
Make changes to dictionary (y/n)? y
```

If the user answers "n," the original file and the dictionary are left unchanged.

Now let's look at the **spellcheck.awk** script, which can be divided into four sections:

- The **BEGIN** procedure, that processes the command-line arguments and executes the **spell** command to create a word list.

- The main procedure, that reads one word at a time from the list and prompts the user to make a correction.

- The END procedure, that saves the working copy of the file, overwriting the original. It also appends words from the exception list to the current dictionary.

- Supporting functions, that are called to make changes in the file.

We will look at each of these sections of the program.

## *BEGIN Procedure*

The **BEGIN** procedure for **spellcheck.awk** is large. It is also somewhat unusual.

```
# spellcheck.awk -- interactive spell checker
#
# AUTHOR: Dale Dougherty
#
```

```
# Usage: nawk -f spellcheck.awk [+dict] file
# (Use spellcheck as name of shell program)
# SPELLDICT = "dict"
# SPELLFILE = "file"

# BEGIN actions perform the following tasks:
#       1) process command-line arguments
#       2) create temporary filenames
#       3) execute spell program to create wordlist file
#       4) display list of user responses

BEGIN {
# Process command-line arguments
# Must be at least two args -- nawk and filename
        if (ARGC > 1) {
        # if more than two args, second arg is dict
                if (ARGC > 2) {
                # test to see if dict is specified with "+"
                # and assign ARGV[1] to SPELLDICT
                        if (ARGV[1] ~ /^\+.*/)
                                    SPELLDICT = ARGV[1]
                        else
                                    SPELLDICT = "+" ARGV[1]
                # assign file ARGV[2] to SPELLFILE
                            SPELLFILE = ARGV[2]
                # delete args so awk does not open them as files
                            delete ARGV[1]
                            delete ARGV[2]
                }
        # not more than two args
                else {
                # assign file ARGV[1] to SPELLFILE
                            SPELLFILE = ARGV[1]
                # test to see if local dict file exists
                        if (! system ("test -r dict")) {
                        # if it does, ask if we should use it
                                printf ("Use local dict file? (y/n)")
                                getline reply < "-"
                        # if reply is yes, use "dict"
                                if (reply ~ /[yY](es)?/){
                                            SPELLDICT = "+dict"
                                }
                        }
                }
        } # end of processing args > 1
        # if args not > 1, then print shell-command usage
        else {
                print "Usage: spellcheck [+dict] file"
                exit 1
        }
# end of processing command line arguments
```

```
# create temporary file names, each begin with sp_
        wordlist = "sp_wordlist"
        spellsource = "sp_input"
        spellout = "sp_out"

# copy SPELLFILE to temporary input file
        system("cp " SPELLFILE " " spellsource)

# now run spell program; output sent to wordlist
        print "Running spell checker ..."
        if (SPELLDICT)
                SPELLCMD = "spell " SPELLDICT " "
        else
                SPELLCMD = "spell "
        system(SPELLCMD spellsource " > " wordlist )

# test wordlist to see if misspelled words turned up
        if ( system("test -s " wordlist ) ) {
        # if wordlist is empty (or spell command failed), exit
                print "No misspelled words found."
                system("rm " spellsource " " wordlist)
                exit
        }

# assign wordlist file to ARGV[1] so that awk will read it.
        ARGV[1] = wordlist

# display list of user responses
        responseList = "Responses: \n\tChange each occurrence,"
        responseList = responseList "\n\tGlobal change,"
        responseList = responseList "\n\tAdd to Dict,"
        responseList = responseList "\n\tHelp,"
        responseList = responseList "\n\tQuit"
        responseList = responseList "\n\tCR to ignore: "
        printf("%s", responseList)

} # end of BEGIN procedure
```

The first part of the **BEGIN** procedure processes the command-line arguments. It checks that **ARGC** is greater than one for the program to continue. That is, in addition to "nawk," a filename must be specified. This file specifies the document that **spell** will analyze. An optional dictionary filename can be specified as the second argument. The **spellcheck** script follows the command-line interface of **spell**, although none of the obscure **spell** options can be invoked from the **spellcheck** command line. If a dictionary is not specified, then the script executes a **test** command to see if the file *dict* exists. If it does, the prompt asks the user to approve using it as the dictionary file.

Once we've processed the arguments, we delete them from the **ARGV** array. This is to prevent their being interpreted as filename arguments.

The second part of the **BEGIN** procedure sets up some temporary files, because we do not want to work directly with the original file. At the end of the program, the user will have the option of saving or discarding the work done in the temporary files. The temporary files all begin with "sp_" and are removed before exiting the program.

The third part of the procedure executes **spell** and creates a word list. We test to see that this file exists and that there is something in it before proceeding. If for some reason the **spell** program fails, or there are no misspelled words found, the **wordlist** file will be empty. If this file does exist, then we assign the filename as the second element in the **ARGV** array. This is an unusual but valid way of supplying the name of the input file that awk will process. Note that this file did not exist when awk was invoked! The name of the document file, which was specified on the command line, is no longer in the **ARGV** array. We will not read the document file using awk's main input loop. Instead, a **while** loop reads the file to find and correct misspelled words.

The last task in the **BEGIN** procedure is to define and display a list of responses that the user can enter when a misspelled word is displayed. This list is displayed once at the beginning of the program as well as when the user enters "Help" at the main prompt. Putting this list in a variable allows us to access it from different points in the program, if necessary, without maintaining duplicates. The assignment of **responseList** could be done more simply, but the long string would not be printable in this book. (You can't break a string over two lines.)

## Main Procedure

The main procedure is rather small, merely displaying a misspelled word and prompting the user to enter an appropriate response. This procedure is executed for each misspelled word.

One reason this procedure is short is because the central action—correcting a misspelled word—is handled by two larger user-defined functions, which we'll see in the last section.

```
# main procedure, executed for each line in wordlist.
#       Purpose is to show misspelled word and prompt user
#       for appropriate action.

{
# assign word to misspelling
        misspelling = $1
        response = 1
        ++word
```

```
# print misspelling and prompt for response
        while (response !~ /(^[cCgGaAhHqQ])|^$/ ) {
                printf("\n%d - Found %s (C/G/A/H/Q/):", word, misspelling)
                getline response < "-"
        }
# now process the user's response
# CR - carriage return ignores current word
# Help
        if (response ~ /[Hh](elp)?/) {
        # Display list of responses and prompt again.
                printf("%s", responseList)
                printf("\n%d - Found %s (C/G/A/Q/):", word, misspelling)
                getline response < "-"
        }
# Quit
        if (response ~ /[Qq](uit)?/) exit
# Add to dictionary
        if ( response ~ /[Aa](dd)?/) {
                dict[++dictEntry] = misspelling
        }
# Change each occurrence
        if ( response ~ /[cC](hange)?/) {
        # read each line of the file we are correcting
                newspelling = ""; changes = ""
                while( (getline < spellsource) > 0){
                # call function to show line with misspelled word
                # and prompt user to make each correction
                        make_change($0)
                # all lines go to temp output file
                        print > spellout
                }
        # all lines have been read
        # close temp input and temp output file
                close(spellout)
                close(spellsource)
        # if change was made
                if (changes){
                # show changed lines
                        for (j = 1; j <= changes; ++j)
                                print changedLines[j]
                        printf ("%d lines changed. ", changes)
                # function to confirm before saving changes
                        confirm_changes()
                }
        }
# Globally change
        if ( response ~ /[gG](lobal)?/) {
        # call function to prompt for correction
        # and display each line that is changed.
        # Ask user to approve all changes before saving.
                make_global_change()
        }
} # end of Main procedure
```

The first field of each input line from **wordlist** contains the misspelled word and it is assigned to **misspelling**. We construct a **while** loop inside which we display the misspelled word to the user and prompt for a response. Look closely at the regular expression that tests the value of **response**:

```
while (response !~ /(^[cCgGaAhHqQ])|^$/)
```

The user can only get out of this loop by entering any of the specified letters *or* by entering a carriage return—an empty line. The use of regular expressions for testing user input helps tremendously in writing a simple but flexible program. The user can enter a single letter "c" in lower- or uppercase or a word beginning with "c" such as "Change."

The rest of the main procedure consists of conditional statements that test for a specific response and perform a corresponding action. The first response is "help," which displays the list of responses again and then redisplays the prompt.

The next response is "quit." The action associated with quit is **exit**, which drops out of the main procedure and goes to the **END** procedure.

If the user enters "add," the misspelled word is put in the array **dict** and will be added as an exception in a local dictionary.

The "Change" and "Global" responses cause the program's real work to begin. It's important to understand how they differ. When the user enters "c" or "change," the first occurrence of the misspelled word in the document is displayed. Then the user is prompted to make the change. This happens for each occurrence in the document. When the user enters "g" or "global," the user is prompted to make the change right away, and all the changes are made at once without prompting the user to confirm each one. This work is largely handled by two functions, **make_change()** and **make_global_change()**, which we'll look at in the last section. These are all the valid responses, except one. A carriage return means to ignore the misspelled word and get the next word in the list. This is the default action of the main input loop, so no conditional need be set up for it.

## END Procedure

The **END** procedure, of course, is reached in one of the following circumstances:

- The **spell** command failed or did not turn up any misspellings.
- The list of misspelled words is exhausted.
- The user has entered "quit" at a prompt.

The purpose of the **END** procedure is to allow the user to confirm any permanent change to the document or the dictionary.

```
# END procedure makes changes permanent.
# It overwrites the original file, and adds words
# to the dictionary.
# It also removes the temporary files.

END {
# if we got here after reading only one record,
# no changes were made, so exit.
        if (NR <= 1) exit
# user must confirm saving corrections to file
        while (saveAnswer !~ /([yY](es)?)|([nN]o?)/ ) {
                printf "Save corrections in %s (y/n)? ", SPELLFILE
                getline saveAnswer < "-"
        }
# if answer is yes then mv temporary input file to SPELLFILE
# save old SPELLFILE, just in case
        if (saveAnswer ~ /^[yY]/) {
                system("cp " SPELLFILE " " SPELLFILE ".orig")
                system("mv " spellsource " " SPELLFILE)
        }
# if answer is no then rm temporary input file
        if (saveAnswer ~ /^[nN]/)
                system("rm " spellsource)

# if words have been added to dictionary array, then prompt
# to confirm saving in current dictionary.
        if (dictEntry) {
                printf "Make changes to dictionary (y/n)? "
                getline response < "-"
                if (response ~ /^[yY]/){
# if no dictionary defined, then use "dict"
                        if (! SPELLDICT) SPELLDICT = "dict"

# loop through array and append words to dictionary
                        sub(/^\+/, "", SPELLDICT)
                        for ( item in dict )
                                print dict[item] >> SPELLDICT
                        close(SPELLDICT)
# sort dictionary file
                        system("sort " SPELLDICT "> tmp_dict")
                        system("mv " "tmp_dict " SPELLDICT)
                }
        }
# remove word list
        system("rm sp_wordlist")
} # end of END procedure
```

The **END** procedure begins with a conditional statement that tests that the number of records is less than or equal to 1. This occurs when the **spell** program does not generate a word list or when the user enters "quit" after seeing just the first record. If so, the **END** procedure is exited as there is no work to save.

Next, we create a **while** loop to ask the user about saving the changes made to the document. It requires the user to respond "y" or "n" to the prompt. If the answer is "y," the temporary input file replaces the original document file. If the answer is "n," the temporary file is removed. No other responses are accepted.

Next, we test to see if the **dict** array has something in it. Its elements are the words to be added to the dictionary. If the user approves adding them to the dictionary, these words are appended to the current dictionary, as defined above, or if not, to a local *dict* file. Because the dictionary must be sorted to be read by **spell**, a **sort** command is executed with the output sent to a temporary file that is afterwards copied over the original file.

## Supporting Functions

There are three supporting functions, two of which are large and do the bulk of the work of making changes in the document. The third function supports that work by confirming that the user wants to save the changes that were made.

When the user wants to "Change each occurrence" in the document, the main procedure has a **while** loop that reads the document one line at a time. (This line becomes $0.) It calls the **make_change()** function to see if the line contains the misspelled word. If it does, the line is displayed and the user is prompted to enter the correct spelling of the word.

```
# make_change -- prompt user to correct misspelling
#                 for current input line.  Calls itself
#                 to find other occurrences in string.
#         stringToChange -- initially $0; then unmatched substring of $0
#         len -- length from beginning of $0 to end of matched string
# Assumes that misspelling is defined.

function make_change (stringToChange, len, # parameters
        line, OKmakechange, printstring, carets)   # locals
{
# match misspelling in stringToChange; otherwise do nothing
   if ( match(stringToChange, misspelling) ) {
   # Display matched line
        printstring = $0
        gsub(/\t/, " ", printstring)
        print printstring
        carets = "^"
        for (i = 1; i < RLENGTH; ++i)
                carets = carets "^"
        if (len)
                FMT = "%" len+RSTART+RLENGTH-2 "s\n"
        else
                FMT = "%" RSTART+RLENGTH-1 "s\n"
        printf(FMT, carets)
```

```
      # Prompt user for correction, if not already defined
              if (! newspelling) {
                       printf "Change to:"
                       getline newspelling < "-"
              }
      # A carriage return falls through
      # If user enters correction, confirm
              while (newspelling && ! OKmakechange) {
                       printf ("Change %s to %s? (y/n):", misspelling, newspelling)
                       getline OKmakechange < "-"
                       madechg = ""
              # test response
                       if (OKmakechange ~ /[yY](es)?/ ) {
                       # make change (first occurrence only)
                                madechg = sub(misspelling, newspelling, stringToChange)
                       }
                       else if ( OKmakechange ~ /[nN]o?/ ) {
                                # offer chance to re-enter correction
                                printf "Change to:"
                                getline newspelling < "-"
                                OKmakechange = ""
                       }
              } # end of while loop

      # if len, we are working with substring of $0
              if (len) {
              # assemble it
                       line = substr($0,1,len-1)
                       $0 = line stringToChange
              }
              else {
                       $0 = stringToChange
                       if (madechg) ++changes
              }

      # put changed line in array for display
              if (madechg)
                       changedLines[changes] = ">" $0

      # create substring so we can try to match other occurrences
              len += RSTART + RLENGTH
              part1 = substr($0, 1, len-1)
              part2 = substr($0, len)
      # calls itself to see if misspelling is found in remaining part
              make_change(part2, len)

      } # end of if

   } # end of make_change()
```

If the misspelled word is not found in the current input line, nothing is done. If it is found, this function shows the line containing the misspelling and asks the user if it should be corrected. Underneath the display of the current line is a row of carets that indicates the misspelled word.

```
Two other utlities that are found on the UNIX system
          ^^^^^^^^^^
```

The current input line is copied to **printstring** because it is necessary to change the line for display purposes. If the line contains any tabs, each tab in this copy of the line is temporarily replaced by a single space. This solves a problem of aligning the carets when tabs were present. (A tab counts as a single character when determining the length of a line but actually occupies greater space when displayed, usually five to eight characters long.)

After displaying the line, the function prompts the user to enter a correction. It then follows up by displaying what the user has entered and asks for confirmation. If the correction is approved, the **sub()** function is called to make the change. If not approved, the user is given another chance to enter the correct word.

Remember that the **sub()** function only changes the first occurrence on a line. The **gsub()** function changes all occurrences on a line, but we want to allow the user to confirm *each* change. Therefore, we have to try to match the misspelled word against the remaining part of the line. And we have to be able to match the next occurrence regardless of whether or not the first occurrence was changed.

To do this, **make_change()** is designed as a recursive function; it calls itself to look for additional occurrences on the same line. In other words, the first time **make_change()** is called, it looks at all of $0 and matches the first misspelled word on that line. Then it splits the line into two parts—the first part contains the characters up to the end of the first occurrence and the second part contains the characters that immediately follow up to the end of the line. Then it calls itself to try and match the misspelled word in the second part. When called recursively, the function takes two arguments.

```
make_change(part2, len)
```

The first is the string to be changed, which is initially $0 when called from the main procedure but each time thereafter is the remaining part of $0. The second argument is **len** or the length of the first part, which we use to extract the substring and reassemble the two parts at the end.

The **make_change()** function also collects an array of lines that were changed.

```
# put changed line in array for display
        if (madechg)
                changedLines[changes] = ">" $0
```

The variable **madechg** will have a value if the **sub()** function was successful. $0 (the two parts have been rejoined) is assigned to an element of the array. When all of the lines of the document have been read, the main procedure loops through this array to display all the changed lines. Then it calls the **confirm_changes()** function to ask if these changes should be saved. It copies the temporary output file over the temporary input file, keeping intact the corrections made for the current misspelled word.

If a user decides to make a "Global change," the **make_global_change()** function is called to do it. This function is similar to the **make_change()** function, but is simpler because we can make the change globally on each line.

```
# make_global_change --
#               prompt user to correct misspelling
#               for all lines globally.
#               Has no arguments
# Assumes that misspelling is defined.

function make_global_change(    newspelling, OKmakechange, changes)
{
# prompt user to correct misspelled word
    printf "Globally change to:"
    getline newspelling < "-"

# carriage return falls through
# if there is an answer, confirm
    while (newspelling && ! OKmakechange) {
                printf ("Globally change %s to %s? (y/n):", misspelling,
                                newspelling)
                getline OKmakechange < "-"
        # test response and make change
                if (OKmakechange ~ /[yY](es)?/ ) {
                # open file, read all lines
                        while( (getline < spellsource) > 0){
                        # if match is found, make change using gsub
                        # and print each changed line.
                                if ($0 ~ misspelling) {
                                        madechg = gsub(misspelling, newspelling)
                                        print ">", $0
                                        changes += 1  # counter for line changes
                                }
                        # write all lines to temp output file
                                print > spellout
                        } # end of while loop for reading file

                # close temporary files
                        close(spellout)
                        close(spellsource)
                # report the number of changes
                        printf ("%d lines changed. ", changes)
```

```
                    # function to confirm before saving changes
                            confirm_changes()
                    } # end of if (OKmakechange ~ y)

            # if correction not confirmed,  prompt for new word
                    else if ( OKmakechange ~ /[nN]o?/ ){
                            printf "Globally change to:"
                            getline newspelling < "-"
                            OKmakechange = ""
                    }

            } # end of while loop for prompting user for correction

    } # end of make_global_change()
```

This function prompts the user to enter a correction. A **while** loop is set up to read all the lines of the document and apply the **gsub()** function to make the changes. The main difference is that all the changes are made at once—the user is not prompted to confirm them. When all lines have been read, the function displays the lines that were changed and calls **confirm_changes()** to get the user to approve this batch of changes before saving them.

The **confirm_changes()** function is a routine called to get approval of the changes made when the **make_change()** or **make_global_change()** function is called.

```
# confirm_changes --
#               confirm before saving changes

function confirm_changes(  savechanges) {
# prompt to confirm saving changes
        while (! savechanges ) {
                printf ("Save changes? (y/n)")
                getline savechanges < "-"
        }
# if confirmed, mv output to input
        if (savechanges ~ /[yY](es)?/)
                system("mv " spellout " " spellsource)
}
```

The reason for creating this function is to prevent the duplication of code. Its purpose is simply to require the user to acknowledge the changes before replacing the old version of the document file (**spellsource**) with the new version (**spellout**).

## *The spellcheck Shell Script*

To make it easy to invoke this awk script, we create the **spellcheck** shell script (say *that* three times fast). It contains the following lines:

```
AWKLIB=/usr/local/awklib
nawk -f $AWKLIB/spellcheck.awk $*
```

This script sets up a shell variable **AWKLIB** that specifies the location of the **spellcheck.awk** script. The symbol "$*" expands to all command-line parameters following the name of the script. These parameters are then available to awk.

One of the interesting things about this spell checker is how little is done in the shell script.[*] All of the work is done in the awk programming language, including executing 10 UNIX commands. We're using a consistent syntax and the same constructs by doing it all in awk. When you have to do some of your work in the shell and some in awk, it can get confusing. For instance, you have to remember the differences in the syntax of **if** conditionals and how to reference variables. Modern versions of awk provide a true alternative to the shell for executing commands and interacting with a user. The full listing for **spellcheck.awk** is found in Appendix C, *Supplement for Chapter 12*.

# Generating a Formatted Index

The process of generating an index usually involves three steps:

* Code the index entries in the document.

* Format the document, producing index entries with page numbers.

* Process the index entries to sort them, combining entries that differ only in page number, and then preparing the formatted index.

This process remains pretty much the same whether using **troff**, other coded batch formatters, or a WYSIWYG formatter such as *FrameMaker*, although the steps are not as clearly separated with the latter. However, I will be describing how we use **troff** to generate an index such as the one for this book. We code the index using the following macros:

| Macro | Description |
|-------|-------------|
| .XX   | Produces general index entries. |
| .XN   | Creates "see" or "see also" cross references. |
| .XB   | Creates bold page entry indicating primary reference. |
| .XS   | Begins range of pages for entry. |
| .XE   | Ends range of pages for entry. |

These macros take a single quoted argument, which can have one of several forms, indicating primary, secondary, or tertiary keys:

"*primary* [ : *secondary* [ ; *tertiary* ]]"

---

[*] *UNIX Text Processing* (Dougherty and O'Reilly, Howard W. Sams, 1987) presents a sed-based spell checker that relies heavily upon the shell. It is interesting to compare the two versions.

A colon is used as the separator between the primary and secondary keys. To support an earlier coding convention, the first comma is interpreted as the separator if no colon is used. A semicolon indicates the presence of a tertiary key. The page number is always associated with the last key.

Here is an entry with only a primary key:

```
.XX "XView"
```

The next two entries specify a secondary key:

```
.XX "XView: reserved names"
.XX "XView, packages"
```

The most complex entries contain tertiary keys:

```
.XX "XView: objects; list"
.XX "XView: objects; hierarchy of"
```

Finally, there are two types of cross references:

```
.XN "error recovery: (see error handling)"
.XX "mh mailer: (see also xmh mailer)"
```

The "see" entry refers a person to another index entry. The "see also" is typically used when there are entries for, in this case, "mh mailer," but there is relevant information catalogued under another name. Only "see" entries do not have page numbers associated with them.

When the document is processed by **troff**, the following index entries are produced:

```
XView    42
XView: reserved names    43
XView, packages 43
XView: objects; list of 43
XView: objects; hierarchy of    44
XView, packages 45
error recovery: (See error handling)
mh mailer: (see also xmh mailer)    46
```

These entries serve as input to the indexing program. Each entry (except for "see" entries) consists of the key and a page number. In other words, the entry is divided into two parts and the first part, the key, can also be divided into three parts. When these entries are processed by the indexing program and the output is formatted, the entries for "XView" are combined as follows:

```
XView, 42
        objects; hierarchy of, 44;
          list of, 43
        packages, 43,45
        reserved names, 43
```

To accomplish this, the indexing program must:

- Sort the index by key and page number.

- Merge entries that differ only in the page number.

- Merge entries that have the same primary and/or secondary keys.

- Look for consecutive page numbers and combine as a range.

- Prepare the index in a format for display on screen or for printing.

This is what the index program does if you are processing the index entries for a single book. It also allows you to create a master index, an overall index for a set of volumes. To do that, an awk script appends either a roman numeral or an abbreviation after the page number. Each file then contains the entries for a particular book and those entries are uniquely identified. If we chose to use roman numerals to identify the volume, then the above entries would be changed to:

```
XView    42:I
XView: reserved names    43:I
XView: objects; list of 43:I
```

With multivolume entries, the final index that is generated might look like this:

```
XView, I:42; II:55,69,75
        objects; hierarchy of, I:44;
          list of, I:43; II: 56
        packages, I:43,45
        reserved names, I:43
```

For now, it's only important to recognize that the index entry used as input to the awk program can have a page number or a page number followed by a volume identifier.

## *The masterindex Program*

Because of the length and complexity of this indexing application,[*] our description presents the larger structure of the program. Use the comments in the program itself to understand what is happening in the program line by line.

---

* The origins of this indexing program are traced back to a copy of an indexing program written in awk by Steve Talbott. I learned this program by taking it apart, and made some changes to it to support consecutive page numbering in addition to section-page numbering. That was the program I described in *UNIX Text Processing*. Knowing that program, I wrote an indexing program that could deal with index entries produced by Microsoft Word and generate an index using section-page numbering. Later, we needed a master index for several books in our X Window System Series. I took it as an opportunity to rethink our indexing program, and rewrite it using nawk, so that it supports both single-book and multiple-book indices. *The AWK Programming Language* contains an example of an index program that is smaller than the one shown here and might be a place to start if you find this one too complicated. It does not, however, deal with keys. That indexing program is a simplified version of the one described in Bell Labs Computing Science Technical Report 128, *Tools for Printing Indexes*, October 1986, by Brian Kernighan and Jon Bentley. [D.D.]

After descriptions of each of the program modules, a final section discusses a few remaining details. For the most part, these are code fragments that deal with nitty-gritty, input-related problems that had to be solved along the way. The shell script **masterindex**\* allows the user to specify a number of different command-line options to specify what kind of index to make and it invokes the necessary awk programs to do the job. The operations of the **masterindex** program can be broken into five separate programs or modules that form a single pipe.

```
input.idx | sort | pagenums.idx | combine.idx | format.idx
```

All but one of the programs are written using awk. For sorting the entries, we rely upon **sort**, a standard UNIX utility. Here's a brief summary of what each of these programs does:

**input.idx**
> Standardizes the format of entries and rotates them.

**sort**
> Sorts entries by key, volume, and page number.

**pagenums.idx**
> Merges entries with same key, creating a list of page numbers.

**combine.idx**
> Combines consecutive page numbers into a range.

**format.idx**
> Prepares the formatted index for the screen or processing by **troff**.

We will discuss each of these steps in a separate section.

## *Standardizing Input*

This **input.idx** script looks for different types of entries and standardizes them for easier processing by subsequent programs. Additionally, it automatically rotates index entries containing a tilde (˜). (See the section "Rotating Two Parts" later in this chapter.)

The input to the **input.idx** program consists of two tab-separated fields, as described earlier. The program produces output records with three colon-separated fields. The first field contains the primary key; the second field contains the secondary and tertiary keys, if defined; and the third field contains the page number.

---

\* This shell script and the documentation for the program are presented in Appendix C. You might want to first read the documentation for a basic understanding of using the program.

Here's the code for **input.idx** program:

```
#!/work/bin/nawk -f
# ------------------------------------------------
# input.idx -- standardize input before sorting
# Author:  Dale Dougherty
# Version 1.1    7/10/90
#
# input is "entry" tab "page_number"
# ------------------------------------------------
BEGIN { FS = "\t"; OFS = "" }

#1 Match entries that need rotating that contain a single tilde
    # $1 ~ /~[^~]/  # regexp does not work and I do not know why
$1 ~ /~/ && $1 !~ /~~/ {
    # split first field into array named subfield
        n = split($1, subfield, "~")
        if (n == 2) {
        # print entry without "~" and then rotated
                printf("%s %s::%s\n", subfield[1], subfield[2], $2)
                printf("%s:%s:%s\n", subfield[2], subfield[1], $2)
        }
        next
}# End of 1


#2 Match entries that contain two tildes
$1 ~ /~~/ {
    # replace ~~ with ~
        gsub(/~~/, "~", $1)
} # End of 2

#3  Match entries that use "::" for literal ":".
$1 ~ /::/ {
    # substitute octal value for "::"
        gsub(/::/, "\\72", $1)
}# End of 3

#4 Clean up entries
{
    # look for second colon, which might be used instead of ";"
        if (sub(/:.*:/, "&;", $1)) {
                sub(/:;/, ";", $1)
        }
    # remove blank space if any after colon.
        sub(/: */, ":", $1)
    # if comma is used as delimiter, convert to colon.
        if ( $1 !~ /:/ ) {
        # On see also & see, try to put delimiter before "("
                if ($1 ~ /\([sS]ee/) {
                        if (sub(/, *.*\(/, ":&", $1))
                                sub(/:, */, ":", $1)
                        else
                                sub(/ *\(/, ":(", $1)
                }
```

```
                    else { # otherwise, just look for comma
                            sub(/, */, ":", $1)
                    }
            }
            else {
                    # added to insert semicolon in "See"
                    if ($1 ~ /:[^;]+ *\([sS]ee/)
                            sub(/  *\(/, ";(", $1)
            }
}# End of 4

#5 match See Alsos and fix for sort at end
$1 ~ / *\([Ss]ee +[Aa]lso/ {
  # add "~zz" for sort at end
            sub(/\([Ss]ee +[Aa]lso/, "~zz(see also", $1)
            if ($1 ~ /:[^; ]+ *~zz/) {
                    sub(/ *~zz/, "; ~zz", $1)
            }
  # if no page number
            if ($2 == "") {
                    print $0 ":"
                    next
            }
            else {
            # output two entries:
            # print See Also entry w/out page number
                    print $1 ":"
            # remove See Also
                    sub(/ *~zz\(see also.*$/, "", $1)
                    sub(/;/, "", $1)
            # print as normal entry
                    if ( $1 ~ /:/ )
                            print $1 ":" $2
                    else
                            print $1 "::" $2
                    next
            }
}# End of 5

#6 Process entries without page number (See entries)
(NF == 1 || $2 == "" || $1 ~ /\([sS]ee/) {
    # if a "See" entry
            if ( $1 ~ /\([sS]ee/ ) {
                    if ( $1 ~ /:/ )
                            print $1 ":"
                    else
                            print $1 ":"
                    next
            }
            else  { # if not a See entry, generate error
                    printerr("No page number")
                    next
            }
}# End of 6
```

```
#7 If the colon is used as the delimiter
$1 ~ /:/ {
   # output entry:page
        print $1 ":" $2
        next
}# End of 7

#8  Match entries with only primary keys.
{
        print $1 "::" $2
}# End of 8

# supporting functions
#
# printerr -- print error message and current record
#                 Arg: message to be displayed

function printerr (message) {
        # print message, record number and record
        printf("ERROR:%s (%d) %s\n", message, NR, $0) > "/dev/tty"
}
```

This script consists of a number of pattern-matching rules to recognize different types of input. Note that an entry could match more than one rule unless the action associated with a rule calls the **next** statement.

As we describe this script, we will be referring to the rules by number. Rule 1 rotates entries containing a tilde and produces two output records. The **split()** function creates an array named **subfield** that contains the two parts of the compound entry. The two parts are printed in their original order and are then swapped to create a second output record in which the secondary key becomes a primary key.

Because we are using the tilde as a special character, we must provide some way of actually entering a tilde. We have implemented the convention that two consecutive tildes are translated into a single tilde. Rule 2 deals with that case, but notice that the pattern for rule 1 makes sure that the first tilde it matches is not followed by another tilde.[*]

The order of rules 1 and 2 in the script is significant. We can't replace "~~" with "~" until after the procedure for rotating the entry.

---

[*] In the first edition, Dale wrote, "For extra credit, please send me mail if you can figure out why the commented regular expression just before rule 1 does not do the job. I used the compound expression as a last resort." I'm ashamed to admit that this stumped me also. When Henry Spencer turned on the light, it was blinding: "The reason why the commented regexp doesn't work is that it doesn't do what the author thought. ☺ It looks for tilde followed by a non-tilde character ... but the second tilde of a ~~ combination is usually followed by a non-tilde! Using /[^~]~[^~]/ would probably work." I plugged this regular expression in to the program, and it worked just fine. [A.R.]

Rule 3 does a job similar to that of rule 2; it allows "::" to be used to output a literal ":" in the index. However, since we use the colon as an input delimiter throughout the input to the program, we cannot allow it to appear in an entry as finally output until the very end. Thus, we replace the sequence "::" with the colon's ASCII value in octal. (The **format.idx** program will reverse the replacement.)

Beginning with rule 4, we attempt to recognize various ways of coding entries—giving the user more flexibility. However, to make writing the remaining programs easier, we must reduce this variety to a few basic forms.

In the "basic" syntax, the primary and secondary keys are separated by a colon. The secondary and tertiary keys are separated by a semicolon. Nonetheless the program also recognizes a second colon, in place of a semicolon, as the delimiter between the secondary and tertiary keys. It also recognizes that if no colon is specified as a delimiter, then a comma can be used as the delimiter between primary and secondary keys. (In part, this was done to be compatible with an earlier program that used the comma as the delimiter.) The **sub()** function looks for the first comma on the line and changes it to a colon. This rule also tries to standardize the syntax of "see" and "see also" entries. For entries that are colon-delimited, rule 4 removes spaces after the colon. All of the work is done using the **sub()** function.

Rule 5 deals with "see also" entries. We prepend the arbitrary string "~zz" to the "see also" entries so that they will sort at the end of the list of secondary keys. The **pagenums.idx** script, later in the pipeline, will remove "~zz" after the entries have been sorted.

Rule 6 matches entries that do not specify a page number. The only valid entry without a page number contains a "see" reference. This rule outputs "see" entries with ":" at the end to indicate an empty third field. All other entries generate an error message via the **printerr()** function. This function notifies the user that a particular entry does not have a page number and will not be included in the output. This is one method of standardizing input—throwing out what you can't interpret properly. However, it is critical to notify the user so that he or she can correct the entry.

Rule 7 outputs entries that contain the colon-delimiter. Its action uses **next** to avoid reaching rule 8.

Finally, rule 8 matches entries that contain only a primary key. In other words, there is no delimiter. We output "::" to indicate an empty second field.

Here's a portion of the contents of our *test* file. We'll be using it to generate examples in this section.

```
$ cat test
XView: programs; initialization 45
XV_INIT_ARGS~macro      46
Xv_object~type  49
Xv_singlecolor~type      80
graphics: (see also server image)
graphics, XView model   83
X Window System: events 84
graphics, CANVAS_X_PAINT_WINDOW 86
X Window System, X Window ID for paint window    87
toolkit (See X Window System).
graphics: (see also server image)
Xlib, repainting canvas 88
Xlib.h~header file       89
```

When we run this file through **input.idx**, it produces:

```
$ input.idx test
XView:programs; initialization:45
XV_INIT_ARGS macro::46
macro:XV_INIT_ARGS:46
Xv_object type::49
type:Xv_object:49
Xv_singlecolor type::80
type:Xv_singlecolor:80
graphics:~zz(see also server image):
graphics:XView model:83
X Window System:events:84
graphics:CANVAS_X_PAINT_WINDOW:86
X Window System:X Window ID for paint window:87
graphics:~zz(see also server image):
Xlib:repainting canvas:88
Xlib.h header file::89
header file:Xlib.h:89
```

Each entry now consists of three colon-separated fields. In the sample output, you can find examples of entries with only a primary key, those with primary and secondary keys, and those with primary, secondary, and tertiary keys. You can also find examples of rotated entries, duplicate entries, and "see also" entries.

The only difference in the output for multivolume entries is that each entry would have a fourth field that contains the volume identifier.

## *Sorting the Entries*

Now the output produced by **input.idx** is ready to be sorted. The easiest way to sort the entries is to use the standard UNIX **sort** program rather than write a custom script. In addition to sorting the entries, we want to remove any duplicates and for this task we use the **uniq** program.

Here's the command line we use:

```
sort -bdf -t: +0 -1 +1 -2 +3 -4 +2n -3n | uniq
```

As you can see, we use a number of options with the **sort** command. The first option, *-b*, specifies that leading spaces be ignored. The *-d* option specifies a dictionary sort in which symbols and special characters are ignored. *-f* specifies that lower- and uppercase letters are to be *folded* together; in other words, they are to be treated as the same character for purposes of the sort. The next argument is perhaps the most important: *-t:* tells the program to use a colon as a field delimiter for sort keys. The "+" options that follow specify the number of fields to skip from the beginning of the line. Therefore, to specify the first field as the primary sort key, we use "+0." Similarly, the "-" options specify the end of a sort key. "-1" specifies that the primary sort key ends at the first field, or the beginning of the second field. The second sort field is the secondary key. The fourth field ("+3") if it exists, contains the volume number. The last key to sort is the page number; this requires a numeric sort (if we did not tell **sort** that this key consists of numbers, then the number 1 would be followed by 10, instead of 2). Notice that we sort page numbers after sorting the volume numbers. Thus, all the page numbers for Volume I are sorted in order before the page numbers for Volume II. Finally, we pipe the output to **uniq** to remove identical entries. Processing the output from **input.idx**, the **sort** command produces:

```
graphics:CANVAS_X_PAINT_WINDOW:86
graphics:XView model:83
graphics:~zz(see also server image):
header file:Xlib.h:89
macro:XV_INIT_ARGS:46
toolkit:(See X Window System).:
type:Xv_object:49
type:Xv_singlecolor:80
X Window System:events:84
X Window System:X Window ID for paint window:87
Xlib:repainting canvas:88
Xlib.h header file::89
XView:programs; initialization:45
XV_INIT_ARGS macro::46
Xv_object type::49
Xv_singlecolor type::80
```

## Handling Page Numbers

The **pagenums.idx** program looks for entries that differ only in page number and creates a list of page numbers for a single entry. The input to this program is four colon-separated fields:

```
PRIMARY:SECONDARY:PAGE:VOLUME
```

The fourth is optional. For now, we consider only the index for a single book, in which there are no volume numbers. Remember that the entries are now sorted.

The heart of this program compares the current entry to the previous one and determines what to output. The conditionals that implement the comparison can be extracted and expressed in pseudocode, as follows:

```
PRIMARY = $1
SECONDARY = $2
PAGE = $3
if (PRIMARY == prevPRIMARY)
        if (SECONDARY == prevSECONDARY)
                print PAGE
        else
                print PRIMARY:SECONDARY:PAGE
else
        print PRIMARY:SECONDARY:PAGE
prevPRIMARY = PRIMARY
prevSECONDARY = SECONDARY
```

Let's see how this code handles a series of entries, beginning with:

```
XView::18
```

The primary key doesn't match the previous primary key; the line is output as is:

```
XView::18
```

The next entry is:

```
XView:about:3
```

When we compare the primary key of this entry to the previous one, they are the same. When we compare secondary keys, they differ; we output the record as is:

```
XView:about:3
```

The next entry is:

```
XView:about:7
```

Because both the primary and secondary keys match the keys of the previous entry, we simply output the page number. (The **printf** function is used instead of **print** so that there is no automatic newline.) This page number is appended to the previous entry so that it looks like this:

```
XView:about:3,7
```

The next entry also matches both keys:

```
XView:about:10
```

Again, only the page number is output so that entry now looks like:

```
XView:about:3,7,10
```

In this way, three entries that differ only in page number are combined into a single entry.

The full script adds an additional test to see if the volume identifier matches. Here's the full **pagenums.idx** script:

```
#!/work/bin/nawk -f
# -------------------------------------------------
# pagenums.idx -- collect pages for common entries
# Author:  Dale Dougherty
# Version 1.1    7/10/90
#
# input should be PRIMARY:SECONDARY:PAGE:VOLUME
# -------------------------------------------------

BEGIN { FS = ":"; OFS = ""}

# main routine -- apply to all input lines
{
    # assign fields to variables
         PRIMARY = $1
         SECONDARY = $2
         PAGE = $3
         VOLUME = $4

    # check for a see also and collect it in array
         if (SECONDARY ~ /\([Ss]ee +[Aa]lso/) {
         # create tmp copy & remove "~zz" from copy
                 tmpSecondary = SECONDARY
                 sub(/~zz\([Ss]ee +[Aa]lso */, "", tmpSecondary)
                 sub(/\) */, "", tmpSecondary)
         # remove secondary key along with "~zz"
                 sub(/^.*~zz\([Ss]ee +[Aa]lso */, "", SECONDARY)
                 sub(/\) */, "", SECONDARY)
         # assign to next element of seeAlsoList
                 seeAlsoList[++eachSeeAlso] = SECONDARY "; "
                 prevPrimary = PRIMARY
         # assign copy to previous secondary key
                 prevSecondary = tmpSecondary
                 next
         } # end test for see Also

    # Conditionals to compare keys of current record to previous
    #  record.  If Primary and Secondary keys are the same, only
    #  the page number is printed.

    # test to see if each PRIMARY key matches previous key
         if (PRIMARY == prevPrimary) {
```

```
                # test to see if each SECONDARY key matches previous key
                    if (SECONDARY == prevSecondary)
                    # test to see if VOLUME matches;
                    # print only VOLUME:PAGE
                            if (VOLUME == prevVolume)
                                    printf (",%s", PAGE)
                            else {
                                    printf ("; ")
                                    volpage(VOLUME, PAGE)
                            }
                    else{
                    # if array of See Alsos, output them now
                            if (eachSeeAlso) outputSeeAlso(2)
                    # print PRIMARY:SECONDARY:VOLUME:PAGE
                            printf ("\n%s:%s:", PRIMARY, SECONDARY)
                            volpage(VOLUME, PAGE)
                    }
            } # end of test for PRIMARY == prev
            else { # PRIMARY != prev
                    # if we have an array of See Alsos, output them now
                    if (eachSeeAlso) outputSeeAlso(1)
                    if (NR != 1)
                            printf ("\n")
                    if (NF == 1){
                            printf ("%s:", $0)
                    }
                    else {
                            printf ("%s:%s:", PRIMARY, SECONDARY)
                            volpage(VOLUME, PAGE)
                    }
            }
            prevPrimary = PRIMARY
            prevSecondary = SECONDARY
            prevVolume = VOLUME

} # end of main routine

# at end, print newline
END {
    # in case last entry has "see Also"
        if (eachSeeAlso) outputSeeAlso(1)
        printf("\n")
}

# outputSeeAlso function -- list elements of seeAlsoList
function outputSeeAlso(LEVEL) {
        # LEVEL - indicates which key we need to output
        if (LEVEL == 1)
                printf ("\n%s:(See also ", prevPrimary)
        else {
                sub(/;.*$/, "", prevSecondary)
                printf ("\n%s:%s; (See also ", prevPrimary, prevSecondary)
        }
```

```
                sub(/; $/, ".):", seeAlsoList[eachSeeAlso])
                for (i = 1; i <= eachSeeAlso; ++i)
                        printf ("%s", seeAlsoList[i])
                eachSeeAlso = 0
        }

        # volpage function -- determine whether or not to print volume info
        #       two args: volume & page

        function volpage(v, p)
        {
           # if VOLUME is empty then print PAGE only
                if ( v == "" )
                        printf ("%s", p)
                else
           # otherwise print VOLUME^PAGE
                        printf ("%s^%s",v, p)
        }
```

Remember, first of all, that the input to the program is sorted by its keys. The page numbers are also in order, such that an entry for "graphics" on page 7 appears in the input before one on page 10. Similarly, entries for Volume I appear in the input before Volume II. Therefore, this program need do no sorting; it simply compares the keys and if they are the same, appends the page number to a list. In this way, the entries are reduced.

This script also handles "see also" entries. Since the records are now sorted, we can remove the special sorting sequence "~zz." We also handle the case where we might encounter consecutive "see also" entries. We don't want to output:

```
Toolkit (see also Xt) (See also XView) (See also Motif).
```

Instead we'd like to combine them into a list such that they appear as:

```
Toolkit (see also Xt; XView; Motif)
```

To do that, we create an array named **seeAlsoList**. From **SECONDARY**, we remove the parentheses, the secondary key if it exists and the "see also" and then assign it to an element of **seeAlsoList**. We make a copy of **SECONDARY** with the secondary key and assign it to **prevSecondary** for making comparisons to the next entry.

The function **outputSeeAlso()** is called to read all the elements of the array and print them. The function **volpage()** is also simple and determines whether or not we need to output a volume number. Both of these functions are called from more than one place in the code, so the main reason for defining them as functions is to reduce duplication.

Here's an example of what it produces for a single-book index:

```
X Window System:Xlib:6
XFontStruct structure::317
Xlib::6
```

```
Xlib:repainting canvas:88
Xlib.h header file::89,294
Xv_Font type::310
XView::18
XView:about:3,7,10
XView:as object-oriented system:17
```

Here's an example of what it produces for a master index:

```
reserved names:table of:I^43
Xt:example of programming interface:I^44,65
Xt:objects; list of:I^43,58; II^40
Xt:packages:I^43,61; II^42
Xt:programs; initialization:I^45
Xt:reserved names:I^43,58
Xt:reserved prefixes:I^43,58
Xt:types:I^43,54,61
```

The "^" is used as a temporary delimiter between the volume number and the list
of page numbers.

## Merging Entries with the Same Keys

The **pagenums.idx** program reduced entries that were the same except for the
page number. Now we'll to process entries that share the same primary key. We
also want to look for consecutive page numbers and combine them in ranges.

The **combine.idx** is quite similar to the **pagenums.idx** script, making another pass
through the index, comparing entries with the same primary key. The following
pseudocode abstracts this comparison. (To make this discussion easier, we will
omit tertiary keys and show how to compare primary and secondary keys.) After
the entries are processed by **pagenums.idx**, no two entries exist that share the
same primary and secondary keys. Therefore, we don't have to compare secondary keys.

```
PRIMARY = $1
SECONDARY = $2
PAGE = $3
if (PRIMARY == prevPRIMARY)
        print :SECONDARY:
else
        print PRIMARY:SECONDARY
prevPRIMARY = PRIMARY
prevSECONDARY = SECONDARY
```

If the primary keys match, we output only the secondary key. For instance, if there
are three entries:

```
XView:18
XView:about:3, 7, 10
XView:as object-oriented system:17
```

they will be output as:

```
XView:18
:about:3, 7, 10
:as object-oriented system:17
```

We drop the primary key when it is the same. The actual code is a little more difficult because there are tertiary keys. We have to test primary and secondary keys to see if they are unique or the same, but we don't have to test tertiary keys. (We only need to know that they are there.)

You no doubt noticed that the above pseudocode does not output page numbers. The second role of this script is to examine page numbers and combine a list of consecutive numbers. The page numbers are a comma-separated list that can be loaded into an array, using the **split( )** function.

To see if numbers are consecutive, we loop through the array comparing each element to 1 + the previous element.

```
eachpage[j-1]+1 == eachpage[j]
```

In other words, if adding 1 to the previous element produces the current element, then they are consecutive. The previous element becomes the first page number in the range and the current element becomes the last page in the range. This is done within a **while** loop until the conditional is not true, and the page numbers are not consecutive. Then we output the first page number and the last page number separated by a hyphen:

```
23-25
```

The actual code looks more complicated than this because it is called from a function that must recognize volume and page number pairs. It first has to split the volume from the list of page numbers and then it can call the function (**rangeOfPages( )**) to process the list of numbers.

Here is the full listing of **combine.idx**:

```
#!/work/bin/nawk -f
# ------------------------------------------------
# combine.idx -- merge keys with same PRIMARY key
#                and combine consecutive page numbers
# Author:  Dale Dougherty
# Version 1.1   7/10/90
#
# input should be PRIMARY:SECONDARY:PAGELIST
# ------------------------------------------------

BEGIN   { FS = ":"; OFS = ""}
```

```
# main routine -- applies to all input lines
#   It compares the keys and merges the duplicates.
{
    # assign first field
        PRIMARY=$1
    # split second field, getting SEC and TERT keys.
        sizeOfArray = split($2, array, ";")
        SECONDARY = array[1]
        TERTIARY = array[2]
    # test that tertiary key exists
        if (sizeOfArray > 1) {
        # tertiary key exists
                isTertiary = 1
        # two cases where ";" might turn up
        # check SEC key for list of "see also"
                if (SECONDARY ~ /\([sS]ee also/){
                        SECONDARY = $2
                        isTertiary = 0
                }
        # check TERT key for "see also"
                if (TERTIARY ~ /\([sS]ee also/){
                        TERTIARY = substr($2, (index($2, ";") + 1))
                }
        }
        else # tertiary key does not exist
                isTertiary = 0
    # assign third field
        PAGELIST = $3

    # Conditional to compare primary key of this entry to that
    #  of previous entry. Then compare secondary keys.  This
    #  determines which non-duplicate keys to output.
        if (PRIMARY == prevPrimary) {
                if (isTertiary && SECONDARY == prevSecondary)
                        printf (";\n::%s", TERTIARY)
                else
                        if (isTertiary)
                                printf ("\n:%s; %s", SECONDARY, TERTIARY)
                        else
                                printf ("\n:%s", SECONDARY)
        }
        else {
                if (NR != 1)
                        printf ("\n")
                if ($2 != "")
                        printf ("%s:%s", PRIMARY, $2)
                else
                        printf ("%s", PRIMARY)

                prevPrimary = PRIMARY
        }

        prevSecondary = SECONDARY
} # end of main procedure
```

```
# routine for "See" entries (primary key only)
NF == 1 { printf ("\n") }

# routine for all other entries
#  It handles output of the page number.

NF > 1  {
        if (PAGELIST)
        # calls function numrange() to look for
        # consecutive page numbers.
                printf (":%s", numrange(PAGELIST))
        else
                if (! isTertiary || (TERTIARY && SECONDARY)) printf (":")

} # end of NF > 1

# END procedure outputs newline
END {  printf ("\n") }

# Supporting Functions

# numrange -- read list of Volume^Page numbers, detach Volume
#                from Page for each Volume and call rangeOfPages
#                to combine consecutive page numbers in the list.
#         PAGE = volumes separated by semicolons; volume and page
#                separated by ^.

function numrange(PAGE,      listOfPages, sizeOfArray)
{
  # Split up list by volume.
        sizeOfArray = split(PAGE, howManyVolumes,";")
  # Check to see if more than 1 volume.
        if (sizeOfArray > 1) {

        # if more than 1 volume, loop through list
                for (i = 1; i <= sizeOfArray; ++i) {
                # for each Volume^Page element, detach Volume
                # and call rangeOfPages function on Page to
                # separate page numbers and compare to find
                # consecutive numbers.
                        if (split(howManyVolumes[i],volPage,"^") == 2)
                                listOfPages = volPage[1] "^"
                                        rangeOfPages(volPage[2])
                # collect output in listOfPages
                        if (i == 1)
                                result = listOfPages
                        else
                                result=result ";" listOfPages
                } # end for loop
        }
        else { # not more than 1 volume

        # check for single volume index with volume number
        # if so, detach volume number.
```

```
                # Both call rangeOfPages on the list of page numbers.
                    if (split(PAGE,volPage,"^") == 2 )
                    # if Volume^Page, detach volume and then call rangeOfPages
                            listOfPages = volPage[1] "^" rangeOfPages(volPage[2])
                    else # No volume number involved
                            listOfPages = rangeOfPages(volPage[1])
                    result = listOfPages
            } # end of else

            return result  # Volume^Page list

    } # End of numrange function

    # rangeOfPages -- read list of comma-separated page numbers,
    #                 load them into an array, and compare each one
    #                 to the next, looking for consecutive numbers.
    #        PAGENUMBERS = comma-separated list of page numbers

    function rangeOfPages(PAGENUMBERS, pagesAll, sizeOfArray,pages,
                          listOfPages, d, p, j) {
        # close-up space on troff-generated ranges
            gsub(/ - /, ",-", PAGENUMBERS)

        # split list up into eachpage array.
            sizeOfArray = split(PAGENUMBERS, eachpage, ",")
        # if more than 1 page number
            if (sizeOfArray > 1){
            # for each page number, compare it to previous number + 1
                p = 0  # flag indicates assignment to pagesAll
            # for loop starts at 2
                    for (j = 2; j-1 <= sizeOfArray; ++j) {
                    # start by saving first page in sequence (firstpage)
                    # and loop until we find last page (lastpage)
                            firstpage = eachpage[j-1]
                            d = 0  # flag indicates consecutive numbers found
                    # loop while page numbers are consecutive
                            while ((eachpage[j-1]+1) == eachpage[j] ||
                                        eachpage[j] ~ /^-/) {
                            # remove "-" from troff-generated range
                                    if (eachpage[j] ~ /^-/) {
                                            sub(/^-/, "", eachpage[j])
                                    }
                                    lastpage = eachpage[j]
                            # increment counters
                                    ++d
                                    ++j
                            } # end of while loop
                    # use values of firstpage and lastpage to make range.
                            if (d >= 1) {
                            # there is a range
                                    pages = firstpage "-" lastpage
                            }
                            else # no range; only read firstpage
                                    pages = firstpage
```

```
                        # assign range to pagesAll
                             if (p == 0) {
                                     pagesAll = pages
                                     p = 1
                             }
                             else {
                                     pagesAll = pagesAll "," pages
                             }
                     }# end of for loop

             # assign pagesAll to listOfPages
                     listOfPages = pagesAll

             } # end of sizeOfArray > 1

             else # only one page
                     listOfPages = PAGENUMBERS

         # add space following comma
             gsub(/,/, ", ", listOfPages)
         # return changed list of page numbers
             return listOfPages
     } # End of rangeOfPages function
```

This script consists of minimal **BEGIN** and **END** procedures. The main routine does the work of comparing primary and secondary keys. The first part of this routine assigns the fields to variables. The second field contains the secondary and tertiary keys and we use **split()** to separate them. Then we test that there is a tertiary key and set the flag **isTertiary** to either 1 or 0.

The next part of the main procedure contains the conditional expressions that look for identical keys. As we said in our discussion of the pseudocode for this part of the program, entries with wholly identical keys have already been removed by the **pagenums.idx**.

The conditionals in this procedure determine what keys to output based on whether or not each is unique. If the primary key is unique, it is output, along with the rest of the entry. If the primary key matches the previous key, we compare secondary keys. If the secondary key is unique, then it is output, along with the rest of the entry. If the primary key matches the previous primary key, and the secondary key matches the previous secondary key, then the tertiary key must be unique. Then we only output the tertiary key, leaving the primary and secondary keys blank.

The different forms are shown below:

    primary
    primary:secondary
    :secondary

```
:secondary:tertiary
::tertiary
primary:secondary:tertiary
```

The main procedure is followed by two additional routines. The first of them is executed only when **NF** equals one. It deals with the first of the forms on the list above. That is, there is no page number so we must output a newline to finish the entry.

The second procedure deals with all entries that have page numbers. This is the procedure where we call a function to take apart the list of page numbers and look for consecutive pages. It calls the **numrange( )** function, whose main purpose is to deal with a multivolume index where a list of page numbers might look like:

```
I^35,55; II^200
```

This function calls **split( )** using a semicolon delimiter to separate each volume. Then we call **split( )** using a "^" delimiter to detach the volume number from the list of page numbers. Once we have the list of pages, we call a second function **rangeOfPages( )** to look for consecutive numbers. On a single-book index, such as the sample shown in this chapter, the **numrange( )** function really does nothing but call **rangeOfPages( )**. We discussed the meat of the **rangeOfPages( )** function earlier. The **eachpage** array is created and a **while** loop is used to go through the array comparing an element to the one previous. This function returns the list of pages.

Sample output from this program follows:

```
Xlib:6
:repainting canvas:88
Xlib.h header file:89, 294
Xv_Font type:310
XView:18
:about:3, 7, 10
:as object-oriented system:17
:compiling programs:41
:concept of windows differs from X:25
:data types;  table of:20
:example of programming interface:44
:frames and subframes:26
:generic functions:21
:Generic Object:18, 24
:libraries:42
:notification:10, 35
:objects:23-24;
:: table of:20;
:: list of:43
:packages:18, 43
:programmer's model:17-23
:programming interface:41
```

```
:programs;  initialization:45
:reserved names:43
:reserved prefixes:43
:structure of applications:41
:subwindows:28
:types:43
:window objects:25
```

In particular, notice the entry for "objects" under "XView." This is an example of a secondary key with multiple tertiary keys. It is also an example of an entry with a consecutive page range.

## Formatting the Index

The previous scripts have done nearly all of the processing, leaving the list of entries in good order. The **format.idx** script, probably the easiest of the scripts, reads the list of entries and generates a report in two different formats, one for display on a terminal screen and one to send to **troff** for printing on a laser printer. Perhaps the only difficulty is that we output the entries grouped by each letter of the alphabet.

A command-line argument sets the variable **FMT** that determines which of the two output formats is to be used.

Here's the full listing for **format.idx**:

```
#!/work/bin/nawk -f
# -----------------------------------------------
# format.idx -- prepare formatted index
# Author:  Dale Dougherty
# Version 1.1   7/10/90
#
# input should be PRIMARY:SECONDARY:PAGE:VOLUME
# Args:  FMT = 0 (default) format for screen
#        FMT = 1 output with troff macros
#        MACDIR = pathname of index troff macro file
# -----------------------------------------------
BEGIN {        FS = ":"
               upper = "ABCDEFGHIJKLMNOPQRSTUVWXYZ"
               lower = "abcdefghijklmnopqrstuvwxyz"
}

# Output initial macros if troff FMT
NR == 1 && FMT == 1 {
               if (MACDIR)
                       printf (".so %s/indexmacs\n", MACDIR)
               else
                       printf (".so indexmacs\n")
               printf (".Se \"\" \"Index\"\n")
               printf (".XC\n")
} # end of NR == 1
```

```
# main routine - apply to all lines
# determine which fields to output
{
   # convert octal colon to "literal" colon
   # make sub for each field, not $0, so that fields are not parsed
        gsub(/\\72/, ":", $1)
        gsub(/\\72/, ":", $2)
        gsub(/\\72/, ":", $3)


   # assign field to variables
        PRIMARY = $1
        SECONDARY = $2
        TERTIARY = ""
        PAGE = $3
        if (NF == 2) {
                SECONDARY = ""
                PAGE = $2
        }
   # Look for empty fields to determine what to output
        if (! PRIMARY) {
                if (! SECONDARY) {
                        TERTIARY = $3
                        PAGE = $4
                        if (FMT == 1)
                                printf (".XF 3 \"%s", TERTIARY)
                        else
                                printf ("  %s", TERTIARY)
                }
                else
                        if (FMT == 1)
                                printf (".XF 2 \"%s", SECONDARY)
                        else
                                printf ("  %s", SECONDARY)
        }
        else { # if primary entry exists
            # extract first char of primary entry
                firstChar = substr($1, 1, 1)
            # see if it is in lower string.
                char = index(lower, firstChar)
            # char is an index to lower or upper letter
                if (char == 0)  {
                # if char not found, see if it is upper
                        char = index(upper, firstChar)
                        if (char == 0)
                                char = prevChar
                }
                # if new char, then start group for new letter of alphabet
                if (char != prevChar) {
                        if (FMT == 1)
                                printf(".XF A \"%s\"\n", substr(upper, char, 1))
                        else
                                printf("\n\t\t%s\n", substr(upper, char, 1))
                        prevChar = char
                }
```

```
                        # now output primary and secondary entry
                        if (FMT == 1)
                                if (SECONDARY)
                                        printf (".XF 1 \"%s\" \"%s", PRIMARY, SECONDARY)
                                else
                                        printf (".XF 1 \"%s\" \"", PRIMARY)
                        else
                                if (SECONDARY)
                                        printf ("%s, %s", PRIMARY, SECONDARY)
                                else
                                        printf ("%s", PRIMARY)
                }

        # if page number, call pageChg to replace "^" with ":"
        # for multi-volume page lists.
                if (PAGE) {
                        if (FMT == 1) {
                                # added to omit comma after bold entry
                                if (! SECONDARY && ! TERTIARY)
                                        printf ("%s\"", pageChg(PAGE))
                                else
                                        printf (", %s\"", pageChg(PAGE))
                        }
                        else
                                printf (", %s", pageChg(PAGE))
                }
                else if (FMT == 1)
                        printf("\"")

                printf ("\n")

} # End of main routine

# Supporting function

# pageChg -- convert "^" to ":" in list of volume^page
#       Arg: pagelist -- list of numbers

function pageChg(pagelist) {
        gsub(/\^/, ":", pagelist)
        if (FMT == 1) {
                gsub(/[1-9]+\*/, "\\fB&\\P", pagelist)
                gsub(/\*/, "", pagelist)
        }
        return pagelist
}# End of pageChg function
```

The **BEGIN** procedure defines the field separator and the strings **upper** and **lower**. The next procedure is one that outputs the name of the file that contains the **troff** index macro definitions. The name of the macro directory can be set from the command line as the second argument.

The main procedure begins by converting the "hidden" colon to a literal colon. Note that we apply the **gsub()** function to each field rather than the entire line because doing the latter would cause the line to be reevaluated and the current order of fields would be disturbed.

Next we assign the fields to variables and then test to see whether the field is empty. If the primary key is not defined, then we see if the secondary key is defined. If it is, we output it. If it is not, then we output a tertiary key. If the primary key is defined, then we extract its first character and then see if we find it in the **lower** string.

```
firstChar = substr($1, 1, 1)

char = index(lower, firstChar)
```

The **char** variable holds the position of the letter in the string. If this number is greater than or equal to 1, then we also have an index into the **upper** string. We compare each entry and while **char** and **prevChar** are the same, the current letter of the alphabet is unchanged. Once they differ, first we check for the letter in the **upper** string. If **char** is a new letter, we output a centered string that identifies that letter of the alphabet.

Then we look at outputting the primary and secondary entries. Finally, the list of page numbers is output, after calling the **pageChg()** function to replace the "^" in volume-page references with a colon.

Sample screen output produced by **format.idx** is shown below:

```
                 X
 X Protocol, 6
 X Window System, events, 84
   extensibility, 9
   interclient communications, 9
   overview, 3
   protocol, 6
   role of window manager, 9
   server and client relationship, 5
   software hierarchy, 6
   toolkits, 7
   X Window ID for paint window, 87
   Xlib, 6
 XFontStruct structure, 317
 Xlib, 6
   repainting canvas, 88
 Xlib.h header file, 89, 294
 Xv_Font type, 310
 XView, 18
   about, 3, 7, 10
   as object-oriented system, 17
   compiling programs, 41
```

```
concept of windows differs from X, 25
data types;  table of, 20
example of programming interface, 44
frames and subframes, 26
generic functions, 21
Generic Object, 18, 24
```

Sample **troff** output produced by **format.idx** is shown below:

```
.XF A "X"
.XF 1 "X Protocol" "6"
.XF 1 "X Window System" "events, 84"
.XF 2 "extensibility, 9"
.XF 2 "interclient communications, 9"
.XF 2 "overview, 3"
.XF 2 "protocol, 6"
.XF 2 "role of window manager, 9"
.XF 2 "server and client relationship, 5"
.XF 2 "software hierarchy, 6"
.XF 2 "toolkits, 7"
.XF 2 "X Window ID for paint window, 87"
.XF 2 "Xlib, 6"
.XF 1 "XFontStruct structure" "317"
.XF 1 "Xlib" "6"
.XF 2 "repainting canvas, 88"
.XF 1 "Xlib.h header file" "89, 294"
.XF 1 "Xv_Font type" "310"
.XF 1 "XView" "18"
.XF 2 "about, 3, 7, 10"
.XF 2 "as object-oriented system, 17"
```

This output must be formatted by **troff** to produce a printed version of the index. The index of this book was originally done using the **masterindex** program.

## *The masterindex shell script*

The **masterindex** shell script is the glue that holds all of these scripts together and invokes them with the proper options based on the user's command line. For instance, the user enters:

```
$ masterindex -s -m volume1 volume2
```

to specify that a master index be created from the files *volume1* and *volume2* and that the output be sent to the screen.

The **masterindex** shell script is presented in Appendix C with the documentation.

# Spare Details of the masterindex Program

This section presents a few interesting details of the **masterindex** program that might otherwise escape attention. The purpose of this section is to extract some interesting program fragments and show how they solve a particular problem.

## How to Hide a Special Character

Our first fragment is from the **input.idx** script, whose job it is to standardize the index entries before they are sorted. This program takes as its input a record consisting of two tab-separated fields: the index entry and its page number. A colon is used as part of the syntax for indicating the parts of an index entry.

Because the program uses a colon as a special character, we must provide a way to pass a literal colon through the program. To do this, we allow the indexer to specify two consecutive colons in the input. However, we can't simply convert the sequence to a literal colon because the rest of the program modules called by **masterindex** read three colon-separated fields. The solution is to convert the colon to its octal value using the **gsub( )** function.

```
#< from input.idx
# convert literal colon to octal value
$1 ~ /::/ {
        # substitute octal value for "::"
        gsub(/::/, "\\72", $1)
```

"\\72" represents the octal value of a colon. (You can find this value by scanning a table of hexadecimal and octal equivalents in the file */usr/pub/ascii.*) In the last program module, we use **gsub( )** to convert the octal value back to a colon. Here's the code from **format.idx**.

```
#< from format.idx
# convert octal colon to "literal" colon
# make sub for each field, not $0, so that fields are not parsed
        gsub(/\\72/, ":", $1)
        gsub(/\\72/, ":", $2)
        gsub(/\\72/, ":", $3)
```

The first thing you notice is that we make this substitution for each of the three fields separately, instead of having one substitution command that operates on $0. The reason for this is that the input fields are colon-separated. When awk scans an input line, it breaks the line into fields. If you change the contents of $0 at any point in the script, awk will reevaluate the value of $0 and parse the line into fields again. Thus, if you have three fields prior to making the substitution, and the substitution makes one change, adding a colon to $0, then awk will recognize four fields. By doing the substitution for each field, we avoid having the line parsed again into fields.

## Rotating Two Parts

Above we talked about the colon syntax for separating the primary and secondary keys. With some kinds of entries, it makes sense to classify the item under its secondary key as well. For instance, we might have a group of program statements or user commands, such as "sed command." The indexer might create two entries: one for "sed command" and one for "command: sed." To make coding this kind of entry easier, we implemented a coding convention that uses a tilde (˜) character to mark the two parts of this entry so that the first and second part can be swapped to create the second entry automatically.[*] Thus, coding the following index entry

```
.XX "sed~command"
```

produces two entries:

```
sed command     43
command: sed    43
```

Here's the code that rotates entries.

```
#< from input.idx
# Match entries that need rotating that contain a single tilde
$1 ~ /~/ && $1 !~ /~~/ {
        # split first field into array named subfield
        n = split($1, subfield, "~")
        if (n == 2) {
        # print entry without "~" and then rotated
                printf("%s %s::%s\n", subfield[1], subfield[2], $2)
                printf("%s:%s:%s\n", subfield[2], subfield[1], $2)
        }
        next
}
```

The pattern-matching rule matches any entry containing a tilde but not two consecutive tildes, which indicate a literal tilde. The procedure uses the **split()** function to break the first field into two "subfields." This gives us two substrings, one before and one after the tilde. The original entry is output and then the rotated entry is output, both using the **printf** statement.

---

[*] The idea of rotating index entries was derived from *The AWK Programming Language*. There, however, an entry is automatically rotated where a blank is found; the tilde is used to prevent a rotation by "filling in" the space. Rather than have rotation be the default action, we use a different coding convention, where the tilde indicates where the rotation should occur.

Because the tilde is used as a special character, we use two consecutive tildes to represent a literal tilde in the input. The following code occurs in the program after the code that swaps the two parts of an entry.

```
#< from input.idx
# Match entries that contain two tildes
$1 ~ /~~/ {
        # replace ~~ with ~
        gsub(/~~/, "~", $1)
}
```

Unlike the colon, which retains a special meaning throughout the **masterindex** program, the tilde has no significance after this module so we can simply output a literal tilde.

## *Finding a Replacement*

The next fragment also comes from **input.idx**. The problem was to look for two colons separated by text and change the second colon to a semicolon. If the input line contains

```
class: class initialize: (see also methods)
```

then the result is:

```
class: class initialize; (see also methods)
```

The problem is fairly simple to formulate—we want to change the second colon, not the first one. It is pretty easy to solve in sed because of the ability to select and recall a portion of what is matched in the replacement section (using \( . . . \) to surround the portion to match and \1 to recall the first portion). Lacking the same ability in awk, you have to be more clever. Here's one possible solution:

```
#< from input.idx
#  replace 2nd colon with semicolon
if (sub(/:.*:/, "&;", $1))
        sub(/:;/, ";", $1)
```

The first substitution matches the entire span between two colons. It makes a replacement with what is matched (&) followed by a semicolon. This substitution occurs within a conditional expression that evaluates the return value of the **sub()** function. Remember, this function returns 1 if a substitution is made—it does not return the resulting string. In other words, if we make the first substitution, then we make the second one. The second substitution replaces ":;" with ";". Because we can't make the replacement directly, we do it indirectly by making the context in which the second colon appears distinct.

## A Function for Reporting Errors

The purpose of the **input.idx** program is to allow variations (or less kindly, inconsistencies) in the coding of index entries. By reducing these variations to one basic form, the other programs are made easier to write.

The other side is that if the **input.idx** program cannot accept an entry, it must report it to the user and drop the entry so that it does not affect the other programs. The **input.idx** program has a function used for error reporting called **printerr( )**, as shown below:

```
function printerr (message) {
        # print message, record number and record
        printf("ERROR:%s (%d) %s\n", message, NR, $0) > "/dev/tty"
}
```

This function makes it easier to report errors in a standard manner. It takes as an argument a **message**, which is usually a string that describes the error. It outputs this message along with the record number and the record itself. The output is directed to the user's terminal "/dev/tty." This is a good practice since the standard output of the program might be, as it is in this case, directed to a pipe or to a file. We could also send the error message to standard error, like so:

```
print "ERROR:" message " (" NR ") " $0 | "cat 1>&2"
```

This opens a pipe to **cat**, with **cat**'s standard output redirected to the standard error. If you are using gawk, mawk, or the Bell Labs awk, you could instead say:

```
printf("ERROR:%s (%d) %s\n", message, NR, $0) > "/dev/stderr"
```

In the program, the **printerr( )** function is called as follows:

```
printerr("No page number")
```

When this error occurs, the user sees the following error message:

```
ERROR:No page number (612) geometry management:set_values_almost
```

## Handling See Also Entries

One type of index entry is a "see also." Like a "see" reference, it refers the reader to another entry. However, a "see also" entry may have a page number as well. In other words, this entry contains information of its own but refers the reader elsewhere for additional information. Here are a few sample entries.

```
error procedure  34
error procedure (see also XtAppSetErrorMsgHandler) 35
error procedure (see also XtAppErrorMsg)
```

The first entry in this sample has a page number while the last one does not. When the **input.idx** program finds a "see also" entry, it checks to see if a page number ($2) is supplied. If there is one, it outputs two records, the first of which is the entry without the page number and the second of which is an entry and page number without the "see also" reference.

```
#< input.idx
# if no page number
        if ($2 == "") {
                print $0 ":"
                next
        }
        else {
        # output two entries:
        # print See Also entry w/out page number
                print $1 ":"
        # remove See Also
                sub(/ *~zz\(see also.*$/, "", $1)
                sub(/;/, "", $1)
        # print as normal entry
                if ( $1 ~ /:/ )
                        print $1 ":" $2
                else
                        print $1 "::" $2
                next
        }
```

The next problem to be solved was how to get the entries sorted in the proper order. The **sort** program, using the options we gave it, sorted the secondary keys for "see also" entries together under "s." (The *-d* option causes the parenthesis to be ignored.) To change the order of the sort, we alter the sort key by adding the sequence "~zz" to the front of it.

```
#< input.idx
# add "~zz" for sort at end
        sub(/\([Ss]ee [Aa]lso/, "~zz(see also", $1)
```

The tilde is not interpreted by the sort but it helps us identify the string later when we remove it. Adding "~zz" assures us of sorting to the end of the list of secondary or tertiary keys.

The **pagenums.idx** script removes the sort string from "see also" entries. However, as we described earlier, we look for a series of "see also" entries for the same key and create a list. Therefore, we also remove that which is the same for all entries, and put the reference itself in an array:

```
#< pagenums.idx
# remove secondary key along with "~zz"
        sub(/^.*~zz\([Ss]ee +[Aa]lso */, "", SECONDARY)
        sub(/\) */, "", SECONDARY)
```

```
# assign to next element of seeAlsoList
    seeAlsoList[++eachSeeAlso] = SECONDARY "; "
```

There is a function that outputs the list of "see also" entries, separating each of them by a semicolon. Thus, the output of the "see also" entry by **pagenums.idx** looks like:

```
error procedure:(see also XtAppErrorMsg; XtAppSetErrorHandler.)
```

## *Alternative Ways to Sort*

In this program, we chose not to support **troff** font and point size requests in index entries. If you'd like to support special escape sequences, one way to do so is shown in *The AWK Programming Language*. For each record, take the first field and prepend it to the record as the sort key. Now that there is a duplicate of the first field, remove the escape sequences from the sort key. Once the entries are sorted, you can remove the sort key. This process prevents the escape sequences from disturbing the sort.

Yet another way is to do something similar to what we did for "see also" entries. Because special characters are ignored in the sort, we could use the **input.idx** program to convert a **troff** font change sequence such as "\fB" to "˜˜˜" and "\fI" to "˜˜˜˜," or any convenient escape sequence. This would get the sequence through the **sort** program without disturbing the sort. (This technique was used by Steve Talbott in his original indexing script.)

The only additional problem that needs to be recognized in both cases is that two entries for the same term, one with font information and one without, will be treated as different entries when one is compared to the other.

# 13

# A Miscellany
of Scripts

This chapter contains a miscellany of scripts contributed by Usenet users. Each program is introduced with a brief description by the program's author. Our comments are placed inside brackets [like this]. Then the full program listing is shown. If the author did not supply an example, we generate one and describe it after the listing. Finally, in a section called "Program Notes," we talk briefly about the program, highlighting some interesting points. Here is a summary of the scripts:

**uutot.awk**   Report UUCP statistics.

**phonebill**   Track phone usage.

**combine**   Extract multipart uuencoded binaries.

**mailavg**   Check size of mailboxes.

**adj**   Adjust lines for text files.

**readsource**  Format program source files for **troff**.

**gent**        Get a termcap entry.

**plpr**        **lpr** preprocessor.

**transpose**   Perform a matrix transposition.

**m1**          A very simple macro processor.

# *uutot.awk — Report UUCP Statistics*

*Contributed by Roger A. Cornelius*

Here's something I wrote in nawk in response to all the C versions of the same thing which were posted to *alt.sources* awhile back. Basically, it summarizes statistics of **uucp** connections (connect time, throughput, files transmitted, etc.). It only supports HDB-style log files, but will show statistics on a site-by-site, or on an overall (all sites), basis. [It also works with */usr/spool/uucp/SYSLOG.*]

I use a shell wrapper which calls "awk -f" to run this, but it's not necessary. Usage information is in the header. (Sorry about the lack of comments.)

```
# @(#) uutot.awk - display uucp statistics - requires new awk
# @(#) Usage:awk -f uutot.awk [site ...] /usr/spool/uucp/.Admin/xferstats
# Author: Roger A. Cornelius (rac@sherpa.uucp)

#       dosome[];           # site names to work for - all if not set
#       remote[];           # array of site names
#       bytes[];            # bytes xmitted by site
#       time[];             # time spent by site
#       files[];            # files xmitted by site
BEGIN {
        doall = 1;
        if (ARGC > 2) {
                doall = 0;
                for (i = 1; i < ARGC-1; i++) {
                        dosome[ ARGV[i] ];
                        ARGV[i] = "";
                }
        }

        kbyte = 1024    # 1000 if you're not picky
        bang = "!";
        sending = "->";
        xmitting = "->" "|" "<-";

        hdr1 = "Remote     K-Bytes    K-Bytes    K-Bytes " \
                "Hr:Mn:Sc Hr:Mn:Sc AvCPS AvCPS     #    #\n";
        hdr2 = "SiteName     Recv      Xmit      Total    " \
                "Recv     Xmit Recv  Xmit Recv Xmit\n";
```

```
        hdr3 = "-------- --------- --------- --------- -------- " \
               "-------- ----- ----- ---- ----";
        fmt1 = "%-8.8s %9.3f %9.3f %9.3f %2d:%02d:%02.0f " \
               "%2d:%02d:%02.0f %5.0f %5.0f %4d %4d\n";
        fmt2 = "Totals   %9.3f %9.3f %9.3f %2d:%02d:%02.0f " \
               "%2d:%02d:%02.0f %5.0f %5.0f %4d %4d\n";
}
{

        if ($6 !~ xmitting)                   # should never be
                next;
        direction = ($6 == sending ? 1 : 2)

        site = substr($1,1,index($1,bang)-1);
        if (site in dosome || doall) {
                remote[site];
                bytes[site,direction] += $7;
                time[site,direction] += $9;
                files[site,direction]++;
        }
}
END {
        print hdr1 hdr2 hdr3;
        for (k in remote) {
                rbyte += bytes[k,2];       sbyte += bytes[k,1];
                rtime += time[k,2];        stime += time[k,1];
                rfiles += files[k,2];      sfiles += files[k,1];
                printf(fmt1, k, bytes[k,2]/kbyte, bytes[k,1]/kbyte,
                        (bytes[k,2]+bytes[k,1])/kbyte,
                        time[k,2]/3600, (time[k,2]%3600)/60, time[k,2]%60,
                        time[k,1]/3600, (time[k,1]%3600)/60, time[k,1]%60,
                        bytes[k,2] && time[k,2] ? bytes[k,2]/time[k,2] : 0,
                        bytes[k,1] && time[k,1] ? bytes[k,1]/time[k,1] : 0,
                        files[k,2], files[k,1]);
        }

        print hdr3
        printf(fmt2, rbyte/kbyte, sbyte/kbyte, (rbyte+sbyte)/kbyte,
                rtime/3600, (rtime%3600)/60, rtime%60,
                stime/3600, (stime%3600)/60, stime%60,
                rbyte && rtime ? rbyte/rtime : 0,
                sbyte && stime ? sbyte/stime : 0,
                rfiles, sfiles);
}
```

A test file was generated to test Cornelius' program. Here are a few lines extracted
from */usr/spool/uucp/.Admin/xferstats* (because each line in this file is too long to
print on a page, we have broken the line following the directional arrow for display purposes only):

```
isla!nuucp S (8/3-16:10:17) (C,126,25) [ttyi1j] ->
                1131/4.880 secs, 231 bytes/sec
isla!nuucp S (8/3-16:10:20) (C,126,26) [ttyi1j] ->
                149/0.500 secs, 298 bytes/sec
```

```
isla!sue S (8/3-16:10:49) (C,126,27) [ttyi1j] ->
                         646/25.230 secs, 25 bytes/sec
isla!sue S (8/3-16:10:52) (C,126,28) [ttyi1j] ->
                         145/0.510 secs, 284 bytes/sec
uunet!uisla M (8/3-16:15:50) (C,951,1) [cui1a] ->
                         1191/0.660 secs, 1804 bytes/sec
uunet!uisla M (8/3-16:15:53) (C,951,2) [cui1a] ->
                         148/0.080 secs, 1850 bytes/sec
uunet!uisla M (8/3-16:15:57) (C,951,3) [cui1a] ->
                         1018/0.550 secs, 1850 bytes/sec
uunet!uisla M (8/3-16:16:00) (C,951,4) [cui1a] ->
                         160/0.070 secs, 2285 bytes/sec
uunet!daemon M (8/3-16:16:06) (C,951,5) [cui1a] <-
                         552/2.740 secs, 201 bytes/sec
uunet!daemon M (8/3-16:16:09) (C,951,6) [cui1a] <-
                         102/1.390 secs, 73 bytes/sec
```

Note that there are 12 fields; however, the program really only uses fields 1, 6, 7, and 9. Running the program on the sample input produces the following results:

```
$ nawk -f uutot.awk uutot.test
Remote     K-Bytes   K-Bytes   K-Bytes Hr:Mn:Sc Hr:Mn:Sc AvCPS AvCPS    #    #
SiteName     Recv      Xmit      Total     Recv     Xmit  Recv  Xmit Recv Xmit
--------   --------- --------- --------- -------- -------- ----- ----- ---- ----
uunet        0.639     2.458     3.097  0:04:34  2:09:49     2     0    2    4
isla         0.000     2.022     2.022  0:00:00  0:13:58     0     2    0    4
--------   --------- --------- --------- -------- -------- ----- ----- ---- ----
Totals       0.639     4.480     5.119  0:04:34  2:23:47     2     1    2    8
```

## Program Notes for uutot.awk

This nawk application is an excellent example of a clearly written awk program. It is also a typical example of using awk to change a rather obscure UNIX log into a useful report.

Although Cornelius apologizes for the lack of comments that explain the logic of the program, the usage of the program is clear from the initial comments. Also, he uses variables to define search patterns and the report's layout. This helps to simplify conditional and print statements in the body of the program. It also helps that the variables have names which aid in immediately recognizing their purpose.

This program has a three-part structure, as we emphasized in Chapter 7, *Writing Scripts for awk*. It consists of a **BEGIN** procedure, in which variables are defined; the body, in which each line of data from the log file is processed; and the **END** procedure, in which the output for the report is generated.

# *phonebill — Track Phone Usage*

*Contributed by Nick Holloway*

The problem is to calculate the cost of phone calls made. In the United Kingdom, charges are made for the number of "units" used during the duration of the call (no free local calls). The length of time a "unit" lasts depends on the charge band (linked to distance) and the charge rate (linked to time of day). You get charged a whole unit as soon as the time period begins.

The input to the program is four fields. The first field is the date (not used). The second field is "band/rate" and is used to look up the length a unit will last. The third field is the length of the call. This can either be "ss," "mm:ss," or "hh:mm:ss." The fourth field is the name of the caller. We keep a stopwatch (old cheap digital), a book, and a pen. Come bill time this is fed through my awk script. This only deals with the cost of the calls, not the standing charge.

The aim of the program was to enable the minimum amount of information to be entered by the callers, and the program could be used to collect together the call costs for each user in one report. It is also written so that if British Telecom changes its costs, these can be done easily in the top of the source (this has been done once already). If more charge bands or rates are added, the table can be simply expanded (wonders of associative arrays). There are no real sanity checks done on the input data. The usage is:

> phonebill [ *file* ... ]

Here is a (short) sample of input and output.

**Input:**

```
29/05    b/p       5:35    Nick
29/05    L/c    1:00:00    Dale
01/06    L/c      30:50    Nick
```

**Output:**

```
Summary for Dale:
        29/05    L/c  1:00:00   11 units
Total: 11 units @ 5.06 pence per unit = $0.56
Summary for Nick:
        29/05    b/p     5:35   19 units
        01/06    L/c    30:50    6 units
Total: 25 units @ 5.06 pence per unit = $1.26
```

The listing for **phonebill** follows:

```
#!/bin/awk -f
#-------------------------------------------------------------------
#   Awk script to take in phone usage - and calculate cost for each
#   person
```

```
#--------------------------------------------------------------------
#    Author: N.Holloway (alfie@cs.warwick.ac.uk)
#    Date  : 27 January 1989
#    Place : University of Warwick
#--------------------------------------------------------------------
#    Entries are made in the form
#        Date   Type/Rate   Length   Name
#
#    Format:
#        Date           : "dd/mm"              - one word
#        Type/Rate      : "bb/rr"  (e.g. L/c)
#        Length         : "hh:mm:ss", "mm:ss", "ss"
#        Name           : "Fred"       - one word (unique)
#--------------------------------------------------------------------
#    Charge information kept in array 'c', indexed by "type/rate",
#    and the cost of a unit is kept in the variable 'pence_per_unit'
#    The info is stored in two arrays, both indexed by the name. The
#    first 'summary' has the lines that hold input data, and number
#    of units, and 'units' has the cumulative total number of units
#    used by name.
#--------------------------------------------------------------------

BEGIN \
    {
        # --- Cost per unit
        pence_per_unit  = 4.40          # cost is 4.4 pence per unit
        pence_per_unit *= 1.15          # VAT is 15%

        # --- Table of seconds per unit for different bands/rates
        #    [ not applicable have 0 entered as value ]
        c ["L/c"] = 330 ;  c ["L/s"] = 85.0;  c ["L/p"] = 60.0;
        c ["a/c"] =  96 ;  c ["a/s"] = 34.3;  c ["a/p"] = 25.7;
        c ["b1/c"]= 60.0;  c ["b1/s"]= 30.0;  c ["b1/p"]= 22.5;
        c ["b/c"] = 45.0;  c ["b/s"] = 24.0;  c ["b/p"] = 18.0;
        c ["m/c"] = 12.0;  c ["m/s"] = 8.00;  c ["m/p"] = 8.00;
        c ["A/c"] = 9.00;  c ["A/s"] = 7.20;  c ["A/p"] = 0   ;
        c ["A2/c"]= 7.60;  c ["A2/s"]= 6.20;  c ["A2/p"]= 0   ;
        c ["B/c"] = 6.65;  c ["B/s"] = 5.45;  c ["B/p"] = 0   ;
        c ["C/c"] = 5.15;  c ["C/s"] = 4.35;  c ["C/p"] = 3.95;
        c ["D/c"] = 3.55;  c ["D/s"] = 2.90;  c ["D/p"] = 0   ;
        c ["E/c"] = 3.80;  c ["E/s"] = 3.05;  c ["E/p"] = 0   ;
        c ["F/c"] = 2.65;  c ["F/s"] = 2.25;  c ["F/p"] = 0   ;
        c ["G/c"] = 2.15;  c ["G/s"] = 2.15;  c ["G/p"] = 2.15;
    }


    {
        spu = c [ $2 ]                          # look up charge band
        if ( spu == "" || spu == 0 ) {
            summary [ $4 ] = summary [ $4 ] "\n\t" \
                            sprintf ( "%4s  %4s  %7s  ? units",\
                                $1, $2, $3 ) \
                            " - Bad/Unknown Chargeband"
        } else {
            n = split ( $3, t, ":" )  # calculate length in seconds
```

```
                  seconds = 0
                  for ( i = 1; i <= n; i++ )
                      seconds = seconds*60 + t[i]
                  u = seconds / spu    # calculate number of seconds
                  if ( int( u ) == u )   # round up to next whole unit
                      u = int( u )
                  else
                      u = int( u ) + 1
                  units [ $4 ] += u   # store info to output at end
                  summary [ $4 ] = summary [ $4 ] "\n\t" \
                              sprintf ( "%4s  %4s  %7s %3d units",\
                                  $1, $2, $3, u )
              }
          }


  END \
      {
          for ( i in units ) {              # for each person
              printf ( "Summary for %s:", i ) # newline at start
                                            # of summary
              print summary [ i ]                    # print summary details
              # calc cost
              total = int ( units[i] * pence_per_unit + 0.5 )
              printf ( \
                  "Total: %d units @ %.2f pence per unit = $%d.%02d\n\n", \
                          units [i], pence_per_unit, total/100, \
                                  total%100 )
          }
      }
```

## *Program Notes for phonebill*

This program is another example of generating a report that consolidates information from a simple record structure.

This program also follows the three-part structure. The **BEGIN** procedure defines variables that are used throughout the program. This makes it easy to change the program, as phone companies are known to "upwardly revise" their rates. One of the variables is a large array named **c** in which each element is the number of seconds per unit, using the band over the rate as the index to the array.

The main procedure reads each line of the user log. It uses the second field, which identifies the band/rate, to get a value from the array **c**. It checks that a positive value was returned and then processes that value by the time specified in $3. The number of units for that call is then stored in an array named **units**, indexed by the name of the caller ($4). This value accumulates for each caller.

Finally, the **END** routine prints out the values in the **units** array, producing the report of units used per caller and the total cost of the calls.

# combine—Extract Multipart uuencoded Binaries

*Contributed by Rahul Dhesi*

Of all the scripts I have ever written, the one I am most proud of is the "combine" script.

While I was moderating *comp.binaries.ibm.pc*, I wanted to provide users a simple way of extracting multipart uuencoded binaries. I added **BEGIN** and **END** headers to each part to enclose the uuencoded part and provided users with the following script:

```
cat $* | sed '/^END/,/^BEGIN/d' | uudecode
```

This script will accept a list of filenames (in order) provided as command-line arguments. It will also accept concatenated articles as standard input.

This script invokes **cat** in a very useful way that is well known to expert shell script users but not enough used by most others. This allows the user the choice of either providing command-line arguments or standard input.

The script invokes sed to strip out superfluous headers and trailers, except for headers in the first input file and trailers in the last input file. The final result is that the uuencoded part of the multiple input files is extracted and uudecoded. Each input file (see postings in *comp.binaries.ibm.pc*) has the following form:

```
headers
BEGIN
uuencoded text
END
```

I have lots of other shell stuff, but the above is simplest and has proved useful to several thousand *comp.binaries.ibm.pc* readers.

## Program Notes for combine

This one is pretty obvious but accomplishes a lot. For those who might not understand the use of this command, here is the explanation. A Usenet newsgroup such as *comp.binaries.ibm.pc* distributes public-domain programs and such. Binaries, the object code created by the compiler, cannot be distributed as news articles unless they are "encoded." A program named **uuencode** converts the binary to an ASCII representation that can be easily distributed. Furthermore, there are limits on the size of news articles and large binaries are broken up into a series of articles (1 of 3, 2 of 3, 3 of 3, for example). Dhesi would break up the encoded binary into manageable chunks, and then add the **BEGIN** and **END** lines to delimit the text that contained encoded binary.

A reader of these articles might save each article in a file. Dhesi's script automates the process of combining these articles and removing extraneous information such as the article header as well as the extra **BEGIN** and **END** headers. His script removes lines from the first **END** up to and including the next **BEGIN** pattern. It combines all the separate encoded parcels and directs them to **uudecode**, which converts the ASCII representation to binary.

One has to appreciate the amount of manual editing work avoided by a simple one-line script.

# *mailavg — Check Size of Mailboxes*

*Contributed by Wes Morgan*

While tuning our mail system, we needed to take a "snapshot" of the users' mailboxes at regular intervals over a 30-day period. This script simply calculates the average size and prints the arithmetic distribution of user mailboxes.

```
#! /bin/sh
#
# mailavg - average size of files in /usr/mail
#
# Written by Wes Morgan, morgan@engr.uky.edu, 2 Feb 90
ls -Fs /usr/mail | awk '
    { if(NR != 1) {
        total += $1;
        count += 1;
        size = $1 + 0;
        if(size == 0) zercount+=1;
        if(size > 0 && size <= 10) tencount+=1;
        if(size > 10 && size <= 19) teencount+=1;
        if(size > 20 && size <= 50) uptofiftycount+=1;
        if(size > 50) overfiftycount+=1;
        }
    }
    END { printf("/usr/mail has %d mailboxes using %d blocks,",
            count,total)
        printf("average is %6.2f blocks\n", total/count)
        printf("\nDistribution:\n")
        printf("Size       Count\n")
        printf(" 0              %d\n",zercount)
        printf("1-10           %d\n",tencount)
        printf("11-20          %d\n",teencount)
        printf("21-50          %d\n",uptofiftycount)
        printf("Over 50        %d\n",overfiftycount)
        }'
exit 0
```

Here's a sample output from **mailavg**:

```
$ mailavg
/usr/mail has 47 mailboxes using 5116 blocks,
average is 108.85 blocks
Distribution:
Size      Count
  0         1
1-10       13
11-20      1
21-50      5
Over 50    27
```

## Program Notes for mailavg

This administrative program is similar to the **filesum** program in Chapter 7. It processes the output of the **ls** command.

The conditional expression "NR != 1" could have been put outside the main procedure as a pattern. While the logic is the same, using the expression as a pattern clarifies how the procedure is accessed, making the program easier to understand.

In that procedure, Morgan uses a series of conditionals that allow him to collect distribution statistics on the size of each user's mailbox.

# adj—Adjust Lines for Text Files

*Contributed by Norman Joseph*

[Because the author used his program to format his mail message before sending it, we're preserving the linebreaks and indented paragraphs in presenting it here as the program's example. This program is similar to the BSD **fmt** program.]

> Well, I decided to take you up on your offer. I'm sure there are
> more sophisticated gurus out there than me, but I do have a nawk script
> that I'm kind of fond of, so I'm sending it in.
>
> Ok, here's the low down. When I'm writing e-mail, I often make a
> lot of changes to the text (especially if I'm going to post on the net).
> So what starts out as a nicely adjusted letter or posting usually ends up
> looking pretty sloppy by the time I'm done adding and deleting lines. So
> I end up spending a lot of time joining and breaking lines all through my
> document so as to get a nice right-hand margin. So I say to myself,
> "This is just the kind of tedious work a program would be good for."
>
> Now, I know I can use **nroff** to filter my document through and
> adjust the lines, but it has lousy defaults (IMHO) for simple text like

this.  So, with a view to sharpening my nawk skills I wrote **adj.nawk**
and the accompanying shell script wrapper **adj**.

Here's the syntax for the nawk filter **adj**:

**adj** [*-l* | *c* | *r* | *b*] [*-w n*] [*-i n*] [*files  . . .* ]

The options are:

*-l*      Lines are left adjusted, right ragged (default).

*-c*      Lines are centered.

*-r*      Lines are right adjusted, left ragged.

*-b*      Lines are left and right adjusted.

*-w n*  Sets line width to *n* characters (default is 70).

*-i n*   Sets initial indent to *n* characters (default is 0).

So, whenever I'm finished with this letter (I'm using **vi**) I will
give the command :%!**adj -w73** (I like my lines a little longer) and
all the breaking and joining will be done by a program (the way the Good
Lord intended :-).  Indents and blank lines are preserved, and two spaces
are given after any end-of-sentence punctuation.

The program is naive about tabs, and when computing line lengths,
it considers a tab character to be one space wide.

The program is notable for its use of command-line parameter
assignment, and some of the newer features of awk (nawk), such as the
match and split built-in functions, and for its use of support functions.

```
#! /bin/sh
#
# adj - adjust text lines
#
# usage: adj [-l|c|r|b] [-w n] [-i n] [files ...]
#
# options:
#    -l    - lines are left adjusted, right ragged (default)
#    -c    - lines are centered
#    -r    - lines are right adjusted, left ragged
#    -b    - lines are left and right adjusted
#    -w n  - sets line width to <n> characters (default: 70)
#    -i n  - sets initial indent to <n> characters (default: 0)
#
# note:
#    output line width is -w setting plus -i setting
#
# author:
#    Norman Joseph (amanue!oglvee!norm)
```

```
adj=l
wid=70
ind=0

set -- `getopt lcrbw:i: $*`
if test $? != 0
then
    printf 'usage: %s [-l|c|r|b] [-w n] [-i n] [files ...]' $0
    exit 1
fi

for arg in $*
do
    case $arg in
    -l) adj=l;  shift;;
    -c) adj=c;  shift;;
    -r) adj=r;  shift;;
    -b) adj=b;  shift;;
    -w) wid=$2;  shift 2;;
    -i) ind=$2;  shift 2;;
    --) shift;  break;;
    esac
done

exec nawk -f adj.nawk type=$adj linelen=$wid indent=$ind $*
```

Here's the **adj.nawk** script that's called by the shell script **adj**.

```
# adj.nawk -- adjust lines of text per options
#
# NOTE:  this nawk program is called from the shell script "adj"
#     see that script for usage & calling conventions
#
# author:
#     Norman Joseph (amanue!oglvee!norm)

BEGIN  {
    FS = "\n"
    blankline  = "^[ \t]*$"
    startblank = "^[ \t]+[^ \t]+"
    startwords = "^[^ \t]+"
}

$0 ~ blankline {
    if ( type == "b" )
        putline( outline "\n" )
    else
        putline( adjust( outline, type ) "\n" )
    putline( "\n" )
    outline = ""
}

$0 ~ startblank {
    if ( outline != "" ) {
        if ( type == "b" )
```

```
                putline( outline "\n" )
        else
            putline( adjust( outline, type ) "\n" )
    }


    firstword = ""
    i = 1
    while ( substr( $0, i, 1 ) ~ "[ \t]" ) {
        firstword = firstword substr( $0, i, 1 )
        i++
    }
    inline = substr( $0, i )
    outline = firstword

    nf = split( inline, word, "[ \t]+" )

    for ( i = 1;  i <= nf;  i++ ) {
        if ( i == 1 ) {
            testlen = length( outline word[i] )
        } else {
            testlen = length( outline " " word[i] )
            if ( match( ".!?:;", "\\" substr( outline,
                    length( outline ), 1 )) )
                testlen++
        }

        if ( testlen > linelen ) {
            putline( adjust( outline, type ) "\n" )
            outline = ""
        }

        if ( outline == "" )
            outline = word[i]
        else if ( i == 1 )
            outline = outline word[i]
        else {
            if ( match( ".!?:;", "\\" substr( outline,
                    length( outline ), 1 )) )
                outline = outline "  " word[i]      # 2 spaces
            else
                outline = outline " " word[i]       # 1 space
        }
    }
}


$0 ~ startwords  {
    nf = split( $0, word, "[ \t]+" )

    for ( i = 1;  i <= nf;  i++ ) {
        if ( outline == "" )
            testlen = length( word[i] )
        else {
            testlen = length( outline " " word[i] )
            if ( match( ".!?:;", "\\" substr( outline,
```

```
                             length( outline ), 1 )) )
                     testlen++
             }

             if ( testlen > linelen ) {
                 putline( adjust( outline, type ) "\n" )
                 outline = ""
             }

             if ( outline == "" )
                 outline = word[i]
             else {
                 if ( match( ".!?:;", "\\" substr( outline,
                         length( outline ), 1 )) )
                     outline = outline "  " word[i]      # 2 spaces
                 else
                     outline = outline " " word[i]       # 1 space
             }
         }
     }

END  {
     if ( type == "b" )
         putline( outline "\n" )
     else
         putline( adjust( outline, type ) "\n" )
}



#
# -- support functions --
#

function putline( line,    fmt )
{
     if ( indent ) {
         fmt = "%" indent "s%s"
         printf( fmt, " ", line )
     } else
         printf( "%s", line )
}



function adjust( line, type,    fill, fmt )
{
     if ( type != "l" )
         fill = linelen - length( line )

     if ( fill > 0 ) {
         if      ( type == "c" ) {
             fmt = "%" (fill+1)/2 "s%s"
             line = sprintf( fmt, " ", line )
         } else if ( type == "r" ) {
             fmt = "%" fill "s%s"
```

```
                        line = sprintf( fmt, " ", line )
            } else if ( type == "b" ) {
                line = fillout( line, fill )
            }
        }
    }

    return line
}


function fillout( line, need,     i, newline, nextchar, blankseen )
{
    while ( need ) {
        newline = ""
        blankseen = 0

        if ( dir == 0 ) {
            for ( i = 1;  i <= length( line );  i++ ) {
                nextchar = substr( line, i, 1 )
                if ( need ) {
                    if ( nextchar == " " ) {
                        if ( ! blankseen ) {
                            newline = newline " "
                            need--
                            blankseen = 1
                        }
                    } else {
                        blankseen = 0
                    }
                }
                newline = newline nextchar
            }

        } else if ( dir == 1 ) {
            for ( i = length( line );  i >= 1;  i-- ) {
                nextchar = substr( line, i, 1 )
                if ( need ) {
                    if ( nextchar == " " ) {
                        if ( ! blankseen ) {
                            newline = " " newline
                            need--
                            blankseen = 1
                        }
                    } else {
                        blankseen = 0
                    }
                }
                newline = nextchar newline
            }
        }

        line = newline
```

```
        dir = 1 - dir
    }

    return line
}
```

## *Program Notes for adj*

This small text formatter is a nifty program for those of us who use text editors. It allows you to set the maximum line width and justify paragraphs and thus can be used to format mail messages or simple letters.

The **adj** shell script does all the option setting, although it could have been done by reading **ARGV** in the **BEGIN** action. Using the shell to establish command-line parameters is probably easier for those who are already familiar with the shell.

The lack of comments in the **adj.awk** script makes this script more difficult to read than some of the others. The **BEGIN** procedure assigns three regular expressions to variables: **blankline**, **startblank**, **startwords**. This is a good technique (one that you'll see used in **lex** specifications) because regular expressions can be difficult to read and the name of the variable makes it clear what it matches. Remember that modern awks lets you supply a regular expression as a string, in a variable.

There are three main procedures, which can be named by the variable they match. The first is **blankline**, a procedure which handles collected text once a blank line is encountered. The second is **startblank**, which handles lines that begin with white-space (spaces or tabs). The third is **startwords**, which handles a line of text. The basic procedure is to read a line of text and determine how many of the words in that line will fit, given the line width, outputting those that will fit and saving those that will not in the variable **outline**. When the next input line is read, the contents of **outline** must be output before that line is output.

The **adjust( )** function does the work of justifying the text based on a command-line option specifying the format type. All types except "l" (left-adjusted, right-ragged) need to be filled. Therefore, the first thing this function does is figure out how much "fill" is needed by subtracting the length of the current line from the specified line length. It makes excellent use of the **sprintf( )** function to actually do the positioning of the text. For instance, to center text, the value of **fill** (plus 1) is divided by 2 to determine the amount of padding needed on each side of the line. This amount is passed through the **fmt** variable as the argument to **sprintf( )**:

```
fmt = "%" (fill+1)/2 "s%s"
line = sprintf( fmt, " ", line )
```

Thus, the space will be used to pad a field that is the length of half the amount of fill needed.

If text is right-justified, the value of **fill** itself is used to pad the field. Finally, if the format type is "b" (block), then the function **fillout** is called to determine where to add spaces that will fill out the line.

In looking over the design of the program, you can see, once again, how the use of functions helps to clarify what a program is doing. It helps to think of the main procedure as controlling the flow of input through the program while procedures handle the operations performed on the input. Separating the "operations" from the flow control makes the program readable and more easily maintained.

In passing, we're not sure why **FS**, the field separator, is set to newline in the **BEGIN** procedure. This means that the field and record separators are the same (i.e., $0 and $1 are the same). The **split()** function is called to break the line into fields using tabs or spaces as the delimiter.

```
nf = split( $0, word, "[ \t]+" )
```

It would seem that the field separator could have been set to the same regular expression, as follows:

```
FS = "[ \t]+"
```

It would be more efficient to use the default field parsing.

Finally, using the **match()** function to find punctuation is inefficient; it would have been better to use **index()**.

# *readsource — Format Program Source Files for troff*

*Contributed by Martin Weitzel*

I am often preparing technical documents, especially for courses and training. In these documents, I often need to print source files of different kinds (C programs, **awk** programs, shell scripts, makefiles). The problem is that the sources often change with time and I want the most recent version when I print. I also want to avoid typos in print.

As I'm using **troff** for text processing, it should be easy to include the original sources into the text. But there are some characters (especially " " and "." and "," at the beginning of a line) that I must escape to prevent interpretation by **troff**.

I often want excerpts from sources rather than a complete file. I also need a mechanism for setting page breaks. Well, perhaps I'm being a perfectionist, but I don't want to see a C function printed nearly complete on one page, but only the two last lines appear on the next. As I frequently change the documents, I cannot hunt for "nice" page breaks—this must be done automatically.

To solve these set of problems, I wrote a filter that preprocesses any source for inclusion as text in **troff**. This is the **awk** program I send with this letter. [He didn't offer a name for it so it is here named **readsource**.]

The whole process can be further automated through *makefiles*. I include a preprocessed version of the sources into my **troff** documents, and I make the formatting dependent on these preprocessed files. These files again are dependent on their originals, so if I "make" the document to print it, the preprocessed sources will be checked to see if they are still current; otherwise they will be generated new from their originals.

My program contains a complete description in the form of comments. But as the description is more for me than for others, I'll give you some more hints. Basically, the program simply guards some characters, e.g., "\" is turned into "\e" and "\&" is written before every line. Tabs may be expanded to spaces (there's a switch for it), and you may even generate line numbers in front of every line (switch selectable). The format of these line numbers can be set through an environmental variable.

If you want only *parts* of a file to be processed, you can select these parts with two regular expressions (with another switch). You must specify the first line to be included and the first line not to be. I've found that this is often practical: If you want to show only a certain function of a C program, you can give the first line of the function definition and the first line of the next function definition. If the source is changed such that new functions are inserted between the two or the order is changed, the pattern matching will not work correctly. But this will accommodate the more frequently made, smaller changes in a program.

The final feature, getting the page breaks right, is a bit tricky. Here a technique has evolved that I call "here-you-may-break." Those points are marked by a special kind of line (I use "/*!" in C programs and "#!" in awk, shell, makefiles, etc.). How the points are marked doesn't matter too much, you may have your own conventions, but it must be possible to give a regular expression that matches exactly this kind of line and no others (e.g., if your sources are written so that a page break is acceptable wherever you have an empty line, you can specify this very easily, as all you need is the regular expression for empty lines).

Before all the marked lines, a special sequence will be inserted which again is given by an environmental variable. With **troff**, I use the technique of opening a "display" (.DS) before I include such preprocessed text, and inserting a close (.DE) and new open (.DS) display wherever I would accept a page break. After this, **troff** does the work of gathering as many lines as fit onto the current page. I suppose that suitable techniques for other text processors exist.

```
#! /bin/sh
# Copyright 1990 by EDV-Beratung Martin Weitzel, D-6100 Darmstadt
# ==================================================================
# PROJECT:        Printing Tools
# SH-SCRIPT:      Source to Troff Pre-Formatter
# ==================================================================

#!
# ------------------------------------------------------------------
# This programm is a tool to preformat source files, so that they
# can be included (.so) within nroff/troff-input. Problems when
# including arbitrary files within nroff/troff-input occur on lines,
# starting with dot (.) or an apostrophe ('), or with the respective
# chars, if these are changed, furthermore from embedded backslashes.
# While changing the source so that none of the above will cause
# any problems, some other useful things can be done, including
# line numbering and selecting interesting parts.
# ------------------------------------------------------------------
#!
  USAGE="$0 [-x d] [-n] [-b pat] [-e pat] [-p pat] [file ...]"
#
# SYNOPSIS:
# The following options are supported:
#        -x d      expand tabs to "d" spaces
#        -n        number source lines (see also: NFMT)
#        -b pat    start output on a line containing "pat",
#                  including this line (Default: from beginning)
#        -e pat    end output on a line containing "pat"
#                  excluding this line (Default: upto end)
#        -p pat    before lines containing "pat", page breaks
#                  may occur (Default: no page breaks)
# "pat" may be an "extended regular expression" as supported by awk.
# The following variables from the environment are used:
#        NFMT      specify format for line numbers (Default: see below)
#        PBRK      string, to mark page breaks. (Default: see below)
#!
# PREREQUISITES:
# Common UNIX-Environment, including awk.
#
# CAVEATS:
# "pat"s are not checked before they are used (processing may have
# started, before problems are detected).
# "NFMT" must contain exactly one %d-format specifier, if -n
# option is used.
# In "NFMT" and "PBRK", embedded double quotes must be guarded with
# a leading backslash.
# In "pat"s, "NFMT" and "PBRK" embedded TABs and NLs must be written
# as \t and \n. Backslashes that should "go thru" to the output as
# such, should be doubled. (The latter is only *required* in a few
# special cases, but it does no harm the other cases).
#
#!
# BUGS:
# Slow - but may serve as prototype for a faster implementation.
```

```
# (Hint: Guarding backslashes the way it is done by now is very
# expensive and could also be done using sed ·'s/\\/\\e/g', but tab
# expansion would be much harder then, because I can't imagine how
# to do it with sed. If you have no need for tab expansion, you may
# change the program. Another option would be to use gsub(), which
# would limit the program to environments with nawk.)
#
# Others bugs may be, please mail me.
#!
# AUTHOR:        Martin Weitzel, D-6100 DA (martin@mwtech.UUCP)
#
# RELEASED:      25. Nov 1989, Version 1.00
# ------------------------------------------------------------------

#! CSOPT
# ------------------------------------------------------------------
#        check/set options
# ------------------------------------------------------------------

xtabs=0 nfmt= bpat= epat= ppat=
for p
do
case $sk in
1) shift; sk=0; continue
esac
case $p in
-x)     shift;
        case $1 in
        [1-9]|1[0-9]) xtabs=$1; sk=1;;
        *) { >&2 echo "$0: bad value for option -x: $1"; exit 1; }
        esac
        ;;
-n)     nfmt="${NFMT:-<%03d>\•}"; shift ;;
-b)     shift; bpat=$1; sk=1 ;;
-e)     shift; epat=$1; sk=1 ;;
-p)     shift; ppat=$1; sk=1 ;;
--)     shift; break ;;
*)      break
esac
done

#! MPROC
# ------------------------------------------------------------------
#        now the "real work"
# ------------------------------------------------------------------

awk '
#. prepare for tab-expansion, page-breaks and selection
BEGIN {
        if (xt = '$xtabs') while (length(sp) < xt) sp = sp " ";
        PBRK = "'"${PBRK-'.DE\n.DS\n'}"'"
        '${bpat:+' skip = 1; '}'
} #! limit selection range
{
```

```
            '${epat:+' if (!skip && $0 ~ /'"$epat"'/) skip = 1; '}'
            '${bpat:+' if (skip && $0 ~ /'"$bpat"'/) skip = 0; '}'
            if (skip) next;
    }
    #! process one line of input as required
    {
            line = ""; ll = 0;
            for (i = 1; i <= length; i++) {
                    c = substr($0, i, 1);
                    if (xt && c == "\t") {
                            # expand tabs
                            nsp = 8 - ll % xt;
                            line = line substr(sp, 1, nsp);
                            ll += nsp;
                    }
                    else {
                            if (c == "\\") c = "\\e";
                            line = line c;
                            ll++;
                    }
            }
    }
    #! finally print this line
    {
            '${ppat:+' if ($0 ~ /'"$ppat"'/) printf("%s", PBRK); '}'
            '${nfmt:+' printf("'"$nfmt"'", NR) '}'
            printf("\\&%s\n", line);
    }
    ' $*
```

For an example of how it works, we ran **readsource** to extract a part of its own program.

```
$ readsource -x 3 -b "process one line" -e "finally print" readsource
\&#! process one line of input as required
\&{
\&    line = ""; ll = 0;
\&    for (i = 1; i <= length; i++) {
\&        c = substr($0, i, 1);
\&        if (xt && c == "\\et") {
\&            # expand tabs
\&            nsp = 8 - ll % xt;
\&            line = line substr(sp, 1, nsp);
\&            ll += nsp;
\&        }
\&        else {
\&            if (c == "\\e\\e") c = "\\e\\ee";
\&            line = line c;
\&            ll++;
\&        }
\&    }
\&}
```

## Program Notes for readsource

This program is, first of all, quite useful, as it helped us prepare the listings in this book. The author does really stretch (old) awk to its limits, using shell variables to pass information into the script. It gets the job done, but it is quite obscure.

The program does run slowly. We followed up on the author's suggestion and changed the way the program replaced tabs and backslashes. The original program uses an expensive character-by-character comparison, obtaining the character using the **substr()** function. (It is the procedure that is extracted in the example above.) Its performance points out how costly it is in awk to read a line one character at a time, something that is very simple in C.

Running **readsource** on itself produced the following times:

```
$ timex readsource -x 3 readsource > /dev/null
real        1.56
user        1.22
sys         0.20
```

The procedure that changes the way tabs and backslashes are handled can be rewritten in nawk to use the **gsub()** function:

```
#! process one line of input as required
{
        if ( xt && $0 ~ "\t" )
                gsub(/\t/, sp)
        if ($0 ~ "\\")
                gsub(/\\/, "\\e")
}
```

The last procedure needs a small change, replacing the variable **line** with "$0". (We don't use the temporary variable **line**.) The nawk version produces:

```
$ timex readsource.2 -x 3 readsource > /dev/null
real        0.44
user        0.10
sys         0.22
```

The difference is pretty remarkable.

One final speedup might be to use **index()** to look for backslashes:

```
#! process one line of input as required
{
        if ( xt && index($0, "\t") > 0 )
                gsub(/\t/, sp)
        if (index($0, "\\") > 0)
                gsub(/\\/, "\\e")
}
```

# *gent — Get a termcap Entry*

*Contributed by Tom Christiansen*

Here's a sed script I use to extract a **termcap** entry. It works for any **termcap**-like file, such as disktab. For example:

```
$ gent vt100
```

extracts the vt100 entry from termcap, while:

```
$ gent eagle /etc/disktab
```

gets the eagle entry from disktab. Now I know it could have been done in C or Perl, but I did it a long time ago. It's also interesting because of the way it passes options into the sed script. I know, I know: it should have been written in *sh* not *csh*, too.

```
#!/bin/csh -f

set argc = $#argv

set noglob
set dollar = '$'
set squeeze = 0
set noback="" nospace=""

rescan:
    if ( $argc > 0 && $argc < 3 ) then
        if ( "$1" =~ -* ) then
            if ( "-squeeze" =~ $1* ) then
                set noback='s/\\//g' nospace='s/^[   ]*//'
                set squeeze = 1
                shift
                @ argc --
                goto rescan
            else
                echo "Bad switch: $1"
                goto usage
            endif
        endif

        set entry = "$1"
        if ( $argc == 1 ) then
            set file = /etc/termcap
        else
            set file = "$2"
        endif
    else
        usage:
            echo "usage: `basename $0` [-squeeze] entry [termcapfile]"
            exit 1
    endif
```

```
sed -n -e \
"/^${entry}[|:]/ {\
    :x\
    /\\${dollar}/ {\
    ${noback}\
    ${nospace}\
    p\
    n\
    bx\
    }\
    ${nospace}\
    p\
    n\
    /^	/ {\
        bx\
    }\
    }\
/^[^	]*|${entry}[|:]/ {\
    :y\
    /\\${dollar}/ {\
    ${noback}\
    ${nospace}\
    p\
    n\
    by\
    }\
    ${nospace}\
    p\
    n\
    /^	/ {\
        by\
    }\
    }" < $file
```

## Program Notes for gent

Once you get used to reading awk scripts, they seem so much easier to understand than all but the simplest sed script. It can be a painstaking task to figure out what a small sed script like the one shown here is doing.

This script does show how to pass shell variables into a sed script. Variables are used to pass optional sed commands into the script, such as the substitution commands that replace backslashes and spaces.

This script could be simplified in several ways. First of all, the two regular expressions don't seem necessary to match the entry. The first matches the name of the entry at the beginning of a line; the second matches it elsewhere on the line. The loops labeled **x** and **y** are identical and even if the two regular expressions were necessary, we could have them branch to the same loop.

# *plpr — lpr Preprocessor*

*Contributed by Tom Van Raalte*

I thought you might want to use the following script around the office. It is a preprocessor for **lpr** that sends output to the "best" printer. [This shell script is written for a BSD or Linux system and you would use this command in place of **lpr**. It reads the output of the **lpq** command to determine if a specific printer is available. If not, it tries a list of printers to see which one is available or which is the least busy. Then it invokes **lpr** to send the job to that printer.]

```sh
#!/bin/sh
#
#set up temp file
TMP=/tmp/printsum.$$
LASERWRITER=${LASERWRITER-ps6}
#Check to see if the default printer is free?
#
#
FREE=`lpq -P$LASERWRITER | awk '
{ if ($0 == "no entries")
   {
        val=1
        print val
        exit 0
   }
   else
   {
        val=0
        print val
        exit 0
   }
}'`
#echo Free is $FREE
#
#If the default is free then $FREE is set, and we print and exit.
#
if [ $FREE -eq 1 ]
then
        SELECT=$LASERWRITER
#echo selected $SELECT
        lpr -P$SELECT $*
        exit 0
fi
#echo Past the exit
#
#Now we go on to see if any of the printers in bank are free.
#
BANK=${BANK-$LASERWRITER}
#echo bank is $BANK
#
#If BANK is the same as LASERWRITER, then we have no choice.
```

```
#otherwise, we print on the one that is free, if any are free.
#
if [ "$BANK" =  "$LASERWRITER" ]
then
        SELECT=$LASERWRITER
        lpr -P$SELECT $*
        exit 0
fi
#echo past the check bank=laserprinter
#
#Now we check for a free printer.
#Note that $LASERWRITER is checked again in case it becomes free
#during the check.
#
#echo now we check the other for a free one
for i in $BANK $LASERWRITER
do
FREE=`lpq -P$i | awk '
{ if ($0 == "no entries")
  {
        val=1
        print val
        exit 0
  }
  else
  {
        val=0
        print val
        exit 0
  }
}'`
if [ $FREE -eq 1 ]
then
#    echo in loop for $i
        SELECT=$i
#    echo select is $SELECT
#    if [ "$FREE" != "$LASERWRITER" ]
#    then
#          echo "Output redirected to printer $i"
#    fi
        lpr -P$SELECT $*
        exit 0
fi
done
#echo done checking for a free one
#
#If we make it here then no printers are free.  So we
#print on the printer with the least bytes queued.
#
#
for i in $BANK $LASERWRITER
do
val=`lpq -P$i | awk ' BEGIN {
        start=0;
```

```
}
/^Time/ {
        start=1;
        next;
}
(start == 1){
        test=substr($0,62,20);
        print test;
} ' | awk '
BEGIN {
        summ=0;
}
{
        summ=summ+$1;
}
END {
        print summ;
}''
echo "$i $val" >> $TMP
done

SELECT=`awk '(NR==1) {
        select=$1;
        best=$2
}
($2 < best) {
        select=$1;
        best=$2}
END {
        print select
}
' $TMP `
#echo $SELECT
#
rm $TMP
#Now print on the selected printer
#if [ $SELECT != $LASERWRITER ]
#then
#    echo "Output redirected to printer $i"
#fi
lpr -P$SELECT $*
trap 'rm -f $TMP; exit 99' 2 3 15
```

## Program Notes for *plpr*

For the most part, we've avoided scripts like these in which most of the logic is
coded in the shell script. However, such a minimalist approach is representative of
a wide variety of uses of awk. Here, awk is called to do only those things that the
shell script can't do (or do as easily). Manipulating the output of a command and
performing numeric comparisons is an example of such a task.

As a side note, the **trap** statement at the end should be at the top of the script, not at the bottom.

# *transpose—Perform a Matrix Transposition*

*Contributed by Geoff Clare*

**transpose** performs a matrix transposition on its input. I wrote this when I saw a script to do this job posted to the Net and thought it was horribly inefficient. I posted mine as an alternative with timing comparisons. If I remember rightly, the original one stored all the elements individually and used a nested loop with a **printf** for each element. It was immediately obvious to me that it would be much faster to construct the rows of the transposed matrix "on the fly."

My script uses ${1+"$@"} to supply file names on the awk command line so that if no files are specified awk will read its standard input. This is much better than plain $* which can't handle filenames containing whitexspace.

```
#! /bin/sh
# Transpose a matrix: assumes all lines have same number
# of fields

exec awk '
NR == 1 {
        n = NF
        for (i = 1; i <= NF; i++)
                row[i] = $i
        next
}
{
        if (NF > n)
                n = NF
        for (i = 1; i <= NF; i++)
                row[i] = row[i] " " $i
}
END {
        for (i = 1; i <= n; i++)
                print row[i]
}' ${1+"$@"}
```

Here's a test file:

```
1 2 3 4
5 6 7 8
9 10 11 12
```

Now we run **transpose** on the file.

```
$ transpose test
1 5 9
2 6 10
3 7 11
4 8 12
```

### Program Notes for transpose

This is a very simple but interesting script. It creates an array named **row** and appends each field into an element of the array. The **END** procedure outputs the array.

# m1 — Simple Macro Processor

*Contributed by Jon Bentley*

The **m1** program is a "little brother" to the **m4** macro processor found on UNIX systems. It was originally published in the article *m1: A Mini Macro Processor*, in *Computer Language*, June 1990, Volume 7, Number 6, pages 47-61. This program was brought to my attention by Ozan Yigit. Jon Bentley kindly sent me his current version of the program, as well as an early draft of his article (I was having trouble getting a copy of the published one). A PostScript version of this paper is included with the example programs, available from O'Reilly's FTP server (see the Preface). I wrote these introductory notes, and the program notes below. [A.R.]

A macro processor copies its input to its output, while performing several jobs. The tasks are:

1.  Define and expand macros. Macros have two parts, a name and a body. All occurrences of a macro's name are replaced with the macro's body.

2.  Include files. Special include directives in a data file are replaced with the contents of the named file. Includes can usually be nested, with one included file including another. Included files are processed for macros.

3.  Conditional text inclusion and exclusion. Different parts of the text can be included in the final output, often based upon whether a macro is or isn't defined.

4.  Depending on the macro processor, comment lines can appear that will be removed from the final output.

If you're a C or C++ programmer, you're already familiar with the built-in preprocessor in those languages. UNIX systems have a general-purpose macro processor called **m4**. This is a powerful program, but somewhat difficult to master, since macro definitions are processed for expansion at definition time, instead of at expansion time. **m1** is considerably simpler than **m4**, making it much easier to learn and to use.

Here is Jon's first cut at a very simple macro processor. All it does is define and expand macros. We can call it **m0a**. In this and the following programs, the "at" symbol (@) distinguishes lines that are directives, and also indicates the presence of macros that should be expanded.

```
/^@define[ \t]/ {
        name = $2
        $1 = $2 = ""; sub(/^[ \t]+/, "")
        symtab[name] = $0
        next
}
{
        for (i in symtab)
                gsub("@" i "@", symtab[i])
        print
}
```

This version looks for lines beginning with "@define." This keyword is $1 and the macro name is taken to be $2. The rest of the line becomes the body of the macro. The next input line is then fetched using **next**. The second rule simply loops through all the defined macros, performing a global substitution of each macro with its body in the input line, and then printing the line. Think about the tradeoffs in this version of simplicity versus program execution time.

The next version (**m0b**) adds file inclusion:

```
function dofile(fname) {
        while (getline <fname > 0) {
                if (/^@define[ \t]/) {              # @define name value
                        name = $2
                        $1 = $2 = ""; sub(/^[ \t]+/, "")
                        symtab[name] = $0
                } else if (/^@include[ \t]/)         # @include filename
                        dofile($2)
                else {                               # Anywhere in line @name@
                        for (i in symtab)
                                gsub("@" i "@", symtab[i])
                        print
                }
        }
        close(fname)
}
BEGIN {
        if (ARGC == 2)
                dofile(ARGV[1])
        else
                dofile("/dev/stdin")
}
```

Note the way **dofile()** is called recursively to handle nested include files.

With all of that introduction out of the way, here is the full-blown **m1** program.

```
#! /bin/awk -f
# NAME
#
# m1
#
# USAGE
#
# awk -f m1.awk [file...]
#
# DESCRIPTION
#
# M1 copies its input file(s) to its output unchanged except as modified by
# certain "macro expressions."  The following lines define macros for
# subsequent processing:
#
#     @comment Any text
#     @@                        same as @comment
#     @define name value
#     @default name value       set if name undefined
#     @include filename
#     @if varname               include subsequent text if varname != 0
#     @unless varname           include subsequent text if varname == 0
#     @fi                       terminate @if or @unless
#     @ignore DELIM             ignore input until line that begins with DELIM
#     @stderr stuff             send diagnostics to standard error
#
# A definition may extend across many lines by ending each line with
# a backslash, thus quoting the following newline.
#
# Any occurrence of @name@ in the input is replaced in the output by
# the corresponding value.
#
# @name at beginning of line is treated the same as @name@.
#
# BUGS
#
# M1 is three steps lower than m4.  You'll probably miss something
# you have learned to expect.
#
# AUTHOR
#
# Jon L. Bentley, jlb@research.bell-labs.com
#

function error(s) {
        print "m1 error: " s | "cat 1>&2"; exit 1
}

function dofile(fname,  savefile, savebuffer, newstring) {
        if (fname in activefiles)
                error("recursively reading file: " fname)
        activefiles[fname] = 1
        savefile = file; file = fname
        savebuffer = buffer; buffer = ""
```

```
                while (readline() != EOF) {
                        if (index($0, "@") == 0) {
                                print $0
                        } else if (/^@define[ \t]/) {
                                dodef()
                        } else if (/^@default[ \t]/) {
                                if (!($2 in symtab))
                                        dodef()
                        } else if (/^@include[ \t]/) {
                                if (NF != 2) error("bad include line")
                                dofile(dosubs($2))
                        } else if (/^@if[ \t]/) {
                                if (NF != 2) error("bad if line")
                                if (!($2 in symtab) || symtab[$2] == 0)
                                        gobble()
                        } else if (/^@unless[ \t]/) {
                                if (NF != 2) error("bad unless line")
                                if (($2 in symtab) && symtab[$2] != 0)
                                        gobble()
                        } else if (/^@fi([ \t]?|$)/) { # Could do error checking here
                        } else if (/^@stderr[ \t]?/) {
                                print substr($0, 9) | "cat 1>&2"
                        } else if (/^@(comment|@)[ \t]?/) {
                        } else if (/^@ignore[ \t]/) { # Dump input until $2
                                delim = $2
                                l = length(delim)
                                while (readline() != EOF)
                                        if (substr($0, 1, 1) == delim)
                                                break
                        } else {
                                newstring = dosubs($0)
                                if ($0 == newstring || index(newstring, "@") == 0)
                                        print newstring
                                else
                                        buffer = newstring "\n" buffer
                        }
                }
        close(fname)
        delete activefiles[fname]
        file = savefile
        buffer = savebuffer
}

# Put next input line into global string "buffer"
# Return "EOF" or "" (null string)

function readline(  i, status) {
        status = ""
        if (buffer != "") {
                i = index(buffer, "\n")
                $0 = substr(buffer, 1, i-1)
                buffer = substr(buffer, i+1)
        } else {
                # Hume: special case for non v10: if (file == "/dev/stdin")
```

```
                        if (getline <file <= 0)
                                status = EOF
                }
                # Hack: allow @Mname at start of line w/o closing @
                if ($0 ~ /^@[A-Z][a-zA-Z0-9]*[ \t]*$/)
                        sub(/[ \t]*$/, "@")
                return status
        }

function gobble(  ifdepth) {
        ifdepth = 1
        while (readline() != EOF) {
                if (/^@(if|unless)[ \t]/)
                        ifdepth++
                if (/^@fi[ \t]?/ && --ifdepth <= 0)
                        break
        }
}

function dosubs(s,  l, r, i, m) {
        if (index(s, "@") == 0)
                return s
        l = ""  # Left of current pos; ready for output
        r = s   # Right of current; unexamined at this time
        while ((i = index(r, "@")) != 0) {
                l = l substr(r, 1, i-1)
                r = substr(r, i+1)         # Currently scanning @
                i = index(r, "@")
                if (i == 0) {
                        l = l "@"
                        break
                }
                m = substr(r, 1, i-1)
                r = substr(r, i+1)
                if (m in symtab) {
                        r = symtab[m] r
                } else {
                        l = l "@" m
                        r = "@" r
                }
        }
        return l r
}

function dodef(fname,  str, x) {
        name = $2
        sub(/^[ \t]*[^ \t]+[ \t]+[^ \t]+[ \t]*/, "")  # OLD BUG: last * was +
        str = $0
        while (str ~ /\\$/) {
                if (readline() == EOF)
                        error("EOF inside definition")
                x = $0
                sub(/^[ \t]+/, "", x)
                str = substr(str, 1, length(str)-1) "\n" x
```

```
            }
            symtab[name] = str
    }

BEGIN {  EOF = "EOF"
         if (ARGC == 1)
                 dofile("/dev/stdin")
         else if (ARGC >= 2) {
                 for (i = 1; i < ARGC; i++)
                         dofile(ARGV[i])
         } else
                 error("usage: m1 [fname...]")
    }
```

## Program Notes for m1

The program is nicely modular, with an **error()** function similar to the one presented in Chapter 11, *A Flock of awks*, and each task cleanly divided into separate functions.

The main program occurs in the **BEGIN** procedure at the bottom. It simply processes either standard input, if there are no arguments, or all of the files named on the command line.

The high-level processing happens in the **dofile()** function, which reads one line at a time, and decides what to do with each line. The **activefiles** array keeps track of open files. The variable **fname** indicates the current file to read data from. When an "@include" directive is seen, **dofile()** simply calls itself recursively on the new file, as in **m0b**. Interestingly, the included filename is first processed for macros. Read this function carefully—there are some nice tricks here.

The **readline()** function manages the "pushback." After expanding a macro, macro processors examine the newly created text for any additional macro names. Only after all expanded text has been processed and sent to the output does the program get a fresh line of input.

The **dosubs()** function actually performs the macro substitution. It processes the line left-to-right, replacing macro names with their bodies. The rescanning of the new line is left to the higher-level logic that is jointly managed by **readline()** and **dofile()**. This version is considerably more efficient than the brute-force approach used in the **m0** programs.

Finally, the **dodef()** function handles the defining of macros. It saves the macro name from $2, and then uses **sub()** to remove the first two fields. The new value of $0 now contains just (the first line of) the macro body. The *Computer Language* article explains that **sub()** is used on purpose, in order to preserve whitespace in the macro body. Simply assigning the empty string to $1 and $2 would rebuild the record, but with all occurrences of whitespace collapsed into single occurrences of the value of **OFS** (a single blank). The function then proceeds to gather the rest of the macro body, indicated by lines that end with a "\". This is an additional improvement over **m0**: macro bodies can be more than one line long.

The rest of the program is concerned with conditional inclusion or exclusion of text; this part is straightforward. What's nice is that these conditionals can be nested inside each other.

**m1** is a very nice start at a macro processor. You might want to think about how you could expand upon it; for instance, by allowing conditionals to have an "@else" clause; processing the command line for macro definitions; "undefining" macros, and the other sorts of things that macro processors usually do.

Some other extensions suggested by Jon Bentley are:

1.  Add "@shell DELIM shell line here," which would read input lines up to "DELIM," and send the expanded output through a pipe to the given shell command.

2.  Add commands "@longdef" and "@longend." These commands would define macros with long bodies, i.e., those that extend over more than one line, simplifying the logic in **dodoef( )**.

3.  Add "@append MacName MoreText," like ".am" in **troff**. This macro in **troff** appends text to an already defined macro. In **m1**, this would allow you to add on to the body of an already defined macro.

4.  Avoid the V10 */dev/stdin* special file. The Bell Labs UNIX systems[*] have a special file actually named */dev/stdin*, that gives you access to standard input. It occurs to me that the use of "-" would do the trick, quite portably. This is also not a real issue if you use gawk or the Bell Labs awk, which interpret the special file name */dev/stdin* internally (see Chapter 11).

As a final note, Jon often makes use of awk in two of his books, *Programming Pearls*, and *More Programming Pearls—Confessions of a Coder* (both published by Addison-Wesley). These books are both excellent reading.

---

[*] And some other UNIX systems, as well.

# A

# *Quick Reference for sed*

## *Command-Line Syntax*

The syntax for invoking sed has two forms:

> **sed** [*-n*][*-e*] '*command*' *file(s)*
> **sed** [*-n*] *-f scriptfile file(s)*

The first form allows you to specify an editing command on the command line, surrounded by single quotes. The second form allows you to specify a *scriptfile*, a file containing sed commands. Both forms may be used together, and they may be used multiple times. The resulting editing script is the concatenation of the commands and script files.

The following options are recognized:

*-n*

Only print lines specified with the **p** command or the **p** flag of the **s** command.

*-e cmd*

Next argument is an editing command. Useful if multiple scripts are specified.

**-f** *file*

Next argument is a file containing editing commands.

If the first line of the script is "#n", sed behaves as if *-n* had been specified.

Frequently used sed scripts are usually invoked from a shell script. Since this is the same for sed or awk, see the section "Shell Wrapper for Invoking awk" in Appendix B, *Quick Reference for awk.*

# Syntax of sed Commands

Sed commands have the general form:

> [*address*[, *address*]][!]*command* [*arguments*]

Sed copies each line of input into a pattern space. Sed instructions consist of addresses and editing commands. If the address of the command matches the line in the pattern space, then the command is applied to that line. If a command has no address, then it is applied to each input line. If a command changes the contents of the space, subsequent command-addresses will be applied to the current line in the pattern space, not the original input line.

## Pattern Addressing

*address* can be either a line number or a *pattern*, enclosed in slashes (/*pattern*/). A pattern is described using a regular expression. Additionally, \n can be used to match any newline in the pattern space (resulting from the **N** command), but not the newline at the end of the pattern space.

If no pattern is specified, the command will be applied to all lines. If only one address is specified, the command will be applied to all lines matching that address. If two comma-separated addresses are specified, the command will be applied to a range of lines between the first and second addresses, inclusively. Some commands accept only one address: **a**, **i**, **r**, **q**, and **=**.

The **!** operator following an address causes sed to apply the command to all lines that do not match the address.

Braces ({}) are used in sed to nest one address inside another or to apply multiple commands at the same address.

> [/*pattern*/[,/*pattern*/]]{
> *command1*
> *command2*
> }

The opening curly brace must end a line, and the closing curly brace must be on a line by itself. Be sure there are no spaces after the braces.

## Regular Expression Metacharacters for sed

The following table lists the pattern-matching metacharacters that were discussed in Chapter 3, *Understanding Regular Expression Syntax*.

Note that an empty regular expression "//" is the same as the previous regular expression.

*Table A–1: Pattern-Matching Metacharacters*

| Special Characters | Usage |
|---|---|
| . | Matches any single character except *newline*. |
| * | Matches any number (including zero) of the single character (including a character specified by a regular expression) that immediately precedes it. |
| [...] | Matches any one of the class of characters enclosed between the brackets. All other metacharacters lose their meaning when specified as members of a class. A circumflex (^) as the first character inside brackets reverses the match to all characters except newline and those listed in the class. A hyphen (-) is used to indicate a range of characters. The close bracket (]) as the first character in the class is a member of the class. |
| \{*n,m*\} | Matches a range of occurrences of the single character (including a character specified by a regular expression) that immediately precedes it. \{*n*\} will match exactly *n* occurrences, \{*n*,\} will match at least *n* occurrences, and \{*n,m*\} will match any number of occurrences between *n* and *m*. (sed and grep only). |
| ^ | Locates regular expression that follows at the beginning of line. The ^ is only special when it occurs at the beginning of the regular expression. |
| $ | Locates preceding regular expression at the end of line. The $ is only special when it occurs at the end of the regular expression. |
| \ | Escapes the special character that follows. |
| \( \) | Saves the pattern enclosed between "\(" and "\)" into a special holding space. Up to nine patterns can be saved in this way on a single line. They can be "replayed" in substitutions by the escape sequences "\1" to "\9". |
| \*n* | Matches the *n*th pattern previously saved by "\(" and "\)", where *n* is a number from 1 to 9 and previously saved patterns are counted from the left on the line. |
| & | Prints the entire matched text when used in a replacement string. |

# *Command Summary for sed*

: *:label*

Label a line in the script for the transfer of control by **b** or **t**. *label* may contain up to seven characters. (The POSIX standard says that an implementation can allow longer labels if it wishes to. GNU sed allows labels to be of any length.)

=   [*address*]=
    Write to standard output the line number of addressed line.

a   [*address*]a\
    *text*

    Append *text* following each line matched by *address*. If *text* goes over more than one line, newlines must be "hidden" by preceding them with a backslash. The *text* will be terminated by the first newline that is not hidden in this way. The *text* is not available in the pattern space and subsequent commands cannot be applied to it. The results of this command are sent to standard output when the list of editing commands is finished, regardless of what happens to the current line in the pattern space.

b   [*address1*[,*address2*]]b[*label*]
    Transfer control unconditionally (branch) to :*label* elsewhere in script. That is, the command following the *label* is the next command applied to the current line. If no *label* is specified, control falls through to the end of the script, so no more commands are applied to the current line.

c   [*address1*[,*address2*]]c\
    *text*

    Replace (change) the lines selected by the address with *text*. When a range of lines is specified, all lines as a group are replaced by a single copy of *text*. The newline following each line of *text* must be escaped by a backslash, except the last line. The contents of the pattern space are, in effect, deleted and no subsequent editing commands can be applied to it (or to *text*).

d   [*address1*[,*address2*]]d
    Delete line(s) from pattern space. Thus, the line is not passed to standard output. A new line of input is read and editing resumes with first command in script.

D   [*address1*[,*address2*]]D
    Delete first part (up to embedded newline) of multiline pattern space created by **N** command and resume editing with first command in script. If this command empties the pattern space, then a new line of input is read, as if the **d** command had been executed.

g   [*address1*[,*address2*]]g
    Copy (get) contents of hold space (see **h** or **H** command) into the pattern space, wiping out previous contents.

G  [*address1*[,*address2*]]G

Append newline followed by contents of hold space (see **h** or **H** command) to contents of the pattern space. If hold space is empty, a newline is still appended to the pattern space.

h  [*address1*[,*address2*]]h

Copy pattern space into hold space, a special temporary buffer. Previous contents of hold space are wiped out.

H  [*address1*[,*address2*]]H

Append newline and contents of pattern space to contents of the hold space. Even if hold space is empty, this command still appends the newline first.

i  [*address1*]i\
   *text*

Insert *text* before each line matched by *address*. (See **a** for details on *text*.)

l  [*address1*[,*address2*]]l

List the contents of the pattern space, showing nonprinting characters as ASCII codes. Long lines are wrapped.

n  [*address1*[,*address2*]]n

Read next line of input into pattern space. Current line is sent to standard output. New line becomes current line and increments line counter. Control passes to command following **n** instead of resuming at the top of the script.

N  [*address1*[,*address2*]]N

Append next input line to contents of pattern space; the new line is separated from the previous contents of the pattern space by a newline. (This command is designed to allow pattern matches across two lines. Using \n to match the embedded newline, you can match patterns across multiple lines.)

p  [*address1*[,*address2*]]p

Print the addressed line(s). Note that this can result in duplicate output unless default output is suppressed by using "#n" or the -*n* command-line option. Typically used before commands that change flow control (**d**, **n**, **b**) and might prevent the current line from being output.

P  [*address1*[,*address2*]]P

Print first part (up to embedded newline) of multiline pattern space created by **N** command. Same as **p** if **N** has not been applied to a line.

q  [*address*]q

Quit when *address* is encountered. The addressed line is first written to output (if default output is not suppressed), along with any text appended to it by previous **a** or **r** commands.

**r**   [*address*]**r** *file*

Read contents of *file* and append after the contents of the pattern space. Exactly one space must be put between **r** and the filename.

**s**   [*address1*[,*address2*]]**s**/*pattern*/*replacement*/[*flags*]

Substitute *replacement* for *pattern* on each addressed line. If pattern addresses are used, the pattern // represents the last pattern address specified. The following flags can be specified:

**n**       Replace *n*th instance of /*pattern*/ on each addressed line.  *n* is any number in the range 1 to 512, and the default is 1.

**g**       Replace all instances of /*pattern*/ on each addressed line, not just the first instance.

**p**       Print the line if a successful substitution is done. If several successful substitutions are done, multiple copies of the line will be printed.

**w** *file*   Write the line to *file* if a replacement was done. A maximum of 10 different *files* can be opened.

**t**   [*address1*[,*address2*]]**t** [*label*]

Test if successful substitutions have been made on addressed lines, and if so, branch to line marked by :*label*. (See **b** and :.) If label is not specified, control falls through to bottom of script.

**w**   [*address1*[,*address2*]]**w** *file*

Append contents of pattern space to *file*. This action occurs when the command is encountered rather than when the pattern space is output. Exactly one space must separate the **w** and the filename. A maximum of 10 different files can be opened in a script. This command will create the file if it does not exist; if the file exists, its contents will be overwritten each time the script is executed. Multiple write commands that direct output to the same file append to the end of the file.

**x**   [*address1*[,*address2*]]**x**

Exchange contents of the pattern space with the contents of the hold space.

**y**   [*address1*[,*address2*]]**y**/*abc*/*xyz*/

Transform each character by position in string *abc* to its equivalent in string *xyz*.

# B

# Quick Reference
# for awk

This appendix describes the features of the awk scripting language.

## Command-Line Syntax

The syntax for invoking awk has two basic forms:

> **awk** [*-v var=value*] [*-Fre*] [*--*] '*pattern { action }*' *var=value datafile(s)*
> **awk** [*-v var=value*] [*-Fre*] *-f scriptfile* [*--*] *var=value datafile(s)*

An awk command line consists of the command, the script and the input filename. Input is read from the file specified on the command line. If there is no input file or "-" is specified, then standard input is read. The *-F* option sets the field separator (**FS**) to *re*.

The *-v* option sets the variable *var* to *value* before the script is executed. This happens even before the **BEGIN** procedure is run. (See the discussion below on command-line parameters.)

Following POSIX argument parsing conventions, the "--" option marks the end of command-line options. Using this option, for instance, you could specify a *datafile* that begins with "-", which would otherwise be confused with a command-line option.

You can specify a script consisting of *pattern* and *action* on the command line, surrounded by single quotes. Alternatively, you can place the script in a separate file and specify the name of the *scriptfile* on the command line with the *-f* option.

Parameters can be passed into awk by specifying them on the command line after the script. This includes setting system variables such as **FS**, **OFS**, and **RS**. The *value* can be a literal, a shell variable ($*var*) or the result of a command ('*cmd*'); it must be quoted if it contains spaces or tabs. Any number of parameters can be specified.

Command-line parameters are not available until the first line of input is read, and thus cannot be accessed in the **BEGIN** procedure. (Older implementations of awk and nawk would process leading command-line assignments before running the **BEGIN** procedure. This was contrary to how things were documented in *The AWK Programming Language*, which says that they are processed when awk would go to open them as filenames, i.e., after the **BEGIN** procedure. The Bell Labs awk was changed to correct this, and the *-v* option was added at the same time, in early 1989. It is now part of POSIX awk.) Parameters are evaluated in the order in which they appear on the command line up until a filename is recognized. Parameters appearing after that filename will be available when the next filename is recognized.

### Shell Wrapper for Invoking awk

Typing a script at the system prompt is only practical for simple, one-line scripts. Any script that you might invoke as a command and reuse can be put inside a shell script. Using a shell script to invoke awk makes the script easy for others to use.

You can put the command line that invokes awk in a file, giving it a name that identifies what the script does. Make that file executable (using the **chmod** command) and put it in a directory where local commands are kept. The name of the shell script can be typed on the command line to execute the awk script. This is preferred for easily used and reused scripts.

On modern UNIX systems, including Linux, you can use the #! syntax to create self-contained awk scripts:

```
#! /usr/bin/awk -f
script
```

Awk parameters and the input filename can be specified on the command line that invokes the shell script. Note that the pathname to use is system-dependent.

## Language Summary for awk

This section summarizes how awk processes input records and describes the various syntactic elements that make up an awk program.

## Records and Fields

Each line of input is split into fields. By default, the field delimiter is one or more spaces and/or tabs. You can change the field separator by using the *-F* command-line option. Doing so also sets the value of **FS**. The following command-line changes the field separator to a colon:

```
awk -F: -f awkscr /etc/passwd
```

You can also assign the delimiter to the system variable **FS**. This is typically done in the **BEGIN** procedure, but can also be passed as a parameter on the command line.

```
awk -f awkscr FS=: /etc/passwd
```

Each input line forms a record containing any number of fields. Each field can be referenced by its position in the record. "$1" refers to the value of the first field; "$2" to the second field, and so on. "$0" refers to the entire record. The following action prints the first field of each input line:

```
{ print $1 }
```

The default record separator is a newline. The following procedure sets **FS** and **RS** so that awk interprets an input record as any number of lines up to a blank line, with each line being a separate field.

```
BEGIN { FS = "\n"; RS = "" }
```

It is important to know that when **RS** is set to the empty string, newline *always* separates fields, in addition to whatever value **FS** may have. This is discussed in more detail in both *The AWK Programming Language* and *Effective AWK Programming*.

## Format of a Script

An awk script is a set of pattern-matching rules and *actions*:

*pattern* { *action* }

An action is one or more statements that will be performed on those input lines that match the pattern. If no pattern is specified, the action is performed for every input line. The following example uses the **print** statement to print each line in the input file:

```
{ print }
```

If only a pattern is specified, then the default action consists of the **print** statement, as shown above.

Function definitions can also appear:

> **function** *name* (*parameter list*) { *statements* }

This syntax defines the function *name*, making available the list of parameters for processing in the body of the function. Variables specified in the parameter-list are treated as local variables within the function. All other variables are global and can be accessed outside the function. When calling a user-defined function, no space is permitted between the name of the function and the opening parenthesis. Spaces are allowed in the function's definition. User-defined functions are described in Chapter 9, *Functions*.

### Line termination

A line in an awk script is terminated by a newline or a semicolon. Using semi-colons to put multiple statements on a line, while permitted, reduces the readability of most programs. Blank lines are permitted between statements.

Program control statements (**do**, **if**, **for**, or **while**) continue on the next line, where a dependent statement is listed. If multiple dependent statements are specified, they must be enclosed within braces.

```
if (NF > 1) {
        name = $1
        total += $2
}
```

You cannot use a semicolon to avoid using braces for multiple statements.

You can type a single statement over multiple lines by escaping the newline with a backslash ( \ ). You can also break lines following any of the following characters:

```
, { && ||
```

Gawk also allows you to continue a line after either a "?" or a ":". Strings cannot be broken across a line (except in gawk, using "\" followed by a newline).

### Comments

A comment begins with a "#" and ends with a newline. It can appear on a line by itself or at the end of a line. Comments are descriptive remarks that explain the operation of the script. Comments cannot be continued across lines by ending them with a backslash.

# Patterns

A pattern can be any of the following:

*/regular expression/*
*relational expression*
**BEGIN**
**END**
*pattern, pattern*

1. Regular expressions use the extended set of metacharacters and must be enclosed in slashes. For a full discussion of regular expressions, see Chapter 3, *Understanding Regular Expression Syntax.*

2. Relational expressions use the relational operators listed under "Expressions" later in this chapter.

3. The **BEGIN** pattern is applied before the first line of input is read and the **END** pattern is applied after the last line of input is read.

4. Use ! to negate the match; i.e., to handle lines not matching the pattern.

5. You can address a range of lines, just as in sed:

   *pattern, pattern*

   Patterns, except **BEGIN** and **END**, can be expressed in compound forms using the following operators:

   &&      Logical And
   | |      Logical Or

   Sun's version of nawk (SunOS 4.1.x) does not support treating regular expressions as parts of a larger Boolean expression. E.g., "/cute/ && /sweet/" or "/fast/ | | /quick/" do not work.

   In addition the C conditional operator ?: (*pattern* ? *pattern* : *pattern*) may be used in a pattern.

6. Patterns can be placed in parentheses to ensure proper evaluation.

7. **BEGIN** and **END** patterns must be associated with actions. If multiple **BEGIN** and **END** rules are written, they are merged into a single rule before being applied.

# Regular Expressions

Table B-1 summarizes the regular expressions as described in Chapter 3. The metacharacters are listed in order of precedence.

*Table B-1: Regular Expression Metacharacters*

| Special Characters | Usage |
|---|---|
| *c* | Matches any literal character *c* that is not a metacharacter. |
| \ | Escapes any metacharacter that follows, including itself. |
| ^ | Anchors following regular expression to the beginning of string. |
| $ | Anchors preceding regular expression to the end of string. |
| . | Matches any single character, including *newline*. |
| [...] | Matches any *one* of the class of characters enclosed between the brackets. A circumflex (^) as the first character inside brackets reverses the match to all characters except those listed in the class. A hyphen (-) is used to indicate a range of characters. The close bracket (]) as the first character in a class is a member of the class. All other metacharacters lose their meaning when specified as members of a class, except \, which can be used to escape ], even if it is not first. |
| *r1* | *r2* | Between two regular expressions, *r1* and *r2*, it allows either of the regular expressions to be matched. |
| (*r1*)(*r2*) | Used for concatenating regular expressions. |
| *r** | Matches any number (including zero) of the regular expression that immediately precedes it. |
| *r*+ | Matches one or more occurrences of the preceding regular expression. |
| *r*? | Matches 0 or 1 occurrences of the preceding regular expression. |
| (*r*) | Used for grouping regular expressions. |

Regular expressions can also make use of the escape sequences for accessing special characters, as defined in the section "Escape sequences" later in this appendix.

Note that ^ and $ work on *strings*; they do not match against newlines embedded in a record or string.

Within a pair of brackets, POSIX allows special notations for matching non-English characters. They are described in Table B-2.

*Table B-2: POSIX Character List Facilities*

| Notation | Facility |
|---|---|
| [.*symbol*.] | Collating symbols. A collating symbol is a multi-character sequence that should be treated as a unit. |
| [=*equiv*=] | Equivalence classes. An equivalence class lists a set of characters that should be considered equivalent, such as "e" and "è". |
| [:*class*:] | Character classes. Character class keywords describe different classes of characters such as alphabetic characters, control characters, and so on. |

*Table B–2: POSIX Character List Facilities (continued)*

| Notation | Facility |
|----------|----------|
| [:alnum:] | Alphanumeric characters |
| [:alpha:] | Alphabetic characters |
| [:blank:] | Space and tab characters |
| [:cntrl:] | Control characters |
| [:digit:] | Numeric characters |
| [:graph:] | Printable and visible (non-space) characters |
| [:lower:] | Lowercase characters |
| [:print:] | Printable characters |
| [:punct:] | Punctuation characters |
| [:space:] | Whitespace characters |
| [:upper:] | Uppercase characters |
| [:xdigit:] | Hexadecimal digits |

Note that these facilities (as of this writing) are still not widely implemented.

# Expressions

An expression can be made up of constants, variables, operators and functions. A constant is a string (any sequence of characters) or a numeric value. A variable is a symbol that references a value. You can think of it as a piece of information that retrieves a particular numeric or string value.

## Constants

There are two types of constants, string and numeric. A string constant must be quoted while a numeric constant is not.

## Escape sequences

The escape sequences described in Table B-3 can be used in strings and regular expressions.

*Table B–3: Escape Sequences*

| Sequence | Description |
|----------|-------------|
| \a | Alert character, usually ASCII BEL character |
| \b | Backspace |
| \f | Formfeed |
| \n | Newline |

*Table B–3:  Escape Sequences  (continued)*

| Sequence | Description |
|----------|-------------|
| \r | Carriage return |
| \t | Horizontal tab |
| \v | Vertical tab |
| \\*ddd* | Character represented as 1 to 3 digit octal value |
| \x*hex* | Character represented as hexadecimal value[a] |
| \\*c* | Any literal character *c* (e.g., \" for ")[b] |

[a] POSIX does not provide "\x", but it is commonly available.
[b] Like ANSI C, POSIX leaves it purposely undefined what you get when you put a backslash before any character not listed in the table.  In most awks, you just get that character.

## Variables

There are three kinds of variables: user-defined, built-in, and fields. By convention, the names of built-in or system variables consist of all capital letters.

The name of a variable cannot start with a digit. Otherwise, it consists of letters, digits, and underscores. Case is significant in variable names.

A variable does not need to be declared or initialized. A variable can contain either a string or numeric value. An uninitialized variable has the empty string ("") as its string value and 0 as its numeric value. Awk attempts to decide whether a value should be processed as a string or a number depending upon the operation.

The assignment of a variable has the form:

> *var* = *expr*

It assigns the value of the expression to *var*. The following expression assigns a value of 1 to the variable **x**.

```
x = 1
```

The name of the variable is used to reference the value:

```
{ print x }
```

prints the value of the variable **x**. In this case, it would be 1.

See the section "System Variables" below for information on built-in variables. A field variable is referenced using **$***n*, where *n* is any number 0 to **NF**, that references the field by position. It can be supplied by a variable, such as **$NF** meaning the last field, or constant, such as **$1** meaning the first field.

## Arrays

An array is a variable that can be used to store a set of values. The following statement assigns a value to an element of an array:

   *array*[*index*] = *value*

In awk, all arrays are *associative* arrays. What makes an associative array unique is that its index can be a string or a number.

An associative array makes an "association" between the indices and the elements of an array. For each element of the array, a pair of values is maintained: the index of the element and the value of the element. The elements are not stored in any particular order as in a conventional array.

You can use the special **for** loop to read all the elements of an associative array.

   **for** (*item* **in** *array*)

The index of the array is available as *item*, while the value of an element of the array can be referenced as *array*[*item*].

You can use the operator **in** to test that an element exists by testing to see if its index exists.

   **if** (*index* **in** *array*)

tests that *array*[*index*] exists, but you cannot use it to test the value of the element referenced by *array*[*index*].

You can also delete individual elements of the array using the **delete** statement.

## System variables

Awk defines a number of special variables that can be referenced or reset inside a program, as shown in Table B-4 (defaults are listed in parentheses).

*Table B-4: Awk System Variables*

| Variable | Description |
| --- | --- |
| **ARGC** | Number of arguments on command line |
| **ARGV** | An array containing the command-line arguments |
| **CONVFMT** | String conversion format for numbers (%.6g). (POSIX) |
| **ENVIRON** | An associative array of environment variables |
| **FILENAME** | Current filename |
| **FNR** | Like **NR**, but relative to the current file |
| **FS** | Field separator (a blank) |
| **NF** | Number of fields in current record |

*Table B-4: Awk System Variables (continued)*

| Variable | Description |
|----------|-------------|
| NR | Number of the current record |
| OFMT | Output format for numbers (%.6g) |
| OFS | Output field separator (a blank) |
| ORS | Output record separator (a newline) |
| RLENGTH | Length of the string matched by **match( )** function |
| RS | Record separator (a newline) |
| RSTART | First position in the string matched by **match( )** function |
| SUBSEP | Separator character for array subscripts (\ 034) |

## Operators

Table B-5 lists the operators in the order of precedence (low to high) that are available in awk.

*Table B-5: Operators*

| Operators | Description |
|-----------|-------------|
| =  +=  -=  *=  /=  %=  ^=  **= | Assignment |
| ?: | C conditional expression |
| \| \| | Logical OR |
| && | Logical AND |
| ~  !~ | Match regular expression and negation |
| <  <=  >  >=  !=  == | Relational operators |
| (blank) | Concatenation |
| +  - | Addition, subtraction |
| *  /  % | Multiplication, division, and modulus |
| +  -  ! | Unary plus and minus, and logical negation |
| ^  ** | Exponentiation |
| ++ -- | Increment and decrement, either prefix or postfix |
| $ | Field reference |

*NOTE*        While "**" and "**=" are common extensions, they are not part of POSIX awk.

## Statements and Functions

An action is enclosed in braces and consists of one or more statements and/or expressions. The difference between a statement and a function is that a function returns a value, and its argument list is specified within parentheses. (The formal syntactical difference does not always hold true: **printf** is considered a statement, but its argument list can be put in parentheses; **getline** is a function that does not use parentheses.)

Awk has a number of predefined arithmetic and string functions. A function is typically called as follows:

> *return = function(arg1, arg2)*

where *return* is a variable created to hold what the function returns. (In fact, the return value of a function can be used anywhere in an expression, not just on the right-hand side of an assignment.) Arguments to a function are specified as a comma-separated list. The left parenthesis follows after the name of the function. (With built-in functions, a space is permitted between the function name and the parentheses.)

# Command Summary for awk

The following alphabetical list of statements and functions includes all that are available in POSIX awk, nawk, or gawk. See Chapter 11, *A Flock of awks*, for extensions available in different implementations.

atan2()     atan2(*y*, *x*)

                 Returns the arctangent of $y/x$ in radians.

break       Exit from a **while**, **for**, or **do** loop.

close()     close(*filename-expr*)

                 close(*command-expr*)

                 In most implementations of awk, you can only have a limited number of files and/or pipes open simultaneously. Therefore, awk provides a close( ) function that allows you to close a file or a pipe. It takes as an argument the same expression that opened the pipe or file. This expression must be identical, character by character, to the one that opened the file or pipe—even whitespace is significant.

continue    Begin next iteration of **while**, **for**, or **do** loop.

cos( )          cos(*x*)

                Return cosine of *x* in radians.

delete          delete *array*[*element*]

                Delete element of an array.

do              do

                    *body*

                while (*expr*)

                Looping statement. Execute statements in *body* then evaluate *expr* and
                if true, execute *body* again.

exit            exit [*expr*]

                Exit from script, reading no new input. The **END** rule, if it exists, will
                be executed. An optional *expr* becomes awk's return value.

exp( )          exp(*x*)

                Return exponential of *x* (*e* ^ *x*).

for             for (*init-expr*, *test-expr*, *incr-expr*) *statement*

                C-style looping construct. *init-expr* assigns the initial value of the
                counter variable. *test-expr* is a relational expression that is evaluated
                each time before executing the statement. When *test-expr* is false, the
                loop is exited. *incr-expr* is used to increment the counter variable
                after each pass.

                for (*item* in *array*) *statement*

                Special loop designed for reading associative arrays. For each element
                of the array, the *statement* is executed; the element can be referenced
                by *array*[*item*].

getline         Read next line of input.

                **getline** [*var*] [<*file*]

                *command* | **getline** [*var*]

                The first form reads input from *file* and the second form reads the out-
                put of *command*. Both forms read one line at a time, and each time
                the statement is executed it gets the next line of input. The line of
                input is assigned to $0 and it is parsed into fields, setting **NF**, **NR**, and
                **FNR**. If *var* is specified, the result is assigned to *var* and the $0 is not
                changed. Thus, if the result is assigned to a variable, the current line
                does not change. **getline** is actually a function and it returns 1 if it
                reads a record successfully, 0 if end-of-line is encountered, and -1 if
                for some reason it is otherwise unsuccessful.

| | |
|---|---|
| gsub() | gsub(*r*, *s*, *t*) |

Globally substitute *s* for each match of the regular expression *r* in the string *t*. Return the number of substitutions. If *t* is not supplied, defaults to $0.

| | |
|---|---|
| if | if (*expr*) *statement1* |

[ **else** *statement2* ]

Conditional statement. Evaluate *expr* and, if true, execute *statement1*; if **else** clause is supplied, execute *statement2* if *expr* is false.

| | |
|---|---|
| index() | index(*str*, *substr*) |

Return position (starting at 1) of substring in string.

| | |
|---|---|
| int() | int(*x*) |

Return integer value of *x* by truncating any digits following a decimal point.

| | |
|---|---|
| length() | length(*str*) |

Return length of string, or the length of $0 if no argument.

| | |
|---|---|
| log() | log(*x*) |

Return natural logarithm (base *e*) of *x*.

| | |
|---|---|
| match() | match(*s*, *r*) |

Function that matches the pattern, specified by the regular expression *r*, in the string *s* and returns either the position in *s* where the match begins, or 0 if no occurrences are found. Sets the values of **RSTART** and **RLENGTH** to the start and length of the match, respectively.

| | |
|---|---|
| next | Read next input line and begin executing script at first rule. |
| print | print [ *output-expr* ] [ *dest-expr* ] |

Evaluate the *output-expr* and direct it to standard output followed by the value of **ORS**. Each *output-expr* is separated by the value of **OFS**. *dest-expr* is an optional expression that directs the output to a file or pipe. "> *file*" directs the output to a file, overwriting its previous contents. ">> *file*" appends the output to a file, preserving its previous contents. In both of these cases, the file will be created if it does not already exist. "| *command*" directs the output as the input to a system command.

**printf**      printf (*format-expr* [, *expr-list* ]) [ *dest-expr* ]

An alternative output statement borrowed from the C language. It has the ability to produce formatted output. It can also be used to output data without automatically producing a newline. *format-expr* is a string of format specifications and constants; see next section for a list of format specifiers. *expr-list* is a list of arguments corresponding to format specifiers. See the **print** statement for a description of *dest-expr*.

**rand()**      rand()

Generate a random number between 0 and 1. This function returns the same series of numbers each time the script is executed, unless the random number generator is seeded using the **srand()** function.

**return**      return [*expr*]

Used at end of user-defined functions to exit function, returning value of expression.

**sin()**      sin(*x*)

Return sine of *x* in radians.

**split()**      split(*str, array, sep*)

Function that parses string into elements of array using field separator, returning number of elements in array. Value of **FS** is used if no field separator is specified. Array splitting works the same as field splitting.

**sprintf()**      sprintf (*format-expr* [, *expr-list* ] )

Function that returns string formatted according to **printf** format specification. It formats data but does not output it. *format-expr* is a string of format specifications and constants; see the next section for a list of format specifiers. *expr-list* is a list of arguments corresponding to format specifiers.

**sqrt()**      sqrt(*x*)

Return square root of *x*.

**srand()**      srand(*expr*)

Use *expr* to set a new seed for random number generator. Default is time of day. Return value is the old seed.

sub()  sub(*r, s, t*)

Substitute *s* for first match of the regular expression *r* in the string *t*. Return 1 if successful; 0 otherwise. If *t* is not supplied, defaults to $0.

substr()  substr(*str, beg, len*)

Return substring of string *str* at beginning position *beg*, and the characters that follow to maximum specified length *len*. If no length is given, use the rest of the string.

system()  system(*command*)

Function that executes the specified *command* and returns its status. The status of the executed command typically indicates success or failure. A value of 0 means that the command executed successfully. A non-zero value, whether positive or negative, indicates a failure of some sort. The documentation for the command you're running will give you the details. The output of the command is not available for processing within the awk script. Use "*command* | **getline**" to read the output of a command into the script.

tolower()  tolower(*str*)

Translate all uppercase characters in *str* to lowercase and return the new string.*

toupper()  toupper(*str*)

Translate all lowercase characters in *str* to uppercase and return the new string.

while  while (*expr*) *statement*

Looping construct. While *expr* is true, execute *statement*.

## *Format Expressions Used in printf and sprintf*

A format expression can take three optional modifiers following "%" and preceding the format specifier:

*%-width.precision format-specifier*

The *width* of the output field is a numeric value. When you specify a field width, the contents of the field will be right-justified by default. You must specify "-" to get left-justification. Thus, "%-20s" outputs a string left-justified in a field 20 characters wide. If the string is less than 20 characters, the field will be padded with spaces to fill.

---

* Very early versions of nawk, such as that in SunOS 4.1.x, don't support **tolower()** and **toupper()**. However, they are now part of the POSIX specification for awk.

The *precision* modifier, used for decimal or floating-point values, controls the number of digits that appear to the right of the decimal point. For string formats, it controls the number of characters from the string to print.

You can specify both the *width* and *precision* dynamically, via values in the **printf** or **sprintf** argument list. You do this by specifying asterisks, instead of specifying literal values.

```
printf("%*.*g\n", 5, 3, myvar);
```

In this example, the width is 5, the precision is 3, and the value to print will come from **myvar**. Older versions of nawk may not support this.

Note that the default precision for the output of numeric values is "%.6g." The default can be changed by setting the system variable **OFMT**. This affects the precision used by the **print** statement when outputting numbers. For instance, if you are using awk to write reports that contain dollar values, you might prefer to change **OFMT** to "%.2f."

The format specifiers, shown in Table B-6, are used with **printf** and **sprintf** statements.

*Table B-6: Format Specifiers Used in printf*

| Character | Description |
|-----------|-------------|
| c | ASCII character. |
| d | Decimal integer. |
| i | Decimal integer. Added in POSIX. |
| e | Floating-point format ([-]$d.precision$e[+-]$dd$). |
| E | Floating-point format ([-]$d.precision$E[+-]$dd$). |
| f | Floating-point format ([-]$ddd.precision$). |
| g | **e** or **f** conversion, whichever is shortest, with trailing zeros removed. |
| G | **E** or **f** conversion, whichever is shortest, with trailing zeros removed. |
| o | Unsigned octal value. |
| s | String. |
| x | Unsigned hexadecimal number. Uses **a-f** for 10 to 15. |
| X | Unsigned hexadecimal number. Uses **A-F** for 10 to 15. |
| % | Literal %. |

Often, whatever format specifiers are available in the system's *sprintf*(3) subroutine are available in awk.

The way **printf** and **sprintf( )** do rounding will often depend upon the system's C *sprintf*(3) subroutine. On many machines, *sprintf* rounding is "unbiased," which means it doesn't always round a trailing ".5" up, contrary to naive expectations. In unbiased rounding, ".5" rounds to even, rather than always up, so 1.5 rounds to 2 but 4.5 rounds to 4. The result is that if you are using a format that does rounding (e.g., "%.0f") you should check what your system does. The following function does traditional rounding; it might be useful if your awk's **printf** does unbiased rounding.

```
# round --- do normal rounding
#          Arnold Robbins, arnold@gnu.ai.mit.edu
#          Public Domain
function round(x,        ival, aval, fraction)
{
        ival = int(x)      # integer part, int() truncates
        # see if fractional part
        if (ival == x)    # no fraction
                return x
        if (x < 0) {
                aval = -x          # absolute value
                ival = int(aval)
                fraction = aval - ival
                if (fraction >= .5)
                        return int(x) - 1       # -2.5 --> -3
                else
                        return int(x)           # -2.3 --> -2
        } else {
                fraction = x - ival
                if (fraction >= .5)
                        return ival + 1
                else
                        return ival
        }
}
```

# C

# Supplement for Chapter 12

This appendix contains supplemental programs and documentation for the programs described in Chapter 12, *Full-Featured Applications.*

## Full Listing of spellcheck.awk

```
# spellcheck.awk -- interactive spell checker
#
# AUTHOR: Dale Dougherty
#
# Usage: nawk -f spellcheck.awk [+dict] file
# (Use spellcheck as name of shell program)
# SPELLDICT = "dict"
# SPELLFILE = "file"

# BEGIN actions perform the following tasks:
#       1) process command line arguments
#       2) create temporary filenames
#       3) execute spell program to create wordlist file
#       4) display list of user responses

BEGIN {
# Process command line arguments
# Must be at least two args -- nawk and filename
      if (ARGC > 1) {
      # if more than two args, second arg is dict
            if (ARGC > 2) {
            # test to see if dict is specified with "+"
            # and assign ARGV[1] to SPELLDICT
                  if (ARGV[1] ~ /^\+.*/)
                        SPELLDICT = ARGV[1]
```

```
                                else
                                        SPELLDICT = "+" ARGV[1]
                        # assign file ARGV[2] to SPELLFILE
                                SPELLFILE = ARGV[2]
                        # delete args so awk does not open them as files
                                delete ARGV[1]
                                delete ARGV[2]
                        }
                # not more than two args
                        else {
                        # assign file ARGV[1] to SPELLFILE
                                SPELLFILE = ARGV[1]
                        # test to see if local dict file exists
                                if (! system ("test -r dict")) {
                                # if it does, ask if we should use it
                                        printf ("Use local dict file? (y/n)")
                                        getline reply < "-"
                                # if reply is yes, use "dict"
                                        if (reply ~ /[yY](es)?/){
                                                SPELLDICT = "+dict"
                                        }
                                }
                        }
                } # end of processing args > 1
                # if args not > 1, then print shell-command usage
                else {
                        print "Usage: spellcheck [+dict] file"
                        exit 1
                }
        # end of processing command line arguments

        # create temporary file names, each begin with sp_
                wordlist = "sp_wordlist"
                spellsource = "sp_input"
                spellout = "sp_out"

        # copy SPELLFILE to temporary input file
                system("cp " SPELLFILE " " spellsource)

        # now run spell program; output sent to wordlist
                print "Running spell checker ..."
                if (SPELLDICT)
                        SPELLCMD = "spell " SPELLDICT " "
                else
                        SPELLCMD = "spell "
                system(SPELLCMD spellsource " > " wordlist )

        # test wordlist to see if misspelled words turned up
                if ( system("test -s " wordlist ) ) {
```

```
        # if wordlist is empty, (or spell command failed), exit
            print "No misspelled words found."
            system("rm " spellsource " " wordlist)
            exit
    }

# assign wordlist file to ARGV[1] so that awk will read it.
    ARGV[1] = wordlist

# display list of user responses
    responseList = "Responses: \n\tChange each occurrence,"
    responseList = responseList "\n\tGlobal change,"
    responseList = responseList "\n\tAdd to Dict,"
    responseList = responseList "\n\tHelp,"
    responseList = responseList "\n\tQuit"
    responseList = responseList "\n\tCR to ignore: "
    printf("%s", responseList)

} # end of BEGIN procedure

# main procedure, executed for each line in wordlist.
#       Purpose is to show misspelled word and prompt user
#       for appropriate action.

{
# assign word to misspelling
    misspelling = $1
    response = 1
    ++word
# print misspelling and prompt for response
    while (response !~ /(^[cCgGaAhHqQ])|^$/ ) {
            printf("\n%d - Found %s (C/G/A/H/Q/):", word, misspelling)
            getline response < "-"
    }
# now process the user's response
# CR - carriage return ignores current word
# Help
    if (response ~ /[Hh](elp)?/) {
    # Display list of responses and prompt again.
            printf("%s", responseList)
            printf("\n%d - Found %s (C/G/A/Q/):", word, misspelling)
            getline response < "-"
    }
# Quit
    if (response ~ /[Qq](uit)?/) exit
# Add to dictionary
    if ( response ~ /[Aa](dd)?/) {
            dict[++dictEntry] = misspelling
    }
```

```
# Change each occurrence
      if ( response ~ /[cC](hange)?/) {
      # read each line of the file we are correcting
            newspelling = ""; changes = ""
            while( (getline < spellsource) > 0){
            # call function to show line with misspelled word
            # and prompt user to make each correction
                  make_change($0)
            # all lines go to temp output file
                  print > spellout
            }
      # all lines have been read
      # close temp input and temp output file
            close(spellout)
            close(spellsource)
      # if change was made
            if (changes){
            # show changed lines
                  for (j = 1; j <= changes; ++j)
                        print changedLines[j]
                  printf ("%d lines changed. ", changes)
            # function to confirm before saving changes
                  confirm_changes()
            }
      }
# Globally change
      if ( response ~ /[gG](lobal)?/) {
      # call function to prompt for correction
      # and display each line that is changed.
      # Ask user to approve all changes before saving.
            make_global_change()
      }
} # end of Main procedure

# END procedure makes changes permanent.
# It overwrites the original file, and adds words
# to the dictionary.
# It also removes the temporary files.

END {
# if we got here after reading only one record,
# no changes were made, so exit.
      if (NR <= 1) exit
# user must confirm saving corrections to file
      while (saveAnswer !~ /([yY](es)?)|([nN]o?)/ ) {
            printf "Save corrections in %s (y/n)? ", SPELLFILE
            getline saveAnswer < "-"
      }
# if answer is yes then mv temporary input file to SPELLFILE
```

```
# save old SPELLFILE, just in case
      if (saveAnswer ~ /^[yY]/) {
            system("cp " SPELLFILE " " SPELLFILE ".orig")
            system("mv " spellsource " " SPELLFILE)
      }
# if answer is no then rm temporary input file
      if (saveAnswer ~ /^[nN]/)
            system("rm " spellsource)


# if words have been added to dictionary array, then prompt
# to confirm saving in current dictionary.
      if (dictEntry) {
            printf "Make changes to dictionary (y/n)? "
            getline response < "-"
            if (response ~ /^[yY]/){
            # if no dictionary defined, then use "dict"
                  if (! SPELLDICT) SPELLDICT = "dict"

            # loop through array and append words to dictionary
                  sub(/^\+/, "", SPELLDICT)
                  for ( item in dict )
                        print dict[item] >> SPELLDICT
                  close(SPELLDICT)
            # sort dictionary file
                  system("sort " SPELLDICT "> tmp_dict")
                  system("mv " "tmp_dict " SPELLDICT)
            }
      }
# remove word list
      system("rm sp_wordlist")
} # end of END procedure


# function definitions

# make_change -- prompt user to correct misspelling
#                for current input line.  Calls itself
#                to find other occurrences in string.
#     stringToChange -- initially $0; then unmatched substring of $0
#     len -- length from beginning of $0 to end of matched string
# Assumes that misspelling is defined.

function make_change (stringToChange, len,   # parameters
      line, OKmakechange, printstring, carets)   # locals
{
# match misspelling in stringToChange; otherwise do nothing
   if ( match(stringToChange, misspelling) ) {
   # Display matched line
         printstring = $0
         gsub(/\t/, " ", printstring)
```

```
            print printstring
            carets = "^"
            for (i = 1; i < RLENGTH; ++i)
                    carets = carets "^"
            if (len)
                    FMT = "%" len+RSTART+RLENGTH-2 "s\n"
            else
                    FMT = "%" RSTART+RLENGTH-1 "s\n"
            printf(FMT, carets)
    # Prompt user for correction, if not already defined
            if (! newspelling) {
                    printf "Change to:"
                    getline newspelling < "-"
            }
    # A carriage return falls through
    # If user enters correction, confirm
            while (newspelling && ! OKmakechange) {
                    printf ("Change %s to %s? (y/n):", misspelling, newspelling)
                    getline OKmakechange < "-"
                    madechg = ""
            # test response
                    if (OKmakechange ~ /[yY](es)?/ ) {
                    # make change (first occurrence only)
                            madechg = sub(misspelling, newspelling, stringToChange)
                    }
                    else if ( OKmakechange ~ /[nN]o?/ ) {
                            # offer chance to re-enter correction
                            printf "Change to:"
                            getline newspelling < "-"
                            OKmakechange = ""
                    }
            } # end of while loop

    # if len, we are working with substring of $0
            if (len) {
            # assemble it
                    line = substr($0,1,len-1)
                    $0 = line stringToChange
            }
            else {
                    $0 = stringToChange
                    if (madechg) ++changes
            }

    # put changed line in array for display
            if (madechg)
                    changedLines[changes] = ">" $0
```

```
        # create substring so we can try to match other occurrences
                len += RSTART + RLENGTH
                part1 = substr($0, 1, len-1)
                part2 = substr($0, len)
        # calls itself to see if misspelling is found in remaining part
                make_change(part2, len)


        } # end of if


} # end of make_change()


# make_global_change --
#         prompt user to correct misspelling
#         for all lines globally.
#         Has no arguments
# Assumes that misspelling is defined.


function make_global_change(    newspelling, OKmakechange, changes)
{
# prompt user to correct misspelled word
    printf "Globally change to:"
    getline newspelling < "-"


# carriage return falls through
# if there is an answer, confirm
    while (newspelling && ! OKmakechange) {
                printf ("Globally change %s to %s? (y/n):", misspelling,
                        newspelling)
                getline OKmakechange < "-"
        # test response and make change
                if (OKmakechange ~ /[yY](es)?/ ) {
                # open file, read all lines
                        while( (getline < spellsource) > 0){
                        # if match is found, make change using gsub
                        # and print each changed line.
                                if ($0 ~ misspelling) {
                                        madechg = gsub(misspelling, newspelling)
                                        print ">", $0
                                        changes += 1  # counter for line changes
                                }
                        # write all lines to temp output file
                                print > spellout
                        } # end of while loop for reading file


                # close temporary files
                        close(spellout)
                        close(spellsource)
                # report the number of changes
                        printf ("%d lines changed. ", changes)
```

```
                    # function to confirm before saving changes
                            confirm_changes()
                    } # end of if (OKmakechange ~ y)


        # if correction not confirmed,  prompt for new word
                    else if ( OKmakechange ~ /[nN]o?/ ){
                            printf "Globally change to:"
                            getline newspelling < "-"
                            OKmakechange = ""
                    }


        } # end of while loop for prompting user for correction

    } # end of make_global_change()


    # confirm_changes --
    #       confirm before saving changes

    function confirm_changes(  savechanges) {
    # prompt to confirm saving changes
        while (! savechanges ) {
                printf ("Save changes? (y/n)")
                getline savechanges < "-"
        }
    # if confirmed, mv output to input
        if (savechanges ~ /[yY](es)?/)
                system("mv " spellout " " spellsource)
        }
```

# *Listing of masterindex Shell Script*

```
#! /bin/sh
# 1.1 -- 7/9/90
MASTER=""
FILES=""
PAGE=""
FORMAT=1
INDEXDIR=/work/sedawk/awk/index
#INDEXDIR=/work/index
INDEXMACDIR=/work/macros/current
# Add check that all dependent modules are available.
sectNumber=1
useNumber=1
while [ "$#" != "0" ]; do
    case $1 in
    -m*)      MASTER="TRUE";;
    [1-9])    sectNumber=$1;;
    *,*)      sectNames=$1; useNumber=0;;
    -p*)      PAGE="TRUE";;
```

```
        -s*)      FORMAT=0;;
        -*)       echo $1 " is not a valid argument";;
        *)        if [ -f $1 ]; then
                     FILES="$FILES $1"
                  else
                     echo "$1: file not found"
                  fi;;
     esac
     shift
done
if [ "$FILES" = "" ]; then
    echo "Please supply a valid filename."
    exit
fi
if [ "$MASTER" != "" ]; then
    for x in $FILES
    do
    if [ "$useNumber" != 0 ]; then
        romaNum=`$INDEXDIR/romanum $sectNumber`
        awk '-F\t' '
           NF == 1 { print $0 }
           NF > 1  { print $0 ":" volume }
         ' volume=$romaNum $x >>/tmp/index$$
        sectNumber=`expr $sectNumber + 1`
    else
        awk '-F\t' '
           NR == 1 { split(namelist, names, ",");
                        volname = names[volume] }
           NF == 1 { print $0 }
           NF > 1  { print $0 ":" volname }
         ' volume=$sectNumber namelist=$sectNames $x >>/tmp/index$$
        sectNumber=`expr $sectNumber + 1`
    fi
    done
    FILES="/tmp/index$$"
fi
if [ "$PAGE" != "" ]; then
    $INDEXDIR/page.idx $FILES
    exit
fi
$INDEXDIR/input.idx $FILES |
sort -bdf -t:  +0 -1 +1 -2 +3 -4 +2n -3n | uniq |
$INDEXDIR/pagenums.idx |
$INDEXDIR/combine.idx |
$INDEXDIR/format.idx FMT=$FORMAT MACDIR=$INDEXMACDIR
if [ -s "/tmp/index$$" ]; then
    rm /tmp/index$$
fi
```

# Documentation for masterindex

This documentation, and the notes that follow, are by Dale Dougherty.

---

## *masterindex* — indexing program for single and multivolume indexing.

### Synopsis

```
masterindex [-master [volume]]  [-page] [-screen] [filename..]
```

### Description

*masterindex* generates a formatted index based on structured index entries output by *troff.* Unless you redirect output, it comes to the screen.

### Options

*-m* or *-master* indicates that you are compiling a multivolume index. The index entries for each volume should be in a single file and the filenames should be listed in sequence. If the first file is not the first volume, then specify the volume number as a separate argument. The volume number is converted to a roman numeral and prepended to all the page numbers of entries in that file.

*-p* or *-page* produces a listing of index entries for each page number. It can be used to proof the entries against hardcopy.

*-s* or *-screen* specifies that the unformatted index will be viewed on the "screen". The default is to prepare output that contains *troff* macros for formatting.

### Files

*/work/bin/masterindex*
*/work/bin/page.idx*
*/work/bin/pagenums.idx*
*/work/bin/combine.idx*
*/work/bin/format.idx*
*/work/bin/rotate.idx*
*/work/bin/romanum*
*/work/macros/current/indexmacs*

### See Also

Note that these programs require "nawk" (new awk): *nawk (1),* and *sed (1V).*

### Bugs

The new index program is modular, invoking a series of smaller programs. This should allow me to connect different modules to implement new features as well as isolate and fix problems more easily. Index entries should not contain any *troff* font changes. The program does not handle them. Roman numerals greater than eight will not be sorted properly, thus imposing a limit of an eight-book index.

(The sort program will sort the roman numerals 1–10 in the following order: I, II, III, IV, IX, V, VI, VII, VIII, X.)

---

## Background Details

Tim O'Reilly recommends *The Joy of Cooking* (JofC) index as an ideal index. I examined the JofC index quite thoroughly and set out to write a new indexing program that duplicated its features. I did not wholly duplicate the JofC format, but this could be done fairly easily if desired. Please look at the JofC index yourself to examine its features.

I also tried to do a few other things to improve on the previous index program and provide more support for the person coding the index.

## Coding Index Entries

This section describes the coding of index entries in the document file. We use the .XX macro for placing index entries in a file. The simplest case is:

```
.XX "entry"
```

If the entry consists of primary and secondary sort keys, then we can code it as:

```
.XX "primary, secondary"
```

A comma delimits the two keys. We also have a .XN macro for generating "See" references without a page number. It is specified as:

```
.XN "entry (See anotherEntry)"
```

While these coding forms continue to work as they have, *masterindex* provides greater flexibility by allowing three levels of keys: primary, secondary, and tertiary. You'd specify the entry like so:

```
.XX "primary: secondary; tertiary"
```

Note that the comma is not used as a delimiter. A colon delimits the primary and secondary entry; the semicolon delimits the secondary and tertiary entry. This means that commas can be a part of a key using this syntax. Don't worry, though, you can continue to use a comma to delimit the primary and secondary keys. (Be aware that the first comma in a line is converted to a colon, if no colon delimiter is found.) I'd recommend that new books be coded using the above syntax, even if you are only specifying a primary and secondary key.

Another feature is automatic rotation of primary and secondary keys if a tilde (~) is used as the delimiter. So the following entry:

```
.XX "cat~command"
```

is equivalent to the following two entries:

```
.XX "cat command"
.XX "command: cat"
```

You can think of the secondary key as a classification (command, attribute, function, etc.) of the primary entry. Be careful not to reverse the two, as "command cat" does not make much sense. To use a tilde in an entry, enter "˜˜".

I added a new macro, .XB, that is the same as .XX except that the page number for this index entry will be output in bold to indicate that it is the most significant page number in a range. Here is an example:

```
.XB "cat command"
```

When *troff* processes the index entries, it outputs the page number followed by an asterisk. This is how it appears when output is seen in screen format. When coded for *troff* formatting, the page number is surrounded by the bold font change escape sequences. (By the way, in the JofC index, I noticed that they allowed having the same page number in roman and in bold.) Also, this page number will not be combined in a range of consecutive numbers.

One other feature of the JofC index is that the very first secondary key appears on the same line with the primary key. The old index program placed any secondary key on the next line. The one advantage of doing it the JofC way is that entries containing only one secondary key will be output on the same line and look much better. Thus, you'd have "line justification, definition of" rather than having "definition of" indented on the next line. The next secondary key would be indented. Note that if the primary key exists as a separate entry (it has page numbers associated with it), the page references for the primary key will be output on the same line and the first secondary entry will be output on the next line.

To reiterate, while the syntax of the three-level entries is different, this index entry is perfectly valid:

```
.XX "line justification, definition of"
```

It also produces the same result as:

```
.XX "line justification: definition of"
```

(The colon disappears in the output.) Similarly, you could write an entry, such as

```
.XX "justification, lines, defined"
```

or

```
.XX "justification: lines, defined"
```

where the comma between "lines" and "defined" does not serve as a delimiter but is part of the secondary key.

The previous example could be written as an entry with three levels:

```
.XX "justification: lines; defined"
```

where the semicolon delimits the tertiary key. The semicolon is output with the key, and multiple tertiary keys may follow immediately after the secondary key.

The main thing, though, is that page numbers are collected for all primary, secondary, and tertiary keys. Thus, you could have output such as:

```
justification  4-9
  lines 4,6; defined, 5
```

## Output Format

One thing I wanted to do that our previous program did not do is generate an index without the *troff* codes. *masterindex* has three output modes: *troff*, *screen*, and *page*.

The default output is intended for processing by *troff* (via *fmt*). It contains macros that are defined in */work/macros/current/indexmacs*. These macros should produce the same index format as before, which was largely done directly through *troff* requests. Here are a few lines off the top:

```
$ masterindex ch01
.so /work/macros/current/indexmacs
.Se "" "Index"
.XC
.XF A "A"
.XF 1 "applications, structure of  2;  program  1"
.XF 1 "attribute, WIN_CONSUME_KBD_EVENTS  13"
.XF 2 "WIN_CONSUME_PICK_EVENTS  13"
.XF 2 "WIN_NOTIFY_EVENT_PROC  13"
.XF 2 "XV_ERROR_PROC  14"
.XF 2 "XV_INIT_ARGC_PTR_ARGV  5,6"
```

The top two lines should be obvious. The .XC macro produces multicolumn output. (It will print out two columns for smaller books. It's not smart enough to take arguments specifying the width of columns, but that should be done.) The .XF macro has three possible values for its first argument. An "A" indicates that the second argument is a letter of the alphabet that should be output as a divider. A "1" indicates that the second argument contains a primary entry. A "2" indicates that the entry begins with a secondary entry, which is indented.

When invoked with the *-s* argument, the program prepares the index for viewing on the screen (or printing as an ASCII file). Again, here are a few lines:

```
$ masterindex -s ch01
                        A
applications, structure of  2;  program  1
attribute, WIN_CONSUME_KBD_EVENTS  13
  WIN_CONSUME_PICK_EVENTS  13
```

```
WIN_NOTIFY_EVENT_PROC   13
XV_ERROR_PROC   14
XV_INIT_ARGC_PTR_ARGV   5,6
XV_INIT_ARGS   6
XV_USAGE_PROC   6
```

Obviously, this is useful for quickly proofing the index. The third type of format is also used for proofing the index. Invoked using *-p*, it provides a page-by-page listing of the index entries.

```
$ masterindex -p ch01
Page 1
            structure of XView applications
            applications, structure of; program
            XView applications
            XView applications, structure of
            XView interface
            compiling XView programs
            XView, compiling programs
Page 2
            XView libraries
```

## *Compiling a Master Index*

A multivolume master index is invoked by specifying the *-m* option. Each set of index entries for a particular volume must be placed in a separate file.

```
$ masterindex -m -s book1 book2 book3
xv_init() procedure  II: 4; III: 5
XV_INIT_ARGC_PTR_ARGV attribute  II: 5,6
XV_INIT_ARGS attribute  I: 6
```

Files must be specified in consecutive order. If the first file is not Volume 1, you can specify the number as an argument.

```
$ masterindex -m 4 -s book4 book5
```

# Index

## Symbols

& (ampersand)
&& (logical AND) operator, 158
in replacement text, 81, 83
* (asterisk)
** (exponentiation) operator, 148
**= (assignment) operator, 149
*= (assignment) operator, 149
as metacharacter, 28, 39–41
multiplication operator, 148
\ (backslash), 147
\<, \> escape sequences, 50, 265
\', \' escape sequences, 265
character classes and, 35
as metacharacter, 30–31
in replacement text, 81–82
(see also escape sequences, awk)
{} (braces)
\{\} metacharacters, 30, 45
in awk, 13, 20, 173
grouping sed commands in, 61, 79
[] (brackets) metacharacters, 30, 34–39
[::] metacharacters, 38
[..] metacharacters, 38
[= =] metacharacters, 38
^ (circumflex)
^= (assignment) operator, 149
character classes and, 30, 37
exponentiation operator, 148
as metacharacter, 30, 43
in multiline pattern space, 107
: (colon) for labels, 128

$ (dollar sign)
as end-of-line metacharacter, 30, 43
for last input line, 59
in multiline pattern space, 107
$0, $1, $2, . . . , 20, 143
. (dot) metacharacter, 28, 31, 40
= (equal sign)
= = (equal to) operator, 157
for printing line numbers, 95
! (exclamation point), 59, 360
!= (not equal to) operator, 157
!~ (does not match) operator, 145,
157–158
branch command versus, 129
csh and, 7
logical NOT operator, 158
> (greater than sign)
>= (greater than or equal to) operator,
157
for redirection, 18, 62, 239
relational operator, 157
– (hyphen)
–= (assignment) operator, 149
–– (decrement) operator, 149–150
character classes and, 36–37
subtraction operator, 148
< (less than sign)
<= (less than or equal to) operator, 157
relational operator, 157
# for comments, 80, 142, 368
#n for suppressing output, 80
#!, invoking awk with, 252–254, 366

# About the Authors

**Dale Dougherty** is President and CEO of Songline Studios, an affiliate of O'Reilly & Associates specializing in the development of online content. The founding editor of the Nutshell series, Dale has written, in addition to *sed & awk*, *DOS Meets UNIX* (with Tim O'Reilly), *Using UUCP & Usenet* (with Grace Todino), and *Guide to the Pick System*.

**Arnold Robbins**, an Atlanta native, is a professional programmer and technical author. He has been working with UNIX systems since 1980, when he was introduced to a PDP-11 running a version of Sixth Edition UNIX. He has been a heavy awk user since 1987, when he became involved with gawk, the GNU project's version of awk. As a member of the POSIX 1003.2 balloting group, he helped shape the POSIX standard for awk. He is currently the maintainer of gawk and its documentation. The documentation is available from the Free Software Foundation and has also been published by SSC as *Effective AWK Programming*.

# Colophon

Our look is the result of reader comments, our own experimentation, and feedback from distribution channels. Distinctive covers complement our distinctive approach to technical topics, breathing personality and life into potentially dry subjects.

The animal featured on the cover of *sed & awk* is a slender loris. Lorises are nocturnal, tree-dwelling, tailless primates with thick, soft fur and large, round eyes. They are found in Southern India and Ceylon, where they live in trees, rarely descending to the ground. Lorises have been observed urinating on their hands and feet—it is thought that they do this to improve their grip while climbing and to leave a scent trail.

A small animal, the slender loris is generally between 7 and 10 inches in size and weighs 12 ounces or less. It subsists on a diet of fruit, leaves, and shoots and small animals that it captures by hand.

Edie Freedman designed the cover of this book, using a 19th-century engraving from the Dover Pictorial Archive. The cover layout was produced with Quark XPress 3.3 using the ITC Garamond font.

The inside layout was designed by Nancy Priest and Mary Jane Walsh. Text was prepared in SGML using the DocBook 2.1 DTD. The print version of this book was created by translating the SGML source into a set of gtroff macros using a filter developed at ORA by Norman Walsh. Steve Talbott designed and wrote the underlying macro set on the basis of the GNU troff -gs macros; Lenny Muellner adapted them to SGML and implemented the book design. The GNU groff text formatter version 1.09 was used to generate PostScript output. The text and heading fonts are ITC Garamond Light and Garamond Book; the constant-width font used in this book is Letter Gothic. The illustrations that appear in the book were created in Macromedia Freehand 5.0 by Chris Reilley.

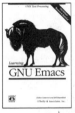

# UNIX Basics *(continued)*

## sed & awk, 2nd Edition

By Dale Dougherty & Arnold Robbins
*2nd Edition Winter 1997*
*450 pages (est.), ISBN 1-56592-225-5*

*sed & awk*, one of the most popular
books in O'Reilly & Associates' Nutshell
series, describes two text processing programs that are mainstays of the UNIX programmer's toolbox. The book lays a foundation for both programs by describing
how they are used and by introducing the
fundamental concepts of regular expressions and text matching.
This new edition covers the *sed* and *awk* programs as they are
now mandated by the POSIX standard. It also includes a discussion of the GNU versions of both programs, which have extensions beyond their UNIX counterparts. Many examples are used
throughout the book to illustrate the concepts discussed..

## SCO UNIX in a Nutshell

By Ellie Cutler & the staff of O'Reilly &
Associates
*1st Edition February 1994*
*590 pages, ISBN 1-56592-037-6*

The desktop reference to SCO UNIX and
Open Desktop®, this version of *UNIX in a
Nutshell* shows you what's under the hood
of your SCO system. It isn't a scaled-down
quick reference of common commands, but
a complete reference containing all user,
programming, administration, and networking commands.

## UNIX in a Nutshell: System V Edition

By Daniel Gilly & the staff of O'Reilly &
Associates
*2nd Edition June 1992*
*444 pages, ISBN 1-56592-001-5*

You may have seen UNIX quick-reference
guides, but you've never seen anything like
*UNIX in a Nutshell*. Not a scaled-down
quick reference of common commands,
*UNIX in a Nutshell* is a complete reference
containing all commands and options, along
with generous descriptions and examples
that put the commands in context. For all but the thorniest UNIX
problems, this one reference should be all the documentation
you need. Covers System V, Releases 3 and 4, and Solaris 2.0.

## What You Need to Know: When You Can't Find Your UNIX System Administrator

By Linda Mui
*1st Edition April 1995*
*156 pages, ISBN 1-56592-104-6*

This book is written for UNIX users, who
are often cast adrift in a confusing environment. It provides the background and
practical solutions you need to solve
problems you're likely to encounter—
problems with logging in, printing, shar-
ing files, running programs, managing
space resources, etc. It also describes the kind of info to gather
when you're asking for a diagnosis from a busy sys admin. And,
it gives you a list of site-specific information that you should
know, as well as a place to write it down.

## Volume 3M: X Window System User's Guide, Motif Edition

By Valerie Quercia & Tim O'Reilly
*2nd Edition January 1993*
*956 pages, ISBN 1-56592-015-5*

The *X Window System User's Guide,
Motif Edition* orients the new user to window system concepts and provides
detailed tutorials for many client programs, including the xtermterminal
emulator and the twm, uwm, and
mwmwindow managers. Later chapters
explain how to customize the X environment. Revised for Motif
1.2 and X11 Release 5.

## What You Need to Know: Using Email Effectively

By Linda Lamb & Jerry Peek
*1st Edition April 1995*
*160 pages, ISBN 1-56592-103-8*

After using email for a few years, you
learn from your own mistakes and from
reading other people's mail. You learn
how to include a message but leave in
only the sections that make your point,
how to recognize if a network address
"looks right," how to successfully sub-
scribe and unsubscribe to a mailing list, how to save mail so that
you can find it again. This book shortens the learning-from-
experience curve for all mailers, so you can quickly be productive and send email that looks intelligent to others.

## O'REILLY™

*TO ORDER:* **800-998-9938** • *order@ora.com* • *http://www.ora.com/*
*OUR PRODUCTS ARE AVAILABLE AT A BOOKSTORE OR SOFTWARE STORE NEAR YOU.*
*FOR INFORMATION:* **800-998-9938** • **707-829-0515** • *info@ora.com*

# Linux

## Linux in a Nutshell

*By Jessica Hekman and the Staff of O'Reilly & Associates*
*1st Edition Fall 1996*
*650 pages (est.), ISBN 1-56592-167-4*

The desktop reference for Linux, *Linux in a Nutshell* covers the core commands available on common Linux distributions. This isn't a scaled-down quick reference of common commands, but a complete reference containing all user, programming, administration, and networking commands. Also documents a wide range of GNU tools.

## Linux Multimedia Guide

*By Jeff Tranter*
*1st Edition September 1996*
*386 pages, ISBN 1-56592-219-0*

Linux is increasingly popular among computer enthusiasts of all types, and one of the applications where it is flourishing is multimedia. This book tells you how to program such popular devices as sound cards, CD-ROMs, and joysticks. It also describes the best free software packages that support manipulation of graphics, audio, and video and offers guidance on fitting the pieces together.

## Running Linux, 2nd Edition

*By Matt Welsh & Lar Kaufman*
*2nd Edition August 1996*
*650 pages, ISBN 1-56592-151-8*

This second edition of *Running Linux* covers everything you need to understand, install, and start using the Linux operating system. It includes a comprehensive installation tutorial, complete information on system maintenance, tools for document development and programming, and guidelines for network and Web site administration.

## Running Linux Companion CD-ROM

*By O'Reilly & Associates and Red Hat Software*
*2nd Edition August 1996*
*Includes two CD-ROMs, 140 pages*
*ISBN 1-56592-212-3*

LINUX is a multi-user, multi-tasking operating system that is in use around the world at research and development organizations as a fully functional, low-cost UNIX workstation. *Running Linux Companion CD-ROM* contains version 3.03 of Red Hat Linux, the most reliable, easy-to-install, and easy-to-upgrade version of the Linux operating system around. This software, together with the popular book, *Running Linux* by Matt Welsh and Lar Kaufman, provides a complete software/documentation package for installing and learning to use the Linux operating system.

## Linux Network Administrator's Guide

*By Olaf Kirch*
*1st Edition January 1995*
*370 pages, ISBN 1-56592-087-2*

A UNIX-compatible operating system that runs on personal computers, Linux is a pinnacle within the free software movement. It is based on a kernel developed by Finnish student Linus Torvalds and is distributed on the Net or on low-cost disks, along with a complete set of UNIX libraries, popular free software utilities, and traditional layered products like NFS and the X Window System. Networking is a fundamental part of Linux. Whether you want a simple UUCP connection or a full LAN with NFS and NIS, you are going to have to build a network.

*Linux Network Administrator's Guide* by Olaf Kirch is one of the most successful books to come from the Linux Documentation Project. It touches on all the essential networking software included with Linux, plus some hardware considerations. Topics include serial connections, UUCP, routing and DNS, mail and News, SLIP and PPP, NFS, and NIS.

# How to stay in touch with O'Reilly

## 1. Visit Our Award-Winning Web Site

### http://www.ora.com/

★ "Top 100 Sites on the Web" —*PC Magazine*
★ "Top 5% Web sites" —*Point Communications*
★ "3-Star site" —*The McKinley Group*

Our web site contains a library of comprehensiveproduct information (including book excerpts and tables of contents), downloadable software, background articles, interviews with technology leaders, links to relevant sites, book cover art, and more. File us in your Bookmarks or Hotlist!

## 2. Join Our Email Mailing Lists

### New Product Releases

To receive automatic email with brief descriptions of all new O'Reilly products as they are released, send email to:
**listproc@online.ora.com**
Put the following information in the first line of your message (*not* in the Subject field):
**subscribe ora-news "Your Name"of "Your Organization"** (for example: subscribe ora-news Kris Webber of Fine Enterprises)

### O'Reilly Events

If you'd also like us to send information about trade show events, special promotions, and other O'Reilly events, send email to:
**listproc@online.ora.com**
Put the following information in the first line of your message (*not* in the Subject field):
**subscribe ora-events "Your Name" of "Your Organization"**

## 3. Get Examples from Our Books via FTP

There are two ways to access an archive of example files from our books:

### Regular FTP
- ftp to:
  **ftp.ora.com**
  (login: anonymous
  password: your email address)
- Point your web browser to:
  **ftp://ftp.ora.com/**

### FTPMAIL
- Send an email message to:
  **ftpmail@online.ora.com**
  (Write "help" in the message body)

## 4. Visit Our Gopher Site
- Connect your gopher to:
  **gopher.ora.com**

- Point your web browser to:
  **gopher://gopher.ora.com/**

- Telnet to:
  **gopher.ora.com**
  **login: gopher**

## 5. Contact Us via Email

**order@ora.com**
To place a book or software order online. Good for North American and international customers.

**subscriptions@ora.com**
To place an order for any of our newsletters or periodicals.

**books@ora.com**
General questions about any of our books.

**software@ora.com**
For general questions and product information about our software. Check out O'Reilly Software Online at **http://software.ora.com/** for software and technical support information. Registered O'Reilly software users send your questions to: **website-support@ora.com**

**cs@ora.com**
For answers to problems regarding your order or our products.

**booktech@ora.com**
For book content technical questions or corrections.

**proposals@ora.com**
To submit new book or software proposals to our editors and product managers.

**international@ora.com**
For information about our international distributors or translation queries. For a list of our distributors outside of North America check out:
**http://www.ora.com/www/order/country.html**

O'Reilly & Associates, Inc.
101 Morris Street, Sebastopol, CA 95472 USA
TEL   707-829-0515 or 800-998-9938
           (6am to 5pm PST)
FAX   707-829-0104

## O'REILLY™

# Titles from O'Reilly

*Please note that upcoming titles are displayed in italic.*

## WEB PROGRAMMING

Apache: The Definitive Guide
Building Your Own Website
CGI Programming for the World Wide Web
Designing for the Web
HTML: The Definitive Guide
JavaScript: The Definitive Guide, 2nd Ed.
Learning Perl
Programming Perl, 2nd Ed.
Mastering Regular Expressions
WebMaster in a Nutshell
*Web Security & Commerce*
*Web Client Programming with Perl*
World Wide Web Journal

## USING THE INTERNET

Smileys
The Future Does Not Compute
The Whole Internet User's Guide & Catalog
The Whole Internet for Win 95
Using Email Effectively
Bandits on the Information Superhighway

## JAVA SERIES

Exploring Java
*Java AWT Reference*
*Java Fundamental Classes Reference*
Java in a Nutshell
*Java Language Reference*
*Java Network Programming*
Java Threads
*Java Virtual Machine*

## SOFTWARE

WebSite™ 1.1
WebSite Professional™
Building Your Own Web Conferences
WebBoard™
PolyForm™
Statisphere™

## SONGLINE GUIDES

NetActivism
Net Law
NetLearning
*Net Lessons*
*NetResearch*
NetSuccess for Realtors
*NetTravel*

## SYSTEM ADMINISTRATION

Building Internet Firewalls
Computer Crime: A Crimefighter's Handbook
Computer Security Basics
DNS and BIND, 2nd Ed.
Essential System Administration, 2nd Ed.
Getting Connected: The Internet at 56K and Up
*Internet Server Administration with Windows NT*
Linux Network Administrator's Guide
Managing Internet Information Services
Managing NFS and NIS
Networking Personal Computers with TCP/IP
Practical UNIX & Internet Security. 2nd Ed.
PGP: Pretty Good Privacy
sendmail, 2nd Ed.
*sendmail Desktop Reference*
System Performance Tuning
TCP/IP Network Administration
termcap & terminfo
Using & Managing UUCP
Volume 8: X Window System Administrator's Guide
*Web Security & Commerce*

## UNIX

Exploring Expect
*Learning VBScript*
Learning GNU Emacs, 2nd Ed.
Learning the bash Shell
Learning the Korn Shell
Learning the UNIX Operating System
Learning the vi Editor
Linux in a Nutshell
Making TeX Work
Linux Multimedia Guide
Running Linux, 2nd Ed.
SCO UNIX in a Nutshell
*sed & awk, 2nd Edition*
*Tcl/Tk Tools*
UNIX in a Nutshell: System V Edition
UNIX Power Tools
Using csh & tsch
When You Can't Find Your UNIX System Administrator
*Writing GNU Emacs Extensions*

## WEB REVIEW STUDIO SERIES

Gif Animation Studio
Shockwave Studio

## WINDOWS

Dictionary of PC Hardware and Data Communications Terms
Inside the Windows 95 Registry
*Inside the Windows 95 File System*
*Win95 & WinNT Annoyances*
*Windows NT File System Internals*
*Windows NT in a Nutshell*

## PROGRAMMING

Advanced Oracle PL/SQL Programming
Applying RCS and SCCS
C++: The Core Language
Checking C Programs with lint
DCE Security Programming
Distributing Applications Across DCE & Windows NT
Encyclopedia of Graphics File Formats, 2nd Ed.
Guide to Writing DCE Applications
lex & yacc
Managing Projects with make
*Mastering Oracle Power Objects*
*Oracle Design: The Definitive Guide*
Oracle Performance Tuning, 2nd Ed.
Oracle PL/SQL Programming
Porting UNIX Software
POSIX Programmer's Guide
POSIX.4: Programming for the Real World
Power Programming with RPC
Practical C Programming
Practical C++ Programming
Programming Python
Programming with curses
Programming with GNU Software
Pthreads Programming
Software Portability with imake, 2nd Ed.
Understanding DCE
Understanding Japanese Information Processing
UNIX Systems Programming for SVR4

## BERKELEY 4.4 SOFTWARE DISTRIBUTION

4.4BSD System Manager's Manual
4.4BSD User's Reference Manual
4.4BSD User's Supplementary Documents
4.4BSD Programmer's Reference Manual
4.4BSD Programmer's Supplementary Documents
X Programming
Vol. 0: X Protocol Reference Manual
Vol. 1: Xlib Programming Manual
Vol. 2: Xlib Reference Manual
Vol. 3M: X Window System User's Guide, Motif Edition
Vol. 4M: X Toolkit Intrinsics Programming Manual, Motif Edition
Vol. 5: X Toolkit Intrinsics Reference Manual
Vol. 6A: Motif Programming Manual
Vol. 6B: Motif Reference Manual
Vol. 6C: Motif Tools
Vol. 8 : X Window System Administrator's Guide
Programmer's Supplement for Release 6
X User Tools
The X Window System in a Nutshell

## CAREER & BUSINESS

Building a Successful Software Business
The Computer User's Survival Guide
Love Your Job!
Electronic Publishing on CD-ROM

## TRAVEL

Travelers' Tales: Brazil
Travelers' Tales: Food
Travelers' Tales: France
Travelers' Tales: Gutsy Women
Travelers' Tales: India
Travelers' Tales: Mexico
Travelers' Tales: Paris
Travelers' Tales: San Francisco
Travelers' Tales: Spain
Travelers' Tales: Thailand
Travelers' Tales: A Woman's World

## O'REILLY™

TO ORDER: **800-998-9938** • **order@ora.com** • **http://www.ora.com/**
OUR PRODUCTS ARE AVAILABLE AT A BOOKSTORE OR SOFTWARE STORE NEAR YOU.
FOR INFORMATION: **800-998-9938** • **707-829-0515** • **info@ora.com**

# International Distributors

## Europe, Middle East and Northern Africa (except France, Germany, Switzerland, & Austria)

**INQUIRIES**
International Thomson Publishing
Europe
Berkshire House
168-173 High Holborn
London WC1V 7AA, United Kingdom
Telephone: 44-171-497-1422
Fax: 44-171-497-1426
Email: itpint@itps.co.uk

**ORDERS**
International Thomson Publishing
Services, Ltd.
Cheriton House, North Way
Andover, Hampshire SP10 5BE,
United Kingdom
Telephone: 44-264-342-832
  (UK orders)
Telephone: 44-264-342-806
  (outside UK)
Fax: 44-264-364418 (UK orders)
Fax: 44-264-342761 (outside UK)
UK & Eire orders: itpuk@itps.co.uk
International orders: itpint@itps.co.uk

## France

Editions Eyrolles
61 Bd Saint-Germain
75240 Paris Cedex 05
France
Telephone: 33 1 44 41 46 16
Fax: 33 1 44 41 11 44

## Australia

WoodsLane Pty. Ltd.
7/5 Vuko Place, Warriewood NSW 2102
P.O. Box 935, Mona Vale NSW 2103
Australia
Telephone: 61-2-9970-5111
Fax: 61-2-9970-5002
Email: info@woodslane.com.au

## Germany, Switzerland, and Austria

**INQUIRIES**
O'Reilly Verlag
Balthasarstr. 81
D-50670 Köln
Germany
Telephone: 49 221 97 31 60 0
Fax: 49 221 97 31 60 8
Email: anfragen@oreilly.de

**ORDERS**
International Thomson Publishing
Königswinterer Straße 418
53227 Bonn, Germany
Telephone: 49-228-97024 0
Fax: 49-228-441342
Email: order@oreilly.de

## Asia (except Japan & India)

**INQUIRIES**
International Thomson Publishing Asia
60 Albert Street #15-01
Albert Complex
Singapore 189969
Telephone: 65-336-6411
Fax: 65-336-7411

**ORDERS**
Telephone: 65-336-6411
Fax: 65-334-1617
thomson@signet.com.sg

## New Zealand

WoodsLane New Zealand Ltd.
21 Cooks Street (P.O. Box 575)
Wanganui, New Zealand
Telephone: 64-6-347-6543
Fax: 64-6-345-4840
Email: info@woodslane.com.au

## Japan

O'Reilly Japan, Inc.
Kiyoshige Building 2F
12-Banchi, Sanei-cho
Shinjuku-ku
Tokyo 160 Japan
Telephone: 81-3-3356-5227
Fax: 81-3-3356-5261
Email: kenji@ora.com

## India

Computer Bookshop (India) PVT. LTD.
190 Dr. D.N. Road, Fort
Bombay 400 001
India
Telephone: 91-22-207-0989
Fax: 91-22-262-3551
Email: cbsbom@giasbm01.vsnl.net.in

## The Americas

O'Reilly & Associates, Inc.
101 Morris Street
Sebastopol, CA 95472 U.S.A.
Telephone: 707-829-0515
Telephone: 800-998-9938 (U.S. &
Canada)
Fax: 707-829-0104
Email: order@ora.com

## Southern Africa

International Thomson Publishing
Southern Africa
Building 18, Constantia Park
240 Old Pretoria Road
P.O. Box 2459
Halfway House, 1685 South Africa
Telephone: 27-11-805-4819
Fax: 27-11-805-3648

# O'REILLY™

TO ORDER: **800-998-9938** • **order@ora.com** • **http://www.ora.com/**
OUR PRODUCTS ARE AVAILABLE AT A BOOKSTORE OR SOFTWARE STORE NEAR YOU.
FOR INFORMATION: **800-998-9938** • **707-829-0515** • **info@ora.com**

O'Reilly & Associates, Inc.
101 Morris Street
Sebastopol, CA 95472-9902
1-800-998-9938

Visit us online at:
http://www.ora.com/
orders@ora.com

## O'REILLY WOULD LIKE TO HEAR FROM YOU

Which book did this card come from?

_____

Where did you buy this book?
- ❏ Bookstore
- ❏ Direct from O'Reilly
- ❏ Bundled with hardware/software
- ❏ Computer Store
- ❏ Class/seminar
- ❏ Other _____

What operating system do you use?
- ❏ UNIX
- ❏ Windows NT
- ❏ Macintosh
- ❏ PC(Windows/DOS)
- ❏ Other _____

What is your job description?
- ❏ System Administrator
- ❏ Network Administrator
- ❏ Web Developer
- ❏ Programmer
- ❏ Educator/Teacher
- ❏ Other _____

❏ Please send me O'Reilly's catalog, containing a complete listing of O'Reilly books and software.

Name _____  Company/Organization _____

Address _____

City _____  State _____  Zip/Postal Code _____  Country _____

Telephone _____  Internet or other email address (specify network) _____

Nineteenth century wood engraving
of a bear from the O'Reilly &
Associates Nutshell Handbook®
*Using & Managing UUCP.*

POST CARD

# BUSINESS REPLY MAIL

FIRST CLASS MAIL   PERMIT NO. 80   SEBASTOPOL, CA

*Postage will be paid by addressee*

### O'Reilly & Associates, Inc.

101 Morris Street
Sebastopol, CA  95472-9902